REMEMBER YOU ARE
AN ENGLISHMAN

Major-General Sir Harry Smith, Bart, of Aliwal, G.C.B.

JOSEPH H. LEHMANN

REMEMBER YOU ARE AN ENGLISHMAN

*A Biography
of Sir Harry Smith
1787–1860*

JONATHAN CAPE
THIRTY BEDFORD SQUARE LONDON

First published 1977
© 1977 by Joseph H. Lehmann

This edition published 1977 by
Jonathan Cape Ltd, 30 Bedford Square, London WC1

British Library Cataloguing in Publication Data

Lehmann, Joseph Herbert
Remember you are an Englishman
Bibl. — Index
ISBN 0–224–01403–x
1. Title
325'.341'09687   DT844.2.S/
Smith, *Sir* Harry George Wakelyn, *bart*

Printed in Great Britain by
Ebenezer Baylis & Son Limited
The Trinity Press, Worcester, and London

Dedicated to
Sunny Lehmann

Contents

Illustrations

PLATES

Frontispiece Sir Harry Smith from a 130-year-old lithograph (Mr J. E. P. Levyns, Pinelands, Republic of South Africa, restored by Mr A. J. Musgrove-Newton)

ix

MAPS

Preface

'The profession of historian is the second oldest in the world,' wrote Professor Hurstfield. 'Like the first it has always had a place in the entertainment industry.' It would be difficult to write a biography of Sir Harry Smith without serving this purpose. In his life are to be found all the elements of a dramatic novel: an unforgettable character involved in romantic love and swashbuckling adventures, whether fighting American back-woodsmen before New Orleans or Napoleon's veterans at Waterloo, fanatical Sikhs in India or Boers and Xhosa tribes-men at the Cape. Even as an administrator and governor, his personality and policies brought a sparkle to the pages of South African history that none have rivalled. Yet, until now, no biography of him has appeared. His autobiography, which was not published until nearly a half century after his death, was neither complete nor wholly reliable, mainly because of deletions and changes made by the editor, his great-nephew. As a participant in some of the most stirring and crucial battles of the British army in the nineteenth century and as an in-fluential figure in shaping the course of South African affairs, an account of his life is long overdue.

Sir Harry Smith left behind a mass of papers that have been scattered throughout England and South Africa. To consult these documents required time and money which were gener-ously provided by DePaul University and the American Philosophical Society. And a special thanks is due to Mr Leslie Ford-Smith, a descendant of Harry's brother Charles, who was kind enough to allow me to use the letters exchanged between Sir Harry Smith and his family and, above all, the correspon-dence with Juana, his wife, which runs to over 200 typescript pages. Since they were not intended for publication, they are most revealing in matters concerning his motives and relation-ships with others, especially his wife, during the Sixth Frontier War in South Africa and immediately after. The discovery of materials such as these makes the biographer's task an exciting one.

The rest of the Smith papers in England were found at the following places: the Cambridge University Library, mainly the manuscript of his autobiography that is often barely legible; the Public Records Office which contains the diary he wrote while in South America, letterbooks kept during the South African and Indian campaigns and letters to his sister Alice and former comrades in arms; the Regimental Museum of the Royal Green Jackets, Peninsular Barracks, Winchester, where, with the permission of the trustees, I was provided with his letters to Tom Payne and George Simmons; the National Army Museum in London, which holds the manuscript orders he issued during the Eighth Frontier War, his diary for 1834 and a manuscript notebook.

In South Africa the Cory Library of Historical Research at Rhodes University in Grahamstown contains a wealth of material dealing not only with Sir Harry's years of service at the Cape but letters he wrote while stationed in India and after he returned to England in 1852. At the Cape Depot of State Archives in Cape Town, Miss Joan Davies made available his letterbooks on the Sixth Frontier War and the volumes of letters exchanged between Sir Harry and Governor D'Urban. A few other letters and memoranda are in the Africana Museum in the Public Library, Johannesburg, and the Kaffrarian Museum, King William's Town.

For making available the papers of persons who knew and wrote about Sir Harry or received letters from him, I wish to express my appreciation to Her Majesty the Queen for access to the Journals of Queen Victoria and the letters of the Duke of Cambridge at the Royal Archives, Windsor Castle; to the Dowager Lady Hardinge for the papers of Viscount Henry Hardinge; to Colonel H. C. B. Cook, O.B.E. (Retd) at the Regimental Museum of the Staffordshire Regiment, Lichfield, for the diaries of General Sir Edward Holdwich; to Mr Davis, Librarian at the Royal Army Medical College, London, for the Sir John Hall papers; to Dr J. M. Fewster, Department of Palaeography, University of Durham, for correspondence in the Earl Grey papers on Sir Harry; and to the staff of the Royal Commonwealth Society Library for the papers of W. C. E. Napier.

Since places are often as informative as documents, I have attempted where possible to study Sir Harry's career on location, from the battlefields of New Orleans and Waterloo to those of Spain. In tracing his steps in the old frontier region of the Eastern Cape, I was fortunate in having as guides Dr and Mrs John Scott, Mr Brian Randles of the Kaffrarian Museum and Professor C. G. Coetzee of Fort Hare University.

For guidance to sources and for offering materials in their possession dealing with the subject, I am most thankful to the late Major Tylden, Mr John L. Sharpe and Major A. J. Smithers, author of the praiseworthy book *The Kaffir Wars, 1779–1877* (Leo Cooper, 1973). In directing me to books and periodicals, especially the regimental histories, I am indebted to Mr C. A. Potts and Mr Henry Jenkins at the Ministry of Defence Library (formerly the War Office Library). For translations from Afrikaans, I thank Professor D. W. Kruger.

Invaluable assistance in preparing this book for publication was contributed by Miss Sally Walker on the staff of the Chicago Historical Society. And for a searching, critical eye in correcting errors in the manuscript I am indebted to Mr Joseph Wydeven at Purdue University.

Last, but by no means least, I give grateful acknowledgment to Mr Graham C. Greene of Jonathan Cape Ltd for encouragement and advice.

J.H.L.

[1]

From the River Plate to the Peninsular War

Wars have brought to prominence some extraordinary characters. None more so, perhaps, than Sir Harry Smith, who in his day was no less celebrated for his military accomplishments on five continents than for his enduring affection for a teenage bride who accompanied him into war. His reputation was that of a man's man, vigorous and combative, capable of raucous humour and given to pungent expletives; yet, he was fair, firm and straightforward, even to the point of admitting freely that he was at times something of a poseur. Always, he appeared to be a man without doubts, confident in himself and the England he served.

There was no military tradition among the Smiths of Whittlesea, a town located deep in the Cambridge fens. Harry, christened Henry George Wakelyn, was born on 28 June 1787, the second son of the local surgeon, John Smith. His mother, Eleanor Moore, who had fourteen children (of whom eleven survived), was the daughter of the local vicar. The Moores, slightly more elevated on the social scale, claimed descent from a saint, Sir Thomas More.

The first and third sons became surgeons like their father, but it was apparent that Harry, even as a child, would follow a more adventurous career. As an athlete and marksman, he took first prizes; his skill as a horseman became legendary. When, for instance, Harry was a mere child of six, his father had a horse so vicious that when purchasers appeared, no one dared to mount him. The reputation of the mettlesome steed drew a military officer to Whittlesea as a potential buyer. When the officer asked to see the charger's paces, the groom who led him held back. Master Harry came forth and insisted that he could control the beast; once placed on the horse's back, he managed it 'like a young Alexander on another Bucephalus'. Blessed with such natural talents and 'a very large organ of courage', as the officer declared, young Harry was bound for the army.

In 1804, all of Britain was under arms to repel Napoleon's expected landing. 'The threat of invasion,' observed one volunteer, 'fired every loyal pair of shoulders for a red coat.' Among those putting on a uniform then was 17-year-old Harry Smith, who was taken into the Whittlesea Troop of the Yeomanry Cavalry. His first encounter with the enemy was as a guard over French prisoners at the Norman Cross Barracks nearby. At the sight of the skinny little trooper, his charges howled with laughter. One of Napoleon's veterans shouted, 'I say leetel fellow, go home with your mama; you must eat more pudding.'

Harry's conduct rather than his size attracted the attention of General William Stewart, to whom he was attached as an orderly dragoon during a review. After the parade, the general turned to his eager attendant and inquired: 'Young gentleman, would you like to be an officer?' 'Of all things', was his reply. 'Well, I will make you a Rifleman, a green jacket,' said Stewart, 'and very smart.'

It was in this offhand manner that Harry was appointed a second lieutenant in the 95th. There were no tests; not even a physical examination was required. Smith qualified by being a gentleman, one of sufficient social standing to exercise command over soldiers. No questions were asked to ascertain the level of his education, though he had received a solid grounding in natural philosophy, algebra, classics and music. That a young man could ride well and withstand the rigours of campaigning were deemed more essential than brains, a condition which once provoked Wellington to observe sourly, 'There is nothing so stupid as a gallant British officer.'

The Smiths were delighted with Harry's commission. Within a month Dr Smith, who spent most of his money on the purchase of fine horses, borrowed £100 to buy his 'pet son', as Harry put it, a promotion to a vacant first lieutenancy. Another loan was necessary to provide a kit. (Thinking of himself, as much as his father, Harry later commented, 'A sort of fatality attends the name of Smith for the accumulation of money.')

The Riflemen's uniforms were the most distinctive in the army. The appearance of bottle-green with black facings, accoutrements and hessian boots, cut a certain dash when compared to the scarlet coats and white pipeclay of ordinary British infantrymen. The sombre colours were suited to their task as skirmishers: the green merged with the foliage while the black eliminated the reflection of light. The French, who watched the Riflemen dart across the countryside, would call them 'the grasshoppers'. To Harry, the colour was right but he thought that the tight uniform and tall narrow cap were not suited to working through hedges and brush. He was further handicapped by the hussar-style braiding on his officer's cap and jacket which tangled in the shrubbery. In addition, the uniform consisted of the officer's red waist-sash, a short, curved sword, and a large cloak, the latter would serve as his bed, for Riflemen were often obliged to sleep in the fields.

Leaving home was an ordeal. The eager anticipation of a career in the army quickly faded as Harry contemplated the possibility of never seeing his parents and five brothers and five sisters again. He recalled:

> I bore up manfully at dinner, then ran to the stables to say good-bye to Jack, a beautiful little horse I had reared from a foal and who, in the hunting field, had kept me ahead of all others. I threw my arms round his neck and had a good cry.

As he was about to climb into the carriage with his father, who insisted on accompanying him to his station, his mother declared that she was happy to see in him 'a force of character which she hoped in greater and more eventful scenes I might evince'. She took her son in her arms and 'wept awfully'. Then suddenly, with an effort that Harry would never forget,

> her tears were dried, she held me at arms length, and gazing at me more intently, said, 'I have two favours to ask of you: one is that you never visit a public billiard-room; the next—our country is at war—if you ever meet your enemy, remember you are born a true Englishman!'

And so Harry was sent off.

Whereas most soldiers learned their trade in the rough-and-ready school of war, Harry learned his at Brabourne Lees in

Kent. The Riflemen, along with the 43rd and 52nd, were specially trained as light infantry under a scientific soldier, Sir John Moore. The brigade, still largely in the experimental stage, was Moore's response to the French sharpshooters who skirmished ahead of their columns of conscripts to fluster and decimate rigid rows of soldiers firing volleys that had neither the accuracy nor the angle to hurt the almost invisible *tirailleurs*. Though severely criticized by traditionalists, Moore insisted upon greater initiative, with a mutual trust between officers and men that depended more upon morale than harsh discipline. Those who could not meet Moore's high standards were weeded out. They were few. In most instances superior recruits were attracted to the novel corps with the green jackets. More than one Rifleman declared that he 'fell in love with their smart, dashing and devil-may-care appearance' and joined forthwith. One officer of the 95th, George Simmons, in replying to his father's observation that the Rifles were a *dangerous regiment*, said that 'the more danger the more honour'. Harry Smith spoke of his comrades as 'proper, saucy fellows', brimming with fun and animal spirits as they skirmished swiftly and relied on individual intelligence without sacrificing the principle of mutual strength. They were described as a pack of trained hounds, running as individuals without any apparent order, but there were no stragglers as they instinctively pursued a common objective.

After Nelson's victory at Trafalgar reduced the danger of a French invasion, the Riflemen began to depart for active service. While the 1st Battalion under Col. Sydney Beckwith left for the low countries to engage the French, Harry remained in England another year to perfect his training. He did so well that though he had never experienced the cut and slash of combat, he was made adjutant to a detachment of the 2nd Battalion which was to embark in the autumn of 1806, destination unknown. Before sailing from Falmouth, Harry bought a notebook to record the deeds that would bring credit to himself and his family. But two months at sea were a terrible bore. His entries were but a pale reflection of what his fiery imagination had led him to expect.

The force being conveyed, 4,500 men under Sir Samuel Auchmuty, was destined to take part in a disastrous sideshow in the River Plate region of South America. The campaign

began as an unauthorized wildcat scheme thought up by Admiral
Home Popham to break the Spanish trade monopoly in the
New World. In the style of Elizabethan buccaneers, they sailed
from Cape Town and audaciously seized Buenos Aires. Apart
from the over one million dollars captured, the economic
opportunities were so promising that an enthusiastic British
government quickly approved Popham's successful attack, and
hundreds of merchant ships were outfitted to exploit the new
sources of riches. The Spaniards, meanwhile, having recovered
from the surprise attack, defeated and captured the small army
of occupation under Col. Beresford. It was into this confused
situation that Auchmuty sailed early in 1807. On his own
initiative, he decided to establish a new footing in the region
with a daring assault on the heavily garrisoned and strongly
fortified town of Montevideo.

Harry Smith and the two Rifle companies were conspicuous
in the final assault on the night of 3 February 1807. Advancing
in absolute darkness, guided only by flashes of enemy cannon
and musket fire, they cleared the way into town with nothing
more than swords and bayonets, for they were ordered not to
load their pieces. Most of the stormers fell, many wounded by
each others' bayonets. 'Having licked them confoundedly,'
Harry noted in his diary, Montevideo was taken.

Harry, who came through the battle unscathed, barely had
time to contemplate his good fortune when he was stricken by
dysentery. He owed his life to the kindness of a Spanish family
in whose home he was quartered. It appears, however, that their
motives were not altogether altruistic, for the daughter of the
family, 'who taught him Spanish' during his long convalescence,
was urged upon him as a bride with a dowry of $20,000, as
many thousand oxen as he wished and a home built to suit his
tastes. Harry politely declined.

Back on duty in June with more spirit than flesh, Harry
continued his role as adjutant with an additional five companies
of the 95th, part of the force that had arrived under Col. Robert
Craufurd. That the initial success of Popham's expedition
inspired some hare-brained schemes is illustrated by the
original orders given to Craufurd: he was to take a convoy of
4,000 men into the Pacific and liberate Chile, then cross the
Andes and establish communications with General Auchmuty
in Argentina almost a thousand miles away. Fortunately,

Craufurd's transports were held up at Cape Horn to return and help in the recovery of Buenos Aires.

Despite the presence of two able commanders, the government decided to send out General John Whitelocke as commander-in-chief, and General Leveson-Gower as second in command — appointments which were more the result of political than military achievement. What reputation Whitelocke had in the army was built largely upon his outbursts of incredible obscenity in dealing with officers and men. One soldier described him as having 'an ungainly figure with a face of brass'.

Whitelocke made preparations to recapture Buenos Aires at the end of June. Craufurd's force, to which Harry was attached, led the attack. After struggling through two miles of mud, they surprised the Spaniards and were on the verge of taking the city when they were recalled to the starting point — Leveson-Gower had a new plan. Violating the basic rules of tactics, Leveson-Gower put forth the novel suggestion that the army be divided into thirteen converging and unconnected columns. The soldiers were to keep their weapons unloaded until their objectives deep in the city were reached. No provision was made for supporting artillery fire. Whitelocke agreed to the plan and then disappeared; he gave no indication as to where he could be found during the battle.

The entire population of Buenos Aires with Gauchos from the pampas rose up against the British columns; ferocious street fighting ensued. Even the women inhabitants, some of them wearing uniforms, contested their advance. While the British struggled to load their weapons, they were sprayed with grapeshot from cannons placed in ditches across the main streets. From every flat-topped roof, musket-shot, bricks, fire-pots, and even boiling oil and water poured down upon them. Suffering heavy casualties, Craufurd's men took refuge in the San Domingo convent, where they were quickly surrounded by 6,000 of the enemy. Whitelocke had 5,400 men in reserve but made no effort to relieve the trapped columns, such as Craufurd's, or to support the two which had successfully taken strong positions. 'Black Bob' Craufurd, a man with a savage temper, loudly cursed Whitelocke and was reported to have ordered his soldiers to shoot the commander-in-chief on sight.

At four o'clock in the afternoon, Craufurd, 'with a bitter pang of heart', was forced to surrender and become a prisoner. The next day, Whitelocke, who still had the strength to retrieve the disaster, agreed to a convention abandoning not only Buenos Aires but Montevideo as well, and to withdraw all of His Majesty's forces from the Plata region within two months in exchange for the release of all British prisoners. One commentator expressed the mood of the army when he wrote: 'This spiritless fool accepted the hard terms ... thereby forever basely staining the glorious annals of England's military history.' Whitelocke was tried by court martial and cashiered. It was popularly believed that he was not executed because of an illegitimate connection with a member of the royal family. For years after, Whitelocke's memory was preserved in the soldier's toast: 'Success to grey hairs, but bad luck to Whitelocks.'

Humiliated by the 'shameful convention' and three days' imprisonment, Harry Smith argued that if the church of San Domingo had not been surrendered 'it would have enabled Whitelocke, from the base of his other successes, to have made an attempt to rescue the force in San Domingo, or again to have moved against the city'. As Harry watched soldiers paint walls with huge letters announcing 'Whitelocke is a traitor', or 'Whitelocke is a coward', he concluded that the real culprit responsible for the defeat and capitulation was 'the overbearing fool' Leveson-Gower. Whitelocke was a scapegoat sacrificed to an angry public. Being a junior officer, Harry was thankful that in no way could his name be associated with the disaster. As for Craufurd, though he was acquitted of wrongdoing, he never got over the experience; in subsequent battles he seemed driven by a desire to prove himself.

Harry had experienced his first campaign. He had, as seasoned soldiers boasted, 'smelled the enemy's powder', and had done so with considerable credit. One impression that never left him, and was later reinforced in Spain, was that a poorly armed but aroused citizenry could be a formidable enemy.

After two months' leave in Whittlesea, Harry Smith reported for duty to Col. Beckwith, who had once more taken command of the regiment. The colonel expressed approval of his conduct in South America and gave him temporary command of a company composed largely of wild Irish recruits. Among the newcomers gathered at Colchester was Rifleman Wilke, who on his way through London climbed St Paul's Cathedral to stop the pendulum of the clock and set all the bells ringing. Lieut. Smith instilled obedience by applying a firm hand and using his powerful lungs. Beckwith was so pleased with Harry's efforts that he rewarded him by giving his brother Tom a commission in the same battalion.

In the meantime the war with Napoleon continued, and it was clear that Britain could use all the help she could get. Therefore, when the king of Sweden appeared ready to join the conflict, the British government eagerly despatched an expedition under Sir John Moore to provide support. Moore soon found out that in his relations with the Swedish king he was dealing with a madman who, among his other peculiarities believed he was the reincarnation of his illustrious forebear, Gustavus Adolphus. Negotiations with the king required all of Sir John's tact and ingenuity, particularly in trying to convince the deranged monarch that an invasion of Russia via Vibourg and St Petersburg was foolhardy. The king finally ordered his men to seize the British general. To evade arrest, Sir John was forced to masquerade as a peasant.

During all this time, the British force of 10,000 men was not allowed to land. Harry, serving once more as adjutant to three companies of the 95th, kept his men in condition by organizing athletic contests. In the long-jump competitions with the 43rd and 52nd, the young adjutant took the prize with the grand leap of 19 feet and 4 inches. Such was Harry's role in the expedition to Sweden! Moore ordered his disappointed men back to England, but they never reached home. The expedition was diverted to join the Spaniards who were resisting Napoleon's efforts to conquer Iberia.

The British army, which was fast becoming the laughing stock of Europe, went from a wild goose chase in Sweden to another misadventure in Spain. Before Moore's force, expanded to 30,000, could join the Spaniards, their new allies were defeated and dispersed. The British were left on their own to face Napoleon's army of 180,000 men. Rather than court disaster by meeting the French head-on, Moore worried and harassed them while desperately hoping that the Spaniards would recover. It was a dangerous game that demanded the utmost from his men, especially the 95th. As 'fighting, thinking' soldiers, they employed rapid movement and accurate fire-power to frustrate the enemy while the redcoats advanced or retreated. With their famous quickstep to conquer distance and time, the 'dashing Rifles' almost invariably appeared at the right place to do the right thing. Harry Smith, with his knowledge of Spanish, was busiest of all. Beckwith sent him forth daily to interrogate the friendly inhabitants, procure rations and find billets.

In danger of being cut off and annihilated by Napoleon's superior numbers, Moore was forced to undertake, in mid-winter, a hasty 250-mile retreat across the Spanish sierras to Corunna, where transports would receive them. 'From the severe attack on our rear-guard at Calcavellos [3 January 1809], where I was particularly distinguished,' related Harry, 'we were daily engaged with a most vigorous enemy, making most terrific long marches (one day 37 miles).' With Riflemen functioning as a disciplined, protective screen, Harry watched as much of the fleeing British army dissolved into 'drunken-ness and disorder'. Handsome, sullen-faced Craufurd, in charge of the Light Brigade, seemed ubiquitous. Embittered by his experience in Buenos Aires, he was 'all fire and intelligence, a master spirit of war' as he strove to maintain order. Never out of the saddle, he rode up and down the lines applying the lash for the slightest infraction of his draconic code. One soldier grudgingly admitted: 'If he flogged two, he saved hundreds from death.'

The transports were delayed by storms, and the French, under Marshal Soult fell remorselessly on their quarry before embarkation could begin. Moore's men, whom Harry described 'as a mass of fugitives and insubordinates', were transformed by the prospect of fighting their pursuers, 'and these fellows licked the French like men'. Afterwards, the British boarded their ships unmolested and sailed for home. Moore, however, died at the hour of victory, his shoulder having been torn off by a round shot.

The British nation was not unaccustomed to the sight of an unsuccessful army returning home, but rarely were the survivors returned in such a deplorable condition as those who landed on 21 January 1809. The sight of Moore's force, reduced 'to a sickly skeleton', horrified the people of Portsmouth. Many soldiers were stricken with typhus and dysentery; all were in filthy rags infested with lice, for the soldiers were unable to change clothes after the baggage had been lost at Calcavellos three weeks before. As they shambled on to the beach, some of the Riflemen joked about their appearance. One commented that they resembled 'the rakings of hell more than the fragments of an army'. On seeing Harry Smith in the George Inn, Col. Beckwith cried out: 'Who the devil's ghost are you, take a place in the coach, and set off home to your father's. I shall soon want again such fellows as you, and I will arrange your leave of absence!'

Huddled in a corner of the coach in tattered clothes and tormented by vermin, Harry reflected on the expedition that had covered itself 'with glory, disgrace, victory and misfortune'. His mother was first to greet him and to her alone did he confide his lousy condition. As she bathed and dressed him, she promised to preserve their mutual secret.

Harry discovered, first as a huntsman and now as a soldier, that he had the boldness and endurance to achieve despite formidable obstacles. Aside from the thrill of being shot at—and missed, his courage gave him a sense of well-being and superiority that qualified him to lead others into battle. He pondered his vanities: a booming voice more common to a man twice his size; an ability to withstand fatigue while seemingly stronger men fell from exhaustion; a manly way of plain-speaking that made for strong friends—and enemies; and though he had a powerful, intimidating, at times uncontrollable temper, in battle he could stay steady and impersonal. Vanity obviously lured men into battle, but it was pride, the pride of high-souled Englishmen—such as himself—that made them conduct themselves with honour.

While being nursed by his parents so that he might return to war, Harry was more effusive than ever in recounting his heroic deeds. (There was no false modesty about Harry.) His parents listened. Their son, so different from the others, was now twenty-one and had grown to manhood. But his short, thin and angular figure continued to give him a boyish look. His face still had no need for a razor. This, however, was no handicap to British soldiers, for they took pride in their clean-shaven faces. Wearing a moustache was a novel affection sported by the French who believed it gave them a terrifying countenance. Englishmen needed no such bluster! Harry's

short-cropped, dark-brown curly hair, which was brushed
forward, contributed to his youthful appearance. In his later,
full-faced years, it combined with his patrician nose—the kind
that Napoleon said indicated a born leader of men—and cleft
chin to give him the visage of a noble Roman of the classical
era. The large, heavy-lidded eyes were dark and shrewd and in
them, at turns, darted the merriment of a prankish boy or the
fury of a basilisk. The thin mouth and determined jaw suggested self-esteem and confidence. His manner was forceful and
blunt, as befitted a soldier, far removed from the social graces
and ready wit that gave rise to a more flaccid charm. In the
strong lines of Harry's face and bearing were stamped the
signet of his success.

After two months at home, Harry decided he was fit enough
to return to his regiment, now preparing to join Wellington's
army in Spain. There were new faces in the battalion, including
that of Johnny Kincaid, a cheery, flippant young subaltern who
proved to be a gallant leader in action and a master of fun and
frivolity in the camp. As they embarked at Dover, Kincaid
noticed how light-heartedly most Riflemen left their women:
'A thorough-going one just gave a kiss to his wife and two to
his sweetheart, if he had not [a wife], and away he went with a
song in his mouth.'

Once more the Light Brigade was under the erratic, sometimes brilliant, Craufurd, whom most men dreaded as much as
the enemy. With a relentless fury, Craufurd drove the Light
Brigade from their landing at Lisbon to the army at Talavera,
deep in the heart of Spain. On little more than sheeptracks,
during the height of an oppressive Iberian summer, his
marches were unparalleled. In the final 28 hours according to
Harry's calculation, the Rifles, carrying heavy packs, marched
56 miles by employing Moore's quickstep, three marching
paces alternating with three running paces.

They appeared a few hours too late to take part in Wellington's hard-fought victory over Marshal Victor at Talavera on
29 July 1809. Advancing across the field with bugle-horns
sounding merrily, Harry was astonished to hear the exhausted
redcoats cheer, 'as if we were demi-gods'. Following some
heavy skirmishing with the retreating enemy, the Rifles were
put to work collecting the dead, who were already putrefying
in the heat. Efforts to burn the piles of dead, however, were

suspended because of the protests of their comrades. Harry and
his burial party were at the inglorious task for days.

Rather than advance to Madrid, Wellington prudently
retired towards Portugal, much to the disappointment of both
his soldiers and the British government. The rest of the year
and throughout the winter, the army remained in quarters
while their Spanish allies rushed on to Madrid—and defeat.
The 95th still served as the 'eyes' of an unmolested army,
active only in battling disease. But there was much time for 'a
jolly set of fellows' such as the Rifles to amuse themselves.
While the rankers found their fun in turning loose a pig with a
greased tail, a prize to any man who caught it, Harry and
Captain James Stewart, no less mad about hunting, 'were
always coursing or shooting, and never sick a day; our more
sedentary comrades many of them distressingly more so'.
Normally they shot red deer and wild boars, but one day in the
company of several subalterns they accidentally flushed a nest of
bandits. Having no shot left, Harry's party retreated firing
buttons plucked from their jackets. On learning that there were
a score or more of these villains who terrorized the district,
Harry returned with a dozen men, some of whom were convalescents who were barely able to march. They fell upon the
bandits, taking a dozen prisoners along with their captain.
Harry feared few men but he was unnerved by the prospect of
encountering the wrath of Craufurd when he reported his
unauthorized 'battle of the Bandits'. The general, however, was
well pleased that he had rid the countryside of these predators.
Harry and his party were rewarded with the spoils, Harry's
share being the captain's beautiful white horse.

In the spring of 1810 Wellington's small army faced
expulsion from Iberia at the hands of Marshal Masséna, a
commander with a large force and formidable reputation.
Napoleon called him 'the spoiled child of Fortune'. It was a
strenuous season for the Light Brigade, which formed the
nucleus of Craufurd's Light Division. Every day had its
demands; speed was essential. The entire division, which
included the 1st and 3rd Caçadores (Portuguese Light Troops)
and the 17th Portuguese Regiment, the 1st German Hussars,
and the Horse Artillery under Captain Hew Ross (the famous
'Chestnut Troop') needed only seven minutes to get under
arms, night or day. As Wellington's forward division, wrote

Harry, 'we prided ourselves upon destroying the enemy *and preserving ourselves.*'

The saga of the 'Light Bobs' was an affair of outposts, minor actions as they were somewhat disparagingly called by others, but often vital to the success and survival of the army. The combat of the Coa was a different sort of contest. It was one of the hardest fought Peninsular battles in which Harry was engaged, and it was nearly a disaster. Heedless of Wellington's warning not to tarry in defending the crossing at the Coa river, the audacious Craufurd was so unadvisedly vain of his *corps d'élite* that he matched 4,000 against Marshal Ney's 24,000. 'But for Beckwith,' wrote Harry, 'the whole force would have been sacrificed' that day, 24 July 1810.

Harry and the 95th held a line before the unfordable river until the mounting pressure of the French became almost irresistible. Unaware that the 52nd was still on the wrong side of the Coa, Craufurd ordered the Rifles to retire across the narrow bridge. Beckwith, realizing the general's mistake, ordered them to hold the crossing while the 43rd counter-attacked so as to give the 52nd enough time to withdraw. According to Captain William Napier of the 43rd: 'Their matchless discipline was their only protection; a phantom hero [Moore] from Corunna saved them!' The bridge was soon piled with dead grenadiers which the Riflemen used as breast-works. Harry's company was the last to leave the scene. By then Harry had been hit by a ball in the ankle. Unable to walk, he feared that he would remain in agony on the spot where he fell until the French made him a prisoner. On seeing his predica-ment, Harry's friend Major MacLeod went to his rescue, put him on his horse and had him taken to the rear. There Harry learned that his brother Tom had been shot through both legs.

Harry soon discovered that the trials endured by the wounded could be more terrible than anything in battle. Unlike the French, the British had no mobile field units or ambulance wagons in the forward area. The moving army sent the dispos-able invalids under escort to the large hospitals far to the rear. The Smith brothers, along with dozens of stricken comrades, improvised as best they could as they shuffled or were trans-ported to the Mondego river, where they would board a ship bound for Lisbon. Harry rode in relative comfort on a gentle-men's sedan chair slung between two mules, while Tom and others more seriously wounded 'suffered excruciating agony' in bullock carts. 'Several of the poor soldiers,' he wrote to his father, 'died upon the road ... Their wounds became completely alive with myriads of large maggots, which really made me shudder.' Those still living groaned all day to the accompaniment of the screeching of ungreased wheels. Carts broke down, sometimes spilling their contents on the road. The cart carrying his friend George Simmons, who had been an assistant surgeon before becoming a combat officer in the 95th, was deserted by the driver, who took the bullocks with him. Harry related,

> As I was the spokesman, the surgeon in charge came to me in great distress. I sent for the village magistrate and actually fixed a rope in my room to hang him if he did not get a pair bullocks (if the Duke of Wellington had known he would have hung *me*).

The bullocks were promptly delivered but they were not broken. 'They ran away with George and nearly jolted him to death, for he was awfully wounded through the thick of the thigh.'

Regulations did not provide for hospital accommodation in Lisbon. Harry, Tom and George settled themselves at an inn known as the Golden Lion, where they had a great feast. The exorbitant cost, however, put out of the question any thought they had of staying there. They found less expensive lodgings in a 'miserable empty house' on the outskirts of the city. The application of leeches, and frequent bleeding and purging were (not surprisingly) to no avail. Tom was sent home.

Wellington, retreating towards the skilfully constructed fortifications around Lisbon, called the Lines of the Torres Vedras, turned and halted his army at the ridge of Busaco to maul his pursuers. Harry and George were elated by the news of a great victory over Masséna and then saddened by the fact that they were not with the Light Division in routing 'Johnny Crappo', as they sometimes called the French. Simmons wept at the thought of not being there. Harry was given a dubious share of the glory forty years later when he was sent a clasp for Busaco. (His name appears in the regimental records as having been there.)

Though insufficiently recovered, Harry and George pleaded with the medical authorities at Belem to allow them to return to their regiment. They were joined by a fellow subaltern, Charlie Eeles. The three cripples—Harry with one foot turned out, George on crutches, and Charlie tottering from fever and missing a thumb—were placed under an Irish major subject to fits. The major gave them the responsibility of watching over a draft of 600 men being returned to the front from the base depot at Belem. They were mostly what the army called the 'Belem Rangers', the worst scoundrels and malingerers, noted for 'every species of skulk'. Scores of them disappeared on the march. On hearing of their desertions, the major went raving mad and fainted. George threw a bucket of cold water over him to hasten his recovery, but it was soon obvious that Harry, a mere lieutenant, would have to take command. To maintain discipline over 'these rascals', Harry relied on two advantages: 'a capital English horse, good at riding over the insubordinate fellow, and a voice of thunder.'

When Harry delivered the men from the Guards to their commander during a heavy rainstorm, 'the commanding officer put his head out of his cottage and said, "Oh, send for the sergeant-major".' Harry roared out, 'We the Light Division men don't do duty with sergeant-majors nor are we told to wait. There are your men, everyone—the only well-conducted in 600 under my charge—and these are your accounts.' He threw down a bundle of papers in the mud and galloped off before the astonished commander could find his voice.

Having placed his charges with their parent regiments, Harry reported to Beckwith. His colonel took a hard look at the injured foot and said, 'You are a mad fool of a boy, coming here with a ball in your leg. Can you dance?' Harry replied, 'No; I can hardly walk but with my toe turned out.' Beckwith thought for a moment and then asked, 'Can you be my A.D.C.?'—'Yes; I can ride and eat', was the answer. Beckwith laughed.

Harry discharged his new duties with credit, but the pain in his foot was often unbearable. Beckwith, suffering himself from intermittent fever,[1] waited until the approaching winter brought a lull in the fighting and then invited Harry and George Simmons to return with him to Lisbon for medical assistance.

Three surgeons examined Harry's sloughing wound. Two of

[1] Probably malaria. One treatment used on an ailing surgeon was to drop buckets of cold water on him from a third-floor window.

them, doubting the success of an operation, warned him that a
stiff leg of his own was better than a wooden one. The third,
named Brownrigg, observed, 'If it were my leg, out should
come the ball.' This is what Harry wanted to hear and shouted,
'Hurrah Brownrigg, you're the doctor for me.'

Before the advent of anaesthesia, it was a point of honour for
British soldiers to show no sign of suffering, no matter how
great the pain, when the surgeon applied his terrible tools: the
probe, the knife and the saw.[1] With Harry there was no need to
exhort him to summon his fortitude, as surgeons often did, for
he cocked up his leg and jauntily declared, 'There it is; slash
away.' The ball lodged in the ankle-joint was jagged, and
tendonous fibres had so grown into it that it took five minutes
of tearing and cutting to remove it. Vinegar was the only
antiseptic. When the surgeon asked for linen to dress the wound,
Harry told George Simmons to tear up a shirt. Looking at
Harry's shirt, George decided, 'No, it is a pity; it is a good
shirt.' With his leg 'aching and smoking', the incident gave
Harry a chance to vent his pent-up feelings by 'damning him a
few' for not tearing up his shirt. By February 1811 Harry had
recovered completely and returned to join the regiment under
Col. Beckwith, himself sufficiently improved to return some
weeks earlier.

The news that his company commander, Captain Leach, had
been taken ill and gone to the rear led to Harry's request for
permission to take charge of the company. The fatherly
Beckwith, always the model of amiability, said: 'Ah, now you
can walk a little, you leave me! Go and be damned to you; but
I love you for your desire.' To Harry, 'Old Sydney' was the
ideal leader. He was never caught napping, in fact, he always
slept in his clothes.

For five months Masséna stubbornly held his position before
the impregnable Torres Vedras, while his army lived off the
country like a plague of locusts. As his army grew weaker,
Wellington's grew stronger. On 6 March the British outposts
learned that the French were retreating across the bleak,
barren country. For the Light Division there was a daily

---

[1] The British had no monopoly on fortitude. One of Napoleon's veterans, who
had been taken prisoner, merely glowered as the surgeon removed his arm. After
the job was done, he seized his amputated appendage, hurled it in the air and
cried: 'Vive l'Empereur! Vive Napoléon!'

association with death as they pressed Marshal Ney and his rearguard.

'That skinny little devil' Smith, indifferent to danger and making enough noise to deafen the enemy, soon gained a reputation that reached headquarters. When a vacancy occurred, a general order was sent appointing him brigade major to the 2nd Light Brigade under Col. Drummond, not, as Harry desired, Beckwith's 1st. On reporting to Drummond with a request for orders regarding the pickets, the colonel let Harry know that 'it is your duty to post the piquets, and mine to have a damned good dinner for you every day'. They understood each other perfectly. 'He cooked dinner often himself,' recalled Harry, 'and I *commanded* the Brigade.'

And so it was. Harry and Beckwith moved into battle with their brigades, handicapped considerably by the absence of Craufurd, who was on leave. Sir William Erskine, Craufurd's replacement sent out from England, was described by Wellington as an exasperating 'madman' and by Harry as 'a near-sighted ass', hopelessly dilatory and confused. Erskine floundered at the battle of Sabugal, Harry's first as a *de facto* brigadier. It was Beckwith who again saved the day. 'Old Sydney', knocked from his horse and with blood streaming down his face in a way that 'excited interest in his appearance', drew his men back a short distance to the face of a hill and then called out in his calm, clear voice, 'Now my men, this will do — let us show them our teeth again.' The French, after repeated attacks, left the disputed field.

That night 'the old rogue', General Picton, stole the supplies of the Light Division for his own 3rd Division. He would never have succeeded, Harry declared, if Craufurd had been in command instead of Erskine. Sir Thomas Picton, whom the Duke described as a fine soldier but 'a rough foul-mouthed devil as ever lived', was a forceful character and a great rival of Craufurd, whom he refused to rescue at the battle of the Coa. While serving as governor of Trinidad, he created a scandal by having a young mulatto girl suspected of theft put to torture, which was legal under the Spanish law that still prevailed in the colony.

Craufurd returned, 'amidst every demonstration of joy', to command his division on the eve of the battle of Fuentes de Oñoro (5 May 1811). The steadiness of his men was such that they successfully held against Masséna's heavily reinforced

3

army. Harry boasted that the 'Light Bobs' were capable of turning the tide of victory any day. The French, however, retired unmolested; their formidable cavalry was too much for the Light Division in open country. An inactive summer followed and, save for an occasional sharp brush that autumn, the year ended quietly.

As a brigade major, Harry proved invaluable to Drummond and his successor, General Vandeleur, whom Harry described as 'a fine gentleman-like old, Irish hero'. All were impressed by the way Harry discharged his duties. In battle or on the march he was rarely off his horse, not resting until his men were properly billeted or settled for the night. 'His devotion to their comforts,' wrote Johnny Kincaid, 'was repaid by their affections.'

As a staff officer, Harry was no stranger at headquarters, where he met officers of high social standing. His own status was no handicap, for he was regarded as a gentleman and, therefore, treated as an equal. The opportunity of cultivating the friendship of senior officers was one that Harry, with little money to buy a promotion, could not ignore. Being eminently plainspoken without a hint of that English virtue of keeping oneself to oneself, he could be most engaging.

Sometimes not. The first time Harry met Sir Lowry Cole, a peppery Irishman, he was sent to act as a guide for the general's 4th Division. It was dark when Harry arrived, so Cole wondered if he was sure that he knew the way. Harry's cool reply was, 'I suppose I should not have been sent if I had not.' It was soon obvious, however, that Harry was confused in the dark. The anxious general kept repeating, 'Are you sure you know the road, sir?' Unable to contain himself any longer, Harry said sharply, 'General Cole, if you will let me alone, I will conduct your Division; if you attract my attention I might miss the road!' Cole exploded with anger as Harry rode off and found the road. As soon as the head of Cole's column reached it, Harry turned and shouted a curt 'Good Night, General', and rode off. Cole shouted in vain for him to come back. (Harry was destined to serve under Cole when the latter became governor of the Cape Colony.)

The young brigade major was by this time no stranger to Wellington. His reputation with horses and hounds during the chase, which was the Duke's great passion, was in itself sufficient to attract the great commander's attention. To his way of thinking, a subaltern who rode well to the hounds would in all likelihood make an excellent officer. The Duke's devotion to the sport is illustrated by an occasion when he was in earnest conversation with General Castanos and they were interrupted by a hare and a pair of hounds that shot across the field. With a loud 'View halloa!' he charged after them in hot pursuit. When the hunt was finished, Wellington resumed his discussion as if nothing had happened. The Spanish general was firmly convinced that the English were as mad as the hares that they pursued with such outrageous abandon.

When Craufurd, 'in one of his mad freaks', reported that the Light Division lacked clothing and other essentials and must go to the rear, Wellington ordered an inspection. The Duke began to ride down the line before Craufurd arrived. On seeing him rush up, the Duke laughed and chided him for being late. Craufurd retorted: 'No, my Lord; you are before your time. My watch is to be depended on.' The tension was broken when Harry's brown mare charged the Duke. The horse was well known. It had belonged to Craufurd, who could not ride her, and was bought by Harry for £120 from another officer that had been thrown by her. 'Hallo Smith,' said the Duke with a stern look, 'your horse masters you.' After the inspection, Wellington announced in his customary abrupt manner of speaking: 'I never saw the Light Division look better or more ready for service. March back to your quarters; I shall soon require you in the field.'

At the beginning of the year 1812, Wellington assigned the Light Division the most disagreeable of all duties, to act as a human battering-ram to breach the walls of Ciudad Roderigo. The town was a stepping stone to Badajoz, the second fortress-city that guarded the frontier of Spain. Wellington could easily take the initiative even in the middle of winter. Carrying his own supplies, he had the advantage of superior mobility. The larger French armies, lumbering in a land stripped of food and abounding in guerillas, worried and laboured to parry the Duke's quick thrusts. More than ever, their generals complained that large armies starved and small ones were defeated.

After marching through deep snow, the British began the investment of Ciudad Roderigo. Following the twelve days of

bombardment, two breaches were pronounced practicable on
19 January 1812. Wellington assigned the larger to Picton's
3rd, called the 'Fighting Division', and the smaller to the
Light, or just *The* Division. Each formed a storming party of
300 men that would be preceded by the 'forlorn hope', an
officer and 25 volunteers. Their purpose was to draw the first
fire and cause the enemy to touch off their mines prematurely.
Plunging into the fiery jaws of the breach called for the most
desperate courage. The French called the volunteers 'Les
Enfants perdus', 'the Lost Children'. Yet, soldiers of the
Peninsular army clamoured to join. There were no rewards;
medals for bravery had not yet been instituted. Only the
subaltern who led them could reckon on a promotion — if
successful. Harry went to Craufurd to ask for the honour of
leading the 'forlorn hope'. 'Black Bob' frowned and said: 'Why
you cannot go; you a Major of the Brigade, a senior Lieutenant,
you are sure to get a Company. No, I must give it to a younger
officer.' The 'forlorn hope' was given to Lieut. Gurwood.

Before the night attack began, Harry had supper with his
brother, Tom, and Captain Uniacke, one of the most active
men in the 95th. When they parted, Uniacke said light-
heartedly, 'Harry, you will be a captain before morning.'
Ironically it turned out that his own death would provide the
vacancy for Harry's promotion.

The three were with the storming party under Major George
Napier of the 43rd when the breach was cleared with bayonets.
Many were down, including Napier,[1] Gurwood, Vandeleur, and
Craufurd. Once through the defences, guided only by fire balls
to show the ground, the stormers swung to the left and to the
right to clear the French from the ramparts. On seeing that the
enemy still defended the larger breach against the 3rd Division,
Harry unceremoniously seized a company of the 43rd from
under the nose of their captain. The captain protested
vehemently and the two exchanged some 'very high words'
over the sounds of battle. The soldiers settled the argument by
following the little brigade major, who attached them to
Uniacke's company. Together they rushed into an explosion
touched off by the defenders. The men were flattened all about.

[1] Waiting for the signal to attack, Napier had the feeling that he would lose an
arm. He asked a surgeon friend to stand by for amputation. His arm was shattered
by grapeshot before he reached the breach.

A much-scorched Harry was blown on to some lighted fuses. A sergeant pulled him to his feet and, on seeing that he had lost his cocked hat, gave him his own catskin forage-cap. They scrambled on to clear the breach just as Picton's Connaught Rangers broke through from the outside. Considering his appearance, one of the Rangers mistook Harry for the enemy. Holding Harry by the throat, he cried out, 'You French bastard!' Harry found sufficient strength to gasp 'damn your eyes' in unmistakable English to avoid being impaled on the Ranger's bayonet.

Most of the men went into town to find drink and plunder, which they believed was their unwritten privilege as stormers. The officers consoled their wounded comrades. Harry found Uniacke, who had a short time to live, his arm torn from its socket. His last words were, 'Remember I was the first man who entered the breach.' But the honour went unfairly, in Harry's jaundiced opinion, to that 'sharp fellow' Gurwood. After being momentarily stunned before the breach, Gurwood dashed off to find the governor of the fort, received his sword in surrender and presented it to the Duke.

Craufurd, mortally wounded, spoke a last few words to Wellington, which led to the Duke's cold comment: 'Craufurd talked to me as they do in a novel.' The great leader of the Light Division was buried with full military honours in the lesser breach, close to where he fell, with the Duke and every available officer present. As the 'Light Bobs' marched back to their camp, they came to a large pool in the road. Remembering the words of Craufurd always to march straight ahead regardless of obstacles, the entire column, officers and men, marched through the deep icy water in a silent unrehearsed tribute to their gallant commander.

Another stage in Harry Smith's life thus came to a close. With Craufurd dead and Beckwith on sick leave in England, never to return, the two men, who had by their instruction and example done so much to shape him as a soldier, were gone. Some years later Harry acknowledged to his friend, Major Powell, 'How much I am indebted to dear old Sydney I cannot with democratical heart use fine autocratical expressions, but I love him with a grateful heart I will avow as I can utter *Rifleman*.'

On 28 February 1812, Harry was gazetted a captain.

⌈2⌉

Campaigning with Juana in the Peninsular War

Grace was in all her steps,
Heaven was in her eye,
In all her gestures dignity
and love.

Paradise Lost

Badajoz the Proud, a tight fist of stone, was the strongest fortress on the Spanish frontier of Portugal. To Wellington its capture would lead to a 'fine campaign in spring'. Twice before he had tried to take it and failed. Since then the defences had been strengthened and 5,000 veterans commanded by General Philippon, an expert on siege warfare, were presently garrisoned there. Napoleon declared repeatedly that the English would never try again to take it. Wellington, however, elated by the capture of Ciudad Roderigo in half the time he had expected, was convinced that he could snatch the rich prize before the scattered French armies could re-group and come to its rescue. To deceive the enemy, the Duke and his men rested and amused themselves while an improvised siege-train of iron guns jolted forward from the coast to Badajoz.

It was a time of year when coursing in this part of Spain was excellent. Harry Smith, with a champion hound named Moro, often supplied the officers' mess with 'hares for soup'. Racing about the countryside, he soon became a familiar figure throughout the army.

These were 'delightful days', with one exception that reminded Harry of the grimmer side of war. After the fall of Ciudad Roderigo, British deserters, some of whom had fought on the walls alongside the French and had been heard in battle deriding the Light Division, were captured and sentenced to death. As major-of-brigade for the day, it was Harry's unpleasant duty to preside over the appalling ceremony that attended a military execution. The provost marshal bungled his assignment by failing to instruct the firing squad properly in the matter of killing seven condemned men at once. Some were only wounded, or completely untouched. Harry ordered the firing squad to reload, run up and put the survivors out of their misery. 'It was an awful scene.' The spectacle of death on the battlefield, assuming a hundred forms, seemed honourable; but to Harry, the slow preparations for an execution revolted and sickened him.[1]

The British soldiers cheered when they were told that they were to assault Badajoz. In long, winding columns they marched full of ardour into a land burgeoning with the fruits of spring. The Light, 3rd and 4th Divisions concentrated at Elvas, four miles from their destination. On 17 March 1812 a cordon of 15,000 men crossed the pontoon bridge over the broad Guadiana, their steps enlivened by drums rolling and bugles blaring appropriately 'St Patrick's Day in the Morning' and other favourite tunes which, said Ensign George Bell, 'made our fellows wild for a dash any time'.

But there was no glory immediately ahead. 'No species in which a soldier is liable to be employed is so galling, or so disagreeable, as a siege,' wrote Lieut. George Glieg. Day and night, the men dug trenches in a lashing rain, which rarely let up, while the French harassed them with shot and shell by day, and incendiary devices by night. An Irishman whose regiment was being relieved by another exclaimed, 'Och! boys SOUDRAD RODRAGO was but a *flay-bite* to this.' Under cover of a dense fog on the 19th, the French burst from their gates and sally-ports to slaughter hundreds of surprised workmen. Often bursting shells scattered about dismembered arms, legs and heads. According to Rifleman Costello, special parties were sent out to collect them 'to prevent any ill-effect their appearance might cause on the courage of the Portuguese'.

The walls of Badajoz slowly began to crumble from the incessant pounding of Wellington's guns. An outlying bastion, Fort Picurina, fell on 24 March, thereby providing sites for the

---

[1] When Harry was at the capture of Montevideo, a deserter, a heavyset Irishman, was captured and hanged. Because of his weight, the rope broke. After some time, he was revived by a priest. With a look of astonishment the Irishman, thinking himself in purgatory, exclaimed, 'What! You here, too, Father!' The general gave him a pardon.

breaching batteries against the bastions of Trinidad and Santa
Maria. As the grand crisis approached, the men of the Light
Division became anxious for fear that the French might tamely
surrender. When it was announced that the assault on three
practical breaches would begin on the night of 6 April, 'so great
was the rage for passports into eternity in our battalion,'
observed Kincaid, 'that even the officers' servants insisted on
taking their places in the ranks.' Buglers who were to remain
behind tried to bribe the bugle-major to gain others' places
in the assault. Many soldiers who had suffered in the trenches
and had seen their comrades mangled became 'incredibly
savage', not only towards the French but towards the inhabitants as well, for it was believed that a sizeable segment
sympathized with the enemy.

No less than seven separate assaults were to be hurled against
Badajoz from different directions. The critical main attack on
the breaches was to be delivered by the 4th at the Trinidad
while the Light Division, under the command of General
Andrew Barnard, devoted itself to the Santa Maria. The time
was fixed for ten p.m.

As was the custom, officers and men cleaned their clothes and
polished their equipment as if they were preparing for a
parade. Wellington, personally, cared little about how his men
appeared, so long as they did not look like the French. By now,
his soldiers had resorted to all sorts of improvisations. One
officer wore a modified monk's cassock.

Some prayed. Prayer meetings led by officers were discouraged by the Duke. His approach to religion was official and
mid-Georgian. Above all, he deplored 'enthusiasm' in religious
observances. Years later he caustically observed that he never
saw soldiers perform an act of religious worship in the Peninsular War, except when 'making the sign of the cross to induce
the people of the country to give them wine'. Similarly, Harry
held formal, High Church views. He never spoke of prayer
before battle; but he came to believe that some special
Providence watched over him *this* day.

While others found it an anxious night and were deep in
thought, or joked to relieve the tension, Harry enjoyed a
simple supper with his friends. They shared a farewell glass and
shook hands. Major Peter O'Hare, 'the ugliest man in the
regiment', who was to lead the division's storming party, saw

to it that his men received a double allowance of grog. O'Hare had risen from the ranks and taken part in all the major battles of the 95th. But this night he had a foreboding of death. As he moved off, he muttered, 'A lieutenant-colonel or *cold meat* in a few hours.' Harry, though it was not part of his assignment as a brigade major, went with him to lead the stormers.

The night was dry and still. Not a sound was to be heard save for the croaking of frogs and an occasional sentry's call, 'Sentinelles! Garde-à-vous!', which the British soldiers rendered 'All's well in *Badahoo*!' Words of command were given in hoarse whispers as the men got into position. The French were aware of their presence and Philippon was not deceived as to where the main assault would fall. Confidently he had the gaps in the walls retrenched on both sides. Mines and barrels of explosives were carefully planted, and various ingenious devices which the British had never encountered before were cunningly prepared. The slopes before the breaches were covered with planks and doors studded with spikes. At the top of the breaches were *chevaux-de-frise*, rows of sword-blades, sharp as razors, set in heavy beams and held fast by iron chains. On the ramparts were 1,200 of Philippon's best men, many with six loaded muskets at hand. Harry, not 50 yards away, could see them looking on quietly as his men brought forward grass-bags and ladders for the ditch, and as four companies under Col. Alister Cameron extended along the counterscarp to draw the French fire. They lay down and waited. General Barnard looked about and then gave the order, '*Now*, Cameron!'

'The first shot brought down on us such a hail of fire as I shall never forget, nor ever saw since,' recalled Harry. 'It was murderous.' To Kincaid, the scene that followed 'furnished as respectable a representation of hell itself as fire, and sword, and human sacrifice could make it, for in one instance, every engine of destruction was in full operation'.

The storming party, with officers shouting 'Come on, my lads', rushed to destruction 'like men going home'. They went into the great yawning ditch illuminated by the eerie, irregular light from explosions and meteoric fireballs. Harry slid down a ladder and was one of the first to reach the breach, his arm locked with an officer of the 'forlorn hope', a method adopted where ascent was difficult and steep. One Rifleman got to the top. 'We made a glorious rush to follow,' Harry wrote, 'but

alas! in vain.' The Rifleman was knocked over. Major O'Hare
fell mortally wounded. 'All were awfully wounded except, I do
believe, myself and little Freer of the 43rd.' Other 'Light Bobs'
came to the ditch, paused at the brink and stared down in
amazement at the smoking floor with its carpet of dead and
dying—and then jumped in. Meanwhile, the men of the 4th
Division, assigned to the breach to the right, leaped into a
ditch that was flooded. Finding the water deeper than expected,
they disappeared holding each other in a deadly grasp. All that
was left to indicate their presence was bubbles rising to the
surface. To avoid this fate, the rest of the 4th crowded into the
mass of struggling men on the Light Division side of the ditch.
They died by the hundreds. The French, on the other hand,
suffered little. Now and again they paused in their deadly
labour to jeer and call out mock invitations to come up the
bloody slope and visit Badajoz.

Miraculously, Harry remained unhurt, though his pockets
were filled 'with chips of stones splintered by musket balls'.
Fearing that some waverers might try to climb back out of the
ditch, he told his fellow officer, Freer, to help him throw down
the ladders so that no soldier could get out. But one of the
soldiers behind cried out, 'Damn your eyes, if you do we will
bayonet you.' Harry was literally pushed up out of the ditch by
the mob. In a few moments, however, those who had reached
the glacis were swept back into the ditch by a fresh brigade of
Portuguese determined to carry the breach. There was another
effort, and another, 'but the more we tried to get up, the more
we were destroyed,' declared Harry. 'Both Divisions were
fairly beaten back, we never carried the breach.' After two hours
and innumerable attempts, the pitiful remnants of the two
divisions sullenly retired, on orders from Wellington. 'There is
no battle, day or night,' wrote Harry, 'I would not willingly
re act [sic] except this.'

Harry was met by Lord Fitzroy Somerset (the future Lord
Raglan who commanded in the Crimean War) who asked,
'Where is Barnard?' Harry did not know, but he assured
Wellington's military secretary that he was among the living
and unhurt. Somerset then told him that it was the Duke's
wish that the two divisions try again to enter the breaches.
Harry was astounded. 'The Devil,' he said, 'why we have had
enough, we are all knocked to pieces.' Somerset thought for a

moment and then spoke, 'I dare say, but you must try again.'
Harry smiled and reasoned, 'If we could not succeed with two
whole fresh and unscathed Divisions, we are likely to make a
poor show of it now ... But we will try again with all our
might.'

The diminished numbers moved off with a steadiness that
resembled the first assault. Crossing over the carnage, they
were about to mount the breach when they heard cheering
within the town, then a cry of 'Blood and 'ounds! Where's the
Light Division? — The town's our own — hurrah!' It was the
men of the 3rd Division. Beyond all expectations, 'Rough Old
Tom' Picton, who had left his sick bed with a wound in the
groin, turned his diversionary attack into victory by capturing
the castle in which were the French reserves of food and
ammunition. A second attack propelled by Picton's voice,
which had 'the power of twenty trumpets' as he 'proclaimed
damnation to everybody', burst through undermanned barricades, for Philippon had concentrated his men at the breaches.

At first light, Harry visited the bloody ground (about 100
square yards) where nearly a third of the Light Division had
fallen. Approximately 1,500 dead, dying and wounded were
strewn before the breach. Many were burned, torn to pieces or
trampled beyond recognition. Only one Rifleman had succeeded
in getting under the hedge of swords: his head had been
battered to bits. O'Hare was found stretched out naked with
three musket balls through his breast. In another spot Harry
found nine slain officers. Some men were still warm but so
desperately injured that they could not be moved without more
assistance than was available. They remained, in the words of
Surgeon Henry, 'stiffening in their gore'.

Harry returned to camp to change his clothes, which had been
cut by musket balls. He discovered that his body had several
contusions, one particularly severe on his left thigh.

The horrors of Badajoz now shifted to inside the walls. It was
still the accepted rule in siege warfare that if a governor did not
capitulate after a practicable breach had been made, the surviving stormers enjoyed the rights to pillage and to gratify
feelings of revenge. No instructions were given to restrain the
men after the fall of Badajoz. Even if there were, it is doubtful
if they would have been obeyed. At first, Barnard, Cameron,
Harry and a few other officers still on their feet kept much of the

Light Division in hand outside the town. Cameron threatened to shoot any man who left the ranks. By mid-morning, on seeing that the entire garrison had surrendered and was being marched out, he released them and told them to enjoy themselves for the rest of the day, but to report as usual for roll call that evening. However, that night, instead of the customary tattoo report of 'all present', it was 'all absent'.

Of all human undertakings, war is one of the most precarious to order: once the system breaks down, chaos and barbarism threaten. Such a breakdown occurred at Badajoz: for two days the soldiers went on the rampage and wantonly sacked the town as no British army had done since the days of Cromwell in Ireland. Virtue and courage abruptly gave way to ignominy. The victorious soldiers sought strong drink as if in a delirium or frenzy, and ignoring pleas for assistance from untended comrades still lying in the field of battle, they became roaring drunk—which only served to increase the overthrow of human decency.

Badajoz and all within it was treated as the soldiers' indisputable property. Though the inhabitants were Spanish, they were considered as sympathetic to the French—and treated accordingly. The soldiers ran amok, plundering, murdering, raping. Neither church nor convent were held sacred, nor priests and nuns spared. In the streets the drunken and the dead lay together.

The men of the 5th Division, having arrived late, looted their inebriated comrades. The army was then joined by criminals released from prison, who acted as guides, and bands of camp followers, women as well as men—'or tigeresses in the shape of women!' They were, if possible, worse than the men.

They stopped at nothing. What they could not carry, they destroyed or burned. Officers, to whom the inhabitants, most of all women, flocked for protection, tried on occasion to stop the violence, and in several cases lost their lives; the officers were totally unable to control the men. Wellington, himself, was approached by revellers firing muskets at random. Holding up broken, jagged-edged bottles they cried, 'Old boy! will you drink. The town's our own—hurrah!' One witness with a gift for understatement reported that the Duke 'did not seem to like it'. Wellington ordered a Portuguese brigade to be marched into the market square and remain under arms as the provost marshal erected a gallows. The effect was magical. The men quickly sobered and the horrors ceased.

Rigorous discipline was everything to Wellington. It was the cement that held his army together and provided the basis on which his great victories were won. The behaviour of his men in Badajoz and at other times when restraints were removed strengthened his opinion that they were 'the scum of the earth'. When people spoke to him 'of their enlisting for their fine military feeling', he scoffed, 'all stuff—no such thing. Some of our men enlist from having got bastard children— some for minor offences—many more for drink!' The events of Badajoz seemed to prove him correct in his estimation of the men. At any rate, discipline was reimposed and the soldiers brought under the control of the officers. The sack of Badajoz was over.

Spain is a land of romance. The luxuriance of the climate with its brilliant sun and clear sky, the unsurpassed beauty of the countryside, the fervency of its people and, above all, the abundance of strikingly attractive women stirred the feelings of the British soldiers. These 'dear little dark creatures with their sweeping eyebrows', as Andrew Barnard saw them, so very graceful and ladylike, so proper in their conduct remained in the minds and imaginations of the soldiers as they lay down at night 'under a canopy of heaven'.

'When the military man approaches,' wrote George Bernard Shaw, 'the world locks up its spoons and packs off its woman-kind.' And so it was when the British soldiers arrived in the Peninsula: they were not welcomed with open arms as allies ready to shed blood for Spain; instead, complained one young officer, the Spaniards had the 'cool effrontry to look upon the English troops as exotic animals', as heretics who had a private quarrel to settle with the French. The British further resented the way the poor Spanish girls were doomed to live entombed in convents like common felons, 'their young hearts blighted forever', as George Simmons commiserated. Conversation with them, if it happened at all, took place through iron grat-ings. George Bell heard them say sadly, 'We are here like birds with clipped wings, powerless.' Some cruel parents, as one officer discovered 'on a certain not too unpleasant occasion', used medieval chastity belts to protect their daughters.

Often yielding-hearted girls were freed from the rigours of 'superstitious bigotry'. Even nuns, wrote Kincaid, who watched the women as closely as he did the enemy, were not averse to 'an elopement without conditions'. The distaff side of the army was soon enlarged beyond the six wives and their children officially allowed rations in most companies. Wives and mistresses by the hundreds — British, Portuguese and Spanish — trailed behind the army with the baggage train.

One Spanish girl, Maria Josefa, the daughter of an influential judge, ran off with a drum-major of the Connaught Rangers. So that she would not be recognized during the search conducted by her angry father, her face was blackened and she was put in the band as a cymbal player. The judge failed to notice that the little 'black', who made more noise than music, was his errant offspring. She and the drum-major were married by a priest, but it was not a happy life. Several attempts were made to assassinate her and her husband. After the drum-major was killed in action, she returned to her father.

As a rule, officers rarely had female companions. Their wives were left at home, or at the base, seldom journeying with them on the march. A few young officers had paramours; but unlike the French generals, who often had mistresses (Masséna was reputed to have debauched himself with a portable harem), the British higher command appears to have travelled without women.

Wellington was no prude, but he did not like women to distract the soldiers from their duties. He limited one officer's leave to Lisbon on the grounds that forty-eight hours was 'as long as any reasonable man can wish to stay in bed with the same woman'. His views on campaign marriages are not recorded but can hardly be imagined as sympathetic. Hard-bitten Picton, as on most subjects, had strong opinions. He once told the Duke with his distinctive growl: 'Soldiers haven't any business wiveing; but if I ever come to it, I'll marry the youngest tit I can get.'

Women caught in the tumult of Badajoz, where rape, mutilation and even death threatened, looked to British officers for their salvation. Two officers, swords in hand, rescued Philippon and his two daughters. Determined parties of officers fought back the intoxicated mob in protecting homes and escorting women to churches where guards had been placed. Some fled to the British camp.

Harry and Kincaid were standing before a tent discussing the events of the previous night when they were interrupted by the sight of two ladies coming directly towards them from the fire and stone of Badajoz. They were dressed in black, a wealth of silk, white gloves and stockings. Their mantillas, thrown length-wise over their heads, were crossed over their full breasts and brought forward so as to cover the entire face, leaving only one small opening before the left eye. Their movements were regal.

The elder of the two threw back her mantilla, revealing more of her shapely figure and a fine-featured face that was care-worn and haggard beyond her years — which to Kincaid (who recorded the event) meant that 'the time for tender thoughts and soft endearments had fled away and gone'. Speaking in the 'confident, heroic manner so characteristic of the high-bred Spanish maiden', she told them they belonged to an old and highly honoured Spanish family that in more prosperous days had provided quarters for Lord Fitzroy Somerset. Her husband, if he were still living, was serving as an officer with the Spanish army in some distant part of the kingdom. Their beautiful home was destroyed, their belongings stolen and their lives in danger unless they were afforded protection. To demonstrate that they had already suffered outrages, she displayed their bleeding ears from which ear-rings had been torn by drunken soldiers. For herself she cared not; but she despaired for her young sister, fresh from a convent, who had been placed in her care. To spare her innocent charge from dishonour worse than death, she adopted the seemingly indelicate course of coming into their camp and appealing for the protection of a British officer. Her faith in the chivalrous character of English gentlemen was such that she knew her 'appeal would not be made in vain, nor the confidence abused'. Her sister's name was Juana Maria de Los Dolores de Leon.[1]

Juana bared her face and blushed. Her face was 'transcendently lovely', Kincaid tells us. Her complexion was of such delicate freshness that it appeared more English than Spanish. But the clear olive skin and the lustrous dark eyes, large and set wide in her oval face, were unmistakably Andalusian. The generous mouth, slightly tilted up at the ends, hinted humour and mischief.

[1] The sisters were lineal descendants of Ponce de Leon, the explorer who discovered Florida while searching for the Fountain of Youth.

A long graceful neck surmounted 'a figure cast in nature's fairest mold'. Her breasts and hips were charmingly rounded, but slender. Her small, typically Spanish feet were what one soldier called 'kissable'. Kincaid found her so irresistibly attractive that merely 'to look at her was to love her'—and he fell in love on the spot! But much to his sorrow, he failed to move quickly and declare his love, for 'a more impudent fellow stepped in and won her!'[1]

Harry confessed to being the 'more impudent fellow'. In hunting, he sought the swiftest horse; in battle, he wanted to be the first to engage the enemy; in love, he wooed and married in two days. Though Juana had just turned fourteen, the age that Juliet fell in love with Romeo, Harry found in her 'an understanding superior to her years, a masculine mind with a force of character no consideration could turn from her own just sense of rectitude'. All this was encased in the

> figure of an angel, with an eye of light and expression which inspired me with maddening love which ... has never abated under many and most trying circumstances. Thus, as good may come out of evil, this scene of devastation and spoil yielded to me a treasure invaluable.

The unexpected discovery of the love-object, the instant crystallization of feelings, followed by a sudden proposal of marriage provide all of the embellishments of romantic fiction. In the cold light of reality, the chances for the success of such a union seemed few indeed. Juana, mature only in a physical sense and fresh from a cloistered existence, was to marry a duty-bound officer in the middle of a war, the horrors of which she so desperately sought to escape. Aside from the incredibly long and difficult marches, to keep pace with a man of the world such as Harry Smith would seem beyond her capabilities. There was also the matter of religion: she was a devout Catholic; he was a staunch Protestant.

Whatever objections Harry's friends offered were apparently dismissed without a second thought. He asked Wellington for permission to marry. Probably because Fitzroy Somerset spoke on their behalf, the Duke agreed to what he must have regarded

[1] It is difficult to feel sorry for the irrepressible Kincaid. He fell in love at first sight with bewildering frequency and always recovered his heart quickly. He died a bachelor at the age of 75.

as an indulgence; he even consented to give the bride away. They were married by a Catholic chaplain from the Connaught Rangers. There was no honeymoon holiday. Harry boasted that, like Wellington, he never took leave. Moreover, the army, which was once more on the move, was woefully short of officers after the slaughter at Badajoz. As for Juana's sister, having accomplished her mission, she left. There is no record of her fate.

For the first time ever recorded, Wellington shed tears when he learned what it cost to take Badajoz: 5,000 casualties. Ciudad Roderigo had cost another 1,500. The two sieges, Wellington later told Lord Canning, cost him the flower of his army. Lacking an adequate siege-train and expert engineers, he saved time by sacrificing men. The methods were brutal but they foiled French efforts to rescue the garrisons and threw their plans for Spain into confusion. When Napoleon heard that Badajoz had fallen, he had one of his fits of rage and ordered all references to it to be suppressed. He turned his back on Spain and prepared his Grande Armée for the invasion of Russia in June.

With Napoleon marching on Russia and the gates to Spain in his control, Wellington was in a position to undertake the offensive. The French still had 250,000 men in Spain to his 45,000, but they were bedevilled by guerillas and cramped by hunger until harvest time. The Duke decided to move towards Salamanca and deliver a blow against the wily Marshal Marmont. Throughout the spring and on into the summer, the commanders, for once evenly matched, sparred for an opening. As Wellington expressed it, 'I shan't fight him without an advantage, nor he me, I believe.'

Meanwhile, the child-bride was plunged into the world of men, her life now regulated by bugles and by shouts in a language totally foreign to her. Her husband was gone most of the day while she waited for him to emerge from the smoke. His 'trusty old groom', West, was assigned to watch over her. A woman was hired to attend to her personal needs. At night she had Harry sleeping at her side under an open sky, some- times on a battlefield. An upsurge of sexual activity un- doubtedly followed the excitement of battle. (At such times, confessed the Duchess of Marlborough, her husband 'pleasured [her] twice with his boots on'.)

4

On reaching Ciudad Roderigo, the Light Division rested for a week in their former cantonments. The weather was benign and the setting serene. 'Our pretty village', as Kincaid saw it, 'stood baking in the sunshine of the plain, while the surrounding forest courted the lovers of solitude to repose within its shady bosom.' Sentiment briefly ruled the world.

Harry now found the time to teach Juana to ride something other than convent donkeys. One of Harry's saddles was converted into a side-saddle and placed on a large Portuguese horse. Though the horse was appropriately timid, Juana's prejudice was such that she wanted no part of anything that came from Portugal. She insisted upon having the thoroughbred Arab, named Tiny, that Harry had acquired from the bandit-captain. Tiny may have fitted her requirements for size and disposition, but it was Harry's favourite charger. He rejected her pleas by saying, 'When you ride as well as you can dance and sing, you shall.' It was the first of many heated disputes, for they both had, as Harry described it, 'the quickest of tempers'. Fortunately, he continued, 'we were both ready to forgive and both intoxicated in happiness.'

The dispute as to how Juana should be mounted was settled by a thunderbolt on the night before the battle of Salamanca. As they were fording the Tormes during a thunderstorm, the Portuguese horse, who even failed to inspire a name, panicked so that Juana could barely stay in the saddle. In words that she never learned in a convent, Juana denounced the cowardly horse and everything Portuguese. She demanded that she be allowed to ride 'her own gallant countryman'. Harry gave way. He recalled:

> It was difficult to say who was the proudest on that morning of the battle, horse, wife or Enrique (as I was always called). She caracoled him among the soldiers, to their delight, for he was broken in like a Mameluke, though very difficult to ride.

When the battle began, West 'who also had a led horse in case of accident, with a little tent and a funny little pair of lanterns', took her off to the rear. With the harsh sounds of battle, 'the pride of her equestrianism was buried in anxiety for him on whom all depended'.

Salamanca (22 July 1812) was Wellington's most brilliant

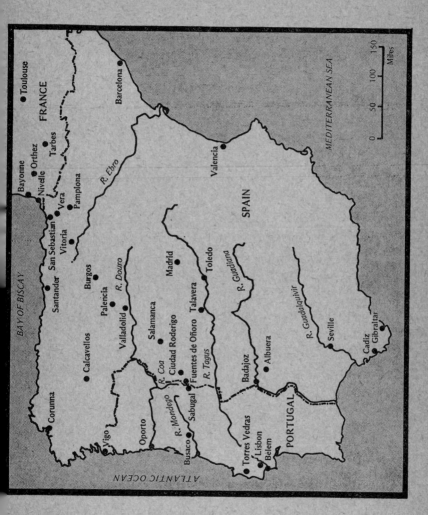

Map 1 The Peninsula

victory. 'There never was an army so beaten in so short a time,' declared the Duke. In forty minutes 40,000 were defeated. Marmont himself was carried off the field on a stretcher. The road to Madrid was open, and an excellent road it was. Anticipating the pleasures to be tasted, British soldiers asked, 'Is this the road to Madrid? Are we really going to the Capital of Spain, the centre of romance?'

Harry had to remain in Salamanca with the casualties. Ever since his first campaign in South America, he had been periodically plagued with boils. After the battle, in which the Light Division played a very small part, he counted eleven immense ones on his knees and thighs. The torment was alleviated by the 'love and excitement' he shared with Juana during his recuperation. After a fortnight, though he had as many boils as ever, he and Juana raced for three days to over-take the Division before it crossed the Guadarrama pass. 'Thank God,' said Harry with relief, 'there was no fighting in my absence.'

Juana, by now, was the darling of the whole Division. She would laugh and talk to all the men, sometimes in broken English. 'Blackguards as many of these poor gallant fellows were,' observed Harry, 'there was not a man who would not have laid down his life to defend her.' Stories were told around the camp of how after the battle of Salamanca she slept on the battlefield on a bed of fresh-cut wheat while holding on to her new horse. During the night he ate her bed from under her, much to her amusement the next morning.

Kincaid later spoke of how his battalion was moving into battle and he, as usual, was 'sternly occupied in calculating' his prospects for killing or being killed, when Juana, whom he thought had retired to a place of safety, emerged from a door-way and grasped his hand. Without saying a word, she pressed it gently and then rushed back into the house. For the rest of the day he 'felt a lightness of heart and buoyancy of spirit which, in such a situation, was no less new than delightful'. He pro-claimed her 'a pattern to her sex and everybody's *beau ideal* of what a wife should be!'

It seemed only natural to Harry's friends — Johnny Kincaid, John Bell and Charlie Beckwith, a nephew of Sydney Beckwith — that now that Juana was with him, he would neglect his responsibilities. 'Alas,' they concluded, 'poor Harry Smith is lost.' Harry soon demonstrated that the reverse was true, 'for my love would excite me to exertions in the hopes of prefer- ment'. Never did she complain when he was gone by saying, 'you might have been with me'; rather she convinced him that she glorified in his duty as much as he did. After a fatiguing day of marching or fighting, 'her first question invariably was "Are you sure you have done your duty?" Then I admit my attention was unbounded and we were very happy.'

Happiness permeated the entire army as they marched into Madrid. The drums and fifes of every regiment were answered by the great bells of the capital and shouts of 'Viva los Engleses! Viva Wellington!' The soldiers were deluged with flowers; wine and sweetmeats were pressed into their hands. Mad with joy, the women and even some of the men with garlic-scented breath and moustaches stiffened with sweat, dust and snuff, smothered the British with kisses almost to suffocation.[1] Officers in particular were singled out. These Madrid women must be infernally fond of kissing, said one astonished officer, when they 'nearly hugged to death such an ill-looking fellow as me'. Harry had difficulty staying on his horse. Some officers, he observed 'actually lost their seats, if not their hearts'. Then Wellington appeared and the chorus of cheers became a deafening roar. The Spaniards kissed his feet, his horse and even the road he passed over.

In the evening the city was illuminated by candles and torches. The celebrations — balls, banquets and bull fights — went on for two months. Harry and his attractive wife, with new ward- robes and comfortable billets, amused themselves like visiting tourists. Dressed in richly embroidered clothes with her long glossy hair clubbed in a bunch and ribbons streaming down her back, Harry's prize of Badajoz showed to greater advantage, as Harry believed, than the most beautiful of the many pretty women in Madrid.

'We flattered ourselves', wrote George Simmons, 'with the hopes of passing a pleasant winter in Madrid.' Wellington, with half of his army, planned to bar the French to the north and west by taking Burgos. But this time the siege failed and the tables were turned. To escape being trapped by the concentric moves of the French armies, he had to abandon Madrid. 'To

---

[1] To be kissed by Spanish men, remembered Private Wheeler, 'was like having a hair broom pushed into one's face that had been daubed in a dirty gutter'.

know when to retreat and to dare to do it,' Wellington concluded, 'was the mark of a great commander.'

The gaiety that had ruled the Spanish capital turned to grief.
The British, who now abandoned Madrid to the French, were
no longer heroes. As one young woman, who had been all
sweetness and affection, told Rifleman Costello, 'Begone, you
cowardly English, you have not the courage to fight the
enemies of our country.' Some Spaniards joined the retreat. A
young padre, Vicar of Vicalbaro, who had befriended the Smiths
during their stay, pleaded with Harry to take him along, for
his anti-French activities were known to the enemy. Harry, to
Juana's amusement, made the priest part of his establishment.
Off they went, Harry on a fine large Andalusian charger,
Juana on Tiny, the padre — whom the soldiers dubbed 'Harry
Smith's confessor' — on a pony. Bringing up the rear were West,
the female servant, a string of assorted horses and mules, and
thirteen hounds and dogs.

The retreat was one of unexpected hardships. Much of the
time there was rain, often in torrents, and men lost their shoes
in the mud. There was little food; when the quartermaster-
general misdirected the rations, many were forced to subsist on
their own meagre supplies. Some men were reduced to eating
acorns and fallen bullocks, roasting the latter as well as they
could over the smoke-fires from wet wood. The sick and the
wounded soon began to fall behind, and dispirited soldiers
became indifferent to life and waited for death or the French to
overtake them.

Harry's padre, who had turned out to be a superb procurer
of supplies — such as chocolates, eggs, and sausages — which
even English money could not buy, was appalled by the misery
and the lack of human compassion which he witnessed. Harry,
who had warned him of the hardships attending a soldier's life,
assured him laughingly that this retreat could in no way compare with the retreat to Corunna and its running battles in the
intense cold weather. The padre was not comforted.

The Light Division, forming the rearguard, was constantly
under arms. They covered the retreat in wonderfully good
order, mocking any effort by the French cavalry to break
through. The Riflemen took advantage of every ground,
always confident, writes Kincaid, 'almost equal to our hope in
Heaven', that the 43rd and 52nd supported them and that

Ross's guns would fire on their pursuers until the last possible moment. Marshal Soult, who had twice their number, balked because of the thick weather and his own sense of caution.

Before the retreat came to a halt at Ciudad Roderigo, Soult struck sharply at the crossing of the Huebra (17 November 1812). While Riflemen held the bed of the river, Harry left Juana with the 52nd, who were to move into bivouac. But, unknown to him, the 52nd was sent into action to prevent a flanking movement. With no time to seek a ford, Juana's party plunged into the swift current. The padre was swept off his pony. The beast drowned but the priest was saved by an air bubble which formed under his great cloak. Juana barely made it by clinging to Tiny. Harry found her 'cold and shivery' from her swim and the heavy rains.

That night Harry looked at his wife and felt sorry for 'this delicate young creature ... wet as a drowned rat, with nothing to eat, and no cover from the deluge'. Not having slept for three nights, 'our rear being in a very ticklish position', Harry fell asleep and rolled over so that he was between her and the fire. The change in temperature awakened her. Trembling with cold, she said sharply, 'How foolish! You must have been nice and warm, and to know that is enough for me.' Years later Harry told her, 'Oh, how I pitied you some days, although I never said so!'

The losses on the retreat, increased sharply by disease, cost Wellington nearly 3,000 men. But he had brought out his army intact in the face of superior forces, in sharp contrast to the disaster that befell Napoleon's army retreating from Russia that winter.

The army rested until spring. It was a time for amusements and, for Harry and Juana, making love. Settled snugly in a cottage in a suburb of Ciudad Roderigo, Juana no longer had to live the life of a gypsy, or a tinker's wife. 'My vivacious little wife was full of animation and happiness,' recalled Harry. 'Every day was an increase in joy.' The padre was kept busy cooking.

In the mornings, Harry attended to his duties and visited the many sick and wounded. Nearly a third of the Division was disabled. Those of Harry's friends who were well went out duck-shooting, standing up to their waists in cold water. Harry, too, continued to live life strenuously. 'At this time,' he confessed,

'I was sporting mad.' He went hunting every day. Following one severe run, his horse collapsed and died; but Harry had four more to choose from. Sometimes the Duke, 'who had a capital pack of fox-hounds', hunted with them. In the company of high-spirited young officers, Wellington's aristocratic hauteur softened and he behaved like a genial country squire engaged in 'the noble science', fox-hunting. He 'made a great deal of noise', according to one who accompanied him, 'and rode violently'. When riders tumbled, the Duke's firm mouth broke forth with a distinctive laugh, something between a great neigh and a prolonged whoop.

The long nights passed with an astonishing tempo of gaiety. Juana and Harry upheld the social circle by attending a continual round of balls, agreeable parties and amateur theatricals. Performances often became riotous when players or the orchestra (the regimental band) became intoxicated. One band disgraced itself by getting drunk before the performance and were found in a room dancing naked save for the pelisses draped over their shoulders. Drinking also could be hazardous on the long journey home. Merrymakers would lose their way and fall into abysses, or plunge into swamps.

Social activities enhanced brotherly feelings and harmony among the officers. 'The Light Division,' wrote Lieut. Gratton, 'had an *esprit de corps* that must be seen to be understood.' Every day the Division grew stronger. The sick returned to duty, and reinforcements, called 'Johnny Newcomes', came out from England. Also came tents, new uniforms and pay, which was months in arrears. Harry, who drew nine shillings and five pence as a captain, had barely enough to pay his debts. It appears, however, that in time of need, he could rely on money from his father. Some were not so fortunate. One subaltern, who had pecuniary differences with his father was so fired up as he charged, sword in hand, into the breach at Ciudad Roderigo that he remarked to an officer alongside him, 'Egad, if I had my father here now, I think I should be able to bring him to terms!'

Wellington began his offensive in May. No longer would he be content with local successes; he was set on driving the French out of Spain. On the night of 20 May 1813 the Light Division was ordered to be ready to leave the next day at sunrise. 'All was cheerfulness, joy and anticipation,' noticed Harry, as the Division marched off with renewed strength for the next

nineteen days. The French appeared surprised by the boldness
of the British advance and they retreated without offering
battle. With no desire to defend Burgos a second time, they
blew up the fortifications, killing in their haste hundreds of their
own men and many civilians. To the British it was as if there
were no war. They strode in sunshine with the regimental
bands playing 'The Downfall of Paris'. Throughout the night
they slept undisturbed in their new tents.

But it was a difficult time for Juana and Harry. Only two of
the five horses were fit to ride. Tiny was lamed before the
advance, so Juana rode Harry's thoroughbred mare. Before the
Division began its triumphal entry into Palencia, the mare
slipped on a grassy bank and fell upon Juana, breaking a small
bone in her foot. 'This was an awful accident,' moaned Harry,
'heretofore health and happiness facilitated all.' He was
tormented by the thought of their being parted, especially if
Juana would have to be left behind without the padre (who had
returned to his parish) to watch over her 'among bigoted
inhabitants' who would not be inspired to tenderness towards
a true Catholic who had married a heretic.

Though Juana was in great pain, the mere hint that she
might be left behind rallied her strength, and she said firmly,
'Get me a mule or an ass, and put a Spanish saddle for a lady on
it; my feet will rest on the footboard, and go I will!' To ensure
her comfort, a dozen officers were in 'immediate requisition',
some testing for the most gentle mule, others rushing from
shop to shop in Palencia in search of the most comfortable
saddle. Her foot healed quickly, and in a few days she was back
on her horse again on the road to Vitoria.

The battle of Vitoria was Wellington's crowning victory in
Spain, the one that sealed Napoleon's fate in that country. King
Joseph, Napoleon's inept brother, who had already abandoned
Madrid in order to prevent being cut off, lost his crown;
Jourdan lost his baton as a marshal of France. The Duke
attacked Joseph's retreating army—now swelled with such
numbers of women that one French general called it 'a mobile
brothel!'—on the morning of 21 June; by evening Wellington
had taken Vitoria and put Joseph in full flight for Pamplona.
Never had a victorious British army seized such vast military
stores and assorted plunder as the French left behind after five
years in Spain.

The Light Division played a leading part in the battle from the first preliminary skirmish to the capture of the last gun. In the middle of the fight, Vandeleur's brigade was called upon to support Lord Dalhousie and his 7th Division. Harry was sent to Dalhousie for orders. He found his lordship, who was unsure of his role in the battle, in deep conversation with his quarter-master-general, a former Rifleman named Drake whom Harry knew. Seeing that Vandeleur's brigade was coming under fire from twelve French guns in a nearby village, Harry wasted no time on ceremony. He interrupted the conversation with a request for orders. Dalhousie ignored him and went on talking. Harry impatiently roared, 'What orders, my Lord?' His lordship, still taking no notice of him commented to a now somewhat animated Captain Drake, 'Better to take the village.' Fully aware that the remark was not addressed to him, Harry shouted, 'Certainly, my Lord', and spurred his horse ahead with both men trying to call him back; but Harry decided it was his turn to ignore them. He galloped back to Vandeleur and told him that he was to take the village immediately. The Riflemen swarmed out in every direction, while the 52nd 'deployed in line as if at Shorncliffe'. They kept up 'a fire that nothing could resist'. Spotting an officer who commanded a battalion of the 7th, Harry raced to him and passed on the spurious order, 'Lord Dalhousie desires you closely to follow this Brigade of the Light Division.' The confused colonel asked, 'Who are you, sir?' — 'Never mind that,' said Harry with a ring of authority, 'disobey my Lord's order at your peril.' The village was taken, along with all of the French guns.

A somewhat perplexed Dalhousie came up to Vandeleur and declared: 'Most brilliantly achieved indeed! Where is the officer you sent to me for orders.' Standing close to Vandeleur, Harry said, 'Here I am, my Lord.' — 'Upon my word, sir, you receive and carry orders quicker than any officer I ever saw.' With unconcealed pride, Harry answered, 'You said, "Take the village", my Lord, there it is, guns and all.' Dalhousie smiled and Drake grinned, 'Well done, Harry.'

The incident was an example of the sort of impertinent initiative that Harry gloried in. He knew only too well that if things had gone wrong, he would in all likelihood have had to face a court martial; but he was so confident in his own assessment of the situation and what his brigade was capable of that he never gave the matter a second thought. It is not on record that Harry ever told Vandeleur what had transpired at Dalhousie's headquarters.

Throughout the afternoon, Harry's brigade chased the French towards Vitoria over fields strewn with their baggage. At one point, the enemy cavalry charged out from behind the baggage and threatened a company of skirmishing Riflemen. By now, however, the system of support developed by the Light Division had become so flawless 'that we never calculated on disaster, but assumed the boldest front and bearing'. The charging dragoons were so roughly handled that they soon scrambled out of sight.

Late in the day Harry was standing with Ross, whose guns were sharply engaged in a duel with enemy artillery, when his horse dropped as if stone dead. Jumping clear of the beast, Harry carefully examined the animal for a wound. Finding none, he gave him a swift kick on the nose. The treatment provided an instant cure. The horse shook his head and as soon as he recovered his feet, Harry was on his back. Artillerymen explained that it was not uncommon for a blast of wind created by a passing cannon-shot to knock out a horse or a man, whose face would be blackened as if he had been in a prize ring for two hours.

Juana, normally so indomitable and gay, was deeply apprehensive when a battle was in progress, as were the rest of the women. Paradoxically, it was more unnerving to be in the rear of the army than at the front. While order and steadiness prevailed among the fighting men, there was generally a scene of uproar and panic among the confused non-combatants. Kincaid remarked,

> The rear of a battle is generally a queer place, the day is won or lost there a dozen times ... fellows who have never seen the enemy in the field, are there to be seen flourishing swords ... while others are flying as if pursued by legions of demons.

The wives and camp followers crowded around men who had been forward, making earnest inquiries about husbands and friends. Juana was told by soldiers who had seen Harry fall from his horse that he had been killed. She rode off with West immediately. They continued their long, fruitless search among

the dead and wounded all along the route of the advancing
army.

In reality, the only injury that Harry sustained that day was
the loss of his voice from cheering. 'It is ridiculous,' he wrote,
'but in no campaign did I ever serve without this little
accident.' At dusk he met Juana on his way back to Division
headquarters. With a croaking, barely audible voice, he tried to
quiet her loud lamentations. Cheered somewhat, Juana
exclaimed, 'Oh then, thank God, you are not killed, only badly
wounded.' — 'Thank God, I am neither,' croaked Harry. But
'in her ecstasy of joy', it was some time before she believed
him.

The sole object the Smiths acquired in a battlefield covered
with treasure was another dog. About to begin the next day's
march, Juana heard moans from the hayloft of the barn they
had slept in. Harry found a ladder and investigated. He discovered twenty French officers more or less severely wounded
and a Spanish lady grieving over one of them who was dying.
Their fears were allayed by Harry's assurance that they were in
safe hands. He gave them all of the food he had, while Juana
comforted her countrywoman as best she could. When a guard
arrived to escort them to the rear, the Spanish lady, as a token
of her gratitude, insisted that Juana accept her little dog. The
animal was named Vitoria. At first, Harry felt that the company
of a pug dog did not quite fit his image, but in the end he
confessed that the dog 'was the most sensible little brute
Nature ever produced, and it and Tiny became most attached
friends'.

There was no respite for the victorious British as they slashed
at a demoralized enemy over the hills and towards France.
Leaving behind a trail of blood and destruction, observed
George Bell, 'they carried along with them the curse of a whole
kingdom!' Villages were left smoking in ruins. Peasants
pressed into service as guides were shot to prevent them from
giving information to the British. Others were tortured until
they revealed where their last morsel of food was hidden.
Priests had their tongues cut out — or worse; women were left
mutilated and dying. To the British, these were truly the
children of the Revolution spreading a Reign of Terror across
the continent. Their acts were merely the final scene of the
horrid spectacle of occupation in Spain and Portugal. 'The seat

of war,' decided Harry, 'is hell on earth even when stripped of the atrocities.'

However, these were but the fleeting reflections of a dedicated soldier. War was Harry's profession and he relished battle. He had a warrior's pride in courage and honour, with the added conviction that the cause he served, England's cause, would alter the course of human events for the better. Unlike so many soldiers in battle who felt humbly insignificant, Harry never doubted that his behaviour would influence the outcome. And as an officer, he knew that his example was crucial. Rifleman Costello found that officers could be divided into two classes: the 'come on', and the 'go on'. Happily, there were few of the latter among the 95th. His comrade Tom Plunket while in action once told one of those few, 'The words "go on" don't befit a leader, Sir.'

Little animosity existed between British and French soldiers; for example, a mutual respect and courtesy prevailed between Riflemen and their opposite numbers. In quiet times it seemed senseless to harass one another while on outpost duty. Enemy sentries frequently conversed and exchanged tobacco and wine. When a French sentry was pointed out to visiting naval officers, they would ask, 'Why don't you shoot him?' One officer of the 95th, who boasted in camp of having ordered a corporal to shoot a French officer during a skirmish so as to obtain his handsome boots, was sent back to England by his brigadier for bringing disgrace to his regiment.

Where possible, efforts were made to protect French stragglers and wounded from savage reprisals by guerillas and camp followers who often tortured and butchered them. One French officer was placed between planks and sawn in two. Two diaries corroborate the grisly story of a camp follower who tried to sell hungry soldiers slices of 'pork' from a French corpse. He fled before he could be seized and shot.

Harry related how he and Juana were guests of a revenge-mad Spanish gentleman during the advance to the Pyrenees. Before dinner he invited Harry to visit his wine cellar. With a fiendish expression the host held up his lantern so that Harry could see four French dragoons stretched out dead on the floor. 'My very frame quivered and my blood was frozen', Harry recalled, as the Spaniard explained how he pretended to be their friend as he got them drunk. Having them thus helpless, he assassinated them by plunging a stiletto into their hearts. Flourishing his dagger once more before Harry's eyes, he cried, 'Thus die all enemies to Spain.' Of the 400,000 men the French were said to have lost in Spain, Harry concluded that more died by this kind of treachery than by any other manner. It disturbed him to see 'the honour and chivalry of arms reduced to the practice of midnight assassins'.

Juana provided an escape from harsh reality. Unlike so many soldiers' wives, she remained unchanged through the horrors and hardships of war. Her playful and gentle manners, her open and unfettered personality always guaranteed to lift his spirits. Some days, between duty and fatigue, there was barely time for more than a word or a kiss, but she never complained of neglect. As he watched them Kincaid reasoned:

> The friendship of man is one thing — the friendship of woman another, and those only who have been on the theatre of fierce warfare, and knowing that such a being was on the spot, watching with earnest and unceasing solicitude over his safety, alike with those most dear to her, can fully appreciate the additional value which it gives to one's existence.

Included among those dear to Juana was the genial Vandeleur. One morning after a forced night-march in the rain over difficult roads, where at times Juana literally had to crawl because both she and Tiny were lame, Harry found her sheltering the general with an umbrella to lessen the pain in his rheumatic shoulder, and laughing heartily as she narrated her night's misadventures.

The transfer of Vandeleur to a cavalry brigade was a great loss to them, all the more so because he was replaced by General Skerrett, who was pompous and aloof, and totally ignorant of the distinctive functions of light infantry. Moreover, his stinginess was such that Harry and Juana were not welcome at his table.

With one last effort to regain his hold on the Peninsula, Napoleon appointed Soult, the Duke of Dalmatia, to supreme command. Soult, whom the British soldiers called the 'Duke of Damnation', miraculously restored the morale of his beaten troops and counter-attacked in an effort to relieve the beleagured garrisons of Pamplona and San Sebastian. Combat followed combat in the bewildering maze of passes and valleys in the Pyrenees. The Light Division was kept deployed between the besieged towns so as to provide assistance where needed most. On failing to relieve San Sebastian, which fell to assault at the end of August, the French retired to recross the border river, Bidossa.

At the battle of Vera (1 September 1813) Skerrett had a chance to cut off a French division retreating towards the only surviving bridge and a ford made difficult by heavy rains. When Harry indicated the importance of holding the crossing, Skerrett laughed at him. He ordered the brigade to retire to a point about a mile away and left only Cadoux's company for picket. Harry fumed and told him 'most *wickedly*', 'We shall repent this before daylight.' Skerrett remained coldly indifferent. Harry was so agitated that he could not sleep. Shortly before dawn, Skerrett received orders from General Alten at division headquarters to do all in his power to hold the passage over the Bidossa. 'Now, General,' crowed Harry, 'let me do so.' Skerrett obstinately wished to discuss the matter. The debate ended abruptly when they heard heavy firing and shouts of 'Vive l'Empereur' announcing the presence of the enemy. Captain Cadoux and his Riflemen repulsed the determined French column time and again, confident that support was at hand. It arrived too late. The Riflemen were finally hurled back and the enemy escaped across the river. Harry found the scene choked with dead, among them Daniel Cadoux with a bullet in his head.

In the beginning, Harry had disliked Cadoux and avoided him, finding him too 'pretty', too 'ladylike' in his manner to be a man's man. But in combat, his conspicuous capabilities and courage soon made them strong friends. Cadoux's death was keenly felt by Harry and he never forgave Skerrett for his failure to support him. Of course, it never occurred to Harry that he might have contributed to Skerrett's obstinacy. In the habit of exercising a free hand with the brigade under the indulgent Vandeleur, he was considerably less than tactful towards a superior wholly unfamiliar with his new assignment.

During a lull in the war that September, Skerrett took sick leave and returned home to a fortune he had inherited. (He did not live long enough to enjoy it; he was killed the next year at

Bergen-op-Zoom.) He was replaced by John Colborne, colonel of the 52nd, who had been Sir John Moore's military secretary. No choice could have pleased Harry more. Colborne thoroughly understood the business of war, most of all the requirements of a light infantry officer which, in Harry's words, called for 'the eye of a hawk and the power of anticipating the enemy's intention'. Though their temperaments differed widely — Colborne was restrained and methodically cool — there was soon a strong mutual attachment.

The British prepared to enter France proud in the knowledge that whereas the French had been beaten by the weather in Russia, they had thrashed them fairly in Spain. Once more the commanders finessed and feinted, but this time it was Soult's turn to hold the Pyrenees. Wellington struck where least expected, at the heights guarding the pass of Vera. In this second combat of Vera (7 October 1813) the Light Division took a leading part. Advancing to the attack, Colborne pointed to the heights above them and told Harry that should he succeed in reaching them without being knocked over, he would be a brevet-major. Harry succeeded without a scratch. The next day Colborne returned from headquarters, smiled broadly and said, 'Well, Major Smith, give me your hand.'

Harry's jubilance was premature. On hearing of his promotion, Colonel Barnard went to Fitzroy Somerset and requested that one of his captains be given a brevet, adding that Smith had been jumped to field rank over the heads of twenty captains. Somerset passed the matter on to the Duke. He weighed the problem and said:

A pity by God! Colborne and the Brigade are so anxious about it and he deserves anything. If Smith will go and serve as Brigade-Major to another Brigade, I will give him the rank after the next battle.

An embarrassed Colborne urged Harry to do so, but he refused. Holding back his disappointment, he said, 'Here I will fight on happily, daily acquiring knowledge from your ability.'

And he did. Before the battle of the Nivelle (10 November 1813) where Wellington hoped to dislodge a firmly entrenched Soult, Colborne took Harry on daily reconnaissance to study the position and give informal tuition on the art of war. One morning the Duke himself, with other officers, joined them. All lay

1 Harry Smith as a lieutenant-colonel in the dark green uniform of a Rifleman shortly after the battle of Waterloo. Portrait attributed to Jean-Baptiste Isaby.

2 Juana Smith as a slender girl of seventeen wearing a pink dress. Portrait attributed to Jean-Baptiste Isaby.

3 The Storming of Badajoz, by Woodville. 'Thus, as good may come out of evil,' observed Harry Smith after the assault, 'this scene of devastation and spoil yielded to me a treasure invaluable'—Juana.

4 General John Colborne (Lord Seaton) noted for being 'calm and collected'. He instructed Harry Smith in the science of warfare.

down as the Duke, who usually kept his thinking to himself, leisurely discussed the situation. Then he dictated his plan to his military secretary. Harry, who for a change said nothing, found it one of the most fascinating scenes he had ever witnessed.

Curiously, it was in the Pyrenees that the soldiers' nerves were strained to the breaking point. There were more desertions at this time than at any other during the long war. It was not the enemy nor the privations but the eeriness of the forbidding mountains enshrouded in mists, and the dark, isolated valleys far below, which threatened. Men accustomed to the plains or town life became fearful. At night they lost their way, or fell from narrow, winding trails into utter blackness. One ordinarily steady soldier of the 85th told Lieut. Gleig that he could face any living thing, but this haunted land was more than he could endure.

Juana, too, was disquieted by the strange surroundings. More and more she became concerned with the fate of 'her man'. What was to become of her if Enrique were killed? Her parents were dead, her only brother had died of wounds in her arms and the whereabouts of her sister were unknown. Other soldiers' wives quickly found another husband. Some already were on their third. Could she marry again?

Not until the battle to control the pass at Vera did Juana actually see her husband in battle. The circumstances were such that she could observe from the window of the cottage where they stayed the uphill advance of the fighting line. At a distance, she mistook for her husband Col. Algeo of the Caçadores, who was mounted on a chestnut horse with the same markings as Harry's war-horse, Old Chap. Suddenly the saddle was empty and the horse was galloping to the rear with the lifeless rider, caught by one foot in the stirrup, dragging along the ground. Screaming, she dashed to intercept the horse. On discovering that it was not Enrique who had been killed, she fell into a deep faint. The effect of this shock was such, said Harry, that she 'did not recover her usual vivacity for several days'. Any loud noise would cause her to flinch and tremble.

A few days before the battle of the Nivelle, Harry and Juana found quarters in a hut with a roof of black-earth sod. Sitting down to supper with Captain Tom Fane, Skerrett's aide who stayed on with the brigade, all was comfort and happiness. But

5

when they retired to their 'nuptial couch', consisting of a hard
mattress on the floor, a sudden storm caused the roof to
collapse, leaving them drenched and as black as chimney
sweeps. Considering 'the ridiculous position we were in made
her laugh herself warm,' said Harry. The servants were turned
out of their tent and the Smiths took their dry beds. Harry was
relieved to find that his giggling young wife had completely
regained her spirits.

He was, however, mistaken. Juana had merely learned to
conceal her fears. Before undertaking the night-march to
positions in preparation for the assault at the Nivelle, Harry
went to say goodbye to his wife, which habit 'had rendered
about as formal as if going on to London out of the country'.
This time it was different, for Juana was clearly depressed, and
insisted that 'you or your horse will be killed tomorrow'.
Harry dismissed the matter with a laugh and commented, 'Well,
of two chances, I hope it may be the horse.' He kissed her and
left.

The charge of the Light Bobs that day, in Harry's opinion,
'was the most beautiful attack ever made in the history of war'.
They swept everything before them. Charging the enemy's last
star-shaped redoubt, Harry's thoroughbred mare was hit.
Turning her around so that she would fall between him and a
hail of bullets, she was hit again and crashed to the ground,
pinning him down before he could jump free. The animal's
blood poured over him like a fountain as he lay helpless and
watched Colborne demand the surrender of the enemy. The
sounds of battle faded and Harry at last succeeded in gaining
the attention of several soldiers. 'Well, damn my eyes if our
old Brigade-Major is killed after all!' remarked one of them.
'Come pull me out!' cried Harry impatiently, 'I'm not even
wounded, only squeezed.'

Freed at last, Harry ran up to Colborne, who was writing a
statement in his notebook that stated in French, 'I surrender
unconditionally'. Colborne passed the note on to Harry to give
to the French commander for his signature. He signed it and
Harry rode off on a borrowed horse to find Wellington.
Covered as he was with blood, the Duke at first did not
recognize him and asked, 'Who are you?' Harry answered, 'The
Brigade-Major, 2nd Rifle Brigade.' Wellington stared at him
for a moment and then inquired if Smith were badly wounded.

'Not at all, sir; it is my horse's blood.' The Duke then read the
note and expressed approval. But on learning from Harry how
many lives it cost to take the last redoubt, he said it was
regrettable, for the French held an untenable position which
they would have had to surrender anyhow. Harry explained that
Colborne's orders at that stage were to 'move on'. A discussion
followed with Alten and other officers as to whether *move on*
implied attack. Harry who had encouraged Colborne to take
the last redoubt, always insisted that it did.

The next day Juana came up with the baggage and saw Harry
unwashed, except for his face. She could not believe that he had
not been terribly wounded. On learning what actually happened,
she reminded him of her prophecy.

It was soon Harry's turn to have a sense of foreboding. It was
during the five days of hard skirmishing before the enemy's
entrenched camp at Bayonne on the Nive river (9–13 December
1813) that Harry had a nightmare. The French were attacking
his home in Whittlesea and his father was carrying his mother
to safety through a door into the garden which the Smith
children called 'the Black Door'. He heard his father call out,
'Now someone shut the door, she is safe and rescued.' Harry
saw and heard everything as clearly as he ever did anything in
his life. He sprang to his feet and roared, 'Stand to your arms!'
Colborne, sleeping near him, bounded to his feet and prepared
to repel the enemy. Harry apologized and told him of his
dream. Colborne tried to calm him by explaining, 'It shows that
asleep or awake, you are intent on your duty.' But Harry found
it impossible to sleep. Taking out his order-book, he jotted the
time: one o'clock, 12 December.

Harry remained in a deep depression, one that he had never
experienced before or never did after. When he received a
letter from his father in their new winter quarters, he knew that
the loss he felt so intensely would be confirmed. It was. His
father described how his mother had died at the precise time of
his dream. Her last words were about her sons' fighting for their
country. (Tom had rejoined the Rifles some time before.)

With his mother gone, Harry felt the loss of 'a friend, a
councellor and a pardoner of offences'. Shortly before his own
death, Harry wrote, 'The real affection and love of a mother is
immortal.' His grief was prolonged and excessive, softened
only by comforting words from Juana.

The resumption of hostilities in February acted as a tonic for Harry. As before every engagement in the past, he recalled his mother's words reminding him that he was 'born a true Englishman'. But now those words had more meaning than ever. At the battle of Orthez (27 February 1814) on the road to Toulouse, Harry's comrades saw him charge ahead as if the devil were after him. In fact, the whole brigade followed him as if nothing could stop them. Soldiers in other units suspected that their zeal was inspired by hopes of plunder. The climax of the action came when the 52nd smartly 'deployed into line like clockwork, and moved on, supported by clouds of sharp-shooters', against the heights held by the French. 'It was the most majestic advance I ever saw,' declared Harry. The divisions on the right and the left took the ground before them and the battle was won. The French lost heavily. Many more deserted.

Juana, coming up with the baggage, began to exhibit a more professional attitude towards the ghastly sights that followed a battle. She described to Harry the dead, dying and wounded, especially the extraordinary number she found shot in the head. She offered food and drink to an artilleryman with both of his arms shot off.

The British continued their advance into the 'sacred country'. The fear that inhabitants might take to guerilla warfare, as Napoleon urged them to do, never materialized. Wellington helped to forestall such resistance by dealing more severely than ever with those responsible for robbery or mayhem. Officers were instructed to do everything in their power to prevent crime. Malefactors were flogged and hanged without trial or mercy. One Spanish muleteer who had entered a home to steal apples was left hanging from a window with an apple in his mouth 'to show what he had coveted'. The more frightful excesses that were committed were usually the work of their own French soldiers. The people, many of them Royalists in this part of France, often welcomed the British as deliverers.

The Light Division fought its last battle as a unit, almost singlehanded, at Tarbes (20 March 1814). As so often in the past, they fought on the defensive against odds — and won. And as always, Harry wrote, we 'prided ourselves in destroying the enemy and preserving ourselves'. Three times the French tried to drive the 95th off a hill. So many fell in the attempt that

Barnard invited Wellington to come and see the sight. 'Well, Barnard,' he said, 'to please you, I will go, but I require no novel proof of the destructive fire of your Rifles.'

Wellington, however, was annoyed that Soult had escaped the trap he had set for him, and taken his much-shaken army behind the protective Garonne and the thick walls of Toulouse. The attack on Toulouse on Easter Sunday, 10 April 1814, was a bloody affair. Years after, Colborne (then Lord Seaton) would give an after-dinner oration on the fine points of the battle, using wine glasses to indicate the various positions. 'It was the worst arranged battle that could be,' he announced, 'nothing but mistakes.' Picton made a diversionary attack, which resulted in a real one that cost 1,500 men. The unsupported Spaniards attacked three times and were repulsed three times. Success was finally achieved by the 4th and 6th Divisions, but the cavalry lost a golden opportunity by failing to punish the enemy's rearguard. 'I think,' concluded Colborne, 'the Duke almost deserved to have been beaten.' The most egregious blunder, as Harry saw it, was the failure to throw in the Light Bobs, who 'literally had done worse than nothing'. The tragedy of so many lives being lost was compounded by the delay in the news that Napoleon had already abdicated. When the Duke was informed, he ejaculated, 'You don't say so, upon my honour. Hurrah!' He then spun round on his heel and snapped his fingers.

'The feeling of no war after six years' perpetual and vigilant war,' observed Harry, 'was so novel that at first it was positively painful.' That there would be no posting of pickets, no alerts, no preparations for attack — and, possibly, no more chances for promotion, gave him a strange, almost depressing sensation. It took him a long time for his subconscious to break the habit of watchfulness. Time and again, he would wake up in the middle of the night in a cold sweat with a dream-inspired feeling that the sentries had not been posted and that they were being overrun by the enemy. War had become a normal state of affairs; peace was abnormal. As Napoleon on one occasion is reported to have said, 'Now look at the fix we are in. Peace has broken out!'

[3]

The Scorching of Washington

True, a new mistress now I chase,
The first foe in the field;
And with a stronger faith embrace
A sword, a horse, a shield.

Robert Lovelace

To the victorious British soldiers and the war-weary French citizens there seemed no end to the gaiety now that the war was over. Because of the drain of conscription on young Frenchmen, there were thousands of unattached females. Captain Cooke recalled:

> There was such an abundance of kissing as probably the like of it was never seen before ... There was kissing in the valleys, and kissing upon the hills, and, in short, there was embracing, kissing, and counter-kissing from Toulouse to Bordeaux.

Harry learned that his comrades had big hearts buttoned inside their close-fitting jackets. 'Most of our gallant fellows were really in love,' he commented, 'or fancied themselves so.' As for himself, 'I had a safeguard in a lovely young wife.' The vanquished French soldiers sulked in their camp while their officers visited Toulouse in plain clothes, picking quarrels with unsuspecting British gentlemen. Duels were frequent.

Ensconced in a luxurious chateau in the suburbs, the Smiths lived a life intent upon the pleasures of theatre-going and parties. As always, the Light Division were as enterprising in amusements as on the battlefield and garnered more than their share of women. 'A woman was a woman in those days,' remarked Kincaid, 'and every officer made it a point of duty to marshal as many as he could to the general assembly, no matter whether they were countesses or *sextonesses*.' After some weeks of quadrilles and soirées, the entertainment came to an end and the army prepared to march in different directions.

Peace meant the end of the Light Division, which some now compared to Napoleon's invincible Imperial Guard. Kincaid went further: 'There never was nor never will be again such a war brigade.' Of the original members who began the campaign, nearly half were gone. Most of those who remained had been wounded at least once. When Harry's brigade gave him a farewell dinner, his separation from all — officers and men — made him feel as if he were leaving home.

As the Portuguese and Spaniards marched south, the British knew they were seeing them for the last time. When they had first met them, they despised them. ('The Spaniard is the mule and Portuguese the ass,' declared Captain Blakeney.) Of the two, the patient Portuguese soldiers were more friendly, while the Spaniards were haughty and unbending. But in the end, Rifleman Costello concluded, the Spaniards had the 'right stuff' in them to make excellent soldiers, 'far superior to the Portuguese'. Harry went further, declaring that he 'never saw better, more orderly, perfectly sober soldiers' in his life. There were 'even deep feelings of regret', Harry recorded, as their allies took their leave. The rest of the Division went on to the coast to embark either for home or for America, where there was another war to finish.

The idea of Harry doing duty in America began with Colborne. Still concerned with Harry's failure to gain promotion, he told him that for the sake of his career he should not remain idle. 'There is a force, a considerable one, going to America. You must go.' Harry agreed. Early the next morning they rode into Toulouse, where Colborne spoke to his old friend General Robert Ross, who was to command the expedition. Ross remembered Smith from the retreat to Corunna and respected his ability. He agreed to take him on as his major-of-brigade.

Nevertheless, Harry rode back to his quarters with a heavy heart. Juana would have to stay behind. Their mutual happiness had to be sacrificed in his pursuit 'of the bubble reputation'. He remembered how she grieved when he spoke of the possibility of their separation.

Juana, at first, took the news bravely. 'It is for your advantage,' she said, 'and neither of us must repine. All your friends have been so kind in arranging the prospect before you satisfactorily.' The word 'friends' caused tears to fill her eyes and she added plaintively: 'You have friends everywhere. I must be expatriated, separated from relatives, go among strangers, while I lose the only thing on earth my life hangs on and clings to.' Harry told her she would be safe with brother Tom, who was returning to England because of his old wound, and who would accompany her to London. Rather than go straight on to his father's house, he asked her to remain in London for some time to master English first. She agreed.

Together they sailed slowly in a skiff down the Garonne to Bordeaux. It was a beautiful city but it failed to suppress the awful thought of parting. On the appointed day, it took all of the strength that Harry could muster. He left Juana 'insensible and in a faint'. He dared not look back. 'God only knows the number of staggering and appalling dangers I had faced, but thank the Almighty, I never was unmanned until now, and I leaped on my horse by that impulse which guides the soldier to do his duty.'

It was an agonizing scene as the army marched to their transports in Bordeaux. Thousands of Portuguese and Spanish women, and their children, who had loved and attached themselves to British soldiers, were left behind in a forlorn and, generally, penniless condition. (The army was seven months arrear of pay.) A general order stated that only those legitimately married to soldiers, with their colonel's permission, would be transported. Such women as returned home would in all probability be rejected as outcasts for having consorted with heretics. Kincaid relates that the Riflemen that landed in Lisbon numbered 1,100 men and one woman. By the time they reached Bordeaux six years later, they had accumulated uncounted hundreds. Some soldiers deserted rather than leave their loved ones. Most were stranded on the beaches where their loud lamentations could be heard by their departing protectors of yesterday.

On boarding the frigate *Royal Oak*, Harry was taken aft to the admiral's cabin. Admiral Malcolm, with unaffected cordiality, offered him a drink. Still thinking of Juana and the lonely days ahead, Harry seized a bottle of gin, poured himself half a tumbler with a splash of water and gulped it down. 'Well done!' said the astonished admiral. 'I have been at sea, man and boy, these forty years, but damn me, if I ever saw a stiffer glass of grog than that in my life.' He invited Harry to join him at his table for the duration of the trip. How things had changed in six years, thought Harry. Formerly it was the naval officer who had been lionized, but Wellington's victories had changed all that. The very words 'Peninsular officer' touched off a reception of enthusiastic cordiality.

The following day General Ross and members of his staff arrived. At 47 years old Ross was an experienced and distinguished soldier with a reputation for stern discipline and great personal courage. Harry was attracted to this even-tempered Irishman, but he soon detected that the responsibilities of his first independent command were breeding caution and diffidence so unlike his daring conduct as a subordinate. How different it would have been if Wellington had been given command, Harry thought. However, in recommending another to the British government, the Duke had pointed out that if they selected a commander with his great reputation, they would be committed to an all-out victory, and geography clearly demonstrated that 'America's heart can be neither pierced nor her head battered in'.

It was a long, uneventful passage from France to the Azores and on to Bermuda, and 'an awful trial' for Harry. In 'a state bordering on despair', his heart yearned for his Spanish bride who loved 'with a force cooler latitudes cannot boast of'; and always his thoughts were troubled with worry for her fate, 'a foreigner in a foreign land' absent from 'that being on whom her life depended'. Harry's days were spent with a sympathetic young naval officer, Lieut. Holmes, who listened and appreciated his grief. At night Admiral Malcolm did the talking, largely on military matters which interested him as much as the sea. He required only four hours of sleep and half that time he continued to speak aloud, though the next day he could not remember a thing he said.

The War of 1812 was a totally unnecessary war. It was a war that the participants, aided by Napoleon's mischievous diplomacy, blundered into and fought in a clumsy fashion until it ended in a draw. The stated aims of the United States were never achieved: curtailment of the impressment of naturalized Americans; recognition of maritime rights; the annexation of Canada; and an end to the threat of Indian raids on the frontier. The unstated objective, however, that British condescension and contempt give way to the respect due to an independent nation, was in good measure accomplished. Though attacks on the almost defenceless Canadian border ended in disaster, the Americans excited admiration through spectacular triumphs in isolated duels with the British navy, the Mistress of the Seas, and in an estimable victory on land at New Orleans.

It was a war that Britain hoped to avoid, and it came at a time, 18 June 1812, when she was fighting for her survival against Napoleon. There were few troops available for a war in North America and the overworked navy, needed elsewhere, was kept busy pursuing American privateers which one Englishman described as being 'manned by a handful of bastards and outlaws'. The insufferable pretensions of the United States not only deprived Wellington's army of a vital source of grain and beef but their offensive privateers began to appear off the coast of Iberia to intercept his supply ships. Not until the spring of 1814 were the British in a position to deal properly with the Americans. 'Now that the tyrant Bonaparte has been consigned to infamy,' observed *The Times* on 15 April 1814, 'there is no public feeling in this country stronger than that of indignation against Americans', whose conduct was 'so black, so loathsome, so hateful'.

At Bermuda, during the last days of July, 1814, the three battalions (4th, 44th and 85th) from Bordeaux were joined by a waiting fourth (the 21st), a battalion of marines, and a company of artillery. Admiral Sir Alexander Cochrane was now in charge of the entire North American station. He would decide the point of attack in retaliation for the wanton destruction the Americans had committed in Upper Canada. The 56-year-old admiral had a long and brilliant record in the Royal Navy and he relished the American war, in which the opportunity to amass a fortune in prize money combined with his desire for revenge—for he hated the Americans, who had killed his brother at Yorktown in 1781. Cochrane was convinced, as he told Lord Melville, that the Americans, like whining spaniels, 'must be drubbed into good manners'. To this end, Cochrane's imaginative mind concocted many a scheme, including one which involved kidnapping certain members of President Madison's administration. Cochrane's second-in-command, Admiral George Cockburn, seems to have found Cochrane's schemes somewhat too fanciful; Cockburn himself was given to decisive action rather than elaborate preparations. Whereas

Cochrane planned and plotted, the self-confident Cockburn desired resolute action.

Cockburn had a career rich in adventure. He went to sea at 12 (he was now 42) and later won the admiration of Nelson for his unremitting zeal. It was this same relentless devotion to duty that since the beginning of 1813 had made him the scourge of Chesapeake Bay as he conducted a campaign of terror and plunder. Cockburn soon made himself the most hated British officer in the war. The American press characteristically denounced him as 'a savage monster ... a modern day Attila ... guilty of inhuman butcheries, savage cruelties—they disgraced human nature'. Unlike Cochrane, however, he had no animosity towards Americans, only towards journalists who defamed him with their outrageous calumnies. Napoleon, whom Cockburn later transported to St Helena and for a year served as his jailer, left the following description of Cockburn: 'He is not a man of bad heart ... but he is rough, overbearing, vain, choleric, and capricious; never consulting anybody; jealous of authority; caring little of the manner in which he exercises it, and sometimes violent without dignity.'

Britain's strength in the Chesapeake was anchored off the mouth of the Patuxent on 18 August 1814. All the senior officers met on board the *Tonnant*. Harry watched as they pored over bad maps and indulged in a long discussion dominated by the fast-talking Cockburn, who flaunted his personal knowledge of the region and of the Americans, having once stayed incognito in a boarding house in Washington. The plan that emerged was to destroy Com. Joshua Barney's flotilla, the only American naval force of consequence now anchored up the Patuxent; from there, if feasible, a descent could be made on Washington, a short distance overland from the town of Benedict. It was hoped that the move against Barney's flotilla would be interpreted by the enemy as the sole objective of the expedition and, thereby, ensure a surprise attack on the federal capital.

As the expedition sailed up the serpentine Patuxent, a thick forest of tall trees closed in on either side. To Harry, looking back from a lead ship, 'the appearance was that of a large fleet stalking through a wood'. They were guided by the shrill pipes of boatswains responding to the cadence of shouted soundings, a harmony that provided a most agreeable sensation. When the water became too shallow for the large transports, the troops were landed near Benedict, 36 miles from Washington.

Ross divided his force of some 4,500 men into three brigades. The light troops were placed under Col. Thornton, the other two under Col. Brooke and Col. Paterson. There was no cavalry, which was a great handicap. The only horses belonged to the general and his staff. Ross gave orders to collect all the horses in the vicinity and eventually managed to harness his artillery (one 6-pounder and two 3-pounders) which until then had been hand-drawn by a party of cursing sailors.

Though there was no opposition from the Americans, the first day's march along the river was exceptionally slow. Weeks at sea had made the soldiers soft. It would take time before they could march any distance with heavy packs. There was also the need to acclimatize to the Maryland summer sultriness. Every day an alarming number of men straggled and fell from the heat and fatigue.

Posted as deputy adjutant-general to the force, Harry was responsible, among other things, for the secret service. All inhabitants who would give information or act as guides were brought to him. The first was a man covered with leprosy called Calder. Keeping his distance, Harry learned that the American was drawn into treason by the hope that British surgeons would give him medical aid. He was soon joined by a healthy-looking younger man named Brown. They both proved useful as guides, but they had no information about enemy troop movements. What they contributed represented the total sum of British intelligence.

The conduct of Ross disturbed Harry, who wrote with a note of disappointment:

> I cannot say my dear friend General Ross inspired me with the opinion he was the officer Colborne regarded him as being. He was very cautious in responsibility—awfully so, and lacking that dashing enterprise so essential to carry a place by a *coup de main*.

On reaching Upper Marlboro, Ross did not know whether to go forward or back. Earl Bathurst, the war secretary, had prohibited any 'extended operations at a distance from the coast'. He was now 30 miles from the sea and 20 miles from the safety of the transports; he had no cavalry, little artillery and scant intelligence concerning the whereabouts of the enemy. His staff of eager young officers, however, urged him on with the argument that Washington was a mere 16 miles ahead. Ross remained reluctant.

The next morning, 23 August, Cockburn arrived in camp from Pig Point on the Patuxent where Com. Barney, rather than risk capture, had blown up his gunboats and withdrawn his 400 sailors to assist in the defence of the capital. Cockburn wasted no time in persuading Ross that Washington could be taken with little difficulty. While the army marched on to Old Fields, Lieut. James Scott, R.N., Cockburn's aide, was sent back to Benedict to inform Admiral Cochrane of their intentions. Cochrane, after lengthy debate with his staff, gave Scott a letter of instructions which was to be eaten if he were in danger of being captured on his return.

Ross and Cockburn were awakened by Scott at 2 a.m. The admiral's message informed them that any attempt to take Washington was far too risky. He ordered them 'to return immediately to Benedict and re-embark'. According to Scott, the irrepressible Cockburn took Ross aside and insisted that the enemy had only raw militiamen incapable of standing up to disciplined veterans. Not to strike a blow would 'be worse than defeat—it will be a stain upon our arms ... There is now no choice left us. We must go on'. Ross, who was by now in a highly agitated state, struck his hand against his forehead and exclaimed, 'Well be it so, we shall proceed.'

By some unknown means, the soldiers had learned that a retreat was contemplated and they grumbled their disappointment as they were ordered to stand to arms just before dawn. When they learned that they were to move forward, Scott wrote, 'a low murmuring burst of enthusiasm involuntarily escaped from the lips of the officers and men'. In less than five minutes the entire army was in full march towards the American capital.

Cockburn was right. Washington was poorly defended. Until June not a single regular was stationed there. Why should the British bother, the Americans reasoned, to take a town of only 6,000 with a much richer prize like Baltimore in the vicinity? Thus, when in mid-August a rider galloped into the capital to announce that the British had entered the Patuxent, confusion and panic ensued. President Madison put out an immediate call for all available regulars and militia in the neighbouring states. On paper this meant a force of over 90,000, but only a humiliating 7,000 could be turned out—and these were mostly undisciplined militia inadequately armed. Civilians fled the unfortified capital as the scattered troops marched and countermarched, still uncertain as to the exact direction of the British thrust.

The president, exercising his authority as commander-in-chief, took the field. James Monroe, the secretary of state and future president, strong on political ambition and short on military knowledge, assumed the duties of an army scout by reconnoitring the Patuxent. No effort was made to impede the British advance by digging trenches, felling trees or placing marksmen in concealment in the thick woods, where they could have created havoc on any troops attempting to pass along the narrow roads. The American army—if such it could be called— was commanded by General William Winder, a Baltimore lawyer with virtually no military experience. Like Ross, Winder was unable to make necessary decisions until options were forced upon him. About all that can be said for the general is that during the British advance he wore out three horses dashing back and forth, and finally injured himself by falling into a ditch.

The opposing armies met at midday on the 24th at Bladensburg, five miles outside Washington. The Americans were taking their positions as the weary redcoats, with sweat in their eyes and dust in their lungs, topped a hill overlooking a branch of the Potomac across which the town lay. Harry could see that the enemy was placed in three widely spaced lines on rising ground above the stream. Calder, the leper, told him that the only approach was across the narrow 90-foot bridge that led into the town, though the shallow water was fordable at various points. Pointing to the breastworks and formidable batteries peering down on the bridge, Harry advised Ross that at least a feint should be made on the American left flank farther up the river. Col. William Thornton interrupted him by asking Ross for permission to attack at once. Harry laughed in his face. To suggest a premature assault with most of the army strung out on the road behind them was the height of folly. Thornton grew red with anger. Then, to Harry's utter amazement, the general approved the precipitate advance. 'Heavens!'

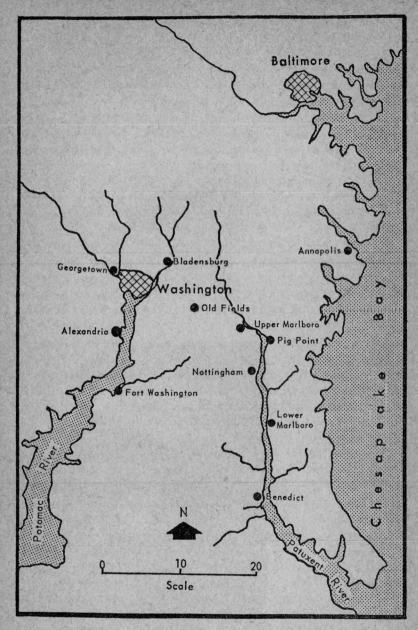

Map 2 The Advance on Washington, 19–24 August 1814

moaned Harry, 'If Colborne were to see this!' It was unthinkable to strike without the slightest effort at reconnaissance to find the enemy's most vulnerable spot. Harry could not hold back the words, 'General Ross, neither of the other Brigades can be up in time to support this mad attack, and if the enemy fight, Thornton's Brigade must be repulsed.'

Without even an advance cloud of sharpshooters, such as the Light Division had invariably used to harass the enemy and put them off their mark, Thornton's men were launched against the bridge. They charged in grand style—and were sharply repulsed. One whole company was nearly wiped out and Thornton was badly wounded. 'There,' declared Harry, 'there is the art of war and all we have learned from the Duke given in full to the enemy.'

As soon as the rest of the army came into sight, an impatient Ross said, 'Now, Smith, do you stop and bring into action the other two Brigades as fast as possible.' Looking for instructions, Harry asked, 'Upon what points, sir?' There was no reply as the gallant general galloped to the head of Thornton's crouching men and shouted, 'Come on, my boys.' He continued to be foremost as his clothes were torn by bullets and his horse was shot from under him. All the while, the fire-eating Cockburn, mounted on a white horse, was by his side. Harry, meanwhile, waved his arms and shouted as he directed the fight for Ross. It was an unnatural position, and not altogether to his liking. As Kincaid used to say, a Rifleman in the rear was like a fish out of water.

The first line of green Yankee militia suddenly dissolved before the onrushing redcoats and the terrifying swish of British rockets trailing fire overhead. The second line soon caved in. There was a general retreat except for Com. Barney and his sailors who kept shouting 'Board 'em, board 'em!' as they stood and served their guns. Working rapidly and with precision, they swept the British before them with grapeshot. Not until they had been outflanked and the commodore himself was seriously wounded were the guns silenced and the battle over. Because of the swiftness with which the nimble Americans took to their heels, few prisoners were taken. The incapable American command disintegrated, for Winder was in a state of collapse. Madison, who barely escaped capture, turned his borrowed horse around and galloped off towards Washington.

5 General Robert Ross who was responsible for military operations against Washington and Baltimore. Kindhearted and vacillating, Ross allowed himself to be overruled by ambitious admirals.

6 Admiral George Cockburn, by J. J. Halls. Known as the 'scourge of the Chesapeake', his sailors burned the White House and other public buildings in Washington.

7 General Sir Edward Pakenham, the high-minded and chivalrous commander at the battle of New Orleans where he dared death once too often.

8 Admiral Sir Alexander Cochrane, by Sir W. Beechey. As the commander of naval operations in North America, he plotted the assault on New Orleans with revenge and plunder in mind.

The British soldiers referred to the battle as the 'Bladensburg Races'. 'Suffice to say,' wrote Harry, 'we licked the Yankees and took all their guns, with a loss of upwards of 300 men, whereas Colborne would have done the same thing with probably a loss of 40 or 50.'

Before resuming the advance, Ross gave his worn men two hours of rest. The wounded were tended and Barney, whose bravery excited British admiration, reported that he was given 'the most marked attention, respect and politeness as if I were a brother'. When Ross and Cockburn rode up to him, Barney said, 'Well, Admiral, you have got hold of me at last.' Cockburn responded by praising him and his men for their noble stand. Most of the enemy casualties (about 150) were dressed not unlike English country folk and spoke the same language! One British officer felt as if they were shooting their own people.

The road to Washington was open, and Ross, leaving his troops at the outskirts, entered the city with a small party that evening. The general hoped for negotiations and the delivery of ransom money into his hands in exchange for his sparing the city. The majority of citizens and members of the government, however, had fled; Ross's party, preceded by a white flag and a drummer to announce their presence, was greeted largely by silence. Near the Capitol in the city's centre, however, there was light sporadic firing from one of the houses in the darkness and four soldiers and the general's horse were hit. Cockburn rushed sailors with rockets into the area to demolish the building. As if in response to the fiery explosions from the rockets, the earth trembled as the Americans blew up the Navy Yard a mile to the south.

Cockburn would gladly have put the torch to the entire city, but Ross refused to allow the destruction of anything but government buildings. Harry, in turn, had no objection to setting fire to works of military value, such as arsenals, barracks, or dockyards, but recalling 'the Duke's humane warfare in the South of France, we [most of the other officers] were horrified at the order to burn the elegant Houses of Parliament and the President's house'.[1] There was strong sentiment, however, in

[1] An angry group of Americans later resolved to retaliate against Ross for devastating Washington by sending a fast vessel to the coast of Ireland. The men were to land at Carlingford Bay and utterly destroy Rosstrevor, his beautiful home. The peace that soon followed put an end to the scheme.

military and government circles at home that the Americans
should be paid back for having sacked and burned York (now
Toronto), the modest capital in Upper Canada. And with
Washington annihilated, it was argued, the seat of government
would be moved to New York, or another northern city where
feeling against the war had always been strong.

At 10.30 p.m. Ross and his staff went down Pennsylvania
Avenue to the White House. Entering the dining-room, they
were amazed to find a table laid with 40 settings, the food warm
and the wine chilled. Madison had been so confident of
victory that he had ordered a supper in celebration. Instead, his
hungry conquerors 'speedily consumed' the feast and toasted the
health of the Prince Regent with what Scott described as a
'super-excellent Madeira'.

Before consigning the residence to flames there was a hunt for
souvenirs, anything from James Madison's love letters to a
pair of rhinestone shoe buckles. Cockburn selected one of
'Jemmy's' (as he called him) old hats. As for Dolly Madison,
who was supposed to have trampled upon the British ensign a
few days before, Cockburn took a cushion from her chair and
jested coarsely about how it would remind him of her 'seat'.
Harry appears to have been satisfied with a clean shirt from the
president's wardrobe. As they left, Harry would 'never forget
the destructive majesty of the flames as the torches were applied
to beds, curtains, etc. Our sailors were artists at their work.'
To him, it would always be a ruthless act unworthy of Englishmen.

Cochrane did not think so. He later criticized Cockburn, saying, 'I am sorry you left a house standing in Washington —
depend upon it, it is mistaken mercy.' Cockburn sincerely
regretted that he could not accommodate his chief. In at least
one instance, he disregarded Ross's order by settling an old
score with *The National Intelligencer*, which had published
slanderous articles about him. Sitting astride his stolen white
mare, Cockburn supervised the destruction of the offices, the
presses and the type. 'Be sure that all the C's are destroyed,' he
called to his sailors, 'so that the rascals cannot any longer abuse
my name.'

Washington was not kind to the invaders who disfigured her.
The accidental explosion of a magazine at Greenleaf Point
killed 12 and wounded 30 others. On the second day a tornado

ripped through the city tearing off roof tops as though they were made of paper. The soldiers, Lieut. Glieg noted in his diary, were dispersed 'as if they had received a total defeat'. Some 30 soldiers were buried in the debris. (The force was further reduced when others were 'poisoned by American whisky'.)

Ross decided to leave that night. There was nothing more to be gained by remaining, and there were rumours of the enemy gathering a large army to retake the city. Harry, meanwhile, had been responsible for collecting 'everything in the shape of transport' that had been left behind by the inhabitants and that had chanced to survive the storm. The wagons were to carry all of the ambulatory wounded and as much flour as Harry could confiscate. Returning to camp after dark, Ross greeted him with the announcement that he had ordered the army to move that night. Harry remonstrated, arguing that the men needed a rest and that proceeding by night along the road beyond Bladensberg would be extremely difficult because of the nature of the terrain. But Ross brushed his arguments aside saying that arrangements had been made and they must march through the night. Harry muttered to himself, 'Oh, for dear John Colborne'. He would have avoided a night march 'as he would the devil'. In Harry's opinion, no time was ever gained by such a move, which so thoroughly fatigued the men; moreover, the confusion and disorder that ensued put them of necessity at the mercy of the enemy. Luckily, he observed, the Yankees were as deficient in the art of war as Ross.

To deceive the Americans, the British subtly let it be known that they intended to bring similar conflagration to Annapolis, and then Baltimore. Inquisitive American gentlemen who came to the British camp ostensibly to inquire about the preservation of private property were sent to Captain Smith. With an air of great curiosity, Harry would pump them for information about the roads, resources and defences of Annapolis and Baltimore. That 'the bait took' was evident when Harry later received reports that the enemy were concentrating their forces at Annapolis.

At 9 p.m. on 25 August after imposing a curfew ordering all inhabitants off the streets, the British left Washington. Campfires burned brightly as they slipped silently out into the darkness. The retreat was organized so cleverly that it was some time before the British soldiers themselves were aware that the entire army had withdrawn.

Retracing their steps into Bladensburg, they were greeted by the spectacle of their unburied dead strewn about and stripped completely naked. The moon had just risen to give an unearthly hue to their swollen bodies whitened by the rain. But there was no time to bury them. More wounded were loaded. Those who could not be moved were entrusted to the care of Com. Barney and his sailors in exchange for their parole. 'The attention and care they received from the Americans,' Harry recorded, 'became the character of a civilized nation.' Harry also managed the distribution of the flour from the barrels with their tops smashed in. 'Soldiers being greedy fellows', observed Harry, completely filled their haversacks.

After pausing an hour, the march continued on a winding road into the dark woods, where all was confusion. Had it not been for weary soldiers throwing flour away by degrees to unconsciously mark the trail, Harry declared, 'the whole column would have lost the road'. At dawn, still only three miles out of Bladensburg, the men were so exhausted that Ross was forced to call a halt. The soldiers were given five hours sleep while Harry and other mounted men went on the lookout for Yankee sharpshooters. The unmolested army continued the retreat to Benedict where they were welcomed with vociferous cheers by the sailors.

Before embarking on the morning of the 30th, Ross called Harry aside and told him that he wanted him to be the bearer of his despatches because his aide, Captain Fall, was too sick to discharge the responsibility. Having so often and freely criticized his commander, Harry never expected that he should have the honour to carry to England the official tidings of victory, an assignment that almost invariably meant promotion. Harry was ecstatic: 'Wife, home, and country, all rushed in my mind at once.'

Cockburn, meanwhile, had but one thought in his mind: a raid on Baltimore. Enlisting the support of Cochrane, he lost no time in pressuring Ross to strike at that 'nest of pirates', by far the richest prize on the Atlantic coast. Ross did not favour the proposal and sought Harry's opinion. Harry warned him against the urgings of admirals 'burning with ambition', and asked Ross to consider the facts of the situation: half the men in his force, which was already too small, were sick from dysentery. The Americans, on the other hand, already forewarned by the false intelligence he had fed them, were concentrating their strength in the area. And even if they should take Baltimore, it would add little to the general effect produced by the seizure of the capital, whereas a defeat would greatly restore the enemy's confidence. Ross agreed. 'Then, sir,' Harry asked, 'may I tell Lord Bathurst you will not go to Baltimore?' The general nodded and said, 'Yes'. Harry was relieved, for he had a presentiment of failure if the attempt were made.

Accompanying Harry to the gangway of the fast frigate, *Iphigenia*, Ross handed him a bundle of letters, including one for his wife. He made Harry promise to visit her at Bath as soon as the despatches were delivered. The general then thanked Harry for his services, adding 'I can ill spare you'. Concern for Ross, so gallant, so amiable — so soft, caused Harry to ask once more if he could assure Bathurst that he would not attempt Baltimore. '*You may*,' he replied firmly.

But as Harry feared, Ross could not for long stand alone against the forceful admirals and his own staff. The attack on Baltimore on 12 September foundered and Ross, riding to the front as usual, was mortally wounded in the breast. While Francis Scott Key was jotting down the words of a future national anthem for his fellow Americans, the body of the general was placed in a barrel of rum so as to preserve it for the voyage to Halifax, Nova Scotia, where he was buried. A monument was later raised to his memory in St Paul's.

Meanwhile, the rapidity of the Atlantic crossing (21 days to Spithead) was such that Harry found it 'consonant to my feeling and in perfect accordance with my character'. At the George Inn, Portsmouth, Harry, West, the ailing Fall and Captain Wainwright, R.N., with naval despatches for the Admiralty, piled into the London coach and hung on to the arm-slings as Harry made the coach-boys 'drive a furiously good pace'. Rattling and careering through a peaceful English countryside was a glorious experience for a soldier who had seen nothing for the past seven years but lands ravaged by war — no burning villages, no starving peasants, no sign of death in its various shapes. Having deposited his despatches at Downing Street, Harry found a room in Parliament Street which had only one bed. He and West shocked the chambermaid by dividing the bed clothes and making a second bed on the floor, Peninsular-style.

Harry was off by dawn to the barracks that he knew quartered some Rifle comrades. On learning from the porter that his friend, Col. John Ross, was staying there, he bolted into his room and shouted: 'Halloa, Ross, stand to arms.' After expressing mutual joy on seeing one another, Harry asked if Juana were alive and well. Ross assured him that she was in every respect. He had seen her just the day before; she was staying in Panton Square, No. 11. 'Oh, thank Almighty God,' said Harry as he burst into tears.

Harry departed as abruptly as he had come. While he was scanning the square for No. 11, Juana recognized his hand on the coach window. 'Oh, Dios, la mano de mi Enrique!' she cried as she ran to him. As they embraced and expressed their gratitude to God, they shared an experience that Harry believed was known only to a very few. Many years later he wrote:

> Oh! you who enter into holy wedlock for the sake of con-
> nexions — tame, cool, amiable, good, I admit — you cannot
> feel what we did. That moment of our lives was worth the
> whole of your apathetic ones for years.

There was no time to linger. His immediate concern for Juana relieved, Harry returned to Downing Street where his presence was demanded. There he was welcomed by Lord Bathurst who told him that the information he had brought with him was of such importance that the Prince Regent wished to see him forthwith. Off they hurried to Carlton House where Harry was ushered into a large room and asked to wait. Sitting alone for nearly half an hour put Harry into deep thought about his interview with royalty. A strange, almost foreign sensation of awe came over him as he thought of himself, an unknown captain, conversing with England's *actual* king. Tossing his head, he recovered his breezy self-confidence by telling himself that he never shrank in the presence of the Duke, 'with his piercing eye', nor would he begin now. General Ross had implored him to talk if he met the Prince, for it was well known that His Royal Highness often complained that 'the bearer of despatches will never talk'. Harry resolved to communicate fully if it were his royal wish.

Bathurst then appeared. 'The Prince will see you.' Harry explained that he knew nothing about court etiquette. The war secretary instructed him to behave as he would to any gentleman; the Prince would soon put him at his ease. As an afterthought, he told Harry to call him 'Sir', and not to turn his back on him. 'No, my Lord,' said Harry, 'I know that; and my profession is one of "show a good front".'

The opulence of the Prince's dressing-room startled him for a moment. There was a marvellous assortment of every variety of dress, perfumes, snuff-boxes and wigs that London could produce. The First Gentleman of Europe made him feel most welcome with his kind words and gracious manner. He spoke of how Ross strongly recommended him as an officer thoroughly informed on the campaigning he came to report, the importance of which was indicated by the Parliament and Tower guns firing at that very moment. Harry could not help but smile to himself at the thought that he, Harry Smith, was sitting with the Prince Regent while all London was celebrating the news he had brought. Harry was then amazed by the Regent's grasp of military matters. Perusing a map of America, the Prince asked incisive questions about the expedition and for details about public buildings burned in Washington. 'In his heart,' observed Harry, 'I fancied I saw he thought it a barbarian act.' The Prince was so skilful in drawing Harry out that he soon found himself relating a few humorous anecdotes that caused the Regent to laugh heartily. As he got up to leave and to back out of his presence, His Highness said appreciatively: 'I and the country are obliged to you all. Ross's recommendations will not be forgotten, and, Bathurst, don't forget this officer's promotion.' To Harry, the interview was the most gentlemanlike and affable he could possibly have imagined.

There was a small dinner party that evening at Bathurst's home on Putney Heath, though Harry would much rather have spent the time with Juana. In the drawing-room he met, much to his surprise, Lord Fitzroy Somerset, who congratulated him on his success in America, and introduced his wife, the niece of the Duke of Wellington, whom he had recently married. Seated between Lord Somerset and an elderly gentleman he did not know, Harry soon discovered he was the lion of the party whom everyone induced to talk. Mounted on his own hobby-horse, he spoke at length about the Duke, who in his eyes was 'something elevated beyond any human being'. Having delivered his tribute, the elderly gentleman next to him said he was glad to hear him speak so well of his brother. He was the Marquis of Wellesley.

One obligation remained, the discharge of which proved to be delightful. Together he and Juana went to Bath to see Mrs Ross. Juana was enchanted by the lush English countryside, though she would sometimes compare it unfavourably with Spain. But she freely admitted that the inns were superior to the Spanish *posadas*. And they stopped when and where they liked, for there were 'no brutal railroads in those days, where all are flying prisoners'.

The general's wife, still unaware of the death of her husband, was in the highest of spirits over his success and the news that the Prince Regent had directed that he be given the insignia of Knight Commander of the Bath. She told them that her husband had promised her that this would be his last campaign.

At the last stage of their journey back to London, Juana looked at a newspaper (she began to read English long before she learned to speak it well) and read of Harry's promotion to the rank of major, which carried with it a grant of £500, 'the reward' she called it, 'of our separation'.

It had been arranged that Harry's father would meet them on their return to London before accompanying them to Whittlesea. Until now Juana refused all entreaties on the part of his family to visit them before Harry's return. Dr John Smith was greeted at the door by Harry. And 'while we mingled our tears for the departed', wrote Harry, Juana was upstairs making herself presentable. There was obviously great curiosity on his father's part regarding the nature and appearance of his 16-year-old daughter-in-law. Pride in his wife and natural inclination to tease induced Harry to arrange a charade. He told his father that his Juana 'was of the stiff Spanish school as stately as a swan and about as proud as a peacock'. Juana, enjoying 'the fun of deception', put on a full Spanish costume with comb and mantilla, and the haughty airs of the hidalgo class. But the pose dissolved before Harry could complete the introduction. Casting aside all restraint, she threw herself into his father's arms, who 'cried like a child' as she, 'showed a heart evidently framed for love.' Her charm was irresistible.

In Whittlesea the rest of the family was equally captivated and she was quickly adopted as one of their own.

Separation was less painful now that Juana was to be accommodated with his family in Whittlesea. She and her father-in-law journeyed with Harry as far as the flat in London. This time Juana did not faint as he took his leave for America. Harry's last glimpse was one of Juana resting her forehead against the mantelpiece in a condition verging on despair, while his father stood by ready to comfort her.

The trip to Portsmouth was made in the company of Dr John Robb, who had been a surgeon with the 95th in the Peninsula and was now inspector-general of the American expedition. To conceal his dejection, Harry spoke glibly and cheerfully of things he expected to do when he returned to England. Robb, a strong-minded realist who said little, finally offered his opinion: 'Oh, that's capital! a fellow going out to be killed by an American Rifleman, talking of what he will do when he comes back.'

[4]

The Battle of New Orleans

*I have it much at heart to give them a complete drubbing
before peace is made.*

Admiral Cochrane

The New Orleans campaign began most inauspiciously for
Harry Smith. Preparing to board ship, he and West discovered
that the wrong portmanteau had been delivered from the coach.
In place of uniforms and boots, they were carrying the dirty
linen—silk stockings, evening pantaloons, etc.—of a Frenchman. Not until three weeks after the battle of New Orleans
were his belongings recovered.

The ship, the frigate *Statira*, was badly overcrowded, Sir
Edward Pakenham's staff and the staffs of the commanders of
the engineers and artillerymen, some thirty in all, were packed
into steerage where they slept on cots. The crew was unhappy
and constantly grumbled, having recently lost their popular
captain, an outstanding sailor who was killed in a duel. His
successor, Captain Swaine, pacific and old-fashioned, was
regarded with contempt by his men.

Pakenham, who was anxious to join his army before the
campaign began, had boarded one of the fastest ships in the
fleet. But the new captain, instead of ensuring all possible speed
night and day, insisted upon making all snug at night by taking
in sail despite the general's protests. Consequently, Pakenham
arrived at New Orleans on 25 December, two weeks after
Admiral Cochrane had deposited some 1,600 men of his army on
the Louisiana shore and two days after his subordinate, General
Sir John Keane, had fought the first battle with the Americans.

That Christmas Eve, on the other side of the Atlantic, the
Treaty of Ghent was signed (but not yet ratified) and for all
practical purposes the war was over. Because of contrary winds,
however, it was not until 14 February that the surviving
combatants were rescued from their ignorance. The unlucky

74

ship, *Statira*, which carried so many passengers destined to be killed before New Orleans, was herself lost on a reef shortly afterwards.

The capture of New Orleans, a first-class military prize, conceived by Admiral Cochrane and endorsed by the Cabinet, was expected to provide a valuable hostage in negotiations and more than pay for the effort in booty. The wealth of the Crescent City, largely in cotton and sugar, was believed to be enormous.

There were certain handicaps, however. The undertaking was stinted in men and supplies by a parsimonious Parliament; then when reinforcements were finally agreed upon, they were sent out in piecemeal fashion. Secrecy was compromised when Cochrane established his advance base in Jamaica, where he assembled an insufficient number of shallow-draught boats and more than enough cargo ships to carry ballast going in and, obviously, loot coming out. Not unlike the Buenos Aires scheme, it was convincing enough on paper, but it failed to recognize that neither the terrain nor the inhabitants would be friendly. (Cochrane was misled by reports that the Creole population was disaffected by American rule to the point of rebellion.)

That New Orleans was well-protected—first by the fortified mouth of the Mississippi, and then by the shallow and unhealthy swamps that all but surround the city—did not deter Cochrane. He found a short cut, one that provided a quick strike against a weakly defended city, such as had been made against Washington.

On 8 December 1814, Cochrane anchored his fleet off the mouth of the shallow lagoon known as Lake Borgne and went in with small vessels to challenge the American gunboats—which were overpowered six days later. The troops were then laboriously conveyed under Admiral Malcolm some 80 miles in rowing boats. On leaving Lake Borgne, they entered the mouth of a creek called Bayou Bienvenue and by various winding bayous and the Villeré canal they arrived at solid ground near the Mississippi and some eight miles from New Orleans. Col. Thornton, with the light troops, wanted to press on as he had so impetuously at Bladensburg. Sir John Keane said no. The men were exhausted and half-frozen. General Andrew Jackson, the future president of the United States, wasted no time while they debated.[1] The next night, the 23rd, his 'dirty shirts' (as the redcoats dubbed them) attacked, but the disciplined British held their ground.

Appearing on the scene that dreary Christmas, Pakenham cursed his luck. He found his army crammed into a neck of land barely a mile wide, with an impenetrable cypress marsh on his right and the broad Mississippi on his left. Two enemy warships continued to drop shells into them at will. Before him was the still invisible prize, New Orleans, the only road to which was blocked by a barricade of mud and cotton bales and manned by uncounted thousands of the enemy. Behind him, distant some twenty hours of hard rowing, was the fleet with all of his supplies and barely enough boats to bring them forward and far too few to withdraw his soldiers should a hasty retreat become necessary. Every day the cold and rain reduced the ranks of his exposed army. The shivering blacks of the two West India regiments, who had no blankets, suffered most and were virtually useless. Had any British commander ever been confronted with such a predicament that was not of his making? Harry asked. To attack or retreat—or even to sit still—was to court disaster.

Pakenham, who had never experienced failure, was not easily discouraged. Born into an aristocratic Anglo-Irish ambit and gazetted a lieutenant at 16, he rose rapidly through purchase and patronage, and by subscribing to what was called the 'daring school' when in battle. At 34 (in 1812) he became one of the youngest major-generals in the service. While serving on the staff of Wellington, who had married his sister Kitty, he temporarily took command of Picton's 3rd Division and smashed the French centre at Salamanca. The Duke remarked that his brother-in-law was not 'the brightest genius, but one of the best we have'. Dazzlingly brave, he was shot in the neck on two occasions. The first gave his head what he described as its 'comical' tilt; the second made it perfectly straight. A great social favourite, his warmth and straightforwardness moved Sir William Napier to write, 'General Pakenham makes me now and then think there are some good

---

[1] Jackson had an active dislike for the British. During the Revolutionary War, in which a brother was killed, he was captured and ordered to shine the boots of an arrogant British officer. When he refused, he was struck on the head with a sword. He carried a scar for the rest of his life.

men in the world.' Having little desire to fight in America, he had hoped to be spared the assignment; but he was too seriously devoted to soldiering to turn it down.

Pakenham's winning ways were not lost on Harry. He had, of course, been acquainted with the general during their Peninsular days, but after the ship-bound intimacy of a long voyage, Harry discovered that he 'was one of the most amusing persons imaginable—a high-minded and chivalrous fellow in every idea, and to our astonishment, very devoutly inclined'. His confidence in Pakenham as a commander began to rise; there was to be no repetition of the distress he had suffered under Ross. Enthusiasm for the coming campaign was increased when Harry heard on landing that the adjutant-general had been shot through the neck and that Pakenham had made him head of the department.

That the presence of the handsome and elegant Pakenham infused new life into the weary force was manifested by cheers wherever he appeared. The Americans who heard them prepared for an immediate attack. But it was not until the 28th that the general moved up his men to reconnoitre in strength, or attack, if feasible. Riding with Harry, Pakenham began to discourse on ground, position and possibilities in a way that reminded Harry of the Duke.

As they drifted close to the enemy lines, Harry detected riflemen stalking them not more than a hundred yards away. Knowing the Americans to be excellent shots, Harry spoke bluntly: 'Ride away, Sir Edward, behind this bank, or you will be shot in a second. By your action you will be recognized as the Commander-in-Chief, and some riflemen are now going to fire.' Pakenham did as he was told. That evening, after giving the incident some thought, a somewhat ruffled Pakenham called Harry aside and asked for an explanation: 'You gentlemen of the Craufurd school are very abrupt and peremptory in your manner to generals. Would you have spoken to Craufurd as you did to me today?' Harry responded:

Most certainly, for if I had not, and one of us had been killed or wounded, and he became aware I observed what I did when I spoke to you, he would have blown me up as I deserved. He taught us to do so.

Pakenham was greatly amused by his answer.

Even with the additional troops Pakenham brought out, the American position seemed impregnable. As they peered through their telescopes, Sir Edward turned suddenly and asked Harry for a 'Light Division opinion'—'What do you say, Smith, as to the practicability of an attack on the enemy's lines.' Flattered, Harry expounded in detail on how the enemy's position was made strong by man and nature, and that any frontal assault over the flat, open ground before an enemy concealed behind formidable breastworks would result in very heavy losses. He suggested that they destroy the two armed ships on the Mississippi and seize the unoccupied right bank, from which they could enfilade the American position. Once they opened fire, those on the left bank could storm the works before them in two, three or more columns.

'You Rifle gentlemen have learnt something, I do believe,' declared Pakenham. At first, Harry thought that the praise might be in jest, 'for he was a most light-hearted fellow'. But later, he told Harry that he concurred entirely with his views. Batteries would be erected to destroy the ships; and when that was done, they would open up on the enemy. Should they destroy any part of the Americans' defences, or silence their batteries, explained Pakenham, the army would attack at once without waiting for the reinforcements expected daily under Sir John Lambert.

British artillery, with improvised red-hot shot, destroyed the schooner *Carolina*. The frigate *Louisiana*, however, managed with tow and sail to escape upstream where men and guns were landed on the opposite bank to continue their chafing fire. In Harry's opinion the *Louisiana*'s escape was a blunder on the part of Col. Alexander Dickson, R.A., chief of artillery. Had the guns been trained on the farthest ship first, the *Louisiana*, 'we might have destroyed both'.

More and heavier guns were needed to breach Jackson's defences. The exertions of overworked sailors and soldiers accomplished an astounding feat, one the Americans thought impossible, by floating and dragging up tons of metals and projectiles. The labour was completed on the night of the 31st, and the army was brought up to attack on the New Year.

The bombardment was a complete failure. The British position was poor: rather than solid earth bulwarks for their defence, the soldiers were forced to use hogsheads of sugar—

for if they dug deeper than eight inches they struck water. The American gunners, on the other hand — among them Laffite's pirates — were well dug in; they ripped their shot through the British hogsheads, knocking over artillerymen and silencing the guns. It was over in an hour. Admiral Codrington, Cochrane's chief of staff, called the one-sided duel 'a blot on the artillery escutcheon'. A 'much mortified' Pakenham was forced to withdraw his troops while the Americans played 'Yankee Doodle'. Only a strong guard was left to protect the remaining guns.

There was a cold drenching rain that evening. Harry was again asked to stay with Pakenham for the night while the rest of his staff went to their usual quarters. Reflecting on the day's debacle, Pakenham said, 'Smith, those guns must be brought back; go and do it.' Knowing how soft the ground had become, Harry pointed out that it would require a large number of men. The general told him to take 600 men from Gibbs's brigade. Harry was given men of the 21st and 44th, who according to Col. Dickson were 'not distinguished for discipline'. Fatigued and dispirited with the mood of failure upon them, they behaved sullenly. Harry's exhortations were simply ignored. Many of the work party stole away into the night. For the first time in his career, Harry was confronted with mass disobedience to orders. To rouse the general from his sleep to report his failure was to Harry 'as bad as the loss of a leg'. But there was no alternative; the guns had to be removed before daybreak.

Concealing his emotion as best he could, Harry told the general that he could not budge the men. Jumping to his feet, Pakenham told Harry to order his horse and turn out Gibbs's entire brigade. By dint of great effort and declarations that 'I am Sir Edward Pakenham, etc., and Commander-in-Chief', most of the guns were brought away by dawn. The heaviest ones were buried (something the general would never have recommended to Harry). 'You see, Smith,' he said as they were riding back, 'exertion and determination will effect anything.' Stung by the remark, Harry protested that he had done his utmost; after all, he had neither the prestige of Pakenham's name, nor the use of the entire brigade. On seeing Harry's great humiliation, Pakenham admitted that what he had said was true and added, 'I admire your mortification; it shows your zeal.'

Harry was consoled by the knowledge that he had not fallen in Sir Edward's estimation.

The galling reverses of the previous week led to grumbling throughout the army. Lieut. Gleig compared it 'to the growling of a chained dog when he sees his adversary, but cannot reach him'. Cold, hungry and stricken with dysentery, these previously successful veterans had come to trounce an enemy who, instead, bombarded them unceasingly and, in a most unchivalrous fashion, hunted their sentries like game. Twice they had been brought to the verge of battle, their blood up for the usual charge, only to be retired and forced to show their backs to the jeering 'dirty shirts'.

If they had any doubt about Pakenham's determination to fight, it was dispelled by the news on the 2nd that Sir John Lambert had landed and was on his way with two elite regiments, the 7th Royal Fusiliers and the 43rd Light Infantry. On the same day the general ordered work to begin on broadening the Villeré canal so as to float large boats that could be brought from the fleet and launched into the Mississippi. These boats would be used to ferry Thornton's brigade to the opposite shore at night where they would capture the American guns and turn them on Jackson's lines.

Lambert's appearance brought with it a measure of unhappiness for Harry. By right of seniority, Major Sir John Tylden, Lambert's assistant adjutant-general, was entitled to take over the department, and Tylden insisted upon it. It meant that Harry would have to take his place with Lambert, a general he had never met before. Transfer from Pakenham's side also meant a sadly diminished role in the impending battle. Pakenham expressed his desire to keep Harry with him, but he could not in justice deny Tylden's claim. Nevertheless, he promised to find work enough for both of them. 'I do believe,' wrote Harry, 'I was more attached to Sir Edward, as a soldier, than I was to John Colborne, *if possible.*'

The assault was to begin as soon as the 1,000 yards of canal was completed. The dirty, exhausting work in the mud continued round the clock. Though they attempted to screen their activities from the Americans, the enemy soldiers were not unaware of their diggings. No attempt, however, was made to stop them, perhaps because Jackson was unwilling to risk his men, mostly militia, against disciplined regulars in the open.

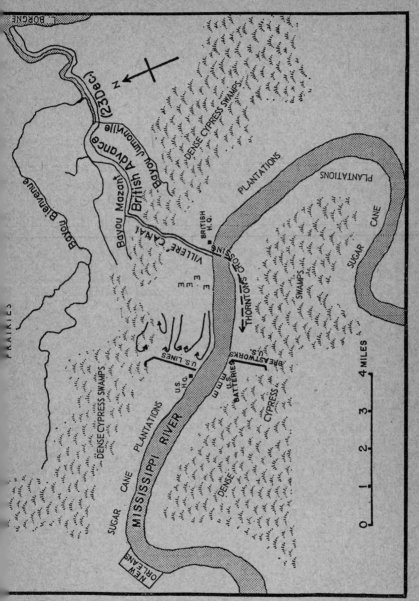

Map 3 The Battle of New Orleans, 8 January 1815

The reinforcements, meanwhile, carried cannon balls in their haversacks to ease the shortage. (One boat capsized on Lake Borgne and seventeen Fusiliers went straight to the bottom.) Struggling knee-deep in mud, the newcomers were depressed by the desolate waste and unsightly marshes 'canopied over with putrid exhalations'. Captain Cooke of the 43rd swore that these 'regions were without doubt the rendezvous of the universe for wild ducks and the resort of hideous floundering alligators'. The 7th and the 43rd were reviewed, but the general-in-chief did not appear—he was up in a pine tree surveying the barricades of the round-hatted Yankees.

All was in readiness by the evening of the 7th. Pakenham inspected the canal and the boats before Thornton's brigade (the 85th, marines and sailors) was to cross over. Examining the dam, Pakenham asked the engineer in charge, 'Are you satisfied the dam will bear the weight of water which will be upon it when the banks of the river are cut?' The engineer replied, 'Perfectly.' Pakenham was not completely satisfied. 'I should be far more so,' Harry heard him say, 'if a second dam was constructed.' The success of the whole project hinged on the sturdiness of the dam.

Harry believed the plan of battle to be excellent. The army of some 6,000 grouped into four brigades (including Thornton's) was to attack at first light on 8 January. The main blow under General Samuel Gibbs (the 4th and 21st) would hit the Americans' left close to the edge of the swamp, which would protect their flank (some light companies and West Indians would go into the swamp) and place them farthest from any enfilading enemy guns. Ahead of the column, under cover of a firing party of 300 Rifles and an equal number of the 44th, the rest of the 44th would carry forward fascines to fill the ditches and ladders to scale the barricades.

The second column under General Keane was divided into two sections. The light companies of the brigade, under Col. Rennie, were to advance on the American right and destroy an unfinished redoubt with two enfilading guns. The bulk of the brigade under Keane (the 93rd and 1st West India) would move parallel to Rennie and storm the centre of the enemy line, or to the left of Gibbs; their movement—essentially a feint to distract the enemy—would be dictated by the outcome of the other assaults and the effects of British artillery.

Lambert's brigade (the 7th and 43rd) were to wait in reserve closer to Gibbs's column than Keane's, ready to exploit the collapse of any part of the American line. (Pakenham told Harry that 'when we are in New Orleans, I can depend upon Lambert's Reserve'.)

After sleeping soundly, for victory seemed certain, the men assembled at four o'clock in the morning. Except for the precautionary warning words of officers, 'steady men', 'steady men', there was silence as they moved to their appointed positions through thick mists. Some American authorities later claimed that in order to put a sharper edge on their appetite for battle, the password given to the British soldiers that day was 'Booty and Beauty', for New Orleans was said to have more than its share of beautiful women. But it is highly unlikely that a man as high-minded as Pakenham would promise his men the sack of the city. The charge was publicly denied by Lambert, Keane, Dickson and other British officers after the war.

There was no hope that they could surprise the Americans. Observation, confirmed by British deserters, alerted Jackson to the coming attack. Militiamen from Louisiana, Tennessee and Kentucky, together with a sprinkling of regular units, stood some 5,000 strong, including reserves, behind earthworks representing two weeks' labour permitted by British procrastination. Though ragged in appearance, as frontiersmen they knew how to use their long rifles and kill if the conditions were favourable. And with a clear line of fire from behind ball-proof concealment, the circumstances were right.

For the British everything went wrong. When Pakenham arose at 5 a.m. and examined the disposition of his forces, he learned that the 44th under Col. Mullins, because of a misunderstanding, had failed in their indispensable work of bringing up the ladders and fascines. Major Tylden, however, reported to the general that the situation had been corrected and that the task would be finished in time for the attack.

As for Thornton's brigade, the dam had burst before the onrushing waters from the broken levee, causing many of the boats to be stranded in the mud. The sailors toiled for hours that night but little was achieved. Thus, only 450 out of 1,400 men had crossed over and they had landed four miles below the guns they were to take, re-align and, on signal, fire across the river when the main force advanced. No one, it appears, had the nerve to rouse the general in the middle of the night (as Harry had done) to report the setback. Quartermaster Surtees recalled, 'Poor Sir Edward seemed like one bereft of his reason, for this failure had blasted all his most sanguine hopes'. According to Col. Dickson, if the general had been acquainted with this difficulty when the boats were first launched, he would have begun the vital operation immediately with fewer boats making more than one trip.

A curious relationship had developed between Pakenham and Harry. A half hour before daylight, on the verge of battle, the general called Harry out of line to discuss his predicament. Harry found Pakenham 'greatly agitated', complaining bitterly:

> Smith, most Commanders-in-Chief have many difficulties to contend with, but surely none like mine. The dam, as you heard me say it would, gave way, and Thornton's people will be of no use whatever to the general attack.

Harry offered the sympathy which seemed to be expected of him:

> So impressed have you ever been, so obvious is it in every military point of view, we should possess the right bank of the river, and thus enfilade and divert the attention of the enemy; there is still time before daylight to retire the columns now. We are under the enemy's fire as soon as discovered.

But the general, concerned for the morale of his troops disagreed: 'This may be, but I have twice deferred the attack. We are strong in numbers now comparatively. It will cost more men, and the assault must be made.'

While Harry continued to press for delay, the first signs of dawn appeared. 'Smith,' said the general, 'order the rockets to be fired.' Harry still tried to dissuade him, but Pakenham dismissed his pleas by observing:

> It is now too late: the columns would be visible to the enemy before they could move out of fire, and would lose more men than it is to be hoped they will in the attack. Fire the rocket, I say, and go to Lambert.

When Harry reached Lambert, he sensed 'the stillness of death and anticipation'. He was sure that the enemy were aware of their proximity.

The incendiary rocket, a blazing harbinger, sputtered and zigzagged. Columns of companies, 60 men abreast and four deep, moved in step to the steady beat of drums, rolling like a great scarlet carpet into the morning fog. A terrible cross-fire of guns, loaded with grape and canister, followed by the discharge of thousands of rifles and muskets, lit up the American lines with rippling orange flashes. Columns crumbled before an unseen enemy. Small streams of soldiers continued towards the flashes that were killing them; others halted to return the fire; some began to fall back. Seeing this, Pakenham rushed forth with his staff to rally his men. As he galloped past, Harry heard him shout, 'That's a terrific fire, Lambert.' Knowing Pakenham's reputation for exposing himself to danger in battle, Harry told Lambert:

> In twenty-five minutes, General, you will command the army. Sir Edward Pakenham will be wounded and incapable, or killed. The troops do not get on a step. He will be at the head of the first Brigade he comes to, and what I say will occur.

And so it was, but it was a matter of seconds rather than minutes. The first troops Pakenham came upon were the 44th fleeing in great confusion. They had failed to get forward in time and then had thrown away their fascines and ladders in every direction. As a result, some Highlanders who had reached the ditch cursed and wept with rage as they stood helpless before the mud rampart. Others retreated or looked for cover. A shot shattered Pakenham's knee as he tried to arrest their flight. A second killed his horse. Helped to his feet, he was hit again in the arm. Mounted with difficulty on a pony by his A.D.C., Major Duncan Macdougall, the general was led forward. The fearless Pakenham waved his hat and was heard to shout, 'For shame! Remember you are British soldiers! Forward, Gentlemen. Forward!' Shot once more in the spine, he fell into Macdougall's arms. His dying words were, 'Have Lambert bring up the reserve.'

Lambert's brigade had advanced about 250 yards from the line when Major Tylden galloped out of the smoke with a loud outburst: 'Sir Edward Pakenham is killed. You command the

Army, and your Brigade must move immediately.' Lambert
was not prepared to act hastily. He had only recently joined the
expedition and knew little of the ground, plans or intentions.
There could be another line, a stronger one beyond. Harry did
not hesitate to speak for the general. Already irked by the way
Tylden had forced his transfer, he informed him caustically, 'If
Sir Edward Pakenham is killed, Sir John Lambert commands,
and will judge what is to be done.'

Harry believed they were beaten. And if the Americans
behaved as the French would in similar circumstances, they
would have counterattacked. Putting a suggestion in the form
of a question, he asked Lambert, 'May I order your Brigade,
sir, to form a line to cover a most irregular retreat, to apply no
other term to it, until you see what has actually occurred to the
attacking columns?' The general agreed. Harry and others of
the staff rode off in different directions.

What Harry saw more than confirmed what he already
believed. The men were either down or dispersed. Meeting
Captain Cooke standing in line with the reserve on his way
back, Harry asked, 'did you ever see such a scene? There is
nothing left but the seventh and forty-third!' Without waiting
for an answer, Harry told him to 'just draw up here for a few
minutes to show front so that the repulsed troops may reform'.
The still unengaged reserve of 1,700 men, according to Cooke's
testimony, did not consider the repulse decisive. They stood
'as cool as cucumbers ... wishing by fresh efforts to wipe off the
stain cast upon His Majesty's uniforms'.

The staff reported. Everywhere the attack had failed and most
of the senior officers had either been killed or wounded. Col.
Rennie, some of whose men briefly held the advance redoubt on
the river, was killed clawing his way to the top of the ramparts.
General Keane, instead of backing Rennie's initial success, had
thrown his support to Gibbs's brigade—in vain. His brigade was
smashed and Keane himself luckily held on to his life with a
dangerous wound in the groin. General Gibbs fell at the head
of his shattered brigade with four balls in him. (He died in
agony that night.) At 10 a.m. it was learned that Thornton's
brigade with 560 men had driven the enemy out of their
unfinished works and wrested control of the opposite bank.
Thornton's was the only success.

Should the expedition be written off as a failure, or another attempt be made to take New Orleans? Lambert called for a council of war to help decide the matter while his brigade held their ground. The evidence regarding this meeting, and possibly another that morning, is fragmentary, confused and sometimes imaginative, according to the source. Harry's version tells of the admirals arriving 'with faces as long as a flying jib'. A lively discussion followed with a wide range of opinions offered. The naval officers, led by Cochrane and 'fighting Macdougall' were not prepared to count the dead and withdraw. With Lambert's brigade, the best of the expedition, still uncommitted and Thornton's success rendering Jackson's position untenable, the basis for victory was laid. Admiral Codrington, responsible for supplying provisions, argued, 'The troops must attack or the whole will be starved.' Appalled by his callousness, Harry said sarcastically, 'Kill plenty more, Admiral; fewer rations will be required.' Sensing by his remarks what Lambert had in mind, Harry jumped up and said to him:

> General, the army are in no state to renew the attack. If success now attended so desperate an attempt, we should have no troops to occupy New Orleans; our success even would defeat our object, and, to take an extreme view, which every soldier is bound to do, our whole army might be the sacrifice of so injudicious an assault.

As for Thornton, Harry continued, the woods on the right bank favoured the American style of warfare and the Yankees would send a superior force to dislodge him. Pointing to the fog that was rolling in, Harry suggested that it would provide cover in recrossing the river and bringing the men back into line. 'The army' he concluded, 'is secure, and no further disaster is to be apprehended.'

Lambert, who had the final say, endorsed this view, supported by most of his officers. Thornton's brigade retired unmolested before a large force of Americans, whom Harry correctly assumed were on their way, could attack them. Thornton was brought back badly wounded and, possibly because of his wound, he later committed suicide.

Strategists, then and now, would debate the soundness of Lambert's decision. On one thing, however, most of the British at the time were in general agreement: the Americans should not be given credit for the victory; rather they were defeated by the failure of Lt.-Col. Mullins and the 44th who had failed to bring forth fascines and ladders essential to the penetration of the enemy lines. Mullins was court-martialled and cashiered from the service for having 'shamefully neglected and disobeyed' his orders. Harry was one of the few who felt that Mullins, like Whitelocke, was 'more abused than he merits'. He placed the full responsibility for failure on his men, who lacked pluck; this was the same 44th that refused Harry's order to remove the guns on the night of 1 January. Sir John Fortescue, the eminent historian of the British army, later argued that Sir Alexander Cochrane, who conceived and planned the expedition for personal profit, was 'the man who should have been tried by court-martial and shot'.

It was Cochrane who fired the last shot of the campaign. Displeased with Lambert's decision, he chose a plan he had discarded earlier and sent warships to the mouth of the Mississippi to force a passage past Fort St Philip. The bombardment from 9 to 17 January had little effect except, perhaps, to create a diversion for the retreating army.

The number of casualties suggested a slaughter rather than a battle. Five British regiments were virtually demolished. The 93rd Highlanders advanced with over 1,000 men and came away with 132 still fit for duty—the carnage resulting from the famous charge of the Light Brigade in the Crimean war was considerably less. The report of the medical director showed that the entire campaign cost over 800 killed, or dead of wounds, and nearly 2,500 wounded, half of whom were permanently disabled.[1] Altogether, nearly half of the effective force was eliminated. In proportion to the numbers engaged, it was one of the heaviest losses ever inflicted on a British army.

On the other side, the Americans in the main battle on the left bank had 6 killed and 7 wounded. For all engagements between 23 December and 8 January, they lost 333 men, only 55 of whom were killed. Within a few weeks, however, almost a thousand of the men from Kentucky and Tennessee contracted yellow fever and died.

[1] Harry discovered, as in the Peninsular War, that soldiers with less than serious wounds in the posterior, which might suggest flight, would not report them.

The stricken lay in the battlefield with the dead for hours. Now and then, a British soldier would find his senses — or nerve — and run to the rear. Some were hurried to their death by the continual fire from the American ramparts.

Late in the afternoon of that raw and gloomy day, Lambert sent Harry forward with a flag of truce and a letter to General Jackson requesting the suspension of hostilities so as to bring in the wounded and bury the dead. The approach was not easy, for the Americans had little appreciation of the military courtesies practised by European armies. They ignored Harry's flag and took pot shots at him. A cannon ball ploughed the ground from under his right foot, which, he reflected, 'would have been a bore indeed to have lost under such circumstances'. Having successfully run the gauntlet, he was at last received and given a message from Jackson agreeing to a cessation of hostilities, on this side of the river only, until noon of the 9th. Jackson insisted, however, as a condition, that neither side send reinforcements to the right bank until midnight of the 9th. (Jackson had already despatched reinforcements.)

Harry was sent out a second time with a large fatigue party and surgeons. Riding ahead, he was greeted by 'a rough fellow', Col. Robert Butler, Jackson's adjutant-general, who strutted about, sword in hand. Harry apologized for keeping him waiting. 'Why now, I calculate as your doctors are tired,' said the American, 'they have plenty to do today.' — '*Do?*' exclaimed Harry as he surveyed the mounds of dead and wounded. He boasted brazenly,

> why this is nothing to us Wellington fellows! The next brush we have with you, you shall see how a Brigade of the Peninsular army (arrived yesterday) will serve you fellows out with a bayonet. They will lie piled on one another like a round shot, if they will only stand.

The colonel pointed out, 'Well, I calculate you must get to them first.' Harry then asked why he carried a drawn sword. 'Because I reckon a scabbard is of no use so long as one of you Britishers is on our soil,' the Yankee said matter-of-factly. 'We don't wish to shoot you, but we must, if you molest our property; we have thrown away the scabbard.' Diminished by the exchange with the American, Harry quietly turned to his work.

All of the dead were British. Except for the shoes, the Americans had not robbed them of their clothes. Harry found many of the dead not more than eighty yards from the enemy lines. 'Had our fellows rushed on,' he believed, 'they would not have lost one half, and victory would have been ours.' Many were blasted by cannon; some had no heads; some he recognized. The contorted forms of the corpses were straightened and their toes were tied together with string. As fast as they could be brought up, they were thrown into a great shallow ditch. When some of the enemy gathered around, speaking French or Spanish, Harry surprised them by conversing with them in their language. Butler became very angry when Harry refused his order to stop fraternizing. Stirred to wrath, Harry swore, 'The next time we meet, Colonel, I hope to receive *you* to bury the dead.'

The wounded, carried on scaling ladders they never had a chance to use, were three times the number Inspector-General Robb was warned to prepare for. Working under the most primitive conditions, he proved most resourceful. With the assistance of Admiral Malcolm, who provided transport to the fleet, Harry vowed that 'not a wounded man was neglected'. The bodies of Pakenham and Gibbs were eviscerated and placed in kegs of rum.[1] By public subscription a life-size monument of them together was placed in St Paul's.

After one of the most trying days of his life, Harry was asked by Lambert to withdraw the troops, out of artillery range. The next morning, the general commented, 'You must have been pretty well done in last night, for I did not see you when I lay down.' Harry admitted that he had had a long day, 'but we Light Division fellows are used to it.' Lambert then said that since Pakenham's military secretary was returning to England with despatches, he would like him to accept the vacant post. 'Me sir!' Harry protested laughingly, 'I write the most illegible scrawl in the world!' But Lambert had the answer: 'You can, therefore, the more readily decipher mine.' He then added, 'Poor Pakenham was much attached to you, and strongly recommended you to me.' Until that moment, Harry had been

[1] Pakenham was officially buried in the family vault, but the legend persists that his cask first became mixed with general provisions being sent from England to a store in Charleston, South Carolina. Much of the rum was said to have been drunk before the grisly contents were discovered.

able to control his feelings; but at the mention of Pakenham's name he sobbed, 'God rest his gallant soul.' In an official despatch dated 28 January 1815, Lambert praised Major Smith's talents and expressed the belief that his qualifications were such as 'to render him hereafter one of the brightest ornaments of his profession'.

To extricate the crippled army from a swamp in the presence of a victorious enemy was a hazardous undertaking. Since there were only enough boats to carry less than half the force at one time, those that remained were in danger of being overpowered by the Americans. The withdrawal, therefore, had to be made in a single, secret movement overland to Lake Borgne.

For the next nine days the men toiled to construct a road of reeds and brush over eight miles of harsh terrain, sometimes carrying boughs of trees great distances in order to bridge over broad ditches. Drenched by rain and coated with mud, the soldiers returned disheartened and miserable to their nighttime camps. The Americans continued rudely to make matters worse by repeating the strains of 'Yankee Doodle' and occasionally offering mock renditions of 'Rule Britannia'. After eating from their meagre supplies, the soldiers shivered their way into bed, where they were kept awake by lob-shots from both sides of the river and frequent alarms caused by enemy raids. 'In short,' wrote Quartermaster Surtees, 'the men's lives began almost to be a burden to them.' Numbers of them deserted, sometimes bribed by promises of land and money which the Americans proffered on printed sheets tossed into pickets.

Aside from information provided by deserters, retreat was indicated to Jackson when the British initiated negotiations for the exchange of prisoners. Lambert selected Harry to make the arrangements. Unlike Col. Butler, Harry found Edward Livingston, Jackson's military secretary (and future secretary of state), 'to be a perfect gentleman, and a very able man'. In the course of their dealings, Harry casually intimated that the British had by no means abandoned the campaign. And when American prisoners were escorted across the battlefield, they were deliberately marched past the soldiers' camps and the gun emplacements. But no sooner had they left the scene, hopefully to report the might and permanence of the British position,

than Dickson hastened the removal of the light guns to the
fleet. Ten heavy guns that could not be moved quickly enough
remained in position to bluff the enemy.

After dark that night (18 January) the British slipped out in
silence with the large guns and dummy sentries silhouetted by
camp-fires. Only a surgeon with 80 severely wounded men
remained behind. The first party of men pounded the reed road
into the mud. Each succeeding, straggling file floundered
deeper in the quagmire. Those who strayed often sank in over
their heads and were lost. Jackson made no attempt to interfere
with the retreat.

The return to the ships was dismal. Those waiting on board
searched the pitifully thinned ranks for glimpses of their friends
or husbands. The cries of those wives who sought in vain were
heard across the water. 'A sullen carelessness, a sort of indifference as to what might happen,' wrote Gleig, 'took
possession of the men's minds.' On board ship, there was an
extraordinary absence of rumours as to their destination.

To return to England disgraced by defeat was unthinkable.
Lambert and Cochrane agreed to launch an attack on Mobile. It
would be an easy victory that would restore flagging spirits and
provide a bridgehead for an overland campaign against New
Orleans which had been deliberated the previous year and
discarded.

On a narrow neck of land at the mouth of Mobile Bay stood
Fort Bowyer, guarding the narrow channel. Early in February
the entire expedition, reinforced by more soldiers and artillery
from England, moved into the area. With the 44th in a forward
position where they could redeem themselves, Lambert
prepared the investment with 1,500 men and heavy calibre
naval guns. Before they opened fire, he gave the commandant
a summons to surrender delivered by Harry Smith.

Because of his experience before Jackson's lines, Harry
approached the fort gingerly. At length he was ushered into the
presence of Major William Lawrence, who 'was as civil as a
vulgar fellow can be'. Following a polite exchange, the
commandant acted puzzled and asked him, 'as one of Wellington's men ... the rules in these cases'. Harry curtly explained:

This belongs to the rule that the weakest goes to the wall,
and if you do not surrender at discretion in one hour, we,

being the stronger, will blow up your fort and burn your wooden walls about your ears.

The commandant offered to accept his advice, provided his men would be allowed to march out honourably with arms and ground them outside the fort at noon the *next day*. He received a flat, 'No!' Judging from the Yankee's 'manner and look under his eyebrows', Harry suspected a trick. Taking a pen and ink, he wrote out the terms whereby a company of British soldiers would occupy the fort immediately and at the same hour the next day the garrison would come out and give up their weapons. When the major demurred, Harry said, 'Good-bye.' Lawrence called him back and agreed to the terms. The British learned afterwards that the fort was to be reinforced from Mobile that night, but adverse winds prevented it.

Rarely was a bloodless conquest celebrated with such ceremony. The formal capitulation at midday, 12 February, of 370 dirty-looking men of the 2nd U.S. Infantry, and 20 women and 16 children, touched off a showy display followed by an elaborate dinner party, arranged by Admiral Codrington on board the flagship. The grandeur of the festivities had the aura of something reserved for the fall of New Orleans — and long since gone stale. It was a poor consolation prize. The comforting tradition that the British can lose every battle but win the last was not fully sustained.

News that the war was over arrived on the 14th. Admiral Cochrane was first to learn of it and Codrington's diary records that he was 'most amazingly cast down by the peace'.[1] The soldiers rejoiced; so did the officers, who normally might be expected to give thought to their prospects as professionals. 'We were all happy enough,' commented Harry, 'for we Peninsular soldiers saw that neither fame nor any military distinction could be acquired in this species of milito-nautico-guerilla-plundering warfare.'

The whole force disembarked on Dauphine Island outside

[1] Cochrane was not officially taken to task for his failure, though he was unemployed for the next six years, receiving no important assignment before his retirement. However, he did win his case that minor spoils taken on the Chesapeake raids belonged to the navy, thus eliminating any division with the army. Cockburn used his money to commission a full-length portrait of himself with Washington in flames as background. Codrington gained fame by annihilating the Turkish fleet at Navarino in 1827.

Mobile Bay and waited. For the next three weeks Harry and his fellow officers 'had great fun in various demi-savage ways', catching and eating alligators (which tasted like coarsely fed pork), hunting and fighting pitched battles between regiments with fir cones while the rest of the army, the generals included, cheered them on. To keep the pesty midges from tormenting him while working on important documents, Harry ordered a private from the 43rd, who was a heavy smoker, under his writing table. (Harry detested tobacco and West only 'chawed'.) When the men began to suffer greatly from dysentery because of the shortage of biscuits, Harry devised a unique means for building ovens by using barrel hoops and mortar made from burned oyster shells. Soon every company had three ovens, and each man over a pound of freshly baked bread daily.

Notice of ratification came on 5 March and Lambert and his staff boarded a sloop-of-war for home. After a stormy crossing, which kept Harry in his bunk much of the time, they encountered a strange sail in a fog at the entrance to the Bristol Channel. The captain of their sloop hailed the trawler to ask if there were any news. 'No, none', was the answer. The vessel was about to disappear in the mist when an afterthought wafted across the water, 'Ho! Bonaparter's back again on the throne of France.'

Harry was overjoyed. With a loud hurrah, he threw his hat up in the air and shouted, 'I will be a Lieutenant-Colonel yet before the year's out!' A somewhat startled Lambert admonished him, 'Really, Smith, you are too vivacious!' Then considering the unexpected news, the general asked, 'How is it possible? It cannot be.' Harry assured him, 'Depend upon it, it's truth; a beast like that skipper could never have invented it, when he did not even regard it as news.'

[5]

Waterloo

How beautifully those English fight! But they *must* give way.
Napoleon at Waterloo

Thoughts of Juana made Harry's anxiety unbearable — for Lambert. Upon landing at Portsmouth, they started the journey for London in a chaise that proved far too slow for Harry. At Guildford he asked for Lambert's permission to board a faster vehicle for home. The mild-mannered general, whom Harry had never seen angry before, suddenly exploded. He had watched Smith fidget for hours, and now he wanted to dash off on his own in the middle of the night. This longing, this driving obsession to join his wife was incomprehensible. Lambert upbraided him for his conduct and then said coolly, 'I will report our arrival; write to me, that I may know your address, for I shall most probably very soon want you again.' Only after Lambert met the Spanish bride would he understand.

Harry paused in London long enough to learn that Juana was well. To add to the lot of Spanish books he had bought for her in Havana, Harry literally ran to buy her a beautiful dressing-case and a heavy gold chain. West carried with him two little white pups he had brought from Cuba, 'a present for the missus'.

West packed everything into a post-chaise Harry ordered and they set off once more. By the time they reached Waltham Cross, Harry decided the pair of horses were not swift enough for his 'galloping ideas', so he added two more horses to the lightweight carriage and 'rattled away' as fast as he could wish.

To keep Juana from being shocked by his sudden appearance, Harry had his father quietly brought to the Falcon Inn in Whittlesea so that Harry could discover her whereabouts and break the news to her gently. Dr Smith told him how Juana

95

went for a stroll with his sisters after church on Sundays. Servants were therefore sent in every direction to fetch her to the house. Unfortunately, 'the fool of a fellow' who found her announced that she must come home directly, for an unknown gentleman had arrived in a chaise-and-four. Thinking that someone had been sent to tell her that her husband had been killed, Juana fell senseless to the ground. Once revived and told the truth, she ran all the way home and flung herself into Harry's waiting arms. He vowed there would never be another separation.

'We were now all happiness,' wrote Harry. But there was no time to enjoy leisurely the comforts of home and the quiet countryside. Napoleon was on the loose. Returning from Elba in March, the French nation rallied to his support; Louis XVIII was forced to flee once more into exile. Bonaparte's overtures for peace were rejected by the Allied Powers, who regarded him as an outlaw. Not daring to risk another defensive campaign in France, Napoleon took the offensive. Closest to Paris and menacing his capital were the British under Wellington and the Prussians under Blücher in Belgium, where most of the people were in sympathy with the French cause. Concentrating forces superior in strength to either Wellington or Blücher, he hoped to defeat them in turn and then be in a position to gain favourable terms for making peace or, if necessary, fall on the flank of the slow-moving Austrians and Russians marching across Germany.

From his headquarters in Brussels, Wellington sent out a call for all available men. As Harry had expected, he received a letter from Lambert telling him to be prepared to join him at a few hours' notice. Knowing that he would serve as Sir John's major-of-brigade, a post which would require at least four horses, he set off to buy new ones, for the faithful Tiny and the battle-bold mare that had carried him in America were too old. And for that 'equestrian artist', as he called Juana, he bought a fine, strong animal named the Brass Mare. Harry's younger brother, Charles, was to accompany them as a Volunteer to serve with the 1st Bn of the 95th.[1] (Tom, who was the adjutant

---

[1] With the commanding officer's permission, a young gentleman unable to obtain a commission was allowed to join as a private. If he served with distinction against the enemy, he might become an officer when a vacancy occurred. Meanwhile, he messed with the officers of his company; and although he carried the weapons of a ranker, he wore the uniform of an officer without any badges of rank.

of the 2nd Bn, was already somewhere in Belgium.) Harry was supremely happy, for he and Juana would be spared all the heartbreak of another separation.

The Smith household began to resemble a military depot — tents, blankets, canteens, boots, and so forth, lay all about. Surveying his wife's baggage, Harry chided 'we could as well have carried our parish church'. Another letter then arrived from Lambert ordering him to Ghent and recommending that he find his own transport for passage via Harwich for Ostend.

On the evening before departure, the entire Smith family took a long, final ride. Mounted on the old mare that had carried him without a fall through the war in America, Harry urged her to make one last leap over a stiff rail with a ditch on either side. The war horse had either lost her strength or failed to measure the leap, for she fell and pinned one of his legs under her shoulder. If she struggled, Harry was sure that his leg would be broken, putting an end to his brigade majorship and possible promotion. Succeeding in drawing his bruised leg free, Harry 'never felt more grateful for an escape'.

Very early the next day they set off for Harwich. Visibly shaken as he bade them all good-bye, Dr Smith said sorrow-fully, 'Napoleon and Wellington will meet, a battle will ensue of a kind never before heard of, and I cannot expect to see you all again.'

In Harwich almost every ship had been commandeered for the transport of troops and supplies. Harry eventually found a small sloop with a captain and his young son as the crew. Measuring the tiny craft with great care, Harry calculated that there was just enough room to carry himself, wife, brother, two grooms, a lady's maid, five horses and all the baggage. For the sake of the horses, he waited a fortnight for a smooth crossing. In Ostend he added another two mules and a Flemish pony to his train to carry the baggage. Harry was now ready for the campaign against Napoleon.

And just in time. After three hurried days' journey, they reached Ghent, where Lambert had arrived the day before. His brigade of all New Orleans regiments consisted of four of the best from the old Peninsulars: the 4th, the 27th and the 40th, and the 81st which was employed for garrison duty in Brussels. Lambert told him that they must be prepared to take the field at a moment's notice.

One of the duties of the British in Ghent was to protect
Louis XVIII and his inglorious Court of idlers. Others may have
found his majesty ugly, lethargic and snuffy, but Harry spoke
of him as 'impressive in manner'. Visiting the Court, Harry
stood near the door when the enormously obese and gouty
Louis waddled in. Royalty laid its hand on his shoulder for
support. As the King spoke of how delighted he was to see
British officers and how great was his debt to their nation,
Harry never beheld a 'more benign countenance ... nor did his
subsequent reign belie the benignity of his expression'. Many
Frenchmen would not agree. They called him Louis the Fat, or
Louis the Pig. They substituted the word 'pig' for the number
'18'. Thus, when money was paid out or soldiers counted off, it
became '15, 16, 17, *pig*, 19, ... '.

While Lambert, an ex-adjutant of the Guards, was working
his regiments into 'beautiful fighting trim', Napoleon with
speed and secrecy struck at the frontier on 15 June. The next
day he mauled Blücher's 80,000 Prussians at Ligny, while his
left wing fought an inconclusive battle with a British force at
Quatre Bras. Detaching Marshal Grouchy with 33,000 to
pursue Blücher, who had barely escaped capture after being
trampled on by French cavalry, Napoleon turned his mighty
host of 73,000 on Wellington, who retired to a strong defensive
position at Waterloo with what he described as his 'infamous
army'. He based his complaint on the fact that his staff was
inexperienced and his men poorly equipped. Far less than half
of his force of 67,000 was British, the rest were Dutchmen,
Belgians or Germans from various minor states. The few who
were veterans had for the most part been in Napoleon's service.
Only the King's German Legion was battle-tested and fully
reliable. Even many of his own British troops were weak
second battalions fleshed out with recruits. Napoleon brusquely
told his generals, 'I tell you Wellington is a bad general, the
English bad troops, and this affair is nothing but a picnic.' If it
was to be a picnic and his army broke, Wellington, rather than
retreat, intended to take his men into the Soignes forest
behind his position where he 'would have defied the devil' to
drive him out.

In less than an hour after the notice, Lambert's brigade was
on the march towards Brussels. Arriving at Asche on the afternoon of the 16th, Harry heard 'rapid and continuous firing at

Quatre Bras, as audible as if we were in a fight'. For the brigade
it was like old times. Once more they were to engage the French
and to fight in the open. This was the kind of warfare they
understood and in which they excelled. The French would not
skulk in a swamp and conceal themselves behind enormous
barricades.

Their hurried pace was slowed when they passed through
Brussels the following day. There, pandemonium reigned.
Rumours that Wellington had been defeated and that Napoleon
had promised his men the sack of the town, drove the civilians
in wild disorder towards Antwerp. The scene created by the
demons of panic 'was an awful novelty to us', wrote Harry.

Rumour affected orders. Just short of the great forest of
Soignes, Lambert was told to halt. The order seemed to
suggest that enemy cavalry was threatening the Duke's line of
communication with Brussels. To lend credence to the possibility, a troop of newly raised Hanoverian Hussars burst
through their position with cries that the French were close on
their heels. Blaring bugles and stentorian shouting put the
brigade on the run towards the alarm-posts. On reporting to
Lambert, Harry found the general calmly sitting down to
dinner with Juana and his A.D.C. With great nonchalance, he
said, 'Let the troops be damned; this is all nonsense; there is
not a French soldier in the rear of his Grace, depend on it, and
sit down to dinner.' Harry remained unconvinced. He dashed
off towards the front where he found a long baggage train
moving quietly through the wood. The alarm was obviously
false. He returned to dismiss the men and to forage through
'the *débris* of a magnificent turbot' that Lambert's butler had
obtained in Brussels.

The rumour that there would be a battle the next day was
more credible. Under makeshift shelter during the storms that
night, veterans playfully comforted the new men with the
remark that the battle would be nothing compared to what they
had experienced in the Peninsula. There was some talk of
omens of victory. So many of the Duke's triumphs were
preceded by thunderstorms and most were on 'Red Sunday' —
Vimiero, Fuentes de Oñoro, Orthez, Vitoria and Toulouse. But
generally there was quiet and thoughtfulness, so unlike the
French side where there was drinking and singing.

That night the Duke ordered Lambert's brigade to take up a

position in front of the forest. However, because the road was choked with overturned wagons and spilled luggage, the men would be required to clear the way first. With a battle imminent and less than an hour's march to get them there, 'the wand of a magician,' said Harry, 'could not have effected a clear course sooner than our 3,000 soldiers of the old school.'

Disregarding her protests, at break of day Harry sent Juana back to Brussels to await the outcome of the battle. Later that morning Lambert sent him to find headquarters and obtain orders from the Duke—no one else. It was a beautiful morning. Everything seemed new and clean without the slightest hint that this land in a matter of hours would become the hub of the world.

At eleven o'clock Harry found the Duke and his staff near the semi-fortified farm called Hougoumont. Harry described Wellington as being 'in high spirits and very animated', and as always he was impressed with the Duke's stately presence, the clear head and keen eye. On seeing Harry ride up he said, 'Hallo, Smith, where are you from last?' Flattered by the Duke's quick recognition, he replied, 'From Lambert's Brigade, and they from America.' In answer to further inquiry about the troops, Harry enumerated the ones that were with him and spoke of the 81st in Brussels. 'Ah, I know, I know,' Wellington said somewhat impatiently, 'but the others, are they in good order?' — 'Excellent, my lord, and very strong,' Harry assured him. 'That's all right,' remarked the Duke, 'for I shall want every man.'

One of the staff then commented, 'I do not think they will attack today.' The Duke corrected him: 'Nonsense, the columns are already forming and I think I have discerned where the weight of the attack will be made. I shall be attacked before an hour.'

Turning to Harry, he asked, 'Do you know anything of my position, Smith?' Harry confessed, 'Nothing, my lord, beyond what I see—the general line, and right and left.' Wellington then gave his orders: 'Go back and halt Lambert's Brigade at the junction of the two great roads from Genappe and Nivelles. Did you observe their junction as you rode up?' — 'Particularly, my lord.' — Wellington continued,

Having halted the head of the Brigade and told Lambert

what I desire, ride to the left of the position. On the
extreme left is the Nassau Brigade—those fellows who
came over to us at Arbonne, you recollect. [Uncertain
allies who had deserted the French cause on 10 December
1813.] Between them and Picton's Division [now the 5th]
I shall most probably require Lambert. There is already
there a Brigade of newly-raised Hanoverians, which
Lambert will give orders to, as they and your Brigade
form the 6th Division. You are the only British staff officer
with it. Find out, therefore, the best and shortest road
from where Lambert is now halted to the left of Picton and
right of the Nassau troops. Do you understand? —

'Perfectly, my lord.' Harry was about to ride off, when the
Duke called him back. 'Now clearly understand that when
Lambert is ordered to move from the fork of the two roads
where he is now halted, you are prepared to conduct him to
Picton's left.'

With his Light Division training, Harry carefully rode over
the ground to prepare himself fully for the conduct of the
troops. Napoleon's best plan, he concluded, was to throw the
weight of his attack on Wellington's left, forcing him to draw
back and break communications with the Prussians, who had
eluded Marshal Grouchy and were expected hourly. But the
Prussians were late, despite the heroic shouts of 'Vorwarts' by
the septuagenarian Blücher, who kept himself going with large
doses of gin and rhubarb juice. Such a flank attack, of course,
would never have succeeded against a Peninsular army capable
of counter manoeuvre, Harry observed. The heterogeneous
mass the Duke now commanded, however, was so diluted with
'young 2nd Battalions ... and intermixed with the rabble of our
allied army' that Harry feared the outcome.

He had barely rejoined Lambert when the battle of Waterloo
began. It commenced with a heavy bombardment at one
o'clock, followed by four great columns of French infantry
advancing like battering rams against Wellington's wall of
men. They were directed towards the centre against Picton's
division, to which the 1st Bn of the 95th under Barnard was
attached. Among them, reflected Harry, were his brother
Charles, Cameron, Leach, Beckwith, Kincaid, Simmons and
other old comrades.

It was not to be 'a battle of science' after all, Harry soon discovered, but 'a stand up fight between two pugilists [who]
"mill away" till one is beaten'. And in his opinion, Napoleon
fought it badly by delivering blows that were 'partial and
and isolated, and enabled the Duke to repel each by concentration'.

Battles in those days were bloody and short. When would
they be committed, Lambert's men, about a half a mile to the
rear, asked? Two hours passed and the call still did not come.
Because of rising ground, their view of the battle was
obstructed. Some fell asleep where they lay only to be wakened
by stray shot that missed its target.

Another great cannonade more intense than any veteran
could remember began about three o'clock. At least 250 French
pieces from a more forward position hurled shells, roundshots,
grape and every object of destruction, including horseshoe nails.
Marshal Ney, thinking that the quick retrograde movement of
Wellington's infantry signified a retreat, launched storms of
cavalry—in truth, Wellington had merely drawn his infantry
behind the crest of a hill to shield them from the bombardment,
and he was fully ready for the cavalry attack. Every regiment
formed squares to meet them. 'The weight of the attack on
Picton,' noted Harry with satisfaction, 'would be resisted by
none but British troops.'

The battle suddenly spilled over towards Lambert's brigade
to the rear. Seemingly from out of nowhere, 'many of the rabble
of Dutch troops were flying towards us,' recalled Harry, 'and to
add to the confusion, soon after came a party of dragoons,
bringing with them three eagles and some prisoners.' Harry
told Lambert, 'We shall have a proper brush immediately, for
it looks as if our left will be immediately turned, and the brunt
of the charge will fall on us.' Within seconds a message arrived
from the Duke ordering them to the exact spot at which he had
told Harry that morning that they would be needed. Moving
forward, they learned that Picton had been killed, shot in the
head, and that Sir John Kempt now commanded the much-
shrivelled 5th Division. Lambert's men were to take their place
with the 95th staying on with them. 'For the two or three
succeeding hours there was no variety with us,' wrote Kincaid,
'but one continual blaze of musketry.'

Layers of grey-blue smoke reduced visibility to less than one hundred yards. At times only the flashes of their weapons distinguished one side from another. The French, in seemingly endless numbers, came on foot and on horse, their officers brandishing swords and gesticulating. They staggered and died, or retired to dissolve in the smoke. As for the British, Kincaid saw the 5th Division, which had begun the fight 5,000 strong, 'dwindled down into a solitary line of skirmishers'. Lambert's 27th 'were lying literally dead in square, a few yards behind us'. Then he wondered, 'I had never heard of a battle in which everybody was killed; but this seemed likely to be an exception, as all were going by turns.' Wellington put it simply to a group of officers as he sought momentary refuge in a square, 'Hard pounding this, gentlemen, but we will see who can pound the longest.'

Charging about with missiles whistling and dancing all around, Harry remained unhurt. His horses were not so fortunate. One was hit in six places and another in seven, but they were not disabled. Towards evening the smoke became so thick, he related, 'that nothing was discernable'. On his right he heard sounds of heavy fighting, but there was no way of telling who was winning. Then there was an abrupt lull. 'Firing ceased on both sides, and we on the left knew that one party or the other was beaten,' said Harry. 'This was the most anxious moment of my life.' A gust of wind crossed the field and lifted the curtain of smoke. 'In a few seconds we saw red-coats in the centre, as stiff as rocks, and the French columns retiring rapidly,' Harry recalled, 'and there was such a British shout as rent the air.'

What they did not know was that Napoleon in one last desperate bid for victory had called up his still unused, magnificent Imperial Guard to deliver the decisive blow up the middle. Led by Ney, 'the bravest of the brave', and in the presence of the Emperor himself, the celebrated Guard moved forward. As volley after volley poured into them, their ranks convulsed, reeled and broke into flight. Wellington then waved his hat to signal the attack.

Harry saw the Duke galloping furiously from the right down the tattered lanes of his soldiers, only one staff officer was still at his side. Harry spurred his horse to meet him. He never saw the Duke more animated. 'Who commands here?' he shouted. 'Generals Kempt and Lambert, my lord,' was Harry's reply.

'Desire them to get into a column of companies of Battalions, and move on immediately.' To be certain of the Duke's intention, Harry asked, 'In which direction, my lord?' — 'Right ahead to be sure,' Wellington answered with vigour.

Men who had stood rooted to the ground all day suddenly sprang to life and bounded across the field. Only the dead and dying remained behind to hold the squares. Their courage soared, for the excitement of the charge dispersed all thoughts of danger. Prussians, who had smashed through from the east, poured in to join them. In their confusion some of the allies fired upon one another. The French became a rabble in flight, incapable of organized resistance. Only a few battalions of the Imperial Guard held their ground long enough to give the Emperor time to escape.

Blücher found Wellington, embraced and kissed him, saying, 'Mein lieber Kamerad.' According to a slightly embarrassed Wellington, the old Prussian then uttered what he thought was probably his entire store of French by commenting, 'Quelle affaire.' The Duke later said of the battle, 'It has been a damned nice thing, the nearest run thing that ever you saw in your life. By God,' he added with no fear of seeming immodest, 'I don't think it would have done if I had not been there!' To Johnny Kincaid it 'was the last, the greatest and the most uncomfortable heap of glory I ever had a hand in'.

The British halted at nightfall. The chase was left to the vengeful Prussians, who in their ardour sabred and shot the panic-stricken French by moonlight. Camping on the ground they had conquered, Harry felt that no picket was required that night. The wounded had to remain where they had fallen. Their groans and pitiful cries for water would reverberate in the memories of survivors for years to come.

During the night Harry was summoned to a nearby cottage where a friend, Captain McCulloch of the 95th, was lying. Harry found him 'in great agony, but very composed', having during the day had his arm shattered and his back severely injured. Harry assisted the surgeon in taking off his arm. 'He recovered,' wrote Harry, 'but was never afterwards able to feed himself or put on his hat, and died, Heaven help him, suddenly of dysentery.'

McCulloch was only one casualty in 'the dreadful tale of killed and wounded'. The list 'was enormous, and every

moment the loss of a dear friend was announced'. Nearly one-
third of the 95th were casualties, among them Colonels Ross,
Barnard and Cameron — all wounded. Among the dead were
many of Harry's old comrades, including Charlie Eeles.

The news that Wellington was without injury was welcomed
by all. But most of his staff were casualties. General Alava, the
Duke's friend and Spanish aide, later described to Harry and
Juana the sombre scene at supper that night. The table had been
laid out for the entire staff, but only he and the commander-in-
chief were present. 'The Duke said very little, ate hastily and
heartily, but every time the door opened he gave a searching
look, evidently in the hope of some of his valuable staff
approaching.' None arrived to relieve the shock of their
absence. After eating, Wellington held up his hands and said,
'The hand of Almighty God has been upon me this day.' His
bed already occupied by a dying member of his staff, the Duke
went to his pallet and fell sound asleep.

For Harry the hand of God was upon the entire Smith family
that day. There being nothing else to eat or drink, Harry was
making tea in a soldier's tin for Lambert, Kempt and himself,
when his brother Tom found him and told him that Charles, too,
except for a slight wound in the neck, was unhurt. When their
father heard the news, it was hard for him to decide whether he
'was more proud of having three sons at Waterloo, or grateful
to Almighty God for their preservation'.

Before daylight the next morning a staff officer awakened
Harry to inform him that the brisk pursuit by the Prussians had
completed the rout of the enemy and that Harry's division
would remain where it was for some hours. Harry hoped to let
Juana know that he was well, but at the moment there was no
way of knowing her whereabouts. Meanwhile, since he was
now confirmed in the post of assistant quartermaster-general,
he took some men from each regiment to succour the living and
bury the dead.

Harry had been over many battlefields but, with the exception
of the breach at Badajoz and one spot at New Orleans, he had
seen nothing to compare with the carnage at Waterloo. The
relatively small field of about two square miles was one great
mass of dead and helplessly wounded, nearly 40,000 men and
10,000 horses. Interspersed among them were detached cannons
and broken ammunition wagons.

'All over the field,' Harry recalled, 'you saw officers, and as many soldiers as were permitted to leave the ranks, leaning and weeping over some dead or dying brother in arms.' The time had not yet arrived when it was considered unmanly to cry openly. In the case of officers of rank who, because of their wounds, could not be moved, a screen of blankets was prepared to shelter them. There were also several Prussian patrols on the ground who mercifully shot their own and other wounded that they believed to be beyond any hope of recovery.

Brother Charles, busily engaged in burying dead green-jackets in a large grave, came upon the body of a French officer 'of delicate mould and appearance'. On closer examination, he found a handsome young woman. When told the story, Harry asked himself was it 'devotion, passion, or patriotism which led to such heroism?' Though the truth would always be a mystery, he was sure that he had the answer: 'Love, depend on it.'

Harry encountered one hideous scene near La Haye Sainte where French cuirassiers and their horses lay in a great mangled heap. Wounded horses struggled on wounded men too weak to move. Faint screams could be heard from unwounded men somewhere underneath. 'The sight was sickening,' wrote Harry, 'and I had no means or power to assist them.'

On all battlefields in those days, the firing had barely subsided when stragglers, camp followers and peasants crept about in their ghoulish pursuit of robbing the dead and wounded, conquerors and conquered. Closing their ears to cries of mercy, they stripped the helpless sufferers. Women plunderers were described as worse than men. The ferocity of these hard-featured harpies was such that they laughed and mocked the pathetic pleas of their disabled victims. They took literally everything, except for the stockings of Highlanders, which were regarded as useless.[1]

That afternoon Harry's division moved forward on the Nivelles road along the line of the French retreat. Cannon, caissons, baggage, muskets and other debris of every kind were strewn about. In the words of General Gneisenau, Blücher's chief of staff, 'it resembled the shore of some great shipwreck'.

---

[1] Even false teeth were taken. Since many were carved from ivory, they could be of value to dentists who would refit them for another's mouth. So many dentures were said to have been salvaged after the battle of Waterloo that for years after, artificial teeth were often referred to as 'Waterloo teeth'.

Seeking Lambert to discuss a military matter, Harry surprised his general as he was changing his shirt. He saw that Lambert had a violent contusion on his right arm, which was immensely swollen and 'black as ebony'. 'My dear General,' Harry exclaimed, 'what an arm! I did not know you had been wounded.' — 'No; nor you never would,' said Lambert firmly, 'if accident had not shown you.' Fearing that Lambert might lose his arm, Harry tried to persuade him to see a surgeon. The general refused and made him promise to say nothing to anyone. Within a few days he was well again.

Duty still would not permit Harry to seek Juana. Each hour he grew more concerned. Not until the third day after the battle would she find him. Those days were for her no less adventurous than they were for Harry, and he recorded the melodramatic tale in his distinctive heroic style as she told it to him in her excited Spanish.

On the morning of Waterloo Juana made her way to Brussels with West and her little dog, Vitty, in her lap. There, like other officers' wives, she would await the outcome of the battle. At the marketplace she found her groom guarding the baggage. Army headquarters, however, had just issued an order to move the baggage train north to Antwerp.

Five miles out of Brussels at 5 p.m., they stopped at an inn, unloaded the baggage and prepared for supper when an alarm was raised: 'The French are coming!' No time was to be lost. Juana and her party must depart at once for Antwerp and safety. In the commotion, the Brass Mare became frightened. With great difficulty West helped Juana on to the rearing, plunging horse and the little pug after her. Juana dropped the rein at the moment West let go of the bridle. With only a snaffle rein in hand, she could not restrain the frantic mare. They flew down the road, passing horsemen and wagons bound for Antwerp. Unable to reach the curb rein, she was carried by the Brass Mare for eight miles until an overturned wagon loomed ahead. Knowing that she could not turn the beast to one side and that the height of the obstacle was beyond the mare's spring, Juana was sure that she 'must inevitably be knocked to pieces'. As the horse gathered itself to jump, Juana caught the loose curb rein and brought it to a sudden halt. Still clutching the pug, she was thrown on to the mare's neck. Juana succeeded in regaining the saddle and holding on the curb, 'and we were then on terms of equality'. Juana, the Brass Mare and Vitty paused to recover their breath.

Having straightened her hair and habit, Juana looked back. Behind her was a party of horsemen. Her first thought was that they were French dragoons, 'although, if I had considered for a moment', she said, 'I should have known that no Dragoon could have come the pace *I* did.' Too exhausted to run, she decided, 'Well, if I am taken, I had better at once surrender.' The first rider to approach her, however, was her groom. Fearing for her safety, he had seized one of the other horses to rescue her.

The three other riders were a commissary, an officer of the Hanoverian Rifles and an English Hussar officer. In all probability they were deserters. She spoke to the Hussar in her halting English, 'Pray, sir, is there any danger?' — 'Danger, mum!' he exclaimed. 'When I left Brussels, the French were in pursuit down the hill.' Shocked by the dreadful news, she asked, 'Oh, sir, what shall I do?' He offered to watch over her and said, 'Come to Antwerp with me.' Another member of the party told her curtly, 'You deserve no pity. You may well be fatigued carrying that dog. Throw it down.' Responding with indignation to his rude remark, Juana said, 'I should deserve no pity if I did.'

Galloping at great speed to escape the French, they reached Antwerp, where the Hussar tried with great difficulty to find a place for her to stay. While he went into the Hôtel de Ville to inquire about a billet, Juana became the object of attention to the curious. She was now covered from head to foot with black mud, with a dirty little dog in her lap. 'On my face,' she recalled, 'the mud had dried, and a flood of tears chasing each other through my cheeks must have given me an odd appearance.'

An English officer of the garrison, on hearing who she was, introduced himself and said he would conduct her to Col. Craufurd, the commandant of the citadel. His wife and daughters, he was sure, would be happy to provide her with accommodation. Juana accepted the offer without hesitation.

The colonel and his family welcomed her and extended every comfort she could wish. Mrs Craufurd provided her with a bath and dry clothes. 'The hospitality of this night ought to have soothed me,' said Juana, 'but the agony of hope, doubt and fear

I was in absorbed every other feeling, although I was so
sensible of kindness.'

The following afternoon Juana learned that the battle had
been fought and won, but there was no word about Harry. She
made up her mind to join her husband, 'whatever shape fate
had reduced him to'. The dismayed Craufurds tried to reason
with her to remain, but she ordered West, who by now had
arrived with the servants, the baggage and spare horses, to be
ready to leave at three o'clock in the morning. Being a veteran
campaigner, Juana led them in light marching order back to
Brussels, reaching that city in four hours.

Among the first soldiers she met was a group of Riflemen.
Eagerly she asked about Harry. They knew Brigade-Major
Smith—he had been killed. Juana had no reason to doubt the
truth of the statement, for her husband was well known
throughout the regiment. 'It was now my turn to ask the Brass
Mare to gallop,' she said. Juana was determined to go to the
battlefield, there 'to die on the body of the only thing I had on
earth to love, and which I loved with a faithfulness which few
can or ever did feel, and none ever exceeded'.

On the road to Waterloo the ugly backwash of war flooded
towards Brussels. Dragging along without any semblance of
order were thousands of fugitives, prisoners and wounded, some
lacking an arm or a leg, conveyed on horses, mules and carts.
Those who had been crushed or died in flight were simply
hurled into ditches along the crammed road. There were, also,
many dead being carried for burial in Brussels and beyond.
Juana glanced at them, expecting that one might be Enrique.
There were other women searching for their men. A traveller
from England, James Simpson, tells of an officer's lady who, on
learning that her husband's head had been shot off, ran about
'hysterical and delirious, with a little boy crying and running
after her. "My husband is not dead, he is just coming; his head
is not shot off"'.'

The gory field of Waterloo was now even more terrible to
behold than it was the day after the battle. Almost all of the
dead were now stark naked, their bodies swollen and dis-
coloured. The stench was overpowering. Looters still prowled
like wolves over the ground, sometimes fighting and robbing
one another, or savagely pouncing on sightseers from Brussels.
A few soldiers were still being nursed; Col. Hay of the 16th

Light Dragoons was not moved from the field for eight days. The French soldiers were being burned and the British buried. When Juana beheld the newly-dug graves, her imagination tormented her further with the thought, 'O God, he has been buried, and I shall never again behold him.'

Seeing from a distance a body that resembled Harry's, she shrieked, 'Oh, there he is!' She spurred her horse over the dead. 'No, it is not he! Find him I will, but whither shall I turn?' There were so many corpses strewn promiscuously about; it seemed an impossible task that she had set for herself.

Roaming more wildly in her heartrending search, Juana thought, remembering her convent training, to appeal to God through Jesus Christ. The next moment a guardian angel, in the form of a friend, Charlie Gore, an aide to Kempt, appeared before her. She cried out, 'Oh, where is he? Where is Enrique?' Gore tried to calm her: 'Why near Bavay by this time, as well as ever he was in his life; not wounded even, nor either of his brothers!' Juana was not convinced. 'Oh, dear Gore, why thus deceive me?' she sobbed reprovingly. 'The soldiers tell me Brigade-Major Smith is killed. Oh, my Enrique!' Gore swore on his honour that he had left Harry in good health, but very anxious about her. It was Charles Smyth, Pack's brigade-major, he explained, who was killed. 'Oh, may I believe you, Charlie! my heart will burst.' — 'Why should you doubt me?' he asked. 'Then God has heard my prayer!' she sighed.

Gore, who had been engaged in a futile search for the grave of Charlie Eeles, offered to ride with her as far as Mons if she could muster the strength to ride that far. 'Strength,' Juana uttered vehemently, 'yes, for anything now!' They reached Mons at midnight. That day she had ridden sixty miles; 'and after all the agony, despair, relief and happiness I had gone through in one day,' she related, 'I ate something and lay down until daylight next morning.'

The distance from Mons to Bavay was not great. Nevertheless, at daybreak Juana pressed on until she reached division headquarters. She saw Lambert and he took her to Harry. 'Soon, O gracious God,' she said in concluding her story, 'I sank into his embrace, exhausted, fatigued, happy and grateful — Oh, how grateful! — to God who had protected him, and sustained my reason through such scenes of carnage, horror, dread, and belief in my bereavement.'

[6]

Keeping the Peace

Paris lay ahead. But Wellington knew better than to relax with Grouchy still in the field and formidable works protecting the French capital. Behind him lay the best of his army, dead or disabled. Encouraged by the excesses committed by the unrestrained Prussians advancing alongside them, many of the allied soldiers with the Duke threatened at any moment to become a plundering mob. And for once the British army was not supplied with its own food. Even the ammunition reserve was dangerously low.

To keep his hungry soldiers, many of whom were in rags and barefooted, in line, Wellington imposed severe measures, far more rigid than any Peninsular veterans could recall. Those who strayed or straggled were pounced upon by special patrols and flogged on the spot. Said the Duke, 'I have no idea of any great effect being produced on British soldiers by anything but the fear of immediate corporal punishment.' The soldiers had little affection for a commander so harsh in discipline, so cold and aloof, but theirs was a grudging admiration best expressed, perhaps, by a veteran who described him as 'that long nosed bastard who beats the French'. However, to junior officers like Harry Smith, who knew the Duke on terms of greater intimacy and equality, he was 'one of the greatest men England or the world ever produced ... I love Wellington with a fervour which cannot be exceeded'. Recalling that Marlborough 'dwindled into imbecility, and became a miser', Harry prayed that the Duke would 'never outlive his mental facilities'.

Opposition began to harden on the outskirts of Paris. While Blücher, who ordered his men to shoot Napoleon on sight as a brigand, fought a bloody action with Grouchy, Wellington

111

found the French strongly entrenched at St Denis. Harry tells of how for a day or two, they fully expected to storm the enemy position. The suspense was relieved by an armistice, after which Napoleon was taken and was soon a prisoner on his way to exile on St Helena.

The army marched into Paris on 7 July. The honour of being first into the capital was given to the 2nd Bn of Rifles with Lieut. Thomas Smith riding out in front, the first British officer to enter the capital.

Harry, too, was honoured by being promoted to quarter-master-general. The 5th and 6th Divisions, along with Brunswickers, who made up the reserve under Kempt, were put in Harry's charge. 'I never felt more proud,' he wrote, 'than in having the movement and arrangement of march of 17,000 soldiers.' A few days later, Tom Fane, one of thousands of Englishmen who had come to France as a visitor, galloped up to Harry and Juana outside their quarters, waving a paper. 'Hurrah, Harry, the *Gazette* has arrived! You are Lieutenant-Colonel, and here is a case for you; it has some order in it, I think.' Excitedly he requested that he be permitted to open it. It was the Order of Companion of the Bath. Assuming an air of indifference, which was so completely out of character, Harry remarked that it 'pleased poor Tom more than it did me'.

Harry and Juana found a billet in the country home of a Parisian lady at Neuilly. It proved a delightful arrangement. The old lady, accustomed to living in great style, introduced Juana to milliners and dressmakers who refitted her in the latest fashions. Harry managed the garden, which yielded an abundance of fruits and vegetables. He had no difficulty with the gardeners after he summoned the head man and said sternly, 'If the garden is not kept in real good order, then I will show you what an Englishman is.' The Frenchman 'was thunderstruck'.

'Our life was now one of continued pleasure and excitement,' wrote Harry; 'nothing but parties at night and races by day.' The officers of the three battalions of Rifles were reunited for a Regimental Dinner to observe the anniversary of the founding of the 95th on 25 August. 'With open windows and all in view of the crowd on the Boulevards,' said the visiting Mr Simpson, 'they caroused, their fine bands playing, and many a spirited toast was drunk with all honours!'

Among Harry's old friends who were now battered convalescents was Charlie Beckwith, who had lost a leg at
Waterloo. The experience led to a religious conversion. 'I was
carried away by the love of glory,' he explained, 'but a good
God said to me, "Stop, you rascal!" and he cut off my leg; and
now I think I shall be happier for it.'

Valiant and cheerful George Simmons, 'a universal favourite
among men and officers', had been shot through the side
and lay on the battlefield for four hours where he was trampled
over many times before he was observed to be alive. In four
days, he claimed, six quarts of blood were taken from him.
Then from twenty-five to thirty leeches were applied daily.
By the third day the flesh on his side was nearly raw from their
biting. 'I kicked, roared, and swore, and tried to drag them off,'
wrote Simmons, 'but my hands were held. Such torture I never
experienced.' More bleeding followed at intervals. Never
doubting the efficacy of this treatment, Harry told him, 'your
presence of mind saved you by making a Brussels surgeon
bleed you'.

Harry was the steward at the races. Because so many
uninvited officers of other nations joined in the fun, Harry
decided to put an end to the confusion that ensued. He stationed
some soldiers at the distance post with instructions to raise a
restraining rope. The first casualty was Marshal Blücher.
Failing to see the rope, he galloped into it, fell and broke his
collar-bone. It was a sombre moment for Harry, for he, like so
many Englishmen of his time, held the gallant old Prussian in
great esteem. Even more distressing were Blücher's moments
of mental derangement. Patting his side, he once told Wellington that he was pregnant and about to give birth to an elephant
fathered by a French soldier. Fortunately for the Duke,
Blücher's bouts of madness did not take place during the
Waterloo campaign.

The behaviour of Blücher and his soldiers was a source of
great annoyance to Wellington who feared that the French
might be provoked into another uprising. He frustrated
Blücher's efforts to blow up the Jena bridge, commemorating
Napoleon's victory over the Prussians in 1806, by posting
Coldstream Guards. (To save the bridge, Louis XVIII declared
that he was prepared to jump off it if that would satisfy the
marshal.) But the Prussian soldiers themselves presented a

more difficult problem. In the words of Sgt Anton, they seemed bent on 'the destruction of every object which they wanted strength to remove, or taste to enjoy'. Russian and Austrian acts of pillage were, at times, no less revolting. The Royalists, too, indulged in an orgy of violence: Ney was shot as a traitor and Voltaire's dead body was desecrated; live eagles, symbols of the Empire, were torn to pieces. These events, wrote Harry, 'kept us all in a state of excitement'. With hatred so openly evinced, the danger of renewed conflict seemed quite real. Lord Castlereagh warned, 'If one shot were fired in Paris, the whole country will rise against us.'

Only the British, though rough in the field, were poor haters. They displayed no animosity towards their former enemies as they walked the conquered streets of Paris. Bad humoured ex-Bonapartist officers, determined to provoke a duel, resorted to insults, of which toe-stamping, as if by accident, was the most common. But such 'accidents' usually went unnoticed, according to Kincaid, for

the natural impulse of an Englishman, on having his toe trodden on, is to make a sort of apology to the person who did it, by relieving him of a portion of the embarrassment which he expects to be the attendant of such awkwardness.

In the end the astonished Frenchman prided himself on having 'done a bold thing—the Englishman a handsome one'. Of course, Kincaid pointed out that 'if the Englishman had clearly understood the Frenchman's intention, he would have been rewarded on the spot by *our* national method—a douse on the chops'. Nevertheless, revengeful French officers, formed into secret societies composed of champion marksmen and swordsmen, often eventually succeeded in forcing an affair of honour. Harry appears to have avoided such confrontations by spending much of his time in the country. His visits to the city were confined largely to the art galleries and theatres. Later in life he boasted that he had never fought a duel, but was quick to add that he had never apologized to any man, except once when he was in the wrong.

On 20 November 1815, by the Second Peace of Paris, the physically and psychologically desolating conflict formally came to a close. To preserve the tranquillity of Europe and prevent further revolutionary convulsions, 'His pottle-belly

Majesty', Louis XVIII was restored once more, but this time the four allied Great Powers established an Army of Occupation, contributing 30,000 men apiece, with another 30,000 made up of contingents from minor states. These soldiers were to remain for five years, with France, in addition to the heavy burden of a war indemnity of 700 million francs, forced to pay the cost. The whole Army of Occupation was put under the command of The Most Illustrious and Most Noble Arthur, Duke, Marquis and Earl of Wellington. William I of the Netherlands made him a prince. On terms of equality with the monarchs of Europe, who called him '*Mon Cousin*', he was by general agreement the most important man of his time.

Only four British divisions were to remain in France on the north-east frontier, and they were reduced in size. Harry lost his staff appointment. Moreover, though he held the rank of lieutenant-colonel in the army, his rank within the regiment, to which he returned as a company-commander, remained that of captain. Lacking seniority and money to purchase promotion, Harry's duties would be considerably less exalted. His critics, who could not help feeling envious over his rapid rise, asked Charlie Beckwith, 'Now, how will Harry Smith, after such extended authority, like to come back to the command of a Company?' His friend responded, 'In the execution of his duty and care of his Company, he will be an example to us all.'

The brigade, once again under Lambert, began to march north in January. As Harry led his men to new quarters, Juana remained behind: having just recovered from a severe illness, she was unable to ride. Driving down in their tilbury, she joined him at Vernais and they continued on together to Cambrai, the Duke's headquarters.

At Cambrai the good life in France was suddenly threatened. Harry's commanding officer, Major Balvaird, a Scotsman with a heavy accent, came to him and said: 'Weel, Harry mi mon, the deevil is in it. I have an order to send a Captain to the depôt at Shorncliffe. You are the first for duty, my lad.' Then he added, 'There is just one chance for you, but you must be prepared.' The thought of serving in England at reduced pay greatly distressed Harry. He said nothing to Juana, fearing that in her delicate condition she might suffer a relapse. And there was still the possibility that there might be a change in his fortunes.

Several nights later, while sleeping in 'a miserable dirty little farmhouse', Harry had another of those strange dreams: The Duke sent for him and said, 'Smith, I have two staff-appointments to give away, you shall have one.' Then, on his way out, the military secretary said, 'You are a lucky fellow, Harry, for the one you are to have is most preferable by far.'

The next day he told Juana of his dream and his premonition that it would come true. And it did, exactly as he had dreamt it. Harry was made the Town-Major of Cambrai, with the pay of an assistant quartermaster-general; Charlie Beckwith, sporting an artificial leg, was given a similar appointment in Valenciennes. But since Cambrai was headquarters, Harry had none of 'that horrid duty, billeting on the inhabitants' that was part of Beckwith's duties.

The Smiths were to be neighbours of the commander-in-chief for the next two years. Not long after they were settled, Wellington sent one of his aides with a note: 'The Duke desires you will come to him immediately, and bring with you the sheet of Cassini's map of the environs of Cambray.' Harry could not imagine what he had in mind. Upon arrival, the Duke briskly asked for the map. Searching it with his keen blue eyes, he asked, 'Now where is my château?' — 'Here, my lord.' — 'Ah, the coverts are very well shown here. Are there foxes in all of these?' — 'Yes my lord, too many in every one.' — 'Well then,' observed the Duke, 'hounds must always know their own country.' Drawing a line across the map with his finger, he announced his decision: 'Now, your hounds hunt that side, mine this.'

Subsequent meetings with the Duke were not unlike those with any other country squire passionately fond of hunting. In such circumstances, as Harry had already noted in Spain, Wellington's demeanour was startlingly different from the battlefield where, as one of his officers remarked, he resembled 'an angry god under whose threatening glance everyone trembled'.

Great coursing parties were held with the Duke, Lord Hill, Sir Hussey Vivian and other generals of the army in attendance. Matches were arranged between Harry and other sportsmen. But he appears to have had all the advantages running with his Spanish hounds, sons of his famous Moro, and a superior mount, the dauntless Lochinvar.[1] 'As a horse,' claimed Harry, 'he was as celebrated as His Grace was a general.' Juana, riding the Brass Mare, was often named by the Duke as one of the umpires.

The fox-hunting was usually disappointing. English hunters frequently complained that French foxes, in contrast to those back home, were stupid, cowardly and apt to run in circles.

One day while he was riding home alone, Harry found himself in an awkward situation. Before him was the Duke riding alone. 'I must either pass him,' he thought, 'or saddle myself on him as companion, neither of which etiquette or delicacy tolerated.' The Duke, on seeing him, solved the problem by inviting Harry to ride towards home with him. Accustomed to seeing his junior officer out with his hounds, the Duke looked around and asked, 'What! no dogs with you?' Harry explained, 'On Sundays, my lord, I never take them out.' The Duke agreed. 'Very proper, although I fear in our late struggle we respected Sunday but little. All our great battles were fought on that holy day which ought to be.' Harry pointed out that so was the disastrous defeat before New Orleans. 'Was it?' asked the Duke. 'You were there, were you not?' Harry told him he was. His professional interest aroused, the great commander asked Harry to give his account. When Harry got to the assault, Wellington interrupted him, saying, 'What! the troops stood and fired in column, did they? What corps?' Harry named them. 'Ah,' he observed, 'they had not been accustomed to victory, but it was quite right to keep two such corps as the 7th Fusiliers and the 43rd in reserve.'

Harry then offered an opinion, 'We ought not to have landed where we did, my lord.' — 'Certainly not,' agreed the Duke, who was strongly critical of Admiral Cochrane. 'I was consulted about those lakes,' the Duke continued. 'Is there navigation there for the purpose of trade?' he asked. When Harry said there was not, Wellington remarked, 'Then it is injudicious to use them to land an army, and craft of any size will never get up to land troops.'

Throughout the discussion of the campaign, Pakenham's name was never mentioned. In referring to him, Harry always

[1] Courage was deemed essential in horses as well as men. When Col. Mainwaring's horse was frightened by a cannon ball, he said angrily: 'You are a coward. I will stop your corn for three days.'

spoke of him as 'the general'. Nor did the Duke ask about him by name. 'How I longed to tell him,' wrote Harry, 'how much I loved and admired his brother-in-law, Sir Edward Pakenham!'

After half-an-hour, in which the Duke fired a series of crisp questions, Harry was impressed by his complete grasp of the subject, and pleased that he had satisfied him with answers. As they prepared to go their separate ways, the Duke said: 'I am glad to have had this conversation with you. It agrees as nearly as may be with the opinion I had previously formed. If you are not engaged, you and Juana come and dine with me today.'

'Our life in Cambray,' wrote Harry, 'was one of successive gaiety.' There was an unceasing, dizzying whirl of balls and parties, along with the pleasures of the hunt. The Duke celebrated each of his military victories. There were so many now that his calendar of feasts, according to one of his officers, began to resemble 'the Romish one with red letter days'. Being the hero of the day, Wellington was visited by England's high society. Even emperors and kings descended from Olympus to visit Cambrai and mingle with such ordinary mortals as the Smiths. 'We were both young,' recalled Harry, 'and my wife was beautiful. We were fêted and petted by every one.'

Harry was enormously proud of his wife. He was 'keenly alive to the general *approbation* she attracted' at every social function: her 'dearest shape ... and full bosom heaving' as she waltzed; the soft, sweet voice as she sang plaintive melodies in the Spanish manner (which one listener likened to 'the last sigh of a dying angel'); her highly animated way of 'describing something or other to the amusement of all', her dark eyes flashing and her 'long fingers flourishing about'. Moreover, Harry knew intimately what others did not: 'the quality of her mind, the generosity of her heart, the *superiority* of her *character over all her sex* so void of all littleness so inherent in the female character.'

It was a pride that Harry now had to share with the Duke, who called her 'my Spanish heroine'. At one of the Duke's many balls, Prince Narinski and his very attractive and most polished wife were his guests. As a compliment to her, Wellington requested that a mazurka be danced. Being unfamiliar with the step, all of the ladies but the Princess remained seated. The Duke went directly to Juana and took her by the hand, saying,

'Come Juana, now for the Russian fandango; you will soon catch the step.' Without hesitation she went on to the floor. The Duke turned her over to a young Russian officer who sprang forward as a partner. 'The Princess danced elegantly,' said Harry, 'and the Duke was as anxious as I was that Juana should acquit herself well.' Being an accomplished dancer, Juana quickly and gracefully mastered the lively step. The Duke 'was as pleased as possible'.

Later, during the annual grand review of the entire Army of Occupation, the Duke spied Juana. He called her to his side and presented her to Alexander I of Russia: 'Voilà, Sire, ma petite guerrière espagnole qui a fait la guerre avec son mari comme la héroïne de Saragosse.' The handsome, dandified Emperor asked her to accompany him for a ride. He plied her with questions about the Spanish war; she responded in fluent French in a manner so knowledgeable it would have done credit to a field officer.

At the ball that night, Alexander continued to single her out; the Grand Duke Michael also waltzed with her. Harry, the forgotten husband, stood to one side in his dull, green Rifle uniform. A Russian courtier, on discovering that Juana was Harry's wife, patronizingly asked, 'Are you aware to whom Madame has been presented?' Already irked by the way the Russians had made Juana their exclusive property, Harry said pertly, 'To be sure, and by *whom* — the greatest man in the world.'

There were more Russians that night, soldiers crowding the road as the Smiths rode home in the cold. Harry was clapping his shoulders, English-style, when Juana noticed that he had lost his Star of the Bath. Having felt something caught on his sleeve, Harry looked back to see a column of Russian cavalry trotting over the dusty road they had just traversed. 'What nonsense!' he said to himself. 'I shall never find it.' At that moment a dragoon's horse kicked the shiny object under Lochinvar's nose. The dent in the Star would remain as a reminder of the day Juana met the Tsar.

The visitor to Cambrai who brought them the greatest happiness was Harry's father. The kindly old Dr Smith spent much of his time in the great garden of the Bishop of Cambrai and, though he was now 63, he still enjoyed the field sports that British officers had introduced to the district. Harry reflected that it was, after all, his father who was responsible for his swift advancement in the service. It was he who had taught him, the favourite son, everything that was manly and to whom Harry was indebted for his expert horsemanship, an accomplishment which first brought him to the attention of his superiors.

At the close of an extended stay of three months, Dr Smith, observing that he and his country had never experienced war and occupation at first hand, announced: 'I shall go home now and pay my taxes with delight. Even were they double, readily would I pay rather than have such a fellow as you and your establishment quartered on me.'

But there were relatively few complaints from the conquered French. Among Harry's duties in Cambrai was the responsibility of dealing with all disputes arising between British officers and the native inhabitants. In most cases he found that his own countrymen were at fault. The Duke dealt hard with wrongdoers. He was uncompromising in the policy he laid down: 'We are Englishmen and pride ourselves on our deportment, and that pride shall not be injured in my keeping.'

The term of occupation was reduced to three years, in good part because of Wellington's influence. His generous endeavours were unaffected by an attempt on his life in Paris by a fanatical Bonapartist. As a reward for his effort, the ex-Emperor left the bungling assassin a legacy of 10,000 francs, proving what every Englishman already knew—that Napoleon was no gentleman. Chafing in idleness, Blücher sent Wellington a crazy message suggesting that he work for the release of Napoleon so that they might engage in another test of strength on the battlefield.

To Harry, looking forward to another two years in France, the news of termination came as a blow. They had lived extravagantly, spending all of his savings, the money left to him by his grandmother and prize-money received for victories in the Peninsula, Washington and Waterloo. He had borrowed money on the assumption that his salary and privileges enjoyed in occupied France would continue. The result, of course, was that he was now in debt. Harry, rationalizing his excessive spending, said:

No wonder, after the life of hardship and privation which

we had led, we should have been somewhat intoxicated by the scene around us, and I spent a lot of money ... All went as fast I could get it.

To pay off some of his debts before leaving, Harry raffled off his thoroughbred, Lochinvar. Juana insisted on buying a ticket in Harry's lottery. 'Oh, nonsense,' said Harry, 'it is only throwing five napoleons away.' His objections notwithstanding, she had her way (as wives always do, commented Harry, most of all Spanish wives). Juana's ticket was the winner. Surprisingly no one protested the outcome.

Creditors were paid and gifts were purchased for M. Watin, their landlord for two years, his brother who lived with him, and their large families. The Watins were sincerely sorry to see them leave. They invited the Smiths to breakfast on their last morning together. Then there were twenty more breakfasts to which Harry and Barnard, the Commandant at Cambrai who was also leaving, accepted invitations. At each they sat down for a few minutes and ate. Thoroughly gorged, Harry felt as though he would never be hungry again. As he and Juana rode their carriage through the streets, there was much waving of handkerchiefs and many adieus.

Harry returned to Shorncliffe to rejoin his old regiment. The Prince Regent was so impressed with their conduct at Waterloo that he ordered the three battalions of the 95th to be removed from the line of numbered regiments and, henceforth, to be known as the Rifle Brigade. Many did not live to enjoy the unprecedented honour conferred upon them. Of the company commanders who survived to stand inspection after returning from France, Kincaid left a colourful description of

a well-shot corps ... Beckwith with a cork leg; Pemberton and Manners each with a shot in the knee, making them as stiff as the other's tree one; Loftus Gray with a gash in the lip and minus a portion of one heel which made him march to the tune of dot and go one; Smith with a shot in the ankle ... Johnstone, in addition to other shot-holes, a stiff elbow, which deprived him of the power of disturbing his friends as a scratcher of Scotch reels upon the violin; Percival with a shot through his lungs; Hope with a grapeshot lacerated leg; and George Simmons with his

riddled body held together by a pair of stays ... which
naturally required such an appendage lest the burst of a
sigh should snap it asunder ...

There were new men in Harry's company to whom he
devoted much time and effort in order to inspire them with 'the
feelings of soldiers'. One of them was Henry Havelock, a
subaltern nicknamed the 'Young Varmint', who was to become
one of Britain's greatest soldiers and win lasting renown for his
relief of Lucknow during the Indian Mutiny. Years later he
recalled how Captain Smith 'was one of the few people who
ever took the trouble to teach me anything'. While others made
him think that soldiering consisted solely of drill and polish,
'he pointed my mind to the nobler part of our glorious profession'. Forty years of experience in the service continually
reaffirmed Havelock's belief that his teacher had 'a natural
talent for war ... There is no species of business which Harry
Smith's mental tact will not enable him to grasp.'
Peace meant sharp cuts in the size of the army. Whole
battalions were disbanded, like the 3rd of the Rifle Brigade;
others were reduced in size. Officers were forced to go on half-
pay or sell their commissions, their new civilian pursuits rarely
giving them the status or opportunities that the service had
offered. Harry, who stayed on, had to struggle along with a
pittance of 12s. 6d. He prayed for another staff appointment to
help solve his financial problems.
It was a sad time of continual farewells. At Gosport, where
the brigade now had its headquarters, 300 veteran green
jackets were discharged, and each had a special good-bye for
Juana. Among them was the faithful West who had watched
over the child-bride like a father. As they stood in the barrack
square an Irishman asked Captain Smith to give them the order
to march off. 'Sure,' he said, 'it's the last after the thousand
your honour has given us.' Harry gave them their last command with tears running down his cheeks. Nor was there a dry
eye among the battle-hardened soldiers as they took their
officers' hands, saying, 'God bless your honour!' With one great
chorus they cheered them. Harry and other officers marched
along the road with the men for some distance, knowing that
after many years of close association they would, in all
probability, never see them again. 'Never was there a Regi-

ment,' wrote Harry, 'in which harmony and unanimity were more perfect.'

As the military establishment dwindled down to normal, political and social unrest increased dangerously. All over Europe there were angry demands for liberty and the correction of social evils. 'The world,' declared an alarmed Metternich in 1819, 'was in perfect health in 1789 compared with what it is today.' In industrial Britain postwar unemployment, high taxes and disastrous harvests led to riots and agrarian crimes to such an extent that a general insurrection appeared to be building up. The strong-nerved hierarchy, the same men whose wealth and leadership had humbled the great Napoleon, were not to be intimidated by mob violence, would-be assassins, or threats of revolution. Repressive measures were enacted and the military called upon to enforce them.

By mid-summer industrial centres like Birmingham, Manchester and Glasgow were seething with discontent. There were cries of 'Bread or Blood!' At St Peter's Fields, Manchester, a force of constables, yeomanry and hussars charged an unarmed crowd of 80,000 men, women and children attending a reform meeting. Several were killed and thousands were injured. It became known as the people's Waterloo, the 'Peterloo Massacre'.

With civilian arrangements for quelling disorders still quite inadequate, soldiers throughout the kingdom waited to be called. Long before the order arrived, Harry's men knew that they would be sent to put down disturbances in Glasgow. He and his company were at target practice when assembly was sounded and their mission announced. 'Hurrah for Glasgow', the men shouted. They boarded a man-of-war on 18 September 1819.

Glasgow in October, Harry complained, is 'a most melancholy, dirty, smoky city, particularly in the end which the barracks are placed'. Because of the turbulence in the city, he and Juana, who travelled north in luxury on a frigate recently fitted for the Duchess of Kent, were forced to live in one room in the barracks. When the situation grew more threatening, Harry arranged to have her stay with Sir Sydney Beckwith's mother in Edinburgh. At 94, Beckwith's mother was still perfectly lucid, though at times eccentric. On learning that Juana was Spanish, she said: 'A Spaniard? Stand up, and let me look at your feet and ankles, for I have always heard your countrywomen celebrated for their neatness.' Juana's shoes and stockings being immaculate and of the finest quality, she gladly raised her flounces. The old lady was more than satisfied. They soon found that they had much in common, for Mrs Beckwith herself had accompanied her soldier-husband on military campaigns. They were delighted by one another's company, and when conversations were concluded the old lady simply said, 'Now go; I am tired.'

Harry's stay in Scotland, meanwhile, was far from amusing. The 'Radical War', as the confrontation in Glasgow was to be called, was a distasteful affair to Harry and his men. It was difficult for old campaigners to look on unemployed, starving weavers, however misdirected and insulting their behaviour, as the foe, or to accept the hard-headed, vindictive bourgeois citizenry as their allies. 'We had neither enemy nor friends,' said Harry. Worse, arrayed against them were old comrades-in-arms, humble heroes of many a battlefield, their means of livelihood cut off in a land dominated by the spirit of *laissez-faire*. Many were rendered useless as soldiers because of the loss of limbs or other debilitating wounds, and reduced to selling leeches and matches, or simply begging. Others were driven by bitter poverty to crime.

Their training as soldiers was not forgotten. Among the old soldiers that Harry recognized was a Rifleman who had lost an arm at New Orleans. From him he learned that they were organized into sixteen battalions indifferently armed with a few muskets and pistols, but mostly just pikes and bricks. Even women were enlisted, to tend the wounded. They were governed by a Central Committee of Delegates, called 'a House of Lords', with a delegate appointed by committee in each district. Regiments, he told Harry, were formed by streets, so that they could turn out quickly—'Ah, just as we did in the towns of Spain and France.' But when it came to a test, the leadership was inept and the organization broke down.

The difficulty of maintaining the peace as policemen rather than acting as soldiers became irksome. One day Harry and his company, along with a score of the 7th Hussars, were ordered to accompany magistrates in arresting a party of delegates. Returning with the prisoners, they were soon surrounded by an angry mob. Harry put those in custody in the centre of his company and told Havelock to march them on to the barracks while he covered their move with mounted men. 'On my word, they were violent,' recalled Harry; bricks, stones and other missiles 'were flying among us half as bad as grapeshot.' Harry directed his troopers to strike back with the broadside of their swords. A sufficient number of heads were left aching to keep the mob at bay. The timorous civil authorities became fearful that their animated, swearing captain, warming to the fight, might order his men to fire, and thereby, put on them the onus of another Peterloo Massacre. Harry, however, was too experienced a soldier to do anything so rash. Well aware that no officer, by law, could open fire in such circumstances without their authority, he told the civil officials calmly, 'You command.'

The commander-in-chief in Scotland, General Sir Thomas Bradford, being present in the city, Harry reported directly to him, as was the custom. Sir Thomas, already apprised of the affair, met him at the door and told him Sir William Rae, the quick-tempered lord advocate, a member of Parliament, disapproved of the supine way he had allowed His Majesty's troops to be insulted with impunity. He wished to speak with Harry immediately.

The lord advocate did not bother to rise as Harry entered the room. Anticipating a dressing-down, Harry wrote, 'my blood was as hot as his'. The thought crossed his mind, 'What! to be rowed by this man, who have ever been approved of by *the Duke*!'

In a bullying, taunting manner, Sir William asked: 'Pray, sir, are you the officer who allowed His Majesty's troops to be insulted in such a manner with arms in hands? *I am surprised, sir*. Why did you thus tamely act?'

In words no less pompous, Harry retorted:

Because my lord, I was acting under the officers of the law, the magistrates, of whom you are the Commander-in-Chief. They would not act, and I did not desire to bring upon my head either the blood of my foolish and misguided countrymen, or the odium of the Manchester magistrates.

He went on to say that if this was not to his liking, he would, on his written order, march the prisoners back through the city. 'A mob will attempt the rescue,' Harry told him, 'and damn

me, my lord, but I will shoot all Glasgow to please you.'
Without waiting for a response, Harry said curtly, 'Good
morning, my lord,' and walked out.

From that day forward, Harry and Sir William worked well
together. As an indication that he favoured Harry over other
officers, Sir William assigned to him some of the most difficult
night-marches that he ever made in his long career.

Harry was unhappy with his role as a 'peace officer' on the
Clydeside and by the state of his finances, which, he wrote to
Colborne, 'has given me such a lesson in adversity I shall be
more careful for the future, I am now a most needy man'. He
pleaded with his former commander to use whatever influence
he had with the Duke or Lord Fitzroy Somerset to obtain for
him an assignment in the Ionian Islands, where there was to be
a vacancy for an inspecting field officer. Whatever efforts, if
any, Colborne made were unsuccessful.

Once more, however, luck came to Harry's aid. When Sir
Hussey Vivian came to Glasgow to take command of the
Western District, his brigade major, Harry's old comrade De
Lacy Evans, resigned in Harry's favour to prepare for a career
in the House of Commons. For the next five years Harry held
a staff appointment in Scotland. Harry's position was further
improved when Vivian was replaced by General Reynell,
who in a matter of weeks was sent to India. The general's post
in Scotland thus vacant, Harry was actually in charge of the
Western District and responsible directly to Bradford, the
commander-in-chief. Harry wrote:

> Of course I was very cautious, fully aware of the delicacy
> of my position as regarded my senior officers, some of
> whom were very jealous of the authority vested in me,
> although personally I had never had a controversial word
> with them.

As for the 'Radical War', slogans became bolder ('Scotland
Free—Or A Desert'), the rumours more absurd (the French
were coming to their aid) and the drilling brisker. Harry and
the army stood on the alert to suppress an uprising. While
there was a great display of rebellion, there was an obvious
reluctance (on both sides) to spill blood. After all, revolution
was against the law. Gradually the tumult faded away.

Life in Scotland turned out to be not so bad after all. Juana rejoined him and he had the 'most delightful duty' of inspecting the various Corps of Yeomanry. With great tact he resolved the differences that at times arose between the army and civil authorities. He wrote:

I was treated *en prince* by the Duke of Montrose, Lord Glasgow, Lord Douglas, Lord-Lieutenants of Counties, Lord Blantrye, etc. The officers of the Corps of Yeomanry, too, all belonged to the aristocracy of the country and their houses were open as their hospitable hearts.

When George IV, whom Harry had met as Prince Regent, made a state visit to Edinburgh in the summer of 1822, Sir Walter Scott and General Bradford drew up the plans for all the processions, while Harry was entrusted with their execution. The occasion demanded that Harry's resolution to save money be broken. He spent an entire year's income to attire himself and Juana as he thought proper.

The King, approving of the arrangements made on his behalf, summoned Harry and asked him to name his reward. With so many hundreds senior to him in his army rank of lieutenant-colonel, he dared not ask for a promotion; nor could he accept a knighthood for organizing parades. Instead, he unselfishly asked that Bradford's deserving aide-de-camp be promoted to lieutenant-colonel. The favour was granted and George IV gave Harry permission to wear the Royal Button. Juana's reward was the royal compliment that she rode a horse admirably.

With tranquillity restored to Glasgow and its environs, most of the army was withdrawn and Harry was put off the staff. The Smiths were once more on the move. The Lord-Provost and Town Councillors publicly expressed their gratitude for his successful efforts in imposing the peace; they awarded him the freedom of the city. 'Glasgow,' Harry wrote years later, 'with all your smoke, your riots, mobs and disaffections, I look back to you with perfect happiness.' He had learned to love the Scots, and recalling the words of his mother that if he were ever in a fight for his country to remember he was born an Englishman, he felt that he could now fight with no less patriotic fervour for the Scottish nation.

In August, 1825, Harry and Juana crossed the Atlantic for Halifax where the battalion was to be stationed. There were special greetings from the governor, Sir James Kempt, Harry's former brigade commander, who still suffered, off and on, from the wound he had received at Badajoz. According to Surgeon Guthrie, there was one period during which Kempt did not sleep at night for an entire year.

While junior officers survived the drastic reduction in the military by accepting such duty as standing guard in North America, transporting convicts to Australia, or searching for illegal stills in Ireland, Kempt was one of the many senior officers selected to govern in a far-flung, ever-expanding empire. Kempt's charm and shrewdness, added to his administrative skills, led to his success as governor in Nova Scotia and a subsequent appointment as governor-general of Canada, replacing another Peninsular general, Lord Dalhousie.

Sir James soon invited Harry to join his personal staff as an aide-de-camp. Harry readily agreed, and the Smiths took up residence in Government House.

Under Kempt, a quiet, unassuming little man, Harry had his first exposure to colonial government. Harry, who had known the governor only as a first-class soldier, was 'perfectly astonished' by Kempt's talents as a statesman. He learned much that was to prove useful when one day he would administer a government of his own. Harry particularly admired how Kempt, in dealing with a strong Whig opposition in the House of Assembly, managed to be firm in his policies without sacrificing popularity.

The agreeable company and climate were soon to be left behind, however, for in November, 1826, Harry was made deputy quartermaster-general in Jamaica, where Sir John Keane was governor. There was the usual round of farewell parties and a great ball at Government House on the last night. A triumphal embarkation followed, all of the officers and gentlemen of Halifax accompanying them on board, and the governor leading the procession with Juana's arm tucked in his. The entire garrison of three regiments voluntarily turned out in columns of sixes to follow. Cheering the loudest were the wrongdoers who, at Harry's request, were released from confinement to barracks for punishment of every description.

Before Harry's departure, Kempt drew him aside and exacted from him a promise 'never to go out snipe-shooting or to ride any more races, in a tropical climate at least'. Flattered by

9 The Duke of Wellington, by T. Lawrence. Harry Smith regarded him as 'the greatest Englishman who ever lived'.

10 General Robert Craufurd, known as 'Black Bob' because of his savage temper. He commanded the Light Division until his death at Ciudad Roderigo.

11 Macomo, by turns Harry Smith's favourite Xhosa chief and bitterest enemy.

12 Sir Benjamin D'Urban, the popular governor of the Cape Colony (1834–7) known as 'Benjamin the Good'. Too circumspect for Harry Smith's temperament, he referred to him as 'Sir Slow'.

Kempt's concern for him, Harry rashly made his promise. Then, with 'tears rolling down his cheeks', Kempt gently pressed money into Harry's hand to pay for the passage to Jamaica — generously giving Harry three times the amount that the army normally allocated.

The brig chartered for the four-week journey into the sun was far superior to the crowded transports Harry was accustomed to. The sea was so calm and the weather so clear that every night but one they dined on deck. Harry's one concern was for the captain's quadrant — the only navigational instrument on board — which was left lying carelessly about the deck. 'I almost worshipped that quadrant,' wrote Harry, and 'watched over it accordingly', fearing that it would be swept overboard and lost — Harry knew the tales of how the loss of a quadrant sometimes resulted in aimless wandering over the surface of the sea.

Landing at Kingston, the Smiths were greeted by Keane and then taken to his residence in Spanish Town, where quarters were prepared for them. The richness and verdure of Jamaica after the barren shores of Nova Scotia in winter were refreshing to their eyes. But unseen in the beauty of their surroundings was a foe who killed more British soldiers than Wellington ever lost engaging the French — yellow fever. Since its conquest in the time of Cromwell, Jamaica was hazardous duty. In one four-year period, 1793–6, in the West Indies, the army lost 80,000 men — 40,000 of whom died — to the terrible scourge. A foretaste of what was to come was the news that shortly after landing, the entire crew, but for one old man, died of the fever.

If the risks from yellow fever were great, so was the importance of Jamaica's strategic position in the Caribbean: a large force was necessary in the West Indies in order to support Canning's policy of preventing the efforts of Spain, backed by other reactionary Powers, to reconquer rebelling colonies in America. In addition, the troops were needed to maintain order in Jamaica itself, for the black population, outnumbering the whites nearly ten to one, was becoming dangerously restless and speaking of emancipation.

Harry went to work immediately. Neither Harry's predecessor nor Keane, whose reputation in the service was built on luck and reckless daring rather than reform, displayed much concern for the soldiers' welfare. Many of the men Harry

10

inspected already had the tell-tale symptoms of a yellow skin, or the sooty hue that indicated the more advanced stage of the disease. Next, Harry examined the barracks. Those of Upper Park near the governor's house were ideally situated, spacious and well-ventilated, with bathrooms. But elsewhere on the island, the dark, dilapidated dwellings into which the soldiers were packed were infamous. The soldiers slept on dirty blankets on the floor, the very feel of which in a tropical climate was loathsome. The wooden floors and walls were crawling with bugs, fleas and various other insects that Harry had never seen before. The soldiers' uniforms, made of the same material that was worn in Canada, were heavy and stifling, causing the men to sweat profusely and become, through exhaustion, prone to disease.

To improve these deplorable conditions, Harry sent a request, approved by the governor, to the office of the commander-in-chief, Wellington, for iron bedsteads and new bedding. As the government was concerned with maintaining a large, healthy garrison on the island, the request was acted upon immediately.

Harry was proud of his achievements. 'Do not call me an egotistical son of a ——,' he told Colborne, as he boasted of how he had not only ameliorated the sleeping facilities of the soldier, but improved his condition 'in fifty other shapes'. Harry reminded Colborne of 'the many days we have mutually laboured for *his* good and that spirit of adhering to the private, I learned under your tuition'.

Disregarding his promise to Kempt, Harry rushed from one station to another. One day, under a tropical sun, he rode 35 miles and travelled another 16 in an open boat. Men were dying everywhere, including the physicians who prescribed bleeding, emetics, purgatives and various stimulants to no avail. Because of overcrowded wards, patients were discharged as soon as their fevers subsided; Harry found that these convalescents often returned to their quarters and immediately indulged in hearty meals washed down with cheap and extremely potent West Indian rum[1] — almost invariably these

---

[1] Harry recalled that at the battle of Busaco Portuguese artillerymen, accustomed only to the weak wine of their country, behaved like madmen after being served West Indian rum. They drew their swords and fought one another while under fire from the French.

meals were followed by relapses from which the soldiers rarely recovered. Given a free hand by the governor, Harry set up convalescent centres for discharged patients. The number who suffered relapses was greatly reduced. Nevertheless, during the three months' epidemic, the ravages of 'yellow jack' swept through the island's five regiments, killing 22 officers and 688 men. Fortunately, neither Harry nor Juana were stricken.

Recognizing that the fatal scourge had a demoralizing effect upon those who survived, thereby making them more prone to succumb, Harry dedicated himself to raising the spirits of the soldiers. As a prophylactic it was certainly more effective than anything provided by the medical men. Apart from frequent visits to the hospitals and convalescent centres, Harry undertook a programme to dispel the gloom that settled over the regiments. Harry began with the hardest hit, the 84th, composed mostly of soldiers who had come directly from England. Only two subalterns were fit for duty; seventeen men died on the very day of his visit. Harry observed:

> The regiment was in a perfect state of despondency, but I cheered them up. I wheeled them into line a time or two, formed close column, and told them, whether a soldier died by yellow fever or on the battle-field, it was all in the service of his country.

Harry went on to promise the terrified young soldiers that they were about to be moved to a new camp and leave yellow fever behind. Having finished his speech, he asked for three cheers for King George.

It was a novel experience for the young soldiers to be addressed in such a manner by a staff officer. 'The poor fellows,' wrote Harry, 'were alive again in no time.' He moved on to the other regiments and continued to make the rounds until the epidemic ran its course.

Pleased with his efforts among the sick and the depressed, Harry wrote to Major Thomas Powell, who was with him at the storming of Ciudad Roderigo, 'I kicked the yellow fever in the A—— [and] blew up all lazy croaking', with the approval of the governor.

It was time for a well-deserved rest. Keane proposed a leisurely tour of inspection around the island. The Smiths drove a four-in-hand while the governor sailed his yacht; each evening the Smiths made rendezvous with the ship and slept on board. There were frequent stops to enjoy the hospitality in the planters' mansions. Contrary to the tales of brutality Harry had heard from emancipationists, he found the slaves on this fertile island 'more happy, better fed, less worked, and better provided for in sickness than any peasants throughout the many parts of the world in which I have been'. Visiting the slaves in their comfortable little huts, he found that they were better housed than the British soldiers had been when he arrived. Following the tour, Harry and Juana found a 'happy retreat' in the mountains, from which he commuted regularly to his office twice a week.

Harry yearned for new employment. He complained to Colborne that he had been in Jamaica now for a year, 'roasting by day and literally boiling by night' with no real opportunity for soldiering, the only trade he knew anything about. Should there be another war soon, which seemed probable, he reminded his old brigade commander of his promise to him: 'If there be a war again, you shall be with me.' He told Colborne that 'behind the scenes, I have been making a bold push to manoeuvre so as to get back in command of 1st Bn, Rifle Brigade, had it, *as I thought* all cut and dry, but I was cruelly disappointed.' He blamed Barnard—the same officer, he grumbled, who had prevented him from getting the brevet of major in 1814 that Colborne had promised him at that time.

Fearing that he would soon be 'roasted alive and rendered an Indian officer, thereby becoming unfit for what you were once kind enough to consider me in the many bloody deeds in which we were once happily associated', he beseeched Colborne to intercede on his behalf to get him transferred—not to Nova Scotia or Canada, 'but the place for me is the Cape of Good Hope'. Juana, he added, was as anxious to leave as he was 'and begs me to say she can campaign as well as ever "pero nole gusta este Paiz".'

At the end of July, 1828, Harry received a letter from Lord Fitzroy Somerset saying that the Duke had praised his exertions in Jamaica and that he had been appointed to replace his old friend, John Bell, who had been moved to the office of colonial secretary, as deputy quartermaster-general at the Cape.

Within 48 hours, without waiting for formal orders, the Smiths sold all of their furnishings, carriages and horses, and flung their belongings on to a transport bound for Nassau. 'As we were all in all to each other,' wrote Harry, 'so were we still in the possession of the world.'

The Smiths were put up as guests for nearly a month by the governor of the Bahamas until they found passage on a brig, the *Euphemia*, bound for Liverpool. It was an uncomfortable month's voyage through tempestuous seas in a ship that 'sailed like a witch'. Harry and Juana had to share a cabin with two officers, having only a piece of canvas as a partition. Battened down most of the time, they had little to eat from the galley and relied on the provisions Harry had taken along. Unfastened boxes were tossed about. Women cried and men cursed as they were flung against the bulkheads. Cockroaches swarmed all over them as they tried to sleep. When the brig entered the Irish Sea, it was so cold that the sailors' hands became frostbitten. There was no grog for the crew, so Harry opened his small cask of fine rum to warm them. The captain of the 'dirty, miserable, exhausted and stinking ship', was an 'ignorant brute' without the foggiest notion of where they were. The *Euphemia* nearly ran down a small Irish smack, which directed them towards the Mersey.

In Liverpool Harry booked a passage on a fine brig, the *Ontario* bound for Calcutta by way of the Cape, which was to depart in a fortnight. He left Juana at the Adelphi Hotel and dashed off to London to confirm his orders and make various necessary arrangements. He met with Lord Fitzroy Somerset and thanked him for his appointment. He found the general not the least bit inconvenienced by the loss of his arm at Waterloo.[1] An appointment was made for Harry to see Wellington, who had become Prime Minister, but the Duke was delayed and Harry had to push on. He also missed seeing Charlie Beckwith, who had now left the army and was embarking upon a totally different kind of career in a Piedmont valley — as an apostle among Waldensian Protestants. (Beckwith had, while looking through the books in the Duke's library at Apsley House, come quite by accident upon a volume about this obscure sect and it had led him to decide to rekindle the evangelical faith. He spent the thirty-five years left to him among the Waldensians.)

---

[1] Somerset, the future Lord Raglan, bore the amputation with exceptional fortitude, making not a sigh nor a groan. As his arm was being taken away, he said simply, 'Hallo, don't carry that arm away till I have taken off the ring.'

Harry squeezed in two days at Whittlesea, where he stayed with his brother Charles, for his father was ill, before returning to Liverpool. The boatman who rowed the Smiths to the brig received all that was left of Harry's cash, half-a-crown. Accustomed to the fare of only three pence, the boatman looked at the coin in disbelief and then protested. 'Keep it,' said Harry, 'and drink to the health of a man banished from his native land.' The Liverpudlian stared at Harry as if he were a convict. Then, sizing him up as a gentleman, he announced, 'I'll drink to your Honour's health, depend on it, and success attend you wherever you go.'

[7]

The Sixth Frontier War

No hour in life is lost that is spent in the saddle.
Winston Churchill

The Smiths arrived at the Cape during the lull between the Fifth and Sixth Frontier Wars. For half a century the settlers of the Eastern Cape region, first under the Dutch and then the British, had pushed eastward, where they clashed with well-organized Xhosa (pronounced 'Cawza') tribes of the Bantu peoples migrating steadily down the east side of the butt-end of Africa. To eliminate friction, the government drew a boundary between them at the Fish river with a buffer of 'ceded' or 'neutral' land from the Fish to the Keiskamma river. Colonists often ignored the boundary and the warlike Xhosas, related to the fierce Zulus and Matabele, whose lands were encroached upon, swept over a hundred-mile-long border to raid cattle and other livestock. Reprisals touched off a succession of minor wars.

Over 500 miles west of the frontier was Cape Town, where Governor Sir Lowry Cole and his lady welcomed the Smiths. They were no strangers. Cole had commanded the Fourth Division in the Peninsula, noted for his orthodox methods and for giving, according to Wellington, 'the best dinners in the army'. Lady Frances Cole, daughter of the Earl of Malmesbury, was no less charming and well remembered as giving the most lively parties during the Occupation. Harry wrote to Colborne that he and Cole, 'who is very popular here and makes a *steady* Governor', agreed upon all points except when they compared the merits of the Fourth and the Light Divisions.

Until they found a home in Rondebosch, the Smiths were put up by John Bell (the governor's brother-in-law) and Lady Catherine. Bell, recalling their days together in Spain as Riflemen, promised, 'You and I and Juana have fared more sparingly together than we will now.'

Though Bell was senior in rank to Harry and experienced in

administrative matters, their strong friendship inhibited any difficulties that might have arisen when Cole named Harry to succeed him should he suffer an accident. Cole explained that earlier experience at the Cape demonstrated that the governor and his successor should be military men.

'No man was ever more happily placed than I was,' Harry announced. As senior member of the Council, commandant of Cape Castle and deputy quartermaster-general, he earned 19s. a day and forage for three horses. His quarters in the Castle, the former residence of the governor, were first class. Six days in the week, as he wrote to Major Powell, he 'laughed, swore, and hunted'; on Sundays he went to church with his garrison. As commander of two 'superb' regiments (the 72nd Highlanders and the 98th) and a company of artillery that might at any time be called to the frontier, Harry said, 'I slap them about ... march them into bivouacks, piquets, sham fights ... as nearly as like the old system' under Craufurd and Colborne.

Working to keep the army fit for war by day, Harry sought, with Juana's help, to improve the social life at Government House at night by eliminating 'a damned old custom here of abusing your neighbour'. He told Powell, 'if I ever report anyone I tell him I intend to do so which makes all fair and above board; so I go to bed, the evil of the day being sufficient thereof.'

Wherever Britons congregated, from the burning sands of India to the snow-covered forests of Canada, hunting and horse-racing flourished. Under Lord Charles Somerset, governor from 1814 to 1827, the breed at the Cape was vastly improved by his importation of thoroughbreds from England. Addicted as Harry was to 'oats and oaths', he diverted much of his immense vitality to breeding and racing a string of splendid hunters. He would travel great distances, on one occasion 140 miles in 30 hours, to buy or merely look at a horse. Because of the peculiar 'elasticity' of the atmosphere at the Cape, he found himself inspired 'to take violent rides'. The excitement of racing cross-country was heightened by danger, for moles 'as big as rabbits' pitted the sand. Falling from a horse that had stepped in a hole was far worse than tripping over a fence back home, for there was no time to jump from the horse. 'You fall like a shot,' said Harry, 'the horse's head first coming to the ground, next yours, and he rolls over you.'

Cole was replaced in January, 1834, by Sir Benjamin D'Urban, who had established a military reputation by shaping up Wellington's Portuguese allies and leading them gallantly into battle. Harry found him no less agreeable than his predecessor, but more deliberate and slow-moving. As a member of the Council, Harry assisted the governor in preparing for the emancipation of the slaves, which by an act of Parliament would take place throughout the Empire on 1 December 1834.

But this was not soldier's work. Harry busied himself much of the time devising more humane methods to deal with military offenders. Punishment for mild infractions was reduced and rations improved (formerly bread, rice and water) for those sentenced to long confinement. His plan for rehabilitation called for avuncular conversations concerning 'the impropriety of their conduct' and efforts to teach prisoners to read and write. Those who were literate were provided with books from the extensive library he brought from England. Good conduct was rewarded by remission of sentences and placement on probation, with orders to report to him every Sunday. Harry was well aware that some of his reforms were not only unfashionable but 'positively contrary to the Royal Warrant'. D'Urban nevertheless gave him full and unqualified support. Like Harry, he was rigid in discipline but opposed to harsh, spirit-breaking punishment.

Among the memoranda Harry wrote at the time, there was one addressed to himself in which he summed up his spectacular military record. Ten years after entering the army, without money, social connections, or fawning to his superiors, he wrote, he had risen to the rank of lieutenant-colonel and filled every staff situation in the field. He went on to enumerate every action in which he had been engaged:

Sieges and storms of fortified towns	4
Sieges and storms of fortified camps	3
Named affairs in despatches and general actions	33
Skirmishes which I *recollect* and sorties	250
Total	290

Now he was middle-aged with 'grey hairs intruding upon my sable brow'. He 'sighed for the past glorious days' and craved

active service that would free him from the strains of peace.
The Xhosa warriors on the frontier soon obliged him.

In December, 1834, when the days were long and warm and
the fields ripening, an irresistible force of 15,000 Xhosas swept
over the frontier on a broad front between the Winterberg
mountains and the sea. Directing them was Macomo, chief of
the Gaika tribe. Two years before he had warned the British
officials who had expelled him from his home in the ceded
territory that this was his country 'and we are to have the
land again'. Highly intelligent, Macomo was an able politician
and warrior, one of the greatest his nation ever produced. And,
according to Harry, by far the ugliest.

Plundering, burning and killing, Macomo's marauders, bred
for speed and strength, caught the military (less than 800
regulars) and the settlers unawares as they prepared for the
Christmas holiday. Most of the frenzied colonists flocked to
Grahamstown, the frontier capital.

The distressing news that the eastern territories were being
devastated reached the governor on 28 December. D'Urban
showed Harry the despatches, which he told his sister Alice
'breathed nothing but despair, inaction, doubt, fear and
desolation'. Harry declared to Sir Benjamin, 'Sir, you must send
me immediately. If I cannot stem the torrent of this invasion,
I shall feel disgraced.' The governor gave him full civil and
military power to restore the peace, and offered him a fast
sloop. Harry insisted he could make better time on horseback.
To reinforce the new commander's frontier force, the governor
ordered a wing of the 72nd, under the veteran Lieut.-Col.
Peddie, who had left an arm at Salamanca, to prepare to sail for
Algoa Bay in two days.

Harry revelled in the assignment. 'I hope to please His
Excellency,' he confided to Juana. 'If exertion will do it, I
cannot fail and work tames the too great vivacity of my
nature — the only thing I have to check.'

To some, the New Year's Eve party at Government House
seemed more convivial than usual. From time to time the
governor absented himself. Not until the next day did his
guests realize that he was being given the latest grim details
of events on the border. Shortly after midnight D'Urban
gave Harry his final instructions. Harry then went home for a
few hours' rest before he began his historic ride.

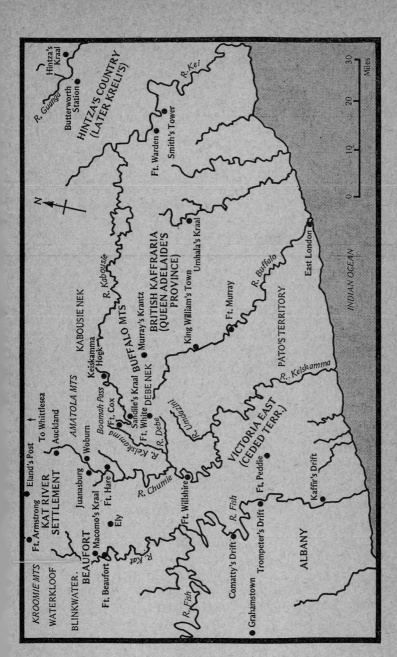

Map 4   The Eastern Frontier of Cape Colony

The first 25 miles were the hardest because of the previous day's exertions and very little sleep. All the while the heat was 'raging like a furnace'. A cup of tea at the first post-house revived him and he 'never felt fagged again'.

Galloping into Caledon at 1 p.m., New Year's Day, Harry called for a fresh horse and dashed off into a thunderstorm. By some strange quirk of nature, he succeeded in riding before the front edge of the downpour. When he finally off-saddled for the day, 94 miles out, Harry found himself completely dry. The hospitable local field cornet provided him with a cup of tea and a bed. At six he ate a 'glorious supper of rice and fowls' followed by brandy, and then retired to bed.

Off by sunrise, Harry had breakfast in Swellendam, 40 miles beyond. The heat was no less intense that second day. Worse, one projected stretch of 20 miles was turned into 30 by a swollen river that forced him through rough country in search of a ford. Harry was so pleased with the performance of the horse assigned to him that he later bought him.

Horses proved to be a problem on the third day. Harry planned to reach George after a hundred-mile ride, but was delayed half-way out by the absence of a mount. All of his swearing in the name of the governor and bullying of the slow-moving field cornet failed to produce one for at least an hour. While waiting, Harry foolishly ate a large noon meal that was being served to burghers enrolling for service in the war.

Suffering from indigestion, for which he took a mixture of calomel and opium, Harry rode the last two stages that day on 'the roughest Diablos that ever were'. Despatch-bearers who rode ahead to prepare his way, alerted the countryside to his coming. Spectators were treated to the unforgettable sight of a little colonel ferociously belabouring and cursing his sluggish mounts. Harry Wakelyn Smith was soon known as 'Hurry Whackalong Smite'.

Though the well-meaning citizens of George had prepared a ceremonial reception, Harry was feeling 'pretty well done' and got rid of them, making straight for a hot tub. He then lay down and dictated letters until eleven that night. He put his own hand to a letter to Juana telling her that he was 'in high spirits because in ten days after my arrival in Graham's Town, or thereabouts, my means will be ample to drive "Solomon's brothers" over the boundary.'

The fourth day Harry had what he called 'a tremendous ride before me'. Overgrown paths to serve as roads, difficult river crossings and mountain passes made his dogged ride treacherous, especially in the uncertain light of the early morning hours.

At midday Harry intercepted the official mail from Grahamstown containing despatches from the commandant, Lieut.-Col. Somerset, and the civil commissioner, Captain Campbell. Alarmed by the gloomy tale of destruction and disaster, and Somerset's statement that he might be forced to abandon the town, Harry resolved to complete the arduous journey in two more days rather than the three he had planned. At the next halt he told Field Commandant Rademeyer that he must send express riders through the night to advise each post that the colonel's mounts be ready a day before they were ordered, so that he might reach Uitenhage the next night.

Stopping for the night about a hundred miles beyond George, Harry wrote to Juana that though he had been at full gallop since four o'clock in the morning, 'I never was in better health than today in my life.' Somehow Harry's light frame and a lifetime in the saddle rendered him insensible to the fatigue that ordinary men would suffer. Harry was well aware that not only would his mere presence on the frontier raise the spirits of the settlers but that his superhuman ride would impress friend and foe alike with his ability to accomplish the seemingly impossible.

Two hours before dawn a solitary rider raced across the desolate land. Far behind was his soldier-servant, a Hottentot named Manie. Again, the country was most difficult. One river was so tortuous in its course that he had to cross it no less than seven times. Drenched with water and sweat, Harry began to steam under the mid-summer sun. His wretched, poorly fed horse, typical of those provided, collapsed. He tried every horseman's trick to make him move on but to no avail.

The stranded rider walked over to the camp of a Dutch farmer with his family and livestock. Obviously they were fleeing the pillaging hordes. Identifying himself, Harry explained his mission and asked for the saddled horse the Boer was leading to carry him to the next relay station, seven miles distant. Knowing the Boers to be a hospitable people, he was astounded when his request was refused. Though the farmer was half again his size, Harry knocked him to the ground, sprang into the saddle and galloped off. The farmer followed him to the next station where Harry was waiting with a remount to be ferried across a river. The Boer was profuse in his apologies, explaining that he had spoken to the guide who followed the colonel and that he was now convinced that Harry was the official he claimed he was.

'The passion, the knocking him down, the heat, etc.,' wrote Harry, 'was very fatiguing.' He reached Uitenhage at four in the afternoon after 'having been beating grass-fed post-horses over some very bad and mountainous roads' for 140 miles. Rather than a well-deserved rest at the end of the day's journey, Harry faced the whole town which had assembled to greet him. A large dinner party had been arranged, but to the amazement of his host Harry dared not eat anything.

Harry looked forward to meeting Col. Cuyler, an American-born soldier of Dutch descent whose Loyalist family had fled New York during the War for Independence. He recognized that Cuyler's extensive experience in frontier warfare could be of great value. But the old warrior was 'as deaf as a beetle', and Harry further exhausted himself shouting into Cuyler's ear.

One young settler, Caesar Andrews, asked to ride into Grahamstown as the colonel's escort. To his astonishment, Harry exploded, 'Escort be damned! I have ridden from Cape Town with my man Manie, and I shall ride into Graham's Town with him tomorrow.' On seeing the expression of disappointment on his face, Harry smiled and said, 'Mr Andrews, although I do not want an escort, I shall be glad for your company.' (Later, on learning that Andrews had served on the frontier as secretary to Commandant-General Stockenström in 1829, Harry made him secretary to the burgher contingent.)

Harry retired to his room with a secretary. There were many interruptions as he dictated letters until midnight for, as he explained to Juana, at one time there were 'forty people in my room, while I am lying on my bed full of tea'.

The last day of the journey was particularly gruelling. The most 'wretched brutes of knocked-up horses' had been laid out for him. Nearing his destination Harry found 'the country in the wildest state of alarm, herds, flocks, families, etc., fleeing like the Israelites. Everything that moved near a bush was a Kaffir.'[1] A party of mounted burghers insisted on acting as his escort. Ten miles outside town there was another escort of six Cape Mounted Rifles waiting for him with one of Somerset's best horses. The luxury of being in the saddle of so fine an animal soon 'perfectly revived me'.

Harry calculated that he had reeled off 600 miles in six days by riding at a rate of 14 miles an hour. There was not the slightest mark on him and he felt fresh enough to fight a general election.

The frightened people of Grahamstown had been waiting to fight a battle for days. The streets of the sprawling town, the colony's second city, were heavily barricaded. 'The whole appearance of the town,' he wrote to John Bell, 'was one of a city long besieged and momentarily awaiting the assault.' The men's faces were lined with worry. They shuffled about in loose order 'like an Irish mob at a funeral'. Had there been an alarm, especially at night, Harry was sure 'it would have set one half of the people shooting the other'.

The scene was so lugubrious that Harry found it difficult to refrain from laughing. But this, he thought, was hardly a fitting way to begin his rule. And he was soon saddened by the sight of burned-out refugees who were destitute in everything they possessed except for the ragged clothes on their backs. Among the thousands who had crowded into the town were the lame, the aged, and the widowed and fatherless.

Somerset was posting men for night duty when he saw the new commander. He escorted Harry to his home, Oatlands, where he was made comfortable. Lieut.-Col. England and Captain Campbell joined him there. Harry questioned them closely on the state of affairs and was obviously displeased with most of the measures that had been adopted. 'Very well,' he finally said, 'I clearly see my way. At as early an hour as possible tomorrow morning I shall declare martial law, and woe betide the man who is not obedient as a soldier!'

Harry's success as a leader was based on the sheer force of his personality. He presented himself as a man all of a piece; a man without doubts; one made for the exercise of authority. Nothing daunted him. Nothing deflected him from his remorseless drive and purpose. Rough manners and a staggering vocabulary

---

[1] The term was applied to black inhabitants of South Africa other than Hottentots and Bushmen. The name became objectionable to them.

suggested a commander aware of his independent strength. His blend of courage, optimism and pure bluff gave the dispirited a badly needed focus. There soon was a transformation of feeling in Grahamstown from panicky self-concern to one of united effort. Order suddenly emerged from confusion.

Straightaway early the next day Harry ordered all able-bodied men to be formed into a corps of volunteers. They would elect their own officers subject to his approval. Within two hours four companies of infantry and one of cavalry, under Lieut.-Col. Sparks, sprang into existence. The principal citizens and officers chosen met in the recently completed St George's church, which served as a military post, powder magazine and council chamber.

On hearing that the meeting was foundering because of an excess of speakers and so few actors, Harry 'deemed this a good opportunity to display my authority which I was resolved on doing most arbitrarily on such a momentous occasion'. Entering the church he saw a body of 'very respectable-looking men'. Harry asked why they were so dilatory in executing his orders. One long-winded gentleman, chairman of the committee of safety, stood up and began to debate the question. In a parade-ground voice, Col. Smith peremptorily declared:

> I am not sent here to argue, but to command. You are now under martial law, and the first gentleman, I care not who he may be, who does not promptly and implicitly obey my command, he shall not even dare to give an opinion; I will try him by a court martial and punish him in five minutes.

The defence of Grahamstown was reorganized. Harry brought the men of the 75th from their garrison some distance out of town, removed the barricades and established new alarm posts. The strength of their defence, he told the citizens, lay not in being cooped up behind walls and barricades but in military resourcefulness and vigilance. He ridiculed the idea of being 'afraid of a lot of black fellows armed with nothing but a knife stuck on the end of a long stick'. Grahamstown's new defences, he assured them, could withstand the assault of 7,000 Frenchmen. By evening he noticed that 'men moved

13 Col. Henry Somerset, commandant of the frontier forces at the Cape. Harry Smith, his rival, called him 'Colonel ass' and advised Governor Sir George Napier that during the Sixth Frontier War Somerset 'never wounded a Kaffir, no, nor ever frightened one'.

14 Hintza, the paramount Xhosa chief, tries to escape from his captor, Col. Smith. The circumstances of his death at the hands of Smith's escort and the alleged removal of his ears afterwards were investigated by a court of enquiry.

15 Lady Smith, by W. Melville. Though quite plump in her middle years, her husband assured a friend that Juana's ankles were 'as trim as ever'.

16 A sample of Harry Smith's handwriting taken from one of his many letters to Juana. The hieroglyphs were part of a code to convey his affections.

like men, and felt that their safety consisted in energetic obedience'.

During the course of the day Harry selected the home of a leading merchant to serve as his temporary headquarters. Admitted by the merchant's wife, he looked over the rooms and announced, 'Ah! This will answer capitally.' — 'But, sir,' remonstrated the lady of the house, 'this is not a hotel as you appear to think, and I am sorry that we shall not be able to accommodate you as you desire.' In the meantime the owner arrived. Recognizing the unexpected guest, he decided it would be best to accede to his request.

Later that day the merchant, who had enrolled as a volunteer, was paraded with his company before the colonel. As Harry passed down the ranks, his host turned his head towards him and touched his hat as a friendly gesture. 'Eyes front, sir,' the colonel barked, 'none of your damned politeness in the ranks.' The offended merchant sulked. And when he learned that he had been placed on the roster for guard duty that night, he indignantly announced that he would be damned before he would obey. His obstinacy was duly reported to his 'house guest'. Harry said, 'Then put him in the guard house till further orders.' After sitting in a prison cell for a couple of days, the merchant-volunteer humbly petitioned to be allowed to return to duty.

Actually, Harry spent most of his time at the government offices, sleeping not more than four hours a night after downing a large draught of porter. He told his wife:

I am an absolute monarch. I sit on a throne almost while my A.D.C. ushers in those who wish to see me, but the work I have done altogether in two days I scarcely believe myself, whom I have astonished, as well as *every other* person.

Harry despised his second in command, Henry Somerset. There was a natural rivalry between them. Somerset, eldest son of Lord Charles Somerset, the former governor, was a direct descendant of John of Gaunt, with the features of a Plantagenet stamped on his face. He had grown up as a page to King George III at St James's Palace. An accomplished horseman, he was with the 10th Hussars in the Peninsula and served as A.D.C. to his uncle, Lord Robert Somerset, during

II

the Waterloo campaign. In 1823 he commanded the Cape
Corps as a major and continued to command after it became
the Cape Mounted Rifles (C.M.R.) in 1827. (The unit was
officered by whites with mostly Hottentots in the ranks.)
His knowledge of the terrain and frontier tribes was second to
none. His policy of firmness and tactics of vigilance in dealing
with Africans, who called him 'Hawk's-eye', made him
immensely popular with many of the settlers. Naturally,
Somerset was resentful of Smith who, with no experience on
the frontier, had been given the command over him.

To Harry 'Hawk's-eye' was an incompetent who owed his
rise to political intrigue and aristocratic connections in the
army, which included his uncle Lord Fitzroy Somerset. He
feared his influence with the Horse Guards and complained
of nepotism in the C.M.R. which Somerset officered with his
sons, sons-in-law and other relatives. Fortunately, he confided
to Juana,

> that little devil Somerset is a contemptible wretch as much
> afraid of *me* as of *responsibility*. His *conduct* has been *puny*,
> *more like a schoolboy* than a man of any *sort of energy* — in
> short they wanted a fellow who could swear a bit and who,
> thank God, bears responsibility as carelessly as, 'Ah,' the
> *dear old Duke himself*.

Nonetheless, Harry had to admit that 'the fellow knows how
to squib about in the bushes capitally'. To inhibit Somerset's
machinations, he kept him as busy as possible chasing about the
frontier. When Harry heard that 'creature Somerset' was
trying to turn the Boers against him he was furious. 'But as
I keep the key of the Gov^t Grog Shop,' he assured his wife, 'he
won't succeed, and I give them every now and then a glass of
grog to drink the King's health.'

Contending that the number of invaders had been exaggerated
by Somerset and others, and that nothing would restore morale
more quickly than to seize the initiative, Harry pressed the
enemy with a few hundred men that were available. As he
explained to Juana, 'it is like fox-hunting; it is all forward,
forward, ah, and *straight forward*, too.'

He promised to 'kick the Kaffirs alive everywhere'. Formidable Fort Willshire, which he felt had been shamefully
abandoned, was reoccupied along with other posts on the

border to help cut off the marauders' retreat. Somerset, with a hundred of his C.M.R. and 200 burghers, struck south and to the rear to restore communications with Algoa Bay and harass the enemy; 60 of the latter were killed. Another small column of 300 men under an old brother Rifleman, Major William Cox, now of the 75th, went forward across the Fish river to destroy the kraals (villages) of chiefs Tyalie and Eno. They were soon sent fleeing for their lives. Eno, 'that double-faced old murderer', escaped by exchanging robes with his daughter, who was seriously wounded while drawing the fire intended for her father. Lieut. Alexander Bisset tells how he rushed forward to save her life, for some men 'smarting from the ruin of hearth and home had no idea of taking prisoners'.

The column under Cox went on deep into the heart of the enemy's country to rescue missionaries and their families, which was accomplished with little opposition. 'This rescue,' Harry recalled, 'was the best thing I ever did during the war, but one which these holy gentlemen and their societies never acknowledged as they ought, though always ready to *censure*.'

As Harry anticipated, nothing would make an enemy laden with spoils, mostly cattle, retire so quickly as a threat to his own territory. By the time the governor arrived on 20 January, peace and order had been restored to most of the eastern province and 400 of the enemy were counted as dead. Harry soon considered the area so safe that when the postmaster asked him for escorts, he 'blew him up and called him an ass'.

In a general order D'Urban lauded Harry's 'indefatigable and most able exertion'. In an official communication to Lord Fitzroy Somerset, the governor repeated his praise and recommended that Harry Smith be promoted to full colonel. Harry wrote to Juana, 'I have gained credit for two things: one, licking the Kaffirs; another, blowing up the lazy rascals who will neither work, fight, nor do anything but draw rations.' More of the enemy might have been destroyed in a 'grand coup', he added, had he not been thwarted by Somerset who let them slip through his fingers.

Harry was eager to launch an offensive into enemy territory as soon as possible. However, '*slow* and *caution*' were the order of the day after His Excellency came on the scene. 'I plainly perceive,' Harry groaned, '*my* watch *loses time*.' D'Urban heartily approved a punitive campaign, but refused to be hurried. 'When things do not fly like lightning,' Harry told Juana, he longed for the domestic life with his 'dear old wife'. On learning that she was suffering from rheumatism, he wished that he were there to massage her 'beautiful legs'.

Concentrating his surplus energy in organizing the burghers, he found them pathetically lacking in one or more essentials such as shoes, shirts and saddles. 'But yet,' he observed, 'when the poor fellows thus dragged from their homes are in the field, they are good-humoured and willing to shoot well enough.' After instilling in them the simple duties of soldiering, he tried to teach them some of the elementary manoeuvres of regular cavalry, but there was such confusion and tumbling of men and horses that he abandoned the idea.

An additional two battalions, each 400 strong, was raised among the aboriginal Hottentots, a tawny-coloured race with Mongoloid features. Captain King pictured them as 'very short and slightly made, lean, and with ugly yellow monkey-looking faces, very prominent cheek bones, small turned-up noses, and little twinkling cunning eyes, and invariably wearing European garments.' They had been drastically reduced in numbers when the Europeans introduced smallpox and liquor. Those whose blood was mixed with the whites were called Griquas, or more coarsely, Bastaards. Except for the inhabitants of southern France, Harry claimed there was no people on earth with 'such a natural turn to become soldiers'. The high-spirited little men quickly took to riding and shooting. Their sharp eyes and natural aptitude for tracking made them almost indispensable auxiliaries in bush warfare. Harry grabbed 'every loose vagabond he could lay his hand on'.

Under Governor Cole 3,000 vagrant Hottentots were settled as a buffer in the ceded area along the fertile Kat river, a land from which Macomo and his tribe had been expelled. As Macomo believed that they would join him as marauders, they were not molested by his warriors during the invasion. Many indeed wavered but in the end most supported the government. 'Their presence in the army,' observed Harry, 'greatly dismayed the Kaffirs who never believed they would fight against them.'

According to a contemporary, Harry admired not only the soldierly qualities of the Hottentots but also the shapeliness of their women. Harry would be the first to admit that he noticed attractive women of any colour. In response to Juana's curiosity about the women in Grahamstown, however, he assured her, 'You are in no danger, alma mia, of being supplanted. This is the most dull, stupid and horrid place on earth, celebrated for the most ugly of the *fair* sex.'

In 1819 the Xhosas had permitted an invading British army to cross into their land and had then fallen upon them from the rear. Before the general advance, therefore, Harry was determined to clear the dense bush along the Fish river border where large parties of the enemy were reported to be lurking. A force of 300 men was given the task under Lieut.-Col. England, a Canadian-born Irishman whose father was an influential general. For two days England blundered about the bush doing little more than burning huts and capturing a few head of cattle. All the while, looking on from safe seclusion were hundreds of the enemy under the wily Macomo himself. England rode back to Grahamstown and complained to Harry that he needed more troops. Amazed that England would desert his command, he took him to D'Urban, who received him coldly and rejected the request.

After the errant colonel left, His Excellency turned to Harry and shook his head, 'God, he has had a licking, and what the devil made him leave his troops? Smith,' he continued, 'this check must be immediately repaired, and you must go yourself. Take with you what you deem sufficient, and lose no time.'

Harry was engaged in despatching reinforcements when Major Cox came to him and spoke of how offended England was that he had been replaced. Privately, Harry 'did not give a straw' for England who, if he had any sense would have been 'ashamed of himself'. Amused by the situation, Harry decided to go to the governor and tell him that England was hurt and, in part, blamed him for his replacement. It was a foolish thing to do. D'Urban was clearly partial to Harry and most indulgent regarding his flippancy, but this time he had gone too far.

His Excellency angrily told Harry, who had never before experienced his wrath, 'I have decided on what I consider the service demands.' In a subdued voice Harry fibbed, 'It was only to serve another, sir.' — 'Yes,' was the reply, 'at the risk of public service.' Nor did England appreciate Harry's 'intervention on his behalf'. More than ever he nursed a grudge against him.[1]

The cleansing operation in the Fish river area began in 'tempestuous rain and wind' on 7 February. The little army of 1,200 men (800 mounted) was divided into three columns of equal strength. The middle column, mainly infantry with several guns, under Harry's immediate command, was to cross at Trompeter's drift and make a broad frontal attack. Meanwhile, the right column (Somerset's) would ford at Kaffir's drift some fifteen miles downstream, while farther upstream the left column (England's) would pass over the river at Commatty's drift. The flanking columns were to move forward and then inwards to cut off the enemy's retreat.

England did not approve of this plan. He scoffed at the idea of catching the enemy with infantry. 'Yes, Colonel,' said Harry emphatically, 'I intend it, and *you shall too.*' But England made up his mind to do nothing of the kind. The campaign was hardly under way when he sent a request to Harry to be allowed to return to Grahamstown. Harry replaced the 'inglorious England' with Major Gregory of the 98th, who happened to be on leave from Cape Town.

Another unforeseen development was the sudden rise of the Fish, normally a shallow, lazy stream. For three days Harry waited, not daring to pit men or animals against a raging, roaring river fed by torrential downpours.

For Harry, war had outgrown battlefields, and he was eager to test tactics in the guerilla warfare peculiar to the Cape frontier. The terrain, which he reconnoitred from a hill overlooking the Fish, told him that the enemy enjoyed a great advantage. Densely wooded and thicketed ground facilitated the defence and complicated the attack. Divested of impedimenta the Xhosas, strong and vigorous in body, could slip through the bush, going where they liked and moving at least twice as fast as regular troops whose scientific appliances were an encumbrance that confined them to narrow trails and footpaths. The enemy was rarely seen except when they

---

[1] In the edited version of Harry's autobiography, Col. England is not mentioned by name but referred to as 'Colonel Z———'. England's subsequent command as general in the Crimean War added little to his reputation. Captain Robert Portal, who served under him, called him a 'terrible fool' who never knew his own mind and took 'an age to get his Division into position'.

scouted a hillside or skimmed along the top. They carefully avoided a pitched battle, preferring to skirmish under cover after springing some cunning artifice that gave them a decided advantage. Harry knew that they were not deficient in courage. Rather than surrender, they would fight fiercely when hemmed in or protecting their cattle. Operating against such a foe, Harry concluded, was like hunting dangerous wild animals.

'The great science of war,' Harry advised D'Urban, 'is to adopt its principles to the enemy you have to contend with and the nature of the country.' Once across the flooded river, he would apply the methods of the old Light Division, which demanded the utmost mobility by sacrificing as many provisions and as much equipment as was feasible. They must move swiftly and hit hard. To prevent small parties from being cut off, a favourite tactic of the Xhosas, he called for unflagging vigilance and cautioned against patrols extending too great a distance from their support. Under no circumstances would he allow the initiative to pass to the enemy. But fighting in the bush must be avoided, for that resulted in a mere test of animal strength and instinct in which the European had no advantage.

On the evening of the 11th the centre column ascended the rugged hills. Col. Smith appeared to be everywhere, his driving, inflexible spirit and example (at one point in the campaign he stayed in the saddle for 26 hours) moving his men through natural obstacles hitherto considered impregnable.

At dawn the alarmed tribesmen and their cattle were driven into open ground. Some of the enemy were armed with muskets, but they lacked the skill to use them properly. The cannon opened fire and the enveloping flanking columns closed in. Troopers rushed up and down short cuts to intercept the now fleeing enemy. Harry wrote to Juana:

> It was a great scene, the screeching of the Kaffirs, their whistling, their women, their dogs, their cattle bellowing. Oh! the noise, the firing in every direction, our guns in action — such an uproar I never witnessed.

Since the enemy had no capital or large population centre to capture and hold, Smith ordered his men to burn their huts, without injuring the women and children, and seize that which they prized most — their cattle. 'This Kaffir war is nothing else than looking for and lifting cattle,' observed Harry. To get an idea of what it was like, Harry suggested that Juana read Walter Scott's tales of the Scottish border: 'You gallop in and half by force, half by stratagem, pounce upon them wherever you can find them; frighten their wives, burn their homes, lift their cattle, and return home quite triumphant.'

Over 2,000 cattle were taken, along with sizeable flocks of sheep and goats. Twenty-five women belonging to chief Bushani were taken; later, as the force marched away, Harry released them and gave them a fat calf. 'Oh, such a kissing of my poor left hand!' Juana was told; 'I thought the poor wretches would have pulled my arm off.'

There was a body count of 73 enemy dead. How many more were wounded or had died in the bush could not be ascertained. It was the Xhosa custom to remove the recently dead, but corpses that had become rigid were left behind.

Three days later, on the 14th, Harry struck again. Though the main body of invaders had already retired towards the Amatola mountains, some 30 more were killed and more livestock was taken.

Smith's loss during the campaign was twelve killed and eleven wounded. It would have been less but for an untoward incident one night when a sleeping 72nd Highlander had his hand stepped on by a horse. He sprang to his feet shouting 'Kaffirs!' Two companies had awakened and commenced firing on each other. Before their officers could stop the panicked men, four had been mortally wounded.

An elated Harry Smith wrote to his wife, 'In four days, I have done what no expedition heretofore in the Kaffir wars *dared ever attempt* and I have beaten an immense number of the enemy.' He had demonstrated to the enemy that regardless of how difficult the ground it could not stop his punitive columns. And he was pleased by the way his men adapted themselves in suffocating heat to bush fighting. The Hotten-tots, in particular, whom Harry now called 'my children', courageously persevered over all obstacles. D'Urban compli-mented his energetic colonel and issued a general order congratulating the troops on their 'complete success'.

Typically, Harry magnified his achievements. His operations beyond the Fish undoubtedly damaged the morale of the enemy, but there was no solid evidence to support his claim that the region had been cleared of the invaders. It is more probable that they had found places of concealment in that extensive tract. Wherever they came from, now that Harry's columns were withdrawn, hundreds were ambushing his patrols and were even so bold as to make an unsuccessful attack on the Hottentots, now considered by the Xhosa as their enemies, in the Kat river settlements. These raids Harry attributed to delay on D'Urban's part, for, as he told Juana, 'wherever we show our noses they will show their tails'.

Once the invasion of Kaffraria was under way, Harry believed the war would be over in a matter of days. But D'Urban insisted on fussing over details. Exasperated, Harry complained, 'I wish my master would be broad awake and finish this slow, tedious and really uninteresting business.' D'Urban worked at his desk all day, including Sundays, Harry wrote to Juana, but he was 'always floundering in the midst of information', much of it supplied by that 'great alarmist Somerset — the damnedest ass on earth'. Though His Excellency was most kind to him, 'this delay is intolerable ... I shall die of *Ennui* ... my hair has grown grey.'

When Harry rode off at the beginning of March to inspect the advance base at Fort Willshire, D'Urban sent a long letter after him advising him that he was in too much of a hurry; he then made a list of what Harry described as 'twenty little silly things with trifling remarks, all of which I have most *vivaciously answered*, and [he] has each time answered right, very right, I was sure it must be so.' Harry penned a no less lengthy message 'with *nine* potent reasons why delay must not be allowed — which I think has touched his honour.' Harry vowed to his wife, 'I will not give way to him. Although I will do all in my power to serve my country, yet no one shall make a tool of me.'

Surely, His Excellency was not himself, thought Harry. He suspected that he was under great pressure from the colonial office, which severely criticized him for the enormous sums he was spending on the war. Back in Grahamstown on 6 March to lead the first troops to Fort Willshire, Harry met with his chief several times and he appeared terribly confused. 'He at one time today did not wish me to go tomorrow, then he urged it, then he was against it, and so on — that I was quite bored.' Yet, despite their differences, it was a combination that worked well: D'Urban ably organized the forces while Smith led them with boldness and imagination.

To escape a desk clogged with paper, Harry busied himself galloping back and forth to Fort Willshire, 45 miles away, and reconnoitring the land beyond. He delighted in racing his fine Swellendam horse and sleeping under an open sky. Bivouacking with his guides and escort gave him an opportunity 'to unbend and not act always the great man', he told Juana. One morning he told his bugler to blow the 'rouse'. He did not know it. 'Damn you, sir,' said Harry, 'blow something.' So he blew a quadrille and Harry began to dance. He thought that Captain Halifax of the 75th 'would have laughed till he died'. Reflecting on the incident, Harry commented: 'What a burlesque upon our school of war!'

As officers and men came forward to the staging area near Fort Willshire, Harry gave a lesson in the art of war. He provided horses for those Boers who needed them and drilled their captains, who were quick to learn. 'I wish I could speak Hollands. I can't, therefore, I drink it [gin],' he punned. When angry he instructed his secretary to the burghers, Andrews, to curse them in their language for him. The colonel was, nevertheless, popular with the Boers. He provisioned them generously, fed them well and gave them grog. Only the Hottentots ate more. According to Captain James Alexander, they could consume six pounds of meat and two loaves of bread at one sitting.

The field commandants were 'capital' when it came to fighting. There was Greyling, Nels, the hatchet-faced 85-year-old veteran Linde, the powerfully built Rademeyer with his bushy black whiskers, who had fought like a demon, hand to hand, when his party was ambushed at Trompeter's pass. There was wily old Van Wyk, old enough to recall how frequently and quickly the British changed their policy towards the blacks. When Harry met him at Grahamstown at the beginning of the war, he asked for a licence. 'A licence for what?' Harry demanded. — 'To shoot Kaffirs, mynheer.' Irritated, Harry informed him that there was a war on and he could shoot as many as he liked. The sturdy Boer shook his head and said: 'I know better than that. I may get myself shot by the government if I do that and all my property confiscated.' Harry became angry and began to shout. Van Wyk stood his ground saying, 'But I must have it in black and white before I draw a trigger.' In the end he got his licence signed by Col. Smith, stating that he could shoot Kaffirs wherever he could find them. Sometimes the Boers could be a nuisance. One 'young, big fat Dutchman' had the temerity to go to the colonel's tent to tell him that he had no blanket and that he was very wet. What should he do? 'Go to the devil and warm yourself you spooney,' cried Harry. 'Make a fire and sing over it. I have given you grog. Why, I never had a blanket campaigning for ten years. You want pluck, sir. Be off.'

Another, he told Juana, 'a great fat stupid-looking Boer', came to his quarters with a request. At first neither Harry nor Andrews could understand him. Finally he mumbled in low voice that he wanted to see his 'vrouw'. Feeling as much distress over that subject as the burgher, Harry said, 'I want to go home to my vrouw but by God I can't. No more shall you. Go to your camp and get ready to shoot Kaffirs.'

'Ah Venus and Mars,' Harry sighed. 'Enough of the latter.' That homesick Boer made his own loneliness more poignant. He said longingly:

Always think of my dear old woman. I feel a void which no tongue can tell or words express, and my Juana stands before me in every shape that I have ever seen her and all combine to make me love her, think of her, *only once dream* (*hang it*) of her — but then I go to bed so tired, not *fatigued*, never that, I sleep like a sailor and I am again as fresh as ever.

By mid-March his letters became longer, laced with passages in Spanish as well as English delineating his great love and devotion. Juana puzzled over his handwriting and his Spanish. In response to her finding fault with his use of her mother tongue, Harry waggishly observed, ''tis you have forgot your own language and not I how to write it.'

Repeatedly her husband spoke of how much he wished she were by his side and reminisced over their happy Peninsular days. He had enough of sleeping alone and the company of men only. 'I have just had a nice bit of wood put on my fire,' he wrote wistfully. 'Oh that you were sitting with me — whereas that ugly beast Balfour [his A.D.C.] is warming his behind at it.'

Juana took him at his word. When she told Enrique she was making plans to join him, he was affectionately blunt. 'So you think *you* could campaign again. I doubt it *old woman*. You would be very much *tired*—think of the *size* and weight you are.' Anyway, Harry promised that the war would be over in a matter of days. When Juana was understandably hurt by his words, Harry lamely tried to make a joke of the matter by writing back, 'if you were, like me, *young*, I should like to have you with me, God knows.' In truth, Harry exhibited the energy of a man half his age. He had his baggage arranged so that in five minutes he could depart for anywhere.

To keep the enemy off balance and provide cattle for an army that was rapidly consuming his forward provisions, Harry took a strong patrol of 400 burghers and 20 C.M.R. out on the morning of 26 March to thrust beyond the Umdazini river some 35 miles away. In twenty hours he returned, having burned 600 huts and captured 1,200 head of cattle. Only one man was wounded, with an assegai—through the rump.

Harry was taken with the beauty of the country he had seen— fertile, well-watered with large forest trees. He told Juana that he intended to have a big grant of land. 'It may do for our children, but *I shall* never *live* upon it with my dear old woman, but sell it probably.' Ever the optimist, after 23 years of a childless marriage with a wife now 37 years old, he still hoped for an heir.

The governor arrived towards the end of March and the field force, 'as highly organized as such a mob of armed inhabitants could be', was ready to move. The 2,000 men (nearly 800 mounted) were divided into four divisions that would advance in column. The original plan, as Harry described it was:

Left	*Left-Centre*	*Centre*	*Right*
Van Wyk	Major Cox	Me myself &	Col. 'ass'
(4th Division)	(3rd Division)	Sir Slow as	(2nd Division
		he goes	under
		(1st Division)	Lieut.-Col.
			Somerset)

'Proud as a Peacock, Lt.-Col. England is to command the ordinary frontier posts and Grahamstown with 1,800 men.'
D'Urban objected to Harry's command of a division on the

grounds that it cramped his power. He ordered that Harry be second in command, continuing as chief of staff. The 1st Division was given to Peddie, who soon grumbled that all of his officers looked up to Col. Smith and not to him. After making an effort to be on good terms with Peddie, Harry concluded, 'the man is an ass and I see I must kick him in order.' On discovering that the one-armed colonel had a taste for liquor, Harry told Juana, 'If he bores me I will stop his grog in *no time*.'

Harry feared that D'Urban might not go very far into Xhosa territory. But when he queried His Excellency on the matter, he was told firmly, 'All the way!'

[8]

The War on Hintza

In planning a war against an uncivilized nation ... your first object should be the capture of whatever they prize most.

Lord Wolseley

It was a motley collection of soldiers that stepped into Kaffraria. They resembled a band of ruffians rather than an army. All the more so in that day, for the sartorial traditions of the tailor king, George IV, still prevailed throughout the British army.

Dashing ahead of the centre column 'to sniff out' the enemy were the native scouts dressed in ornaments that enhanced rather than covered their nakedness.

The Swellendam burghers under Linde rode out in front. They wore broad-brimmed slouch hats and ill-fitting, slovenly clothes of the coarsest material. They carried flint-guns resembling wall-pieces, with great powder horns swinging from their hips. Strapped to their mounts was a sheepskin blanket, biltong (dried meat), and other essentials. Each led a second horse, and some a third horse carrying a little Hottentot servant perched on top like a monkey. The bearded Boers cursed the 'verdoemde Kaffirs!' In turn, Harry would now and then 'blow the fellows up in Dutch (that is my Dutch)', causing D'Urban to hold his sides from laughter. 'I am their man,' he told Juana proudly. 'Somerset has lost most completely their confidence.'

Behind the burghers rode the C.M.R., mostly Hottentots outfitted in dark-green caps and jackets contrasting with their clay-coloured leather pantaloons. Seated on light dragoon saddles, they seemed attached to their hardy little horses. The illusion was heightened by the double-barrelled carbines they often carried across their thighs.

The governor and his chief of staff with their escorts followed. Sir Benjamin wore an oilskin shako and a close-

158

fitting plain blue coat. Harry had a duffle-jacket, sent to him by Juana, and soft brown boots. The staff officers provided a touch of the picturesque, usually having in common a long-backed blue or green jacket. Harry boasted four 'real good horses', one to ride, the others carrying only saddles or fodder. (Four more horses were added later during the campaign.)

Col. Smith's escort consisted of a dozen burghers armed with double-barrelled guns. They watched over him like hawks; wherever he went they surrounded him. At night they mounted sentry over him. Harry had two Hottentot soldier-servants, 'Old Japps, whose very hallao would frighten a Kaffir if his shot did not', and Sgt Manie, who was not well. He nearly died a few days later. 'Poor fellow,' wrote Harry, 'he has never been really the same since that gallop I gave him to Grahamstown.'

The colonel also had the services of a corps of eight 'perfect' guides under Captain Richard Southey. The guides were made up entirely of British colonists whose homes had been destroyed. Crack shots with expert knowledge of the frontier, they were eager to come to grips with the marauders. Southey's men were distinguished by ostrich plumes in their large hats. Those with D'Urban wore a strip of leopard skin on their wide-awakes.

Next in line were the regulars, the 72nd marching to bagpipes. The chief of staff had ordered them to leave their pipe-clay belts behind and to substitute a small pouch for the large cartridge box they normally carried. Their forage caps ended in a large red leather peak, which, Harry wrote, 'makes every man look exactly as if he had sore eyes'. Their red coats were an excellent target in the bush, but Harry felt they served as a reminder to the enemy of a great Power beyond the seas.

The first battalion of Hottentot recruits, officered by 'gentle-men on half pay and respected settlers', were provided with black jackets, trousers and little low-crowned hats. As many bayonets as possible were found for their bright-barrelled muskets, but they soon tossed them into the bush. Feckless and light-hearted, they chattered day and night, almost, but not quite as bad, observed Harry, as the Portuguese. And when they were not talking, they were singing. They soon took to echoing Harry's favourite tune, 'The Girl I Left

Behind Me'. Some of Harry's party soon began to wish that he had taken Juana with him.

To the rear was the royal artillery with six guns (which the Africans called 'fire wagons'), 170 ammunition and provision wagons, and a hundred mounted Boers acting as the rearguard. Each wagon was drawn by twenty bullocks driven by Africans whom Harry had selected. When most compact, the line of march extended over three miles. It took over two hours to pass a given point. Expecting difficulty, Harry took great pains in organizing their movements. Because of his efforts and the excellence of the oxen no serious problems developed during the campaign. Pilfering was kept to a minimum. (Just before the march began, two leaders of the wagons were caught tapping the spirits. Having no time for a court-martial, Harry ordered 50 lashes for each.)

Having described the appearance of the column to Juana, Harry wrote, 'In short, we have costumes of every dye', including 'Kittie' Dutton, the commander's military secretary, who strutted about the camp 'in the paraphernalia of a Kaffir Chieftain's wife or mother'. All the men, he concluded, were badly in need of soap, for 'if we judge from their appearance very few of them make any use of the latter — such dirty brutes as the Boers are I never saw ... In any other country disease would conquer us altho' the Kaffirs cannot.'

All day Harry dashed back and forth along the line singing out 'a very great number of agreeable airs from the irate, civil, ludicrous and probably abusive all in one breath'. By the next day he was reduced to 'whispering and swearing exclusively for my own amusement'.

The weather was perfect. The country was beautiful with fields of ripening maize and millet, and sweet pastures. 'Why,' asked the volunteers, 'do these people plunder our country while theirs is a gardenland?'

Although there was evidence that the region supported a large population, none of the enemy were to be seen. They found only the dead body of one warrior with a leg torn off by some wild animal. He had obviously been shot in a previous skirmish with Col. Smith's patrol. That the hills beyond, however, were alive with warriors was indicated by fire signals and smoke announcing the column's approach.

D'Urban had visions of fighting an old-fashioned, stand-up

battle based upon his experience in the Peninsula. If the enemy refused a pitched battle, his columns would flush them out. While his centre column with the wagon train moved straight on to the Buffalo river, Somerset on the right and Van Wyck on the far left would advance rapidly with their mounted burghers and sweep the enemy in towards the centre. The slower-moving left centre under Cox would clear its designated area while protecting the rear. But aside from the capture of 1,100 cattle and the burning of kraals, there was little actual fighting. The enemy had apparently retired to natural strongholds along the upper Buffalo.

The chief of staff protested against these tactics. He adhered to his maxim: 'Wherever I hear of a Kaffir so soon will *I be at him.*' He argued that their warriors had no more than a hundred muskets and no ammunition—'and a gun does not go off very cleverly without it'. Such a policy as Harry advocated, however, was far too daring and hasty for D'Urban to accept. Commenting on Harry's efforts, he would say, 'Ah that was done in a hurry.' To which Harry would laughingly reply, 'It was *done well.*'

Juana said that her husband was always honest. Not quite. To avoid a head-on clash with His Excellency, which at times engendered heat, Harry tried a different tack: 'When he asks my opinion I chalk out a new course altogether most *extravagant.* I then give in half, so that I approach obtaining what I want.' Of course, he confided to Juana, he hoped the master would grow tired of the campaign 'and leave me to myself—when, whether things go right or wrong, I will have my own way. And I will make some who do not *go where the Kaffirs are* not where they are *not.*'

He was referring to Somerset. When he left his camp he had nearly 1,000 men, yet he deliberately sidestepped a brush with the enemy in the same area Harry had devastated some days before with a force only half that of Somerset's. When the centre column camped at the head of the Buffalo river on 6 April, Somerset rode in and told Harry he had seen a large number of warriors in the hills. 'Where?' asked Harry as he opened his telescope. Scanning the spot indicated by Somerset's finger, he saw nothing but little bushes. 'This is the way these spoonies go on,' Harry bristled, 'everything is Kaffir, Kaffir, Kaffir; whilst I am hunting them and can scarcely find them.'

12

The next day Harry had his wish. Offering D'Urban the
excuse that he should take a strong patrol to meet the 3rd
and 4th Divisions that were converging on the camp, he
ventured up into the nearby mountains with 420 men, trusting
solely to chance in finding the enemy. 'Wonderfully favoured',
Harry had 'the prettiest affair by far of any in the war'.

The enemy, some 600 strong with thousands of cattle, were
ensconced in what they fancied were unassailable heights.
Captain Murray with the light company of the 72nd moved
forward and upwards, while three companies of Hottentots
were sent around to cut off an enemy retreat. As the Highlanders neared the craggy citadel, the defenders jumped up
and shouted defiance. They fired their muskets, using zinc
stripped from farmers' houses as bullets, and hurled assegais
and stones upon them. Five Scots were wounded and Murray
himself was hit. He fought on, unaware of his wound until
one of his men shouted, 'There's ane of them things sticken'
in ye, sir.' Only then did he notice an assegai protruding from
below his ribs.

Try as they might, however, the Highlanders were unable
to ascend any farther. Reminded that this day, the 7th of
April, was the anniversary of the day he had 'a good licking
in Badajoz breaches', Harry decided as had the Duke, to try
something else. 'By God,' he swore, 'I'll have them out yet.'
Searching the rocks above, he found what appeared to be a
practical approach to the top. (He later learned it was the only
one by which they could dislodge the enemy.) The Highlanders, reinforced by a company of Hottentots, pulled one
another up by their muskets and then broke through. With
more Hottentots coming up from the rear, the enemy expended
what little powder they had left and fled under chief Eno,
leaving behind 35 dead. Others were later found who had
jumped to their death from the precipices. The fleeing enemy
left 4,000 cattle behind.

To Harry the affair was an important *coup*. And it happened
on the anniversary of 'that which led to our *blessed union*'.
D'Urban was 'overjoyed'. Murray, a close friend who often
shared Harry's tent, soon recovered. The mountain henceforth
bore his name.

Thousands of captured cattle were now milling round the
camp. 'The noise the devils make is intolerable,' complained

Harry. According to his tally, he had now recovered 10,000 head. If an old law still applied whereby the captors received a dollar a head, it would be 'a pretty thing for my old lady'. (Juana asked John Bell and he informed her that the law had been repealed.) Since his name was Smith and the names of officers in his force were being given to geographical features in this new land, Harry suggested that he might at least be rewarded by having the entire country named 'Smithfield Market'.

Special escorts were organized to return the herds to the colony and, above all, to prevent their theft. To the colonists and the Africans, who were both basically cattle farmers, they represented wealth. Cattle were not only the chief source of riches to the African but, even more than to the Europeans, they represented status. They rarely ate them except on ceremonial occasions. The price of a bride, determined by beauty and social standing, was paid in cattle to her father. Black or white, raiding another's cattle was considered legitimate practice. The loss of a herd could be more painful than the loss of a home or family.

To overtake the dispersed enemy and their herds before they reached the Kei river, beyond which lay the land of paramount chief Hintza,[1] who had remained neutral, Harry urged the governor to push forward with all possible speed. He suggested that the centre column and Somerset's go on straight to the Kei, the latter along a route close to the sea, while Cox and Van Wyk remained behind in the Ciskei to hunt stragglers and thwart any combination that might threaten their communications.

But D'Urban did not want to take any risks. He still thought in terms of general action and, therefore, rejected the idea of dividing his forces as dangerous. As Harry put it, he was 'too scientific ... always full of combinations, reserves, rears and fronts, and too cautious of dangers and faults. The greatest fault one can be guilty of is dash, and yet it is the only thing.' The way D'Urban was conducting the war, Harry opined, 'he will never catch a Kaffir as long as he lives, unless he is inoculated with my guerilla rabidity'.

Harry used all the powers of persuasion at his command,

---

[1] Hintza was theoretically the king of the whole Xhosa nation, whereas in fact he ruled only over the Gealeka tribe beyond the Kei.

without 'assuming towards him a dictatorial manner, and God knows my manner is *"brusque"* enough', and finally his plan was approved. Then again pondering the perils involved, D'Urban countermanded his orders. A lively discussion followed, after which the governor yielded to Harry's views. Then, after two days of short marches, His Excellency called a halt to rest his men and wait for Somerset to come up. Harry remonstrated to no avail. 'My task is *an awful one*,' he wrote to Juana that day (13 April). 'Often do I leave him all prepared to do what I recommend, often do I *return* and *find him quite changed* and *funking* the *responsibility* in a way that *astonishes me*.'

Resolved to act rather than argue, at daybreak on the 15th, Col. Smith appeared with the advance guard before the governor's tent. 'What are your orders, sir?' he asked deferentially. D'Urban said wearily but politely, 'Pray, don't wait for me, Smith, go on.' The entire column soon followed Harry in the descent to the Kei eleven miles away. Harry's next project regarding the governor was to 'stir him up a bit to push into Hintza's Country', he confided to Juana. 'I could give him a good dinner every day.'

Was Hintza friendly or did he secretly conspire with Macomo, Tyalie, Eno and other chiefs who had brought so much suffering and destruction to the colony? There was no direct evidence against him, but the settlers were convinced that he was behind all of the mischief and, in fact, they later called the Sixth Frontier War, Hintza's War. That hundreds of his followers had joined in the invasion, Hintza dismissed by saying that he could not control all of his people; as for stolen cattle brought across the Kei, he claimed that he could not identify them.

In an effort to clarify Hintza's position and come to an agreement with him, the governor sent Van Wyk in January to interview the great chief. Hintza, however, was eloquently evasive. Subsequent messages elicited from him were no less vague. Meanwhile, rumour fed suspicion that he was engaged in clandestine acts of hostility such as the burning of the Methodist missionary station at Butterworth and the murder of a trader.

Exhortations by Harry finally had their effect upon D'Urban, who agreed to confront Hintza with force so as to conclude a satisfactory understanding. Before crossing the Kei, Sir

Benjamin assured Hintza that he did not come with hostile intentions but, unless the colonial cattle driven into his land were returned, he would treat him as an enemy. They would soon make 'the old rascal do whatever we desire of him', Harry promised Juana. 'It is lucky he has not had me to deal with; long ago would I have pounced upon him.'

Riding down to the Kei, Harry saw that the hills beyond were thick with warriors. 'The more there were,' he recalled, 'the more I pushed on.' At the ford, with two pistols in his belt (and a little knit cap on his head from Juana which made him appear as 'something between a Dover smuggler and Robinson Crusoe') he was challenged by a sentinel: 'Hallo, English, do you know what river this is? This is Hintza's country. What do you want here?' — 'To speak with Hintza,' answered Harry. 'We don't want to fight you,' he added, not really speaking for himself.

A conference followed with Buku, a brother of Hintza who held land on either side of the Kei. Through Hermanus, the interpreter, Harry explained to the 'cut-throat looking rascal, just like Duke Constantine of Russia', that they had come as friends and, since the great chief had not come to meet the governor, they would march until he presented himself. By now D'Urban had arrived on the scene and appeared to be in agreement, so Harry said to him, 'Now, sir, let us cross immediately.' But then, 'full of two or three little doubts and fears, military precautions, etc.', D'Urban began to waver. After a time, Harry could stand this indecision no longer. 'Mount,' he roared to his escort. 'Now, General,' he declared, 'I will cross, and you will see every fellow fly before me. Then pray send the whole army on.' It happened as Harry had promised.

Marching through the Transkei, officers were directed to tell their men that they were to abstain from all acts of violence. By the 17th they reached the ruined station at Butterworth. Hintza had been given 36 hours to appear. The governor now extended the time limit to five days. The army halted and waited. Still Hintza did not come, only messengers from time to time to say that their great chief would be there in a few hours. Harry suspected, and rightly, that Hintza was using these days of grace to drive the stolen cattle farther eastward.

The general and his chief of staff also fretted over the tardiness of Somerset and the 2nd Division. Ten times in five days orders were sent to hurry him forward. Harry began to think that Somerset had returned to Grahamstown. D'Urban became livid with anger and swore that Somerset was 'fit for nothing but driving cattle'. Somerset arrived on 20 April with 'the *debris*' of his division. Having mismanaged the forage, his mounted force was reduced to walking. Out of 200 C.M.R. only twelve were still riding. At first it looked as if the stragglers coming into camp had sustained a defeat. Somerset's men had lost all confidence in him.

According to Harry, the other colonel, Peddie, had never given his men any confidence to lose. Officers of the 1st Division referred to him as 'Tom Fool' because his behaviour was 'childish, ridiculous and contemptible'. Harry told Juana, 'His Excellency thinks he must be cracked'.

As a ploy to further delay the British, Hintza sent delegates to their camp with words of friendship and gifts of bullocks and stray horses. At one point, Harry had 35 delegates sitting around him. 'Having their karosses thrown off and naked as they were born,' their champion orator spoke of 'the honour of the British nation'. They then came forward one by one and kissed his hands. 'Humbug,' thought Harry.

A special delegation came in on the 19th headed by Hintza's chief minister, Kuba, 'a sharp wolf-like fellow, with the cunning of satan,' wrote Harry, 'and a set of teeth which made me fear he would bite'. Next to him was one of royal blood, a nephew of Hintza's, who was all grace and good manners, and 'carried his head like the Emperor Alexander of Russia'. They came to assure the governor that Hintza was coming, to which Harry replied, the governor had waited *five days* and was not disposed to wait any longer. But Harry was bluffing, for he knew that D'Urban was inclined to give the chief a little more time. 'The Kaffir must be kicked,' was Harry's view. 'Ah, and bullied, too — and then kicked again and they will do whatever is ordered.'

A number of Hottentot deserters who had left Hintza's service began to drift into the camp, which strengthened Harry's argument that the enemy was becoming disheartened. Soldiers watched Col. Smith as he cross-examined one of them. When Harry asked his name, he discovered it was

Henri Smith! 'By Jupiter,' Harry related to Juana, 'how the fellows laughed. However, I had my jaw too by saying "All Smiths are sharp, active-looking fellows, and so is our deserter rascal".'

When D'Urban learned that a despatch rider, Ensign Armstrong, was killed on the 21st of April he considered the truce broken. On the morning of the 24th a 6-pounder was fired eastwards. Harry waved his cap for all to see. The war on Hintza had begun.

At the same time the governor proclaimed the Fingoes to be British subjects. The Fingoes were landless remnants of once powerful tribes that had fled from Natal when the Zulu king, Shaka, conducted a bloody reign of terror in their land. Having lost their tribal cohesion, they became subordinate to Hintza's people, who addressed them as 'dog'. 'And they think no more of sacrificing one,' Harry observed, 'than killing a dog.' The advent of British power afforded them the chance to throw off their servitude. It was D'Urban's plan to settle 17,000 in the Ciskei, which he intended to annex. Meanwhile, as Harry expressed it, 'We will arm all these Fingoes and use them as an instrument of vengeance against their oppressors.'

The inclusion of 400 Fingo warriors provided another hue to the highly variegated force. Harry wished his wife could see them carrying enormous shields, their heads ornamented with fluttering ostrich plumes and pieces of hide cut to resemble horns. As the amused colonel watched, they gave him a war whoop, held their shields and assegais before them and stomped the earth with their heels. Drumming their shields in unison, they sang their war song 'most melodiously in a deep sonorous voice with a most harmonious base'. They danced and sang all that night to celebrate their freedom from bondage.

With practically no sleep, Harry commenced operations early the next morning. The first day he raced in the direction where Hintza was said to be hiding. He did not find him, but a score of the enemy were killed and great herds were taken. Not bothering to return to camp, the persevering colonel swept on the next morning with 300 mounted men; the infantry and Fingo allies, with few halts, brought up the rear, combing the bush for livestock. When Harry spotted some sign of the enemy, he turned to the Hottentots and Fingoes and 'halloed them on like a pack of hounds'. They rushed along the bed of the Kei and then north and east towards the highlands of the Tsomo river where Hintza had a kraal. Harry's movements could best be traced by the rising smoke from burning huts. The enemy was stunned. Hintza himself barely eluded his grasp.

Few commanders ever demonstrated so well how to make use of a small force. In five days, operating over great distances in extreme heat, Harry took upwards of 15,000 cattle with trifling loss to his troops. Having outdistanced their wagons, they ate freshly slaughtered animals. 'Killing and eating after dark,' he told Juana, who was praying that God might turn Hintza's heart, 'is rather a bore'. One morning he was so famished that he 'could have bit a piece out of his wife's shoulder'. He settled for the offer of a half-chewed joint of goat one of his escorts fished out of a dirty haversack, and gnawed it greedily. Without tents, they slept in the open, unprotected from chilling dews. During those arduous days, Harry never shaved or even combed his hair. His one change of clothes was the replacement of pantaloons literally torn off by thorn bushes. 'The labour I have encountered from the morning of the 24th to the afternoon of the 30th,' he wrote to his wife, 'has astonished everybody nay even myself—nearly equal to my ride up from Cape Town.'

The men, too, suffered great hardship, but always before them was their colonel, his cheery enthusiasm propelling them forward. If they looked grave or worn, he would bound towards them to apply his rough wit or sing to them in what he called 'my beautiful voice'.

Cattle-lifting became more like a sport than war. 'This campaign,' recalled Captain Alexander, 'infected us all with cattle mania.' They learned to judge the pasturage, trace the spoor and find the bovine prize.

Hintza had had enough. The very day that Col. Smith brought his men back into camp twenty miles north-west of Butterworth for a much needed rest, three of Hintza's councillors rode in to announce that the great chief wanted peace. 'Why should Hintza die?' they asked. The governor told them that he wished their chief no harm, but that the war would go on unless he would come in to negotiate.

Then he appeared. His great dignity and carriage set him

off from the rest of his party of 50 councillors and women. In one hand he clutched a bundle of assegais, in the other, a whip of buffalo hide. Under his handsome leopard-skin robe, he was naked except for a brass belt and many bracelets and beads. Harry described him as about 45, a 'very good-looking fellow, and his face, though black, the very image of poor dear George IV'. Though somewhat fleshy, he was a fine physical specimen, nearly six feet tall. Hintza had one annoying habit of not looking directly into the eyes of the person he was talking to, a trait which made him appear shifty.

With his customary courtesy, the governor seated him and his councillor Umtini, 'a man of great repute', on camp stools along with Harry and the interpreter, Shepstone (later Sir Theophilus), the 19-year-old son of a missionary. Then in a clear, strong voice D'Urban read his conditions for peace: 50,000 cattle and 1,000 horses to be returned to the settlers, one half within five days, the rest within a year; delivery of the murderers of Purcell (a trader) and Armstrong, with compensation for their families; and an order to Macomo, Tyalie and other Xhosa chiefs to cease their hostilities and turn over their guns. To ensure fulfilment of these terms, two personages would be held as hostages by the governor. Hintza was given 48 hours to consider the matter.

Weighing the terms before giving an answer, Hintza gesticulated with his right hand 'with more actions in his fingers' than Juana, raised and lowered his eyebrows, and then plunged into subtle discourse. He rejected responsibility for the death of the two white men. And, though he was called the great chief of the Xhosas, it was a mere title; he had no way of restraining the chiefs who ravaged the colony. Then, with a sigh of despondency, he tossed his head and said that he would think over the governor's terms.

To the British witnesses, a revoltingly memorable spectacle followed. To celebrate the occasion, Hintza's men ceremoniously slaughtered a fat ox. Having trussed up the animal, the chief butcher made a long incision, causing a portion of the omentum to protrude. This was cut off and thrown on to the fire. It would be offered to a chief. The butcher then thrust his arm into the bellowing animal and tore out the heart, thereby preserving the blood in the meat, which to their taste added flavour and nutrition. To the disgust of the onlookers, many

of whom felt sick, portions of the tortured beast were consumed while it was still in its last convulsions.

Hintza dined with Harry that night. He ate prodigious
amounts of food, most of all Irish stew, but drank only water.
After dinner they discussed politics through the clever but
stone-faced Shepstone. Harry was impressed with the chief's
astuteness and perfect composure. Though Harry was responsible for his defeat and the burning of his kraal, Hintza was
amiable and said he looked upon the colonel as his father.
'How I bullied, threatened, talked and got around *my wily
son!*' wrote Harry. By midnight, the Xhosa chief agreed to the
terms of the treaty and they swore eternal friendship.

Next morning Hintza appeared before the governor's tent.
A great square of soldiers was drawn up for the ceremony.
He ratified the treaty, and of his own volition, offered himself
and his son, Kreli, as hostages. The chief of staff then stepped
forward, declaring himself to be the chief's patron and thus
responsible to the governor for his good behaviour. Hintza
appeared to be highly pleased by this act. He then shook hands
with the general and his patron. D'Urban formally proclaimed
peace and gave the signal for cannon to be fired. Three were
fired in succession.

'To hear those *three guns*,' declared Harry joyously. 'I am
growing a conceited old rascal and somewhat *proud of myself*',
he confessed to Juana. 'Heaven knows the work I have had
since the 1st January.' Everyone congratulated him on the
success that crowned his exertions, 'except that beast Peddie'.
It would be only a matter of time before Macomo and the
other warring chiefs surrendered, for 'our real friend, Hintza',
promised to show him how to put down these enemies.

There was another dinner that night given by the governor.
Hintza's son, who had just arrived, was invited. For entertainment there was a piper strutting about playing, appropriately,
'The Driving of the Steers'. When asked what he thought of
the music, Hintza said he did not understand it. It put him in
mind of his children at home and that made him cry.

Harry became quite fond of Hintza and prided himself on
their friendship. He bestowed on him various gifts and strung
a necklace of glass beads for his son, 'a very fine young man
about 19 or 20'. 'How you would laugh,' he told Juana, 'to
see me walk about the camp with Hintza leaning on my arm.

There is really something very fine and dignified about this
fellow.' Harry presented him with a blanket for his favourite
wife. He had only fifteen, very few considering that Dingaan,
the present Zulu chief, had 'a small detachment' of 2,000. 'If
I had only one old woman!' Harry moaned. How he longed to
sit and talk with his 'dear old gal'. His absence from her
seemed like ten years.

The smell of Hintza was not always pleasant. Like most of
his people, he did not bathe; rather he smeared his body with
a 'sort of butter', an odoriferous perfume 'that made His
Sable Majesty glisten'. Once in a while he 'washed' his hands,
but Harry wished that he used something other than cow
dung, which was also used, when 'of a particular fine quality',
as a poultice by the medicine men.

On the strength of Hintza's solemn promises, the army
began its return march to the Kei on 2 May. While the main
body remained camped at the Kei and waited for the provisions
of the treaty to be carried out, Somerset would go on with
the captured cattle. With him would go most of the Boers,
who would return to their farms and vrouws. Later when the
time came for them to leave, the Boers crowded around the
little English colonel to say farewell. 'Deeply touched,' Harry
wrote, 'God knows, it is with all my heart I say good-bye.'

Buku came in on the 2nd with all the colonial cattle he could
find, *twenty head*, and many more warriors. At the same time
there was news that Fingoes who were still in the Transkei
were being mutilated and massacred by Hintza's men. Young
women, it was said, had had their breasts cut off. D'Urban
was incensed. When confronted, Hintza denied any responsibility for these acts, but he did not help his cause when he
asked, 'What then, are they not my dogs?' Throwing all
courtesy aside, D'Urban had three ropes placed with nooses
dangling from the branch under which Hintza, Kreli and Buku
were sitting. He threatened to hang all three if the murders
did not cease.

As a precautionary measure, the 150 or so warriors loyal
to Hintza now in camp were ordered to give up their weapons.
They hesitated. Harry bawled out orders to a company of
Highlanders to form up in front, and the corps of guides
behind. Intimidated by the sight of the guns levelled at them,
they dropped their assegais with alacrity. Harry 'laughed like

the devil' as he made the disarmed warriors scramble for the tobacco he threw into their midst.

As Hintza was 'still quite the gentleman', he and his relatives were allowed to keep their weapons. But they acted sullen when they dined with Harry that night. Their host succeeded in making them laugh by suggesting that he marry one of the great chief's daughters to 'cement the *holy alliance* of Kaffir and English'. Hintza caused more laughter by stating that he was too old. Changing the mood, the colonel reminded him that since he had said that he was his father, he expected him to behave like a son and obey his commands. Then he slapped Hintza on the back and sang to him. 'I keep him in a constant state of excitement,' he revealed to Juana, 'and he never quite knows what I am about.'

Hintza was capable of providing a little excitement of his own. A powerful looking servant of the chief, half-Hottentot and half Xhosa, came to the colonel's tent that night denouncing his master as a traitor to his people and asking to serve the British. 'I smelt a rat immediately,' Harry wrote to his sister Alice. Unsatisfactory answers to the questions Harry put to him, confirmed his belief that the man was a liar. 'Scoundrel,' Harry said sharply. 'I will teach you how Englishmen treat runaway servants.' He called Sgt Japps and ordered a good flogging, after which the rogue was to be kicked into Hintza's camp. Japps later returned with a large clasp-knife that he had found concealed on the ruffian and repeated his confession that Hintza had sent him to cut the English colonel's throat. Immediately Harry confronted the chief with what had transpired. Hintza, who had already heard the screams of his servant, treated the matter as a joke and grunted, 'Ugh, Hipps will never wish to be your servant again.'

The next night at dinner, Harry put two pistols before him on the table. Rather than one sentry, he had six placed around his tent. After dinner, he shouted, 'Are you there?' As prearranged, the sentries roared out, 'Yes, sir!'—'By heavens the savages were electrified,' Harry remarked. Then he turned to Hintza and delivered a stern lecture. Again the chief promised to abide by the treaty. Harry could not help but like him. 'If Hintza had been educated and bred amongst well disposed Christians,' he observed to Juana, 'he would have been a *very fine fellow*.' He regretted that he had to frighten

and bully him so, but he saw no other way to bend these people
to his will.

During the cold, rainy days of early May the general and
his chief of staff met in the former's tent to work out the
details involved in extending the British Empire in South
Africa to be facilitated by moving the eastern boundary from
the Fish river to the Kei. The new province in the Ciskei
would henceforth be known as the Province of Queen Adelaide.
Harry had been urging the annexation ever since he had
crossed the Fish, which unlike the Kei, was too overgrown,
the dense vegetation affording too much concealment, to
serve as a boundary. To ensure even greater security, it was
decided that irreclaimable Xhosas such as Macomo and his
followers should be expelled beyond the Kei, and to introduce
Fingoes as new settlers. Though they disagreed on minor
points only, D'Urban could not bear a difference of opinion
for long. Often, after Harry had left, D'Urban would send
him a note in which he submitted to his view. Some days,
Harry complained to Juana, the governor had 'one of his con-
founded little bits of paper humours. Every five minutes I
get some frivolous thing or other.' To smooth their relations,
Harry would agree to trifles, 'but generally get my way when
the objection is worth making'.

On the afternoon of the 5th of May Somerset rode in to
interrupt their discussions. He informed the chief of staff
that there was a great enemy commando preparing to attack
him as he crossed the Kei. Harry laughed and ridiculed the
whole idea by saying he would take thirty of his Hottentots
and then kick the whole for him. Sixteen-year-old Charles
Somerset then came to him and asked to go home with his
father. Charles being, in Harry's opinion, as lacking in veracity
and courage as his father, he was glad to be rid of him. 'Well,
thank heaven he is not my son,' he told Juana. 'I would rather
have Hintza, I declare.'

For meritorious service Harry was to be given a large grant
of beautiful and fertile land, rich in timber and granite, with the
Buffalo river running through it. D'Urban assured him that
one day it would be very valuable. But Harry was not interested
in speculation; he planned to sell it in a year or two after
settlers flocked to the new province. Now 47 years old and in
debt, he could not afford to wait.

'*Money is the word,*' he told Juana. There was now a strong possibility that he would remain on the frontier, hopefully as lieutenant-governor of Adelaide. However, he would insist upon £2,000 a year, with a house and forage for ten horses. Otherwise it would not be worth a life of banishment, living in a hovel, risking life and constitution for an extra 2s. 6d. a day, a sum which hardly covered the additional expenses he now had.

But the time to discuss this matter with the governor was not right. D'Urban confessed to Harry that he had no one else that he could trust. 'You must complete our work or all will be lost,' he said. 'You will remain a Colonel on the Staff.' Harry made no reply. As a soldier he believed it was his duty to willingly obey, regardless of the assignment.

The 10th of May 1835 was to be a day of historical significance. With as much fanfare as could be mustered in the wild surroundings on the banks of the Kei, the governor faced west and formally took possession of the new Province of Queen Adelaide in the presence of the paramount Xhosa chief and his relatives. Three British cheers were given and a royal salute of 21 guns was fired. As described by one British officer present, Hintza and his party stood the whole time 'in a profuse perspiration, either in terror or anxiety', which seemed to increase as the echo of each shot reverberated 'from crag to crag till it was lost in the distant windings of the river'. A soft breeze blew the smoke in Hintza's direction and for some minutes he disappeared in a great cloud.

After the smoke lifted, Hintza entered the governor's tent. D'Urban formally admonished him for not having complied with all the conditions of peace. Nine days had elapsed and very few cattle had been brought in. He, therefore, agreed to the chief's repeated request, supported by Col. Smith, to allow him to return to his people to hasten the collection of the required cattle, while Kreli and Buku would stay with him as hostages. Col. Smith, with 500 men, would act in concert with the chief who, though still a hostage, would continue to be treated with the greatest respect and kindness. Privately D'Urban doubted Hintza's sincerity. He warned Harry, 'he meditates his escape.' He agreed that it might be an opportunity in their favour; 'but depend on it, you have undertaken a laborious task.'

Ascending the heights above the Kei, the colonel called

for a halt to rest his advance party. This included the guides (now increased to fifteen to give him greater protection 'for Juana's sake'), Arthur 'Paddy' Balfour, his A.D.C., an interpreter and Hintza's small party. Watching the C.M.R., the Highlanders and Hottentots struggling up the steep ground below them, Hintza wanted to know how he and his subjects stood in relation to Harry. Choosing his words in a deliberate manner so that there would be no misunderstanding, Harry reminded Hintza that he had offered himself as a hostage and had been his guest for nine days. Now, by his own request, the British allowed him, under Harry's command, to return to his land to fulfil the treaty obligations. If his subjects remained peaceable, no harm would come to them. 'However,' he added, 'look upon me as having full power over you, and if you attempt to escape, you will be assuredly shot.' Hintza replied that his sole object was to live up to the terms of the treaty; he had no intention of trying to escape. That he had placed himself entirely in his father's hands was proof of his sincerity. 'Very well, Hintza,' said Harry emphatically, 'act upon this, and I am your friend. Again I tell you, *if you attempt to escape, you will be shot.*'

But the chief's actions aroused suspicion. As Harry's force proceeded along the old road to Butterworth some natives with cattle were reported nearby. Hintza said that they were afraid to come closer, so he sent one of his mounted men to bring them in. Instead, the messenger went off with them and never returned. Harry questioned his hostage closely about his tribesmen's conduct but failed to get a straight answer. As to the route they should take, Hintza said merely, 'We are going right.'

But not fast enough. It appeared to Harry that the cattle were being driven away from him. To overtake them, he marched well into the night and started again at daybreak. They bivouacked near the Guanga late in the afternoon. After eating with Hintza and Umtini, he asked the chief where he was taking them. Hintza told him that their march should lead them to the mouth of the Bashee. This sounded logical to Harry, for there were indications that cattle were moving in that direction. But Harry was taking no chances: while the chief slept close to him, he 'kept a very Light Division watch over him'.

Beginning the next day's march at noon, Harry continued all that night until eight in the morning. Throughout the forced march, he kept a close watch over the chief, which seemed to annoy Hintza. At breakfast the latter peevishly asked, 'What have the cattle done that you want to take them? or why must I see my subjects deprived of them?' These were strange questions, Harry replied. Surely he recalled that at his own request they were searching for cattle that rightfully belonged to the colonists.

On the march later that morning, Hintza resumed the line of questioning he had begun at breakfast. It was Harry's turn to be irritable. 'I do not want your subjects' cattle; I am sent for the colonial cattle which have been stolen, and which I *will have.*' The chief's mood suddenly changed to one of friendly co-operation. He suggested that Umtini be permitted to ride out to tell his subjects that their chief was present and wished them to drive their cattle in. To this seemingly reasonable request the colonel assented.

They continued along a track that Hintza indicated. As an expert in judging horses, Harry noticed that Hintza was riding a remarkably fine horse, a gift from Somerset, 'which he spared fatigue by leading him up any hill we came across'. Harry was out ahead of the column when he heard the pounding of hoofs behind him, accompanied by the cries of the guides who were guarding Hintza. The chief and his men then swept past him on either side of the path. Harry shouted to Hintza, 'Stop!' At the moment the chief's horse became entangled in the bush and returned to the track with difficulty. Harry came up and drew his pistol, 'at which the chief smiled so ingenuously, I nearly felt regret at my suspicions, and I allowed the chief to ride ahead'. Some guides were now moved in front of Hintza to better guard against any break for freedom. They required no instructions in vigilance. These frontiersmen never trusted the chief, 'author of our misery'. In a most unmilitary fashion they had protested to D'Urban the gentle way he dealt with his hostage.

Reaching clear ground on a high river bank, Harry surveyed the region with his telescope. The high ground continued along the Kebaba, descending in a tongue of land about two miles towards a bend in the river where a few huts stood. There were thousands of cattle in the vicinity. He turned around to watch the progress of the column. There was another cry for Harry's attention. Hintza had bolted in another bid for freedom and was already some 50 yards ahead of the guides. Throwing down his telescope, Harry crouched low in his saddle and raced after him along the tongue of land. His was the only horse capable of overtaking the chief's splendid bay. Spurring his horse violently, Harry had gone half a mile before he was near enough to order the chief to halt. Hintza, now in a frenzy, only urged his long-tailed charger on all the more. Fearing that Hintza might outdistance him, Harry fired a pistol. It snapped. Hintza grinned in derision. Harry pulled out a second pistol; it too snapped. Because of the speed with which he had charged his horse, Harry held back a bit to let him recover his wind. The 'noble animal of best English blood' quickly recovered and brought Harry close to the chief once more. Harry kept towards the river side of him, suspecting (correctly) that Hintza had supporters waiting in the bush below and beyond.

About half a mile from the cluster of huts, Harry was close enough to reach out for the bridle-reins of Hintza's horse, but was frustrated by jabs from Hintza's assegai. Harry commanded him to stop. It was no use, so he hit him on the head with the butt-end of his pistol, but the gun fell to the ground. Harry threw the second pistol after him, but it merely glanced off Hintza's head. 'At this point of desperation,' wrote Harry, 'a whisper came into my ear "Pull him off his horse!" I shall not, nor ever could, forget the peculiarity of that whisper.'

This time Harry got so near that the chief could not manoeuvre his assegai. Clutching him by the collar of his cloak, Harry dragged him from his horse. 'Oh,' he told Juana, 'if I could but describe the countenance of Hintza when I seized him by the throat and he was in the act of falling. A devil could not have breathed more liquid flame.' Hintza hit the ground and was on his feet in an instant. Harry's horse, with a temper to match his master's, refused to halt. As Harry's mount ran away with him, the chief sent a barbed assegai flying after him. When it fell short, the chief darted towards the river bed.

As his horse hurtled straight towards the huts, Harry feared that the warriors were waiting for him to get within range. Fortunately, however, they had gone down towards the river.

13

Dropping the bridle-reins, Harry seized the horse's head and forced the animal around, just in time to see Paddy Balfour and other guides galloping up. Standing in his stirrups, Harry shouted to George Southey (Richard's brother), who was in the lead, to shoot Hintza before he could escape. At 200 yards, Southey wounded the chief in the leg. Hintza fell, picked himself up and continued running. Harry shouted, 'Fire again.' A second ball went through the fugitive's side and chest. To the amazement of his pursuers, Hintza bounded up and disappeared into a thicket.

The colonel ordered his men to investigate the thicket. Southey went upstream, Balfour downstream. Other scouts soon plunged into the bush. Southey heard the sound of an assegai striking on stone behind him. When he turned he saw the top of a warrior's head and an uplifted assegai. Southey fired, and the would-be assailant fell into the shallow water, a bullet in his head. Balfour ran up then, and he and Southey recognized that the warrior was Hintza. Southey took his brass belt and assegais and returned to Harry, crying, 'Hintza is taken.' Delighted by the news, Harry ordered Japps to take the chief's horse and bring him in, but not to be rough about it. Only when Southey came closer did Harry learn 'the melancholy truth' that his hostage was dead. He had hoped to take him alive, but he did not blame his guide. Nor could he feel in any way responsible himself, for he had repeatedly warned the Xhosa chief against trying to escape. By his actions, Hintza had shown himself to be 'the most determined and practised liar'. Writing to his wife afterwards, Harry spoke of 'the pains I took to conciliate and treat kindly that savage! A pack of fox hounds would have followed me all over the world with half of it.'

Harry had neither the tools nor the time to bury the corpse. Ornaments were taken from the body. (Some bracelets along with the assegai thrown at him were sent home to Juana as souvenirs.) Then it was covered with his karosse and placed near the village. Meanwhile, through his telescope, Harry saw an animated Umtini sending out messengers to assemble his warriors. Harry called forward those of Hintza's followers he still held captive and instructed them to tell their tribesmen that their great chief's death was the result of his own treachery, and that he hoped to remain at peace with them.

With the chief no longer alive to guide them or guarantee their safety, many officers thought their colonel would turn back. But that was not Harry's style. Calling his officers before him, as well as influential non-commissioned officers among the Hottentots, he informed them that the Bashee river just beyond the valley was crammed with cattle. Although his troops had been on the road for 14 hours, the colonel pushed on with his cavalry and captured 3,000 head of cattle, most of them belonging to the colonists.

Having noticed at dusk that more were being driven towards the Umtata, he called for his men to saddle up at three in the morning. Those horses and men unable to continue would remain in bivouac under Captain Ross of the C.M.R. to guard the cattle already taken. Ross was instructed to take no chances, for the enemy would more than likely attack.

Taking with him 60 Hottentots to scour the lower Bashee, Harry then went on to the Umtata. The cattle were few, however, and the warriors were growing more numerous and menacing by the hour. On the return march, they attacked the rearguard. But Lieut. Charles Bailie, 'a very sharp fellow', beat them off every time by laying ambuscades under cover of the long grass.

The bivouac of knocked up men, meanwhile, was surrounded and threatened, but the expected attack never came. Ross, however, had bad news for the colonel. His friend, Major White, had gone out for a short distance with a small escort to gather topographical information. They were overwhelmed before Ross, who heard the shots, could come to their aid. White and a corporal were killed.

Positive that the enemy would attempt to retake the cattle as soon as it was dark, Harry exercised every precaution — none too soon, for suddenly, dusky forms swarmed out of the dark. There 'was a low, unearthly growl,' recalled Balfour, 'resembling beings of another world.' A barrage of fire drove them back with heavy loss. About eleven o'clock Captain John Bailie and his 60 Hottentots arrived safely. They had marched all day and into the night, their path beset by many warriors.

Before dawn, related volunteer Jeremiah Goldswain, a picket saw a warrior creeping towards Col. Smith's tent. The picket sent a ball through his neck. The colonel was out of his tent like a shot, crying out, 'Fire away, my lads.' Then he commenced singing 'The Girl I Left Behind Me'.

With no more cattle to be taken and the enemy all around, Harry began his retrograde move to the Kei the next morning. The path was difficult, sometimes only wide enough for one bullock to pass at a time, and through the most ideal hiding places nature could provide. His force, guarding 3,000 cattle and 150 Fingo families who had flocked to him for protection, would be strung out in a highly vulnerable fashion. 'In all my previous service,' Harry declared, 'I was never placed in a position requiring more cool determination and skill.'

Time and again, feinting from one direction, then attacking from another, the Xhosa warriors came forward, now howling like wolves, now hissing like snakes. The Xhosas also indulged in ominous gestures to indicate the pleasure they would take in cutting their enemy's throats. But the troops were too disciplined to be intimidated, too adroit to be attacked with success. The cattle were sometimes confused by the whistles of the enemy to which they had been taught to respond; nevertheless, they were deftly handled by the Hottentot drovers. Without them, said Harry, he could never have brought the cattle in.

They were back to the Kei on 17 May to rejoin D'Urban's main force. In seven days they had marched 218 miles through hostile country, up and down mountains and precipitous ravines.

Two days later Kreli solemnly promised to perform the engagements previously entered into by his father, Hintza, and the governor then proclaimed him ruler of the Transkei. A guard of honour was to escort him back to his homeland while Uncle Buku, a very sullen hostage, had to remain in camp until all the promised cattle arrived. Before he left, Kreli held Harry's hand for five minutes. Tears came to his eyes as he squeezed. 'He may be a hypocrite,' commented Harry, 'but he is a feeling one.'

Macomo, Tyalie and company remained to be subdued. From their strongholds in the Amatola and Buffalo mountains, they continued to make raids, or 'midnight robberies', as Harry called them. While D'Urban established posts and forts, and laid out the capital of the new province, King William's Town, his chief of staff conducted strikes against the enemy to force them across the Kei, out of Adelaide. Moving swiftly in 'the most gigantic marches', he was assisted by chiefs Pato and Kama, who provided an unexpected addition of 1,000 warriors. The sound of Smith's name terrified the enemy. As soon as their scouts spotted Harry's presence, the enemy scattered in disorder. Livestock, huts, great stores of corn and even wives were abandoned.

On 11 June 1835 D'Urban left King William's Town to attend to civil matters in Grahamstown — and from there he would return to Cape Town. He left Harry in command of the troops and placed him in charge of affairs in Adelaide. 'It is now *your province*,' he told him.

⌈9⌉

Inkosi Inkulu of Kaffraria

It is a mistake to make government too dull.

Lord Attlee

For the first time in his career Harry was on his own, in sole command. As 'governor', a term he used in his private correspondence, his primary responsibility was to establish peace. He, therefore, never allowed his troops 'one moment's repose from the furtherance of that object'.

The pressure on the enemy to rout him out of his hiding-places and drive him over the Kei was increased. By now, Macomo had few followers, but Harry always respected their ability to strike back by exploiting a tactical error. He warned his officers many times to exercise every precaution when on patrol. Even so, on 25 June Lieut. Charles Bailie, son of Captain John Bailie, and 30 picked Hottentots were cleverly decoyed, probably by Macomo, and fallen upon. When their ammunition ran out, they fought savagely at close quarters until the last of the patrol was slain. The mystery of their disappearance was not solved for weeks. Not since the outbreak of the war had there been so great a disaster, costing so many lives.

Harry redoubled his efforts to end this guerilla warfare. 'All the fellows wonder what the devil I am made of,' he liked to boast. 'I am here and there and everywhere.' Whatever he was made of, it was less than he had started with when he had left Cape Town. Though he ate well, beginning the day with a large platter of mutton chops, he grew thinner. His face was drawn and sallow; he complained that his rump, what was left of it after riding thousands of miles, was 'as hard as a board'. With administrative duties crowding his time in the field, he finally admitted it would be only 'fair to give my officers a chance of doing something'. They would chase the enemy while he watched and prayed for the safe arrival of 'my life, my love, my soul' — Juana. 'The only holiday I have,' he observed, 'is writing you.' It made him feel so close to her that his heart palpitated. At times he had the sensation of her leaning over him with her 'sweet balmy breath' in his nostrils. Juana encouraged him by declaring his words were her *only food*.

In each succeeding letter Harry's prose grew more ornate and elaborate. 'All the sensations of love, affection, friendship and value,' he averred, 'are concentrated in you.' She in turn doted upon her 'esteem, regard and love for Enrique'. There was one discordant note, a sore point. He told his 'old gal' that if she wanted to show *real affection* for him, she would 'leave off that horrid snuff ... the *only* fault she had in the world'.

In love as in war, Harry did nothing by halves. He and Juana had been married now for 23 years. Yet, he yearned intensely for Juana if they were separated for even a day. At such times, he confessed, when he was home alone, 'I kiss everything I find belonging to you. I take one of your gowns off when I find it hanging up, and I am fool enough to kiss it and fold it in my arms.'

After enduring the torture of separation for four months, the day came in May when Harry could stand it no more and wrote, 'come to the welcoming arms of your faithful husband!' They would rough it together on the frontier, 'and once more we will go together everywhere. As the old man campaigns so well, why should not the old woman?'

In a few days Juana sold off their horses and carriages, packed, and was on her way with a maid, two servants and her dogs. Jolting along in a covered wagon 'over a wild country of bad roads, difficult passes and deep rivers', she averaged 70 miles a day in her 600-mile journey — a rate of speed Harry found worthy of himself.

The time spent waiting for Juana was worse than separation. His thoughts swung erratically between worry for her safety and fantasies of a blissful reunion. In flurries of Spanish as well as English — and even occasionally French — punctuated by coded symbols that only she understood, he bared his innermost feelings in letters that intercepted her *en route*.

'How are you? Where are you?' he asked. 'Few women may

be like you, my love, coming so perfect and so fast to me, making such a long trip in spite of your many illnesses in the middle of winter.' Oh how he wished he could give her the sunshine she deserved. He conjured her 'soft, sweet voice ... her scent like the body of a spirit'. 'Come, come naked,' he implored, 'everything is beautiful for you ... so come ... give me a kiss.' He admitted he was 'a wolf and mad the way I am with you'. Anticipation often stirred him to words explicitly sexual, for her arrival promised 'tongues, lips and hearts and everything put together ... and really we are one — as you are me and I am you'.

When Juana reached Grahamstown, Dr Murray insisted that she rest several days before she resumed her journey. Meanwhile, her husband suffered paroxysms of despair. He was sure that Murray meant well, 'but how dare you interfere, what authority had you?' The dreadful news sent Harry into his little tent where he threw himself into bed. 'I had a most violent hysterical fit, when the Almighty God relieved me of my flood of tears. I tried to pray. I felt wicked and could not. I never slept.' Then he asked his wife reproachfully,

Did anyone stop you after the battle of Waterloo? ... My soul was all anticipation. What am I today? Oh wretch, mad, miserable, mean and wicked. I tremble so, I can scarcely write. I never knew what a broken heart meant. Create another delay, and it is all over with your poor old Enrique.

He concluded his letter: 'My own until we meet here or in heaven.'

The receipt of such a message by Juana took precedence over any physician's advice. It was arranged that they should meet at Fort Willshire, as far as Harry dared to go from his head-quarters. At precisely the same moment they arrived on the crests of opposite ridges overlooking the Keiskamma river and the fort below. In that wildly romantic setting 'we were again united in gratitude to Almighty God'. They relived those tender moments they had experienced in the Peninsula. Then as now, safety existed only within the perimeter of their sentries, for while Major Cox and the main force operated in regions beyond, marauders prowled in the vicinity of their camp as the couple made their way to King William's Town.

Even there, danger was present. Two prowlers were shot in the garden in an attempt to steal Harry's milch cows.

Their residence was the former home of the missionary John Brownlee, which had been partially destroyed at the beginning of the war. The missionary asked Col. Smith, who had taken great pains to rebuild it, to return what was rightfully his. '*Your house*,' said the colonel sharply. 'It is mine by right of conquest.'

The conquest was still incomplete, though by July the starving enemy appeared to be on the verge of surrender. D'Urban, however, was concerned with the cost of further military operations and considered allowing the refractory chiefs to become British subjects in the new province. Harry raised no objections. Preliminary negotiations were begun through Wesleyan missionaries and the wives of Pato and Kama, sisters of Macomo. In mid-August the half-brothers, Macomo and Tyalie, came out of hiding to talk. Meeting with Major Cox and Captain Warden, they presented counter-demands; Macomo was most insolent. Harry decided his presence was required. Riding to Fort Cox, he summoned Macomo to meet with him in two hours outside the fort. If he did not appear at the appointed time, he 'would sweep him off the face of the earth'. Macomo came.

To show that he did not anticipate treachery, the colonel rode out with only his A.D.C., an interpreter, Cox and Warden at his side. They met Macomo and Tyalie within sight of the grave of their father, the great chief Gaika. In a highly theatrical manner, Harry invoked the spirit of Gaika to join the council; he then reminded the chiefs of their father's injunction: never make war with the English. Harry then proceeded to scold them for their cruel and unjust attack on the colonists, and for insulting Cox and Warden. All the while, Macomo, his sharp, restless eyes flashing, appeared highly agitated, but he said not a word as the colonel dictated the conditions for peace. Harry said he would give them half an hour to reach their fellow tribesmen, 'after which I will instantly attack you, and never cease until you are destroyed'. The rakish-looking Tyalie, who was as handsome as his brother was ugly, made an effort to speak, but Harry shut him up. 'I am here to command, not to *listen*.' And if he did not behave, Harry would exclude him from the peace. They

quickly ratified the treaty. 'Such a scene of acting,' he wrote to
Juana. 'You would have laughed to see your old man.'

Demonstrating to the chiefs that he could be as strong in
friendship as he was terrible in war, the colonel invited them
into the fort, where he entertained them royally and showered
them with gifts. The seven guns of the fort were fired that day
(6 September) to mark the end of hostilities. Since D'Urban
now allowed them to become British subjects rather than expel
them, Harry promised Macomo a grant of land and, if he
behaved as a dutiful son, he would build a home upon it.
'*I like Macomo,*' he informed Juana, 'he is a very sensible,
shrewd fellow with a *heart* and, for a savage, wonderfully
clever.' Unfortunately, he was 'early trained to wrong'.

The governor was pleased with Harry's success. He rode
out from Grahamstown 'all power, dignity and determination'
to sign the treaty on 17 September. 'You have done the whole
thing so well,' he told Harry, 'it would have been impossible
to have altered one iota for the better.' He ought to be grateful,
thought Harry, for 'it would never have been finished without
me'. Once the peace was assured, Harry galloped back to 'our
dear little cottage' to share a toast with Juana.

Throughout the war the surveyor-general, Major Mitchell,
had tried to make a sketch of Col. Smith but, as he complained
to the governor, he could not get him to stand still for a
minute. When D'Urban spoke to Harry about Mitchell's
problem, he declared, 'By God, sir, I have not time to stand
still.'

This was no less true in peace than in war. With the same
boundless vitality, flair for the innovative and more than the
usual leavening of the theatrical, Harry applied himself to
civilizing his subjects. 'I joyfully and enthusiastically entered
upon a task of rescuing from barbarism thousands of our
fellow creatures endowed by nature with excellent understanding and powers of reasoning as regards the *present*,' he
wrote in his memoirs. The old colonial system, as he saw it,
was actuated by plunder which led to exploitation and in-
justice. To him the British Empire was a God-given instrument
to extend Christianity and uplift the benighted. British
Kaffraria, he promised, would become a little England in ten
years.

In speaking to the chiefs and their councillors at the 'new

court' in his 'Great Kraal' in King William's Town, he told
them that they were now subjects of 'the most powerful of
nations, whose laws, manners, customs, and institutions were
the admiration of the world'. In reply to their protest that they
were naked and ignorant, he related how the English were
once in the savage state in which the Xhosas now found themselves but, with the help of Almighty God, they had gradually
bettered themselves. 'Do you suppose we have all these things
by lying sleeping all day under a bush?' he asked rhetorically.

Officially no more than the commandant and chief commissioner, Harry planned to rule the province like a benevolent
despot with his authority based on a peculiar blend of martial
law, 'Smith' law (mostly common sense), and what he regarded
as the best of Xhosa customs. True, he was subject to the
commands of the governor, but by force of habit D'Urban
allowed Harry a free hand. Rather than suffer delay, often
Harry did not wait for His Excellency to act or even approve
his measures.

On his own authority, Col. Smith summoned the chiefs to
King William's Town and proclaimed himself their 'Inkosi
Inkulu', — 'very great chief'. Rereading the terms of the treaty,
he held it before them and threatened to rip it to shreds and
wage war if they did not obey. The chiefs were to act as his
magistrates, accountable for the misdeeds, such as cattle theft,
of their people.

The loss of independence and imposition of responsibilities
as defined by the Inkosi Inkulu did not please the chiefs, but
they were reluctant to protest. As Harry explained to D'Urban,
'under this system I gain absolute power over them. I can
now send for an individual or numbers from any part of the
country; he dare as well hang himself as not come.'

The chiefs, however, took pleasure in one aspect of the
system, the ritual the Inkosi Inkulu devised for their investiture which took place in the large room of his residence.
At nine o'clock on the morning of 17 November, a cannon
was fired to assemble the hundreds within hearing distance.
They quickly gathered round the residence and struggled to
peer through the doors and windows. A second gun was fired
to herald the beginning of the investiture. The band played
'God Save the King' and Col. Smith appeared in scarlet and
gold surrounded by his officers. With great decorum, such as

he had admired in Louis XVIII, he ascended the makeshift throne. Harry delivered a long prayer after which the band rendered 'Glory to Thee O God'. Macomo, Umhala and Ganya (Tyalie's proxy) dressed in ill-fitting, semi-military costumes, were ushered to the throne, where they knelt on one knee. Harry took the silver seals of office (specially made by a jeweller in Grahamstown) and suspended them from their necks. An oath of allegiance to the king followed. Harry then drew his sword and ordered them to observe the new boundaries separating the tribes, and to put an end to cattle stealing.

With all this pomp and display, Harry took the opportunity to deliver the 'Word' to the representatives of Kreli. In a speech meant to instil fear, he pointed out that very few of the cattle Kreli was to forfeit had been delivered. 'I thought one of Kreli's men would have fainted,' he wrote in his report to the governor. 'Yesterday's meeting taught me the length of my Political and Magisterial power without resorting to vi et arm [*sic*],' he continued, 'and that I am an *Absolute Monarch.*'

D'Urban was troubled. To give so much authority to the chiefs seemed, to say the least, premature. Harry explained that they were magistrates in a collateral rather than a literal sense, and that he intended to rid himself of the chieftains and the clan system as soon as possible. Until then, he urged the governor to let him go on 'play acting', which would 'lay the foundation for permanent regulations'.

The play acting reached its climax when the new regime was formally inaugurated on 7 January 1836. Harry called it 'the most extraordinary and novel General Assembly that has ever been held in this part of the world.' The troops were paraded and assembled in the great square before Harry's residence. The chiefs came in with 2,000 singing warriors. Another 1,000 Fingoes followed with their great shields. Though it was brutally hot, Macomo and Tyalie wore blue suits and black velvetine waistcoats. Five guns placed all around fired three shots. The colonel raised his cocked hat and led them in shouting, 'Long live the King'. 'Such a roar I never heard,' he told D'Urban, 'with soldiers and wild men.' It was the kind of imperial scene that illustrated journals would use to delight their readers in the Victorian age.

To one group after another, Harry administered the oath of allegiance. The chiefs were addressed singly. The whole then marched off, shouting for joy. It was all done, Harry informed D'Urban, 'to excite to the utmost and inspire them with the power and regularity of all that is English'. That night there was a great dance in which Tyalie was the star performer. (Harry observed that he had 'more brandy than brains in his head'.) Umhala and his people arrived late, so Harry went through the entire ceremony again with them the next day.

Harry asked his 'dear, faithful, adventurous and campaigning wife' to share his throne. Since his subjects called him 'father', he encouraged her to be their 'mother'. She quickly exhibited a missionary impulse to teach the gentle art of needlework along with daily lessons in differentiating right from wrong. Often her husband would find her presiding over a court of her own, attended by the chief's wives and hangers-on.

With the assistance of his commissioners, Captain C. L. Stretch, Richard Southey and Fleetwood Rawstorne, who were also appointed magistrates among the tribes, a census was taken. There were nearly 100,000 inhabitants, but difficulties arose because certain tribes were being relocated at the same time. And many were returning to their old grounds, which Harry had set aside for military purposes or as the sites for future towns. Finding the Xhosas by nature subtle and acute lawyers, Harry had to be adamant in rejecting their appeals. Forced to resort to harsh measures, thousands were herded back to the lands assigned to them as their huts went up in flames.

Harry Smith was the first European administrator to make an effort to codify African law. To assist him in comprehending the ways of the Xhosa people, he selected the venerable and sagacious Ganya, Macomo's councillor and previously Gaika's most trusted adviser. Six hours a day for several days they discussed the customs and traditions. Harry found much that was admirable, most of all that which resembled the laws of Moses.

To establish the habits of civilization Harry encouraged a monetary system to facilitate trade, the cultivation of fields by men rather than women and the burial of the dead. Because of their horror of handling the dead, the Xhosas would take those believed to be dying, be they parent, child or spouse, and cast them outside the kraal to be devoured by wild animals and vultures. To set an example, Harry conducted a Christian funeral service for those who died near his camp. Witnesses were then sent forth to explain the practice and relate how the Inkosi Inkulu promised an ox to any man who brought proof that he had buried a deceased relative.

'The world does not produce a more beautiful race of blacks than these Kaffirs, both men and women,' Harry asserted; 'their figures and eyes are beautiful beyond conception, and they have the gait of princes.' But they showed too much. 'Now that you are British subjects,' he informed them, 'it is sinful to appear naked.' None would be allowed to enter his camp unless they wore a kaross.

More sinful and shocking was the barbarous 'festival of virgins' that old Ganya brought to the Inkosi Inkulu's attention. The orgy, which called for the attendance of nubile maidens, culminated in what Harry described as a kind of 'Rape of the Sabines' in which the females were parcelled out to the chiefs or, should the effort be beyond their capacity, their favoured followers. Like the medieval *droit de seigneur* the girls were sent home with the chief's blessing to marry. Here was a chance, Ganya suggested, to drive a wedge between the chiefs and the fathers of families. The generally unpopular custom was banned by order of the Inkosi Inkulu.

Polygamy for the time being was to be tolerated. Macomo, for one, had eleven attractive wives and was on the look-out for more. However, Harry took a dim view of the practice of purchasing brides, which he saw as leading to many abuses. Gradually he hoped to eliminate the practice by having both parents of the newly married make a contribution, in addition to an offering of his own, to start them off.

There was one local tradition Harry found useful. As a chief, he provided himself with his own distinctive sceptre, a long stick surmounted by a large brass knob. When issuing a ukase, he grabbed the 'gold stick' and waved it as a symbol of his authority. In addition, the native police he had organized were given a similar stick, though shorter with a smaller knob. If a malefactor failed to comply with a tribal law or the Inkosi Inkulu's dictates, the police thrust the stick into the thatch of his hut. 'So long as it remained in the kraal,' wrote Harry, 'the proprietor was under the ban of the Empire, excommunicated, or outlawed.' To lift the ban, it was necessary to return the stick to the authority from which it originated. The system worked well. Only once was it necessary for him to call out his soldiers.

The most vicious of all practices, one that was the greatest threat to 'the system', as Harry called his programme, was witchcraft. To the Africans, sickness and every conceivable misfortune were related to some malevolent influence emanating from a displeased ancestor or, more likely, from a hostile neighbour. To 'smell out' the enemy who cast the evil spell, the victim sought the approval of the chief to enlist the aid of the witch doctor. According to Harry,

> An old hag, perfectly naked, comes forth, the assembled people dance around in a circle. After a variety of gesticulations, this hag approaches the individual already named by the chief, and literally *smells* him, proclaiming him the culprit.

If the doomed were wealthy and contrite, the chief might merely confiscate his property, known as 'eating him up'. Should the chief decide that greater punishment be inflicted, the condemned man was strangled or tossed from the edge of a precipice — or worse. A standard form of punishment was to spread-eagle the victim on the ground where a nest of large, black ants could feast upon him. While other forms of torture were suffered in silence, the pain inflicted by the sting of thousands of ants invariably produced pitiful cries of anguish.

Though it was normally Harry's policy not to interfere directly by outlawing native practices, he condemned witchcraft outright. In the case of the allied art of rain-makers, he tried to discredit them by challenging their powers. Before a large crowd, he poured water on the ground and asked them to put it back into the container. Dismayed, they said, 'We cannot.' Harry demanded, 'Put the rain again in this glass, I say.' As they shook their heads, he turned to the onlookers, 'Now you see how these imposters have deceived you.' Taking his gold stick and placing it violently in the ground, he decreed, 'Any man of my children hereafter who believes in witchcraft, or that any but God the Great Spirit can make rain, I will "eat him up".' To avoid the enmity of the rain-makers, he encouraged them to take up a new and honest profession. To start off, he gave them a gift of many oxen taken from the herd he had accumulated through fines.

The offending chiefs were another matter. The most wilful, the one who gave him more problems than the others put together, was Umhala. Possessed of great intelligence and daring, he never showed the slightest fear, unlike the others, when the Inkosi Inkulu delivered his most violent tirades. The news that Umhala had disobeyed him by 'eating up' a rich man for witchcraft and then brutally roasting him with hot stones, sent Harry into a rage. He summoned the chief to his court. 'Umhala,' he asked sternly, 'did I not give the word — no more witchcraft?' Standing very erect and motionless, the chief gave an affirmative answer. 'Then how dare you, Umhala, one of my magistrates sworn to be obedient to the law, infringe the word?' Umhala denied the charge. Harry then produced the partially charred victim who had somehow survived his ordeal. Thinking him dead, Umhala for once was startled. He admitted having broken the law and promised to make amends. Harry punished him with a fine of ten head of cattle for each one that he had confiscated and deprived him of his medal of office. With all the thunder he could muster, he said, 'Now go and obey my orders!' But there was something about Umhala's demeanour that suggested he would disobey.

Harry decided to make this a test case. He let it be known throughout the province that Umhala had broken the law and must make amends in two days. Two troops of cavalry were called up and held in readiness. On the third day Captain Rawstorne was ordered to 'eat up' the disobedient chief's cattle. Such an act among the Xhosas was tantamount to a declaration of war. Umhala, however, made no effort to resist. And when Harry sent out a call for all the chiefs to assemble at his court, he boldly joined them. As the other chiefs looked on in awe, Unhala betrayed little emotion as Harry chastised him severely. Macomo came forward and spoke eloquently on behalf of the Inkosi Inkulu, who then forgave Umhala. Taking the medal that he had placed under his foot, Harry put it back around the chief's neck. Thenceforth, Harry believed — or wanted to believe — there was a strong bond of affection between them.

Those who claimed to know the chiefs and their advisers repeatedly warned him that they were as skilled at 'play acting' as he was, maybe more, and not to be trusted. But Harry's optimism was such that he insisted on seeing only the good in his chiefs, most of all Macomo. Of all his subjects none pleased him more. Invariably he referred to him as 'my son', as if to satisfy the powerful parental urge of a man who was childless.

Early in April Harry received the astounding news, confirmed by various sources, that Macomo had secretly tried to persuade the other chiefs to desert the province by crossing the Kei. But they all rejected his overtures and said he must be mad. Harry sent for Macomo and showed him the evidence of his treachery. 'The tears stood in his eyes, and he exclaimed, "I shall choke". He would have thrown himself at my feet, had I not prevented him.' The chief then took his hand but was unable to speak. In the end Harry forgave him. After all Macomo, 'my prodigal son', possessed the same stormy, restless spirit he felt in himself. Harry was sure his favourite 'rebel' had learned his lesson.

D'Urban, to whom Harry reported this affair, was doubtful. He had remained suspicious of the chiefs and frequently chided Harry for being partial to Macomo. In November there was an incident involving Ensign Norton, under Captain Geddes Bain's command at Fort Armstrong, who pursued some suspected Xhosa marauders across the border into Adelaide and killed one. On receiving a vigorous protest from Macomo, Harry rode off in the middle of the night to settle the matter. After a hasty inquiry, the colonel arrested Bain and Norton. The ensign was told that he would be cashiered unless Macomo pardoned him for killing one of his people. Macomo, of course, to please Harry, did not press his case, but Harry could not let the matter drop without adding a theatrical touch. He carefully staged a full-dress parade and publicly scolded Norton. 'By God, sir,' said the colonel, 'if any man serves under me he shall be a gentleman of whom I can make a Christian.' Bain, as commanding officer, accepted responsibility for the affair and was held over for court-martial.

Instead of backing Harry, D'Urban supported Bain. Hot with indignation, Harry sent off a letter of resignation. The next day, however, he regretted his rashness and offered to withdraw his request for a court-martial. But D'Urban, to Harry's chagrin, ordered the trial to be held so that the accused could defend his reputation. Bain was subsequently found completely innocent. Harry told Bain he was happy over the outcome and they became friends.

Now that they were apart and unable to smooth over their differences through long conversations, the harmony that had existed between the governor and his colonel began to deteriorate. When Harry's language became bumptious, D'Urban would inform him that his behaviour 'was not appropriate to that of a subordinate'. The nervy colonel would then back down and express his sincerest regrets. But he was never subdued for long and the pattern would soon be repeated. Harry grew more swashing and assertive; D'Urban more touchy and pessimistic. The uncertainty involved in waiting for the reaction of the colonial office to his annexation frayed the governor's temper.

In a letter to Harry dated 8 December, the governor threw aside his studied restraint. He asked,

> Will you have the truth. I have now and then cause for apprehension on account of your *Discretion*, in danger of being thrown overboard by your vivacity—by your imbibing haste and extreme opinions, & acting upon them hastily.

He reminded Smith that he was part of a team working for the good of the system. There were times when his instructions were ignored but, he added sarcastically, 'I am aware that they may appear to be tame and languid to your more vivid imagination ... if they be so *I* am responsible for them. This apprehension and reflection to which it necessarily leads,' he concluded, 'have suggested to me serious doubts as to the safety of trusting very large and extreme power in your hands.'

The reaction was immediate. The reply Harry penned was a mixture of hurt and apology, for D'Urban was too important to his future. He readily acknowledged that at times he was imprudent and given to speedy opinions. 'Surely Your Excellency,' he asked, 'one act of indiscretion [the Bain affair] is not enough to banish me from your confidence.' The only other disagreement that he could recall was over the appointment of the chiefs as magistrates. As to the accusation of 'being regulated by no given rule', he was completely mystified. 'I speak with an humbled heart, but I cannot trace what gives rise to Your Excellency's remark.' It grieved him that the governor assumed that 'I am so self-important as to suppose you cannot do without me, I can bear all with magnanimity but this —— '.

Harry's language may have been unreasonable but his views on policy were not. What were the rules? The powers he exercised on the frontier had never been clearly defined. And D'Urban, rather than back the orders of the man on the spot, allowed colonels like Somerset, envious of the authority of a newcomer of equal rank, to appeal to him directly. Even a lowly captain could challenge him and, worse, succeed in having Harry's decision reversed. Harry, too, waited for a despatch from the colonial office, one that would raise him to the autonomous post of lieutenant-governor.

The long-awaited despatch arrived in Cape Town at the end of March (dated 26 December 1835). The author of the 150-page folio was Lord Charles Glenelg, the third colonial secretary to be appointed within a year. On the basis of evidence supplied 'by the voluntary zeal' of various individuals, he found that in this latest in a series of frontier conflicts, 'the Kaffirs had ample justification for the war'. They had a right to try to regain the lands in the ceded territory from which they had been expelled, and he strongly condemned the spoor law, the procedure used by the colonists and supported by D'Urban to regain stolen cattle. Moreover, it pained him that the governor in his proclamation of 10 May 1835 referred to the Xhosas as 'irreclaimable savages', and that he described them as 'wolves' to the rescued missionaries. Glenelg found this a most unfair description.

Turning to the conduct of the war, Glenelg thought it hardly necessary to employ an army of 5,000 against a dis-organized, poorly armed enemy hiding in the bush. (Actually only 400 regulars had crossed the frontier.) That this was an unequal contest was indicated to him by the fact that hundreds of black men, women and children were killed, whereas the British, up until May, lost only 18. (Actually, before Bailie's patrol was wiped out, they had lost 23 killed, 30 wounded and 7 missing.) That the troops under Col. Smith were motivated by feelings of revenge was apparent to him because of the wanton and indiscriminate manner in which they destroyed the dwellings and food of these virtually defenceless people. Such conduct was unbecoming of soldiers wearing His Majesty's uniform.

Even more reprehensible in the eyes of the colonial secretary was the treatment of Hintza. Contrary to the governor's statement, it appeared highly unlikely that the chief would plot against a formidable British army allied to hostile tribes that surrounded his country; if anything, he would seek the friendship of the British. And he was shocked to learn how the unfortunate chief was 'slain when he had no longer the means of resistance, but covered with wounds and vainly attempting to conceal his person in the water into which he had plunged as a refuge from his pursuers.' There was evidence meriting serious attention

> that Hintza repeatedly cried for mercy, that the Hottentots present granted the boon, and abstained from killing him; that this was then undertaken by Mr Southey, and that then the dead body of the fallen chief was basely and inhumanely mutilated.

It was further reported to him that Hintza's ears were offered publicly for sale in the streets of Grahamstown. Glenelg ordered that an investigation of this affair be undertaken immediately.

'The original justice is on the side of the conquered,' as Glenelg saw it, 'not the victorious party'. Therefore, he called for 'the relinquishment of the newly acquired province' and withdrawal of British troops by the end of the year. Meanwhile, Andries Stockenström was on his way as lieutenant-governor of the Eastern Province to prepare a new approach to frontier government.

Some historians have held that D'Urban had only himself to blame for this hostility emanating from the colonial office. They point to his often tardy, sporadic and confused despatches as the principal cause. But it is likely that even if D'Urban's views had been brilliantly stated and sent to England by the swiftest ships they would have had little effect: in addition to a rising sentiment of philanthropy in Britain there was the fact that a cost-conscious Parliament was in a mood of resistance to the idea of expanding an already over-extended empire.

Opposition to D'Urban's policies began at the Cape. Upon his arrival, he had been instructed to be considerate of the welfare of the non-whites, and he listened sympathetically to the missionaries, especially Dr John Philip of the influential

London Missionary Society. Humane and high-minded, the governor took pleasure in carrying out the abolition of slavery; but these same traits were later outraged by the pillaging and murdering of settlers by 'irreclaimable savages'. But to an evangelical missionary like Dr Philip such words were intolerable. And when D'Urban decided that the invaders must be driven over the Kei, Philip hastened to London to protest.

Glenelg, a mediocre bureaucrat who owed his office to the humanitarian forces, was prepared to listen. Behind the somewhat diffident colonial secretary, in the role of *éminence grise* stood the brilliant James Stephen, a zealous and decisive man who literally ran the colonial empire for some two decades. 'Mr Over-Secretary', or 'King Stephen' as his enemies called the under-secretary, was a dedicated evangelist associated with the Clapham sect of powerful and articulate philanthropists. Stephen believed that with the exception of Cape Town as a staging-post to the East, South Africa was not worth holding.

Hearings on South African affairs were being held at this time before a select parliamentary committee investigating the treatment of indigenous people in the British colonies. The committee was packed with friends and supporters of the autocratic negrophile chairman, Thomas Fowell Buxton. 'If the Irish people were but black,' Daniel O'Connell, the great Irish leader remarked bitterly, Buxton and his followers in the back rows of Commons would have been the greatest advocates of their cause.

The witnesses before the committee, men in most cases who happened to be available in Europe at the time, were mostly ardent champions of the Africans. Their evidence, though largely hearsay, confirmed the prejudices of the committee. Dr Philip himself admitted that he had spent no more than a fortnight in Kaffraria. The one witness who spoke from extensive experience was Stockenström. He told of how unprincipled Europeans on the frontier, who with the false cry of 'stop thief', raised commandos to seek alleged reprisals and enrich themselves at the expense of innocent tribesmen — thereby, ultimately provoking a war. He advocated the return of the land to the chiefs and better protection for the natives on the basis of treaties.

A dramatic high-point was reached with the appearance of 'the native Christian trophies', brought back from South

Africa by Philip: Andries Stoffels, a Hottentot from the Kat river settlement dressed as an English gentleman; and Jan Tshatsu, presented as a great chief from Kaffraria outfitted in the blue and gold uniform of an officer. In reality he was a minor chief with only a 1,000 followers. At the time of his departure, Harry complained to D'Urban that the tractable Tshatsu had been whisked out of Adelaide by Philip without his permission or without even saying good-bye to his wife and family.

The two prize converts praised without stint the good missionaries who taught them the ways of civilization. Other Europeans — starting with D'Urban — robbed, beat and generally abused African people. Tshatsu related how Col. Smith had seized his house at Brownlee's mission station and converted it into stables. (He failed to mention that it was his tribesmen who burned Brownlee's home.) To the select committee they were shining examples of the peace-loving, noble savage struggling heroically to protect his land against predatory white men; truly, these people were worthy of rescue and capable of being elevated to the level of Christian society.

Philip took them on a tour of London and the country, starting with Exeter Hall. Before large, cheering crowds, they thanked God, the missionaries and the English people for their salvation. 'Dr Philip,' in the words of Professor Cory, 'acting as a sort of clerical Barnum was the hero of the hour.' Stoffels and Tshatsu were petted, wined and dined everywhere they went. The effects of their triumphal tour, however, were not so fortunate. Stoffels contracted consumption and died in Cape Town before he reached home. Tshatsu became addicted to wine and was thrown out of the church by Brownlee.

Conditioned by hair-raising tales of atrocities in the press and from the pulpit,[1] the temper of the British people was roused to exaggerated sentimentalism on behalf of the poor native. There was little sympathy for the suffering colonists, who had obviously brought the war on themselves. Crusading philanthropic power was at its height and the public simply

---

[1] One minister, claiming Philip as his authority, told his congregation that two missionaries were tied to the muzzle of a cannon by an officer who promised to blow them to kingdom come if they did not take up arms against the natives. But their lives were miraculously saved when the match was mysteriously extinguished.

believed what they were told. Petitions from the settlers were buried under an avalanche of humanitarian propaganda. Considering the climate of prejudice in Britain at the time, it is difficult to imagine that Glenelg would have written a despatch other than one approved by the 'Saints', as they were dubbed by their opponents. Only the intervention on the part of King William himself, who argued that an honourable soldier like D'Urban should be given a chance to defend himself, prevented a peremptory retrocession.

In Africa, meanwhile, rumour preceded Glenelg's despatch. The *Commercial Advertiser* in Cape Town, edited by Philip's son-in-law, the tenacious John Fairbairn, gleefully proclaimed there would be a reversal in policy. Even Macomo predicted to Harry that the new province would be returned to the chiefs. 'Never!' said Harry stiffly.

On 3 April 1836 Harry received an extract of the 'monstrous' despatch from an angry and bewildered D'Urban. 'It positively paralysed me,' he told the governor. He had no doubts as to who was responsible. 'Those canting ultra philanthropists are gulling the people of England and making a British Minister crawl to their damned Jesuitical procedure.' He was prepared to evacuate the province but, he predicted, it would be 'to the utter discomfiture of the people over whose rights we now preside'.

To defend his conduct and preserve whatever career he had left in the army, Harry wrote to his friend Col. Wade, 'I belched forth a short letter of vindication of 44 papers, which Sir Benjamin forwarded with very strong remarks of his own.' Harry gave a detailed account of his actions during the war from beginning to end. What misery the enemy suffered they brought down upon themselves as unprovoked aggressors. Neither he nor the British soldiers fought with feelings of revenge. However, to enlighten the colonial secretary on the subject, he explained, 'War is not a game of pleasure, but one of retribution and indemnification … The right of conquest had established the boundary beyond the Kei.' History is replete, he argued, with the banishment of tribes and nations, beginning with the Bible, through the Norman Conquest and down to the present moment when aborigines were being ejected from vast territories in Australia and America. The Xhosas originally took this very land from the Hottentots. 'Such have been the usages of nations.' Why, he asked, should the Xhosas be an exception to this rule and favoured by Britain over peaceful settlers whom they attacked, colonists 'who duly paid their taxes and therefore considered that they had a right to be defended?'

Referring to the war with Hintza, 'there is not a Kaffir chief who had not told me that he promoted the war to the utmost, for obvious reasons. The captured cattle were to be driven to him, possession was ensured to the victor, and he could help himself as he pleased.' (Harry later sent Glenelg testimony to this effect taken from Macomo, Eno and others.)

As to the circumstances of Hintza's death, it was inconceivable that the story told by Dr A. G. Campbell of Grahamstown, which he got from two Hottentots who were never near the scene, should be accepted as the truth in preference to the official report of a respected colonel of 31 years' service who had bled and suffered imprisonment for his country. This 'double-faced scoundrel', Dr Campbell, Harry informed Glenelg, lent him the very horse he used to run Hintza down, and afterwards, wrote to him:

> The horse is now more valuable to me as having been the instrument in assisting in the prevention of the escape of Hintza, and when again I ride him it will always bring to my recollection the name of Colonel Smith.

The death of Hintza was his own fault, Harry contended, for he had promised that he would not try to escape. And if he had escaped, he asked, 'what was I to have said to Your Excellency? The mark of disgrace and dishonour would have been stamped upon a brow where heretofore it had not dared to sit.' Hintza was a black-hearted villain 'capable of any guilt', including murder. Harry had since learned that the chief had murdered at least three persons in cold blood: 'one for interrupting him in his *amours*'; another, one of his wives 'whose brains he dashed out with a club'; a third, a brother, whom he had torn to pieces with wild horses.

Summing up his defence, Harry stated that as a member of the Church of England, one principle alone actuated him: 'Fear God and love your neighbour as yourself.' To underscore his point, he wrote, 'Decidedly no revengeful feeling exists either in my mind or practice, but whether in War or

Peace, *Obedience* is the first duty of a Soldier, his next fearlessly, zealously, and conscientiously to perform it.'

Letters and clippings from sister Alice and his friends abroad revealed to Harry that, taking their 'lies' from Philip and his mouthpiece, the *Commercial Advertiser*, he was 'branded as the murderer of Hintza throughout the newspapers of the world'. Even in far off Australia the *Sydney Monitor* condemned Col. Smith for 'a heartless affair' and told how with 'his hands wet with the blood of the gallant Hintza', he expelled a defenceless people from their land 'with fire and sword and rapine'. The *East India Colonial Magazine* recited all the lurid details 'of the consummation of the most gloating barbarism that ever degraded the heart of a Commodus or a Nero'. Was this the same Smith, the writer wanted to know, who when a captain, after stigmatized as a coward by his brother officers, horse-whipped and then shot, without the 'slightest provocation' the most unoffending man, 'poor O'Grady of Dublin', and as punishment was sentenced to two years in Kilmainham prison?

Since he was 'shamefully abandoned by the Minister of Colonies', whose duty it was to sustain him against 'the misled voice of the public', rather than sacrifice him 'at the shrine of cringing party spirit', Harry appealed to Fitzroy Somerset, Kempt, Colborne, Lambert and the Duke himself to intervene on his behalf. But the philanthropist lobby was far more powerful than his friends' combined efforts. The best his supporters could do was guarantee a fair hearing at the court of inquiry held at Fort Willshire in August and September, 1836. The nature of the proceedings and the selection of officers sitting in judgment was discussed by Harry and D'Urban beforehand. Harry's suggestions were given considerable weight.

The investigation, which actually involved the innocence or guilt of George Southey more than Harry Smith, was a minor triumph for the accused. D'Urban, the colonists and the entire anti-Philipine party derived a great satisfaction from its outcome. The sinewy arguments of the accused corroborated by the testimony of officers who were eye-witnesses—Balfour, Bisset, Dr Ford (who examined the body)—could not be shaken by the accusers who offered mere hearsay evidence. Dr Campbell, who apparently joined the Philipine party because he was disgruntled by his failure to be appointed district surgeon of Albany, might have been as clever with his pen as with his scalpel, but he withered under cross-examination. Other witnesses for the prosecution were vague and confused. Klaas, the Hottentot soldier who repeated the story of Hintza's death to Campbell as told to him by two Hottentots, never appeared. The two Hottentots in question, Nicholas, Harry's orderly in the field, and Windvogel, the bugler, swore that they never told Klaas anything. As to Hintza's ears, it was never ascertained who removed them (if they *were* removed); nor were they ever found.

Apologies and expressions of gratitude were not sufficient for Harry. So that he be re-established 'in the eyes of the world', he contended that Glenelg 'was bound, as a man of honour, to have instigated Majesty to have conferred upon me some mark of distinction'. (Harry had knighthood in mind.) The colonial secretary rejected his petition.

D'Urban was encouraged to believe that Glenelg would change his mind and retain the Province of Queen Adelaide. Since the treaties of September, 1835, by which the misbehaving chiefs were permitted to remain in the Ciskei were more in line with the philanthropists' position, it seemed likely that the government would approve his actions. If not, he assured Harry on 13 May 1836 that he would 'overthrow every assumption and every argument put forth by Lord Glenelg by the stubborn facts' in a despatch that he would send in a few days. The glacially slow D'Urban did not send his despatch with its 235 enclosures, 'papers a yard high', until *six months* later. By then, whatever possible impact the 'resounding rejoinder' might have had on the government was lost. It only made D'Urban appear ridiculous. Meanwhile, at the end of May, Glenelg rejected the September treaties on the grounds that the people of Queen Adelaide Province could become British subjects only by an act of the king himself.

At this stage the inhabitants of the province were completely baffled. Rumours began to circulate. One had it that the land would become completely independent. Harry heard that it had been initiated by the missionaries, possibly 'to make Dr Philip Lord Bishop, Judge, Saint and Devil'. Deputations from the Hottentots told the colonel that they would not remain a day after he left. Every Xhosa chief visited him to say, 'Oh our Father stay, we shall be ruined in confusion when

you go.' Some vowed, 'as a great compliment', they would
take him by force and tie him to a stake. When the Inkosi
Inkulu told them that Stockenström would soon arrive to take
his place, they sighed, 'Ah, this is the manner the English
have always treated us. They never adhere to any system, but
are always changing the men with whom we are brought in
contact.' The people, who had never been so protected before,
feared that their chiefs would once more 'eat them up', a sad
fate for those Harry had planned to Christianize and educate.

Now that 'the system' was just beginning to work, Harry
toyed with various schemes to keep him in the province. He
considered returning to England to rally his supporters, but
the cost would be prohibitive. Perhaps he could stay on as the
military commandant by arranging protest meetings on the
frontier of British and Dutch settlers, Hottentots and Xhosa
chiefs, who in 'one unanimous acclamation' would request 'that
officers remain as at present established'. — 'Only say the
word,' he told D'Urban.

The word never came. The governor was too circumspect
to approve such a proposal. In fact D'Urban began to wonder
whether he was on solid legal ground by maintaining martial
law in the province. On 18 August he suddenly abolished it.
Harry objected, 'The sooner we march out of the province
the better, for how am I to "eat up" a Kaffir according to
Blackstone?' It obviously put an end to the annexation experiment. Stockenström, who was on the road from Cape Town,
had no inkling that the governor intended such a move. It was
a blow to his authority, for which he never quite forgave
D'Urban.

The Swedish-born, Cape-bred lieutenant-governor was not
a forgiving man by nature. There was no question that he was
able, but he had a reputation for being tactless and quarrelsome.
His appointment was greeted by widespread dissatisfaction.
'He is very unpopular with all the English,' reported Harry,
'more so the Dutch, and the Kaffirs detest him for many things,
particularly for his exertions in locating the Hottentots on the
Kat River' when he held the post of Commissioner-General,
Eastern Districts. Caustically he remarked to D'Urban,
'Gustavus Vasa — so *called*' thinks he can arrange everything
'by one swoop of his wand or talisman'. Harry, however,
foresaw that Stockenström would 'be thwarted at every turn

by everybody except the annointed of the earth'. As for his
own attitude, he did not hold Stockenström personally
responsible for his misfortune. Proud of what he had accomplished, he tried through co-operation to preserve as much of
'the system' as possible by effecting a smooth transition to the
lieutenant-governor's programme.

Having settled his family in Grahamstown, where angry
colonists openly insulted him, Stockenström went on to King
William's Town on 13 September. The Smiths greeted him
with great courtesy, and he responded to their warmth. He
expressed admiration for all that Col. Smith had done in so
short a time.

There was a great convocation of all the chiefs with the
ostentatious display that Harry so dearly loved. Following
the customary three cheers for the king, he introduced his
successor with a long speech in which he recited all that 'his
children' had accomplished through his teaching. Stockenström,
who thought that Harry would never finish, then said a few
words of his own and solicited questions from the chiefs.
Macomo, who usually curled his lip at the mention of Stockenström's name, spoke with restraint. Tyalie was downright rude.
Harry gave him a severe reprimand and warned him that if he
gave the word, he would be 'eaten up' in a moment. 'The
odium with which they regarded him,' he told D'Urban, 'I
believe I much mitigated.'

At the end of the ceremony there was a great demonstration
of affection for Harry and Juana. For all his bluster, the people
knew that the spirited colonel was a man of good will with
their best interest at heart. Hundreds surrounded his residence;
'some wept aloud, others lay on the ground groaning'. There
were those who declared 'their life was not worth living'. Old
Ganya, a poor man whom Harry rewarded handsomely for his
services, found little comfort in his riches, saying he would as
soon die now that he had lost his father. (He died a few weeks
later.) The normally impassive Umhala, his most stubborn
opponent, was overcome with emotion. Juana, too, was
encircled by sobbing women. With heaving breast, she shed
tears with them.

The next morning Juana and Harry prepared to leave for
Fort Willshire. The soldiers who had campaigned with the
colonel turned out to wish them Godspeed. Thousands of

natives followed the heavy-hearted couple, 'yelling as if in despair'.

The journey to Cape Town, where he was to resume his former duties, took on the appearance of a triumphal procession. All of Grahamstown turned out to acclaim their hero. A banquet and speeches of gratitude followed. How different things looked now, Harry remarked, compared to the day he entered the beleaguered town. There was the same grand reception in every town they passed through. The Smiths travelled slowly, Harry on horseback and Juana in a light, horsedrawn wagon with a comfortable swinging seat. Now and then Harry would dash off to pursue an ostrich or other game he spied. Farmers would ride out to greet him. Offers of food and lodgings were more plentiful than they could accept.

Their welcome in Cape Town was no less enthusiastic. There were public meetings and dinners. Inscribed silver plates, tokens of admiration, began to pour in from citizens and soldiers. Harry calculated their worth at 500 guineas. The two Hottentot battalions varied the pattern with a silver candelabra.

In the following months, other occasions called for ceremony: the accession of Queen Victoria, Harry's promotion to full colonel and the retirement of D'Urban from office (May, 1837). The 'great and good Sir Benjamin', as the South Africans called him, after trying to vindicate his policies (which the colonial office never really regarded as defensible), hastened his removal by using shockingly intemperate and exasperated language in his messages to Glenelg. (D'Urban stayed on in South Africa until given command of the British troops in Canada in 1847, where he died two years later.)

The gloomy forecast Harry made regarding Adelaide soon came true. Never fully supported by the governor or his own subordinates, Stockenström's policy was handicapped from the start. Witchcraft and tribal tyranny returned. Cattle stealing was soon on the increase. Stockenström lost part of his own herds. Much of his energy was diverted by quarrels with the colonists. After losing a libel action against one of them, he sought vindication in London. Instead, he was removed from office by Glenelg's successor and rewarded for his service with a baronetcy. This act and the fall of Glenelg for bungling Canadian affairs, encouraged Harry to request a similar honour because he had been 'unmercifully censured by Glenelg'. But he received only a 'grateful acknowledgement' for his labours from Lord John Russell, the colonial secretary in 1839.

Harry blamed the Glenelg–Stockenström programme for the departure of thousands of Boers. Feeling betrayed by a government that consistently favoured the blacks and cut them off from adjacent lands, the land-hungry Boers sought to preserve their way of life in the vast, unclaimed grasslands of the interior far beyond British jurisdiction. Masses of these disgruntled pastoralists joined what was to be known as the Great Trek. D'Urban deplored the emigration of a 'brave, patient, industrious, orderly, and religious people', the consequences of which were to be more profound than he ever imagined.

Sharing the governor's esteem for the Dutch settlers at the Cape, Harry was positive that if his administration of the chronically unsettled frontier had been allowed to mature, 'not a Boer would have migrated'. 'I am proud to say,' he wrote in his memoirs, 'I had as much influence over the Boers as over the Kaffirs, and by a kind and persuasive manner in expostulation, had they meditated such a step, I could at once have deterred them.'

The new governor, Sir George Napier, who arrived in January, 1838, agreed with Glenelg's policy but, most of all, he struggled to keep the peace and reduce expenditures. Though Napier and Harry were comrades who served together in the Light Division, the new governor relied largely on John Bell, his colonial secretary, for advice. Harry knew Napier to be a good soldier but not particularly bright. (The *Dictionary of National Biography* described him as a dunce at school.) Anyhow, Harry's health was bad after his exertions on the frontier and his interests lay elsewhere—India.

'It would be a fine thing,' Harry told Juana, 'to grow rich in our old days' by receiving a post in India. He asked for and waited to be appointed quartermaster-general to the forces there. Glenelg, before his resignation, and the late king, had endorsed the move. But in Juana's words, he was 'most hardly used by Lord Hill', who gave the office to a favourite. Juana was not too disappointed, for she dreaded the harsh climate of India.

'The hardest duty a soldier has to perform,' Harry told Napier, 'is the listless daily idleness.' He thought of writing the life and adventures of Harry and Juana Smith, and then postponed the project.

Harry began to ask himself if his career had reached a dead-end when the *David Scott*, on its way to Calcutta in the early months of 1840, arrived with new orders from Lord Hill: Col. Smith was to proceed to India and assume the post of adjutant-general to Her Majesty's forces with the local rank of major-general. Without waiting for another ship, the Smiths booked passage on the *David Scott* and were on their way within five days.

Believing he had left South Africa for good, Harry wrote his farewell:

> Oh, Cape of Good Hope, notwithstanding your terrific south-easters in the summer, your dreadful north-westers in winter, your burning sun, your awful sands, I and my wife will ever remember you with an affection yielding alone to that of the 'Land of our Sires!'

[10]

The One Day War: Maharajpore

Unavoidable wars are always just wars.

Napoleon

The observance of the 25th anniversary of Waterloo came close to being the last for the Smiths. The ill-fated *David Scott*, destined soon to burn in Mauritius harbour, encountered a storm of hurricane force in mid-June, 1840, that carried away her top masts, tore her sails to shreds and tossed her about like a log. Harry believed it was a Divine Hand that saved them as it had saved him and his brothers at Waterloo. His horses were so badly battered that one died. Juana barely recovered by the time they arrived in Calcutta. She feared, and rightly, that the storm and its aftermath presaged a series of illnesses in the pestilential East. But wherever Harry was called to soldier, she accepted the fact that he could not trouble himself as to whether the climate would agree with his or her constitution. To do so, observed General Sir William Francis Butler, would have been as absurd as having a missionary 'stop to inquire if his predecessor had disagreed with a cannibal king who had eaten him'.

At Government House they were welcomed as temporary guests by Lord Auckland, the governor-general, and his sisters. To his family, the ruler of India was known as the 'comical dog', but many of his subordinates found no humour in him and thought of him as a 'vacillating bungler'. Harry saw him as 'sensible but timid'.

At army headquarters there were many old friends, officers who had been in the Peninsula and who now acted as guardians of the Empire. The commander-in-chief, Sir Jasper Nicolls, who had served under Craufurd in South America and then at Corunna, was a man noted for his firmness and caution. While commanding the 59th, composed of men trained in the use of

17 A rare profile sketch of Harry Smith. Artist and date unknown.

18 Lord Glenelg, philanthropist and colonial secretary (1835–9), who championed the cause of the Xhosa tribesmen at the Cape. His political opponent, Lord Grey, declared that he was 'not worth a farthing'. Harry Smith would agree.

19 Lord
Ellenborough, the
haughty and
aggressive governor-
general of India
(1841–4). Harry Smith
dubbed him the 'mad
Moghul' because of
his thirst for glory.

20 Lord Gough, the
impetuous and genial
Irishman who
commanded the
British forces in
India (1843–9).
Gough is as 'brave
as *ten* lions,' wrote
Sir Charles Napier,
'each with two sets
of teeth and two
tails.'

grenades, he ordered that they be used without explosives, for in his opinion, the moral effect on the enemy of a lighted grenade alone would be as effective, without causing injury among the grenadiers. Understandably Harry's fame as a fire-eater was a liability, and the tactics of persuasion that he had used so successfully on D'Urban left his new chief unmoved. Rarely would Nicolls ever take him into his confidence.

'The profession of war is an eventful one,' Harry wrote to D'Urban, but that was before he sat at the adjutant-general's desk in Calcutta, where his body was tormented by perspiration, prickly heat and insects of every variety while his head 'must be full of cannon, musquets, sabres, rations, transport ... pipeclay, tobacco, soap, etc., etc.'. To make sure that his desk 'every evening is as clear as an Indian sky', he displayed before him in large letters words taken from Ecclesiastes: 'Whatsoever thy hand findeth to do, do it with all thy might.' His fiery nature found an outlet when officers presented him with what he considered an unreasonable claim or grievance. Accustomed to his easygoing predecessor, they were startled by Harry's tart responses. When Col. Anderson requested the transfer of two of his officers to spare his regiment the scandal of a court-martial, he received a severe letter informing him that 'if the officers named were not fit to serve in the 50th Regiment, they were not fit to serve in any other'.

Sir Jasper sometimes had to intervene, and Harry would back down by thanking his chief for 'having pointed out the error which you were so kind as to consider clerical'. In a rare, confidential mood the chief finally told Harry that his 'rapid style often made me think you were inclined, in your Peninsular manner, to take me by storm or surprise'. After six months in office, Harry wrote to his friend Payne that he had 'very much learned to restrain an impetuosity which never produces so favourable a result as Moderation, for if right, it frequently makes you wrong'.

For an officer who sought active service, no part of the Empire offered greater opportunities than India at the time of Harry Smith's arrival. One army from India was off in China fighting the First Opium War. Another had been sent to Afghanistan to place an unpopular puppet on the throne in Kabul in order to forestall what Auckland believed to be a Russian threat to India. The immediate borders were menaced

by potential enemies in every direction—Burma, Sind, Nepal
and the Mahrattas in the Gwalior State.

The First Afghan War (1839-42) was a story of mismanagement by incompetent commanders and political officers
that led to the greatest single disaster to the British army in
the history of India. In November, 1840, when Harry heard
that General Cotton, commanding at Kabul, was very ill and
might soon be replaced, he told Auckland frankly that his
object in coming to India 'was if possible to be employed in the
Field'. The governor-general advised him that the employment
of an adjutant-general was hindered by a variety of obstacles;
however, he added, there was no officer under his authority
whom 'he was more ready to make use of'. Harry wrote to
D'Urban, 'This was of course enough for me', and he informed
Nicolls that he was 'ready and most willing to accept any
command ... at this critical period'. Sir Jasper waited a few
days before penning a curt answer: 'I received your letter, I
did not answer it; I will not forget though.' Left with 'literally
nothing in the great scale of arrangement', Harry tried again.
This time in his request to the commander-in-chief he enclosed
a long memorandum outlining his strong views on the situation,
to show that he possessed 'an idea beyond a Parchment Certifi-
cate of discharge'. Nicolls, who never approved of Auckland's
risky 'forward' policy, sent back a brief note describing Harry
as 'very pugnacious', and that everything he spoke of 'and more
was under the vigilant eye of Lord Auckland'. Dejected, Harry
concluded that Sir Jasper 'apprehended that if I once got the
command, the wealthy Persia would have been attempted and
my progress alone interrupted by the Caspian Sea'.

Cotton was succeeded by General Elphinstone, whom Harry
described as 'an old Boy near 70, fat, corpulent and wieldy'.
He proved to be the worst possible choice among the general
officers available. Blunder followed blunder. Considering their
position in Kabul untenable, a British army of less than 5,000
retreated towards India in the dead of winter, and were
annihilated in the mountain passes. By mid-January, 1842, only
one, Dr Brydone, escaped death or capture. Elphinstone,
crippled by gout and prematurely senile, died soon after of
dysentery.

'Upon receipt of every disaster,' Harry told D'Urban, 'I
offered my services boldly to undertake the command from the

source to the mouth of the Indus.' Each time Nicolls turned him down. Instead, the command beyond the Indus was divided and given to Generals Nott and Pollock, both of whom were Smith's juniors. Auckland kept Harry's hopes alive by promising a command should the Burmese invade India. But they remained peaceful. In Harry's estimation, Auckland's character, 'though one of ability and judgment, wanted that firmness to judge for himself and (his mind once made up), to prosecute his intentions with inflexibility, which stamps the man as fitted to govern ... ' The government, too, questioned Auckland's fitness and sent out Lord Ellenborough to replace him.

Under a new governor-general, Harry thought there might be a reversal of his fortunes. He boasted to Alice that 'Lord E. has taken a great fancy to me and treats me quite as an old friend'. But Ellenborough refused to give him a command. In Afghanistan, he adopted a policy commonly known in the army as 'Butcher and Bolt', by which it was demonstrated through a punitive expedition that the British always won the last battle. Following different routes, Pollock and Nott pounded their way back into Afghanistan. The enemy was beaten at every turn and General Sale's garrison at Jallalabad was relieved. The armies of retribution met in Kabul in September, 1842, and Pollock blew up the city's bazaar. The country was then abandoned 'to their own barbarism' as an additional sort of punishment meted out by a great civilized Power. Once more independent, the Afghans quickly restored the very ruler the British had originally deposed.

Harry was soon appalled by Ellenborough's 'want of stability'. Though the governor-general was 'passionately fond of soldiers', he apprised D'Urban, he had 'no idea of time, foresight and previous preparations to move the cumbersome machine of war ... Five peremptory orders were sent to Pollock: first *he would* move then he *would not*, then he could not, no transport.' In matters of government, there were things D'Urban would scarcely credit unless he witnessed them himself. 'The Moghul,' as Harry took to calling him because of his love for oriental pomp, 'is steering, if he steers at all, with a very wild helm.' The opinions of respected senior officials he treated with 'both derision and contempt'. In formulating a policy, he 'jumps to the most rabid conclusions without duly weighing the subject at all ... and never by any chance carries out *one subject* but grapples with something new, leaving it unfinished as before'.

While he was turning the government inside out in a vain and despotic manner, Ellenborough enlisted Harry's assistance in preparing a gigantic display, Indian-style, to receive the victorious, avenging army at Ferozepore on 17 December 1842. The war-stained veterans were to be deployed in the form of a huge star with a throne in the centre from which the governor-general would bellow his proclamations. A powerful speaker, Ellenborough had been nicknamed the 'Elephant', which seemed to please him. Elephants, in fact, were given an important role in the ceremony. Gilded and taught to salaam, they were placed in rows to either side of a tottering and tawdry triumphal arch through which the 'heroes of Afghanistan' would march. But the elephants became frightened when the parade began, forgot to salaam and ran off. The whole affair made Ellenborough an object of ridicule. When Wellington heard of the gaudy throne on a field of the cloth of gold, he remarked, 'he ought to sit upon it in a straight-waistcoat'. Harry wrote home, 'Our Moghul is non compos, as sure as eggs are the produce of fowls ... ' The Indian princes whom Ellenborough sought to impress merely laughed.

Ridicule turned to indignation when the governor-general, in a further effort to convert disaster into victory, lavished praise and honours on the returning forces. Peninsular veterans grumbled when Ellenborough designed a special medal for all ranks in the Jallalabad and Afghan campaigns: a bronze star suspended from a rainbow ribbon representing the rising sun. With the exception of the Waterloo campaign, the Duke had successfully opposed such general awards. Harry wrote to D'Urban scornfully:

The Moghul has been overacting the drama of medals, honours and distinctions to a ridiculous extent, and all the martial heroes since the days of St. Michael and Satan must seek shelter in the shade, while the modern renown of the 'Illustrious Garrisons',[1] etc., etc., shows forth with the splendour peculiar to the Dispenser of rays, who

[1] The phrase the governor-general had used to describe the defenders of Jallalabad and which was turned into mockery throughout the army.

evidently regards himself inferior to neither Marlborough, Napoleon or Wellington.

Ellenborough had departed for India with the promise to restore peace to Asia. But Harry foresaw that the possibilities for war had been vastly increased. First, Britain's prestige as a military power to keep the warlike princes in line had sunk to a new low after the Afghan war, 'the most disgraceful as well as disastrous war England was ever connected with'. Second, he told Alice, 'Our Moghul is mad, undoubtedly—a species of military madness.'

Using the pretext that some of the amirs of Sind were plotting hostilities, Ellenborough sent the hasty and fiercely vigorous General Charles Napier,[1] now 60, to deal with them. Napier's persuasions came at the point of a sword. He swiftly conquered the territories of all the amirs by March, 1843. As a pun, Napier sent the governor-general a one-word message in Latin—*Peccavi*, I have Sin[ne]d. He regarded his actions as 'a very advantageous, useful, humane piece of rascality'. Ellenborough, who never made any secret of his desire to control the lower Indus for commercial and military purposes, formally annexed the territories in August. There was, however, a strong negative reaction in Britain. As Mountstuart Elphinstone expressed it, 'Coming after Afghanistan, it put me in mind of a bully who has been kicked in the street and goes home to beat up his wife in revenge.' But unlike Queen Adelaide Province, Sind was retained, for Victorian morality was persuaded that British rule represented tranquillity, justice and social improvement when compared to the tyranny of the amirs who tolerated slavery.

Harry could not help but look on Napier's success with envy. 'My heart sickens with the fever of ambition,' he told Alice. He had come so close to being in the field: Ellenborough had promised him the command in Sind if anything happened to Napier; Auckland told him on leaving that he wished that he had let him take over in Afghanistan; Nicolls, who was soon to retire as commander-in-chief, expressed regrets that he had not backed Harry's appointment. From all quarters old comrades wrote that they could not understand how an officer with Smith's experience should remain so idle. All these great

[1] His younger brothers were the more sedate Sir George and Sir William. Between them they accumulated 23 wounds during the Peninsular War.

military events occurred, he told Alice, while 'your brother was quietly pruning rose-water trees, training jessamine, lopping forest trees ... ' And to think that for conquering Sind, Napier was made governor of the province, and given the G.C.B. and £50,000 as his share of the plunder, 'which ended *his* financial worries'. (Later his statue was placed in Trafalgar Square.)

'For the present,' Harry fretted, 'I am more of a beggar than ever.' Social obligations required more expenditures than at the Cape. And there was still the matter of his debts, on which he continued to pay 11 per cent interest and £100 a month against the principal. His pecuniary difficulties had been aggravated when Alice had become a widow many years before. She earned a little money writing tales for the young, but it was not enough to support herself and her two sons. Harry took on the burden of educating them and continued to give them allowances.

Another relative, a grand-nephew, Weston Holdich (his uncle, Lieut. Edward Holdich, was to become Harry's A.D.C.) was a source of constant embarrassment. Weston took 'to shameful drinking and squandering' which Harry attributed to the Holdich side. To make matters worse, Weston was stationed in India where it was reported to Harry that he was drunk on parade and drunk on duty. 'Never was there so decided an enemy as I am to drunkenness,' Harry announced to Alice. 'I would have broke him if he had been *my only son.*' (Weston died in 1845, presumably of excessive drinking.)

In May, 1842, Harry received a sinecure as colonel of the 3rd regiment, the Buffs. Since he never actually served with the regiment, he received only £75 a year while at head-quarters. It helped. But Harry's one great hope in India, where the climate made Juana ill most of the time and threatened to turn him into 'a crusty old fellow', was prize money at the end of a successful campaign.

A new commander-in-chief could greatly improve his prospects. After a two-year postponement, Nicolls was due to retire in 1843. Harry literally prayed that D'Urban would succeed him. He implored his former chief to 'write the Duke *himself* as well as Sir R. Peel [the Prime Minister]. Now is the time to redeem yourself from ill-usage ... ' For a while D'Urban was under consideration, but the post went to Sir Hugh Gough as a reward for his success in the Opium War.

When Nicolls left, they parted in friendship. The Smiths may have failed to charm Sir Jasper, but they respected him as 'a man of few words, shrewd and decisive'. They hoped that Gough would make full use of his adjutant-general's talents in the field. As for Ellenborough, Harry told D'Urban, 'so fickle is he, no reliance can be placed for *one moment* upon his intention'.

Gough, 63, was another one of those colourful figures who achieved prominence during the Peninsular campaign. A fearless, quick-tempered, but good-natured Irishman, he was frequently accused of employing 'Tipperary tactics' — i.e., rushing to frontal contact with the enemy so as to give them cold steel. Despite heavy casualties, he was immensely popular with his men. Recruits were told how after a battle it was 'a perfect sight to see old Gough shake the bullets out of that white coat', which he always wore in a fight so as to be conspicuous.

The Smiths and the Gough family (wife and youngest daughter) met in Calcutta with a wish to establish a mutual friendship and understanding for the good of the service and their personal ambitions. This proved to be easier than Harry had imagined, for Gough was a 'practical regimental soldier, a finished gentleman, all heart and hospitality'. But as a general, in Harry's estimation, the genial Irishman with the thick brogue was 'a little rusty, if ever polished, in the strategy required'. In their long conversations, Gough's object always appeared to be 'approval of what has been done, rather than seeking a prospective opinion'. Ellenborough went to the other extreme, seeking Harry's views beforehand. He was not the least bit regimental in his ideas. Harry discovered that he 'possesses some intuitive knowledge of strategy which he has improved in observing Napoleon's & Wellington's campaigns ... but sets at defiance all the numerous links between the soldier ... and the ability and renown of a general.' Though the governor-general and the commander-in-chief were soon on excellent terms, Harry feared it would be 'difficult to dovetail two bodies so opposite in formation'. On one thing they were all in complete agreement, the desire for military glory. They did not have to wait long.

The Gwalior campaign, sometimes called the One Day War, had its origins in oriental court intrigues complicated by a powerful but unruly army estimated at 40,000 men. The mischief began when the Mahratta chief, Maharajah Jankoji, died

unmourned in February, 1843, without an heir. His 12-year-old
widow, the Maharani Tara Bai, 'the poor little thing' as
Ellenborough called her, adopted a boy of nine as her son and
successor. The Mama Sahib, maternal uncle of the late
maharajah, became regent with the approval of the British.
However, the young maharani soon bowed to the wishes of the
army and dismissed him. His place was taken by Dada Khasji,
who was also said to be her lover. Reports of the conflict
between Dada and Mama were amusing to the British soldier
but not to the governor-general. He adopted the doctrine,
upheld afterwards by his successors, that the British Raj had
the right to intervene in the domestic affairs of independent
states so as to preserve the general peace. That Ellenborough's
candidate had been expelled was sufficient reason in itself for
intervention. But far more significant was the fact that the
turbulent army was the real power and hostile to the British,
and that army might ally itself with the Sikhs who appeared to
be spoiling for a war. A combination of 120,000 men and 500
guns could conceivably overwhelm the British forces in India.

To restore the situation in the State of Gwalior, Ellenborough called for the formation of an army at Agra in mid-
August. He referred to it as an Army of Observation, for he
wanted it known at home that he still hoped that it would not
become 'necessary to move a man across the frontier'. As
Harry explained it to D'Urban, the Moghul 'so burned his
fingers in the heat of his precipitancy in Scinde that he is now
naturally cautious to avoid being regarded the aggressor'.
Personally, Harry believed that the acquisition of the State of
Gwalior, wedged as it was into British territory, was
strategically vital to their communications in India and that
the menacing attitude of the Mahratta army would soon give
the governor-general cause to act.

After twelve days in Calcutta, the Smiths and Goughs
travelled in the sapping heat to Agra. Harry would be directly
involved in providing 'my *Peace Loving* Lord with a sharp
weapon in his hand' and moving it on to the border.

To collect and move an army in India, Harry noted in his
memoirs, 'requires much arrangement and consideration'. The
size of the country with its primitive roads entailed long and
laborious marches. A column progressed roughly at the rate of
two miles an hour, halting every hour to let the baggage,

always enormous, and rearguard close up, because the line naturally lengthened during the advance. The assembly of a battering train, for they anticipated reducing the fortress-city of Gwalior, the capital, was a staggering task. Each of the heavy guns required a team of twenty bullocks. In addition to the bullocks, there were hundreds of horses, camels and elephants, requiring over 300 pounds of vegetation each day. Harry saw an army on the march become a snorting, shuffling zoo parade.

And then there were the servants. Every fighting man required several to attend to his needs. Field officers thirty or more. (One general in the Afghan War had more than a hundred and required 60 camels to travel in comfort.) Besides the necessary water-carriers, dooley-bearers, grass-cutters, etc., there were cooks, barbers, cobblers, laundrymen, vendors of every kind — and dancing girls, described by Major Thorn as 'far from regarding chastity among the cardinal virtues'. When the column halted, the great migration resembled a Greenwich fair rather than a military camp. As one soldier saw it, 'The magic of the rupee turned them all into (temporary) brethren.'

There was one class of camp follower, the professional plunderers, who fanned out behind the army for miles. No matter how roughly they were handled by flankers who charged them, they were impossible to control. Plucking, grubbing and devouring they left little for their winged brethren, the vultures and the kites.

Accustomed to moving quickly, Harry regarded these traditional encumbrances to a travelling army in India as an intolerable nuisance. Should he remain in India for the rest of his military life, he vowed in a letter to Kempt, he would modernize this army.

'The season of the year must be rigidly attended,' Harry further noted, 'for such is the fickleness of disease and its awful ravages, that it would need an excess of folly to leave it out of account.' Cholera in particular caused grave concern as the troops concentrated at Agra. There were many interesting, if inaccurate, theories as to its origin. For instance, because of the erratic pattern of empty beds when it struck, some soldiers believed that the disease had been introduced by the Wandering Jew, who walked in a figure-eight pattern. The treatment was often no more enlightened. For example, there was the 'rack', which according to Sgt Bennet, was a bed of open webs to which the stricken was secured and roasted over a spirit lamp. If the disease did not kill the patient, the various treatments often would.

In the midst of his preparations, Harry heard that his father, now 87, was reduced to skin and bones, and frequently hallucinating all sorts of terrors. 'Poor old man,' he wrote to Alice, 'all things must end, and our only prayer ought now to be, however painful the blow we must anticipate, "Lord, now lettest Thou Thy servant depart in peace".' At the end of October, he learned that his father had died. In one of his last lucid moments, Alice gained something for his 'darling son'. She spoke his name in a loud voice and the old man said, 'Harry, yes, God bless him.'

In responding to Alice's correspondence, Harry introduced a happy note. Marching with him to war were the sons of his two Waterloo brothers: Hugh, the son of Tom; Harry, the son of Charles.

Ellenborough ordered his Army of Observation to march on 11 December, announcing that they would not stop until order was completely restored in Gwalior. His force of 20,000 was divided into two wings that would converge on the offending state from opposite directions: the right wing, under Gough's immediate command would move straight south from Agra; the left wing under Sir John Grey would come up from the southeast. 'According to the rules of strategy and correct principles of combination,' Harry remarked to D'Urban, 'this division of the threatening or invading forces may with reason be questioned.' However, in this case Gough felt that he could dispense with the rules, because the political agents assured him that since the Mahrattas had chased off their European officers and instructors, they were an undisciplined rabble. The greatest danger, the agents insisted, was that they might disband and become brigands. Harry agreed with Gough's arrangements, 'for strategy is totally unknown to a native army, which usually posts itself on a well-chosen position and awaits an attack'.

Hostilities seemed unlikely. To stop the British, the Mahrattas overthrew Dada and delivered him to the governor-general. Ellenborough was not satisfied. He wanted their army drastically reduced. The maharani let it be known that she was prepared to meet with him and to bring the boy prince with her. Ellenborough reiterated that his aim was peace and that his Army of Observation was merely promenading. Expecting prompt compliance with his wishes, he ordered Gough's force across the border, the Chumbal river, which took place between the 23rd and 26th December, 1843. They would assemble at Hingonah, where a durbar (official audience) would take place. The heavy ordnance was left behind.

Since there was to be peace rather than war, Christmas week was observed with all the normal festivities. The governor-general's party, which included Lady Gough and her daughter, Juana, and Mrs Curtis, wife of the commissary-general, were invited to join his table for Christmas dinner and to celebrate the bloodless victory. During the meal, the ladies suddenly noticed that their host had become preoccupied. Ellenborough had received word that the maharani had cancelled her plans to meet him the following day and that the Mahratta army, outraged by his crossing of the border, was massing to contest the British invasion.

Instructions were sent out to prepare for battle. Grey's force, though considerably smaller, was still regarded as sufficiently strong to fight independently. He was directed to proceed towards the city of Gwalior by an indirect route so as to avoid the dangerous pass at Antri. Gough planned to unite with Grey *en route*. Meanwhile, he would engage the Mahrattas said to be gathering before him.

Staff officers rode out on the morning of the 28th to reconnoitre the enemy's position. Harry, who was in the habit of taking long rides early in the morning to familiarize himself with the ground, could not resist joining a patrol led by the army's quartermaster-general. He returned to report to Gough that the enemy

> appeared to be on the plain in dense masses of troops, his left resting on the broken ground of the Ahsin river, his guns drawn out in front, his right 'en air', as if more troops were coming up to occupy the position selected.

Sir Hugh had a choice of waiting for Grey's 4,000 to reinforce him, or to fight the next morning, which would be 'most desirable in order to enable the pursuit of the fugitives to be protracted, therefore effective, and ensure the capture of every gun'. Gough agreed that it would be better to begin the battle the next day.

At the head of 12,000 men Gough began the march before dawn. Two columns would turn the Mahrattas' left flank while a third under General Littler would make a frontal assault. The columns 'reached their position with utmost precision', a remarkable occurrence, Harry told Kempt, since the army had 'to disengage itself from a mass of laden elephants, camels and bullocks, resembling rather the multitude of Xerxes than anything modern'.

To everyone's astonishment, round shot began to drop on the British. It became quickly apparent that the enemy had moved forward during the night to occupy the village of Maharajpore, where the governor-general and the other civilians, mere onlookers, expected to have their breakfast.

Rarely has a battle begun under more ludicrous circumstances. Ellenborough, who loved war but had never witnessed a battle, was with his staff on elephants close to Littler's batteries. This was believed to be a safe position for him to watch and to encourage the men to engage the enemy. As it turned out, the enemy guns concentrated their fire on these rear batteries first and the troops were treated to the sight of the governor-general rushing out of harm's way.

The officers' ladies also came under fire. They had ridden their elephants at the head of Littler's column to avoid the suffocating clouds of dust. Expecting something in the nature of a social occasion, they were startled to see cannon balls bowling towards them and between their elephants' legs. 'Juana had this command of Amazons,' Harry wrote to Kempt, 'and she was as experienced as they young; her command was anything but satisfactory.' Imposing her will on her panicky companions, she succeeded with difficulty in leading them along the route to safety that Ellenborough and his staff had taken. There was but one casualty: an exploding magazine caused one of the elephants to lose part of an ear. He bounded off with amazing speed.

Gough pondered. Should he change his plan of attack? The little Irishman with white hair and flowing whiskers, dressed in his white fighting coat and hat for all the world to see, paced up and down the line with a single staff officer. Now and then he stopped and looked over the field before him. Much of the view was obstructed by tall crops of corn. But it was obvious that the Mahrattas' position was stronger than anything he had expected. Their guns were heavier and so well posted, as Harry saw it, that each battery flanked and supported the other in what could be a murderous crossfire. To undertake a frontal assault would be playing the enemy's game and would result in heavy losses. Harry rode up and urged Sir Hugh to attack the left flank instead and threaten their rear. But the commander made up his mind to go ahead as planned; he ordered up his howitzers for support.

At half-past eight, Gough began the assault with the words 'On at them!' The British gunners, with the sun in their eyes, could make little impression on the enemy's numerous, well-protected and almost invisible batteries. Ellenborough later wrote to Wellington that their 'batteries kept getting up literally like coveys of partridges'. The infantry suffered cruelly as case and grapeshot decimated their ranks, but with the steady precision of mechanical toy soldiers they plodded forward. They paused on command to fire a volley. A cheer followed as they rushed forward with their bayonets and swept the Mahrattas' main position. The enemy fell back to another position until the redcoats dislodged them once more. The cavalry and horse artillery stove in the flanks and drove them towards the river, uneven ground greatly hindering the pursuit. The cavalry commander, General Thackwell, later charged General Smith, his senior, with deliberately holding them back. Harry had nothing to say on the subject, except to tell Alice that he was on the right flank where he had 'a narrow escape'. A round shot bruised his leg, tore off his stirrup and passed under his charger's chest. The force of the shot threw his horse, 'a noble Arab', over on his side. Harry's leg was so numbed that he thought it was broken. Only after the sensation returned to it could he stand. His toes were black for days.

The desperate Mahratta gunners, reduced to firing old horseshoes for want of ammunition, fought valiantly. Some strange psychological discipline kept them manning their guns until they were cut down. 'A more thorough devotedness to their cause,' Harry told Kempt, 'no soldier could evince.' Within two hours the Mahratta army was broken and scattered, and 56 guns were taken.

The chief criticism that Harry had to offer regarding the battle was that the combined moves of the various arms were 'not quite so scientifically powerful' as they might have been. For this, in large part, he blamed the inexperienced officers of the Indian army rather than Gough. Generally speaking, of course, all were at fault for 'no one gave our foe credit for half his daring and ability'. Why, there had even been talk that horsewhips would be the only weapon needed! He went on to tell Kempt that in this campaign he acquired invaluable experience in Indian warfare and, above all, reconfirmed the need 'to hold in just estimation your enemy, a creed I have ever advocated, and to a certain extent, in every instance practised'. As for the Sepoy battalions (natives serving under British officers), he would give them their full measure of praise, but praise 'rested on the British soldier's example, the want of that "point d'appui" would entail a dire want indeed, that of victory'. Those 'blockheads in the East' who held that India required no British troops were dead wrong. Of Gough's losses, nearly half of the 800 casualties were suffered by two British regiments, the 39th and 40th. Without those two British regiments, in Harry's opinion, the outcome of the battle would have been doubtful.

A second 'soldier's battle' was fought that very day by the left wing at Punniar only a few miles away. Grey allowed himself to be surprised by a superior Mahratta force that marched parallel to and unnoticed by his own column, but the steadiness of his troops led to a complete rout of the enemy. The war was over.

Once all fighting had ceased, a staff officer found Juana and the other ladies and assured them that all danger had passed. He led them on to Sir Hugh's camp, where a tent was pitched on the very ground the enemy had held earlier in the day. After their cheek-twitching experience that morning, the ladies now viewed the cruel visage of war after a battle: the mangled remains of men 'dashed to eternity', the helpless wounded, the groans of amputees in hospital tents outside of which arms and legs had been flung. There were sudden explosions as the engineers touched off earthen jars of spare powder that had been buried by the enemy. The ladies had just settled down in the tent for a cup of tea when soldiers burst in and bundled them off: just in time, for a large mine exploded and the tent was blown to bits. Few slept that night, recalled one officer: 'the dull heavy sound of exploding mines made the hours hideous.'

Sir Charles Napier later wrote a letter of congratulation to Harry and asked:

'How come all the ladies to be in the fight? I suppose you all wanted to be gloriously rid of your wives!'[1] Well there is something in that, but I wonder the women stand so atrocious an attempt. Poor things! I dare say they too had their hopes. They talk of our immoral conduct in Scinde. I am sure there never was any so bad as this. God forgive you all. Read your Bible and wear your laurels.

The unprecedented presence of the governor-general with the conquering army made it possible to conclude a peace in a matter of hours. The maharani and the young prince and their advisers came into the British camp on 31 December. Apart from the regular escort of warriors, the British soldiers were treated to the sight of the maharani surrounded by a female bodyguard, a score or so of attractive young Mahratta girls mounted bareback on horses. A Mahratta chief, carrying the prince in his arms, walked up to Ellenborough and placed the boy in his arms saying, 'He is now your Highness's child. You are his father and protector, and he looks to you for everything.' There was swift submission to all the terms the governor-general imposed. The main condition of the treaty, by which Gwalior became a protected state rather than an annexed province, was the disbandment of the army. A special contingent of 10,000 men was enlisted to serve under British officers. There was no problem in recruiting that number after it was learned that they would receive all arrears in pay.

Ellenborough held a general parade of all forces in Gwalior, the capital. Mahratta troops marched along as their band played what was intended to be 'God Save the Queen'. Their arms and colours were surrendered afterwards.

In keeping with his mania for decorations, Ellenborough ordered medals to be struck from captured guns and distributed to all ranks. The bronze star with the rainbow ribbon

[1] Ellenborough was already rid of his beautiful but scandalous wife. He had divorced her for adultery and she was now living in the desert, the wife of a Bedouin sheikh.

had 'Maharajpore' or 'Punniah' in the centre. The ladies, who moved between the tents of Ellenborough and Gough to enjoy the sumptuous feasts that were held every day, were not forgotten. They too received the star for their unplanned presence on the battlefield. 'As Juana is again a heroine,' Harry informed Alice, 'I want a gold star to be made at the jeweller's who makes mine.' She would wear it as a brooch with the enamel part taking the place of the ribbon.

There was even better news for those at home. Harry was to be made a Knight Commander of the Most Honourable Military Order of the Bath. But he insisted that 'I am Sir *Harry* Smith—none of your Henries.' And so it was recorded on the rolls of the order. A knight required a coat of arms, so he asked Alice, who had 'a fancy in such things', to assist him. The result was a complicated design that included the Waterloo medal, a fleur-de-lis, two martlets, two lions and an elephant. The leg of the elephant had to be corrected by Harry, who observed that it had to be more like man's, for it 'bends precisely forward in the way *old Sudbury* of Whittlesea used to walk'. Regarding the motto, the words should match the deeds,

> for as a boy, as I was a jawing fellow, I always had a great sway among my comrades; and progressively the truth must neutralize the vanity of assertion I have ever been looked up to in my profession. Thus, 'Inter militis miles' — a 'Soldier among soldiers'. And thank heaven *I have served* with soldiers!!!

He had one final request for Alice: 'Try if possible to get allowed to call Juana Lady Harry Smith, or Lady Wakelyn Smith ... Lady Smith is like a title in a bad farce.'

Aware of his debt to posterity, he asked Alice to inquire if it would be proper to leave his letterbook to a museum. He also felt that his deeds should be recorded in an autobiography. This undertaking was begun in Glasgow in 1824. During the two-month period, 11 August to 15 October, 1844, with little else to do while enjoying the bracing coolness of Simla, he brought the work up through the Gwalior campaign. The 600 pages of close foolscap sheets were scrawled from memory at 'full gallop' in straightforward and vigorous prose, the style befitting the man. He never once read over a sheet he had written, 'but rushed ahead as water finds its level'. Calling it

21 Lord Hardinge, the one-handed governor-general of India (1844–1847). Wellington observed: 'He always understands what he undertakes and undertakes nothing but what he understands.'

22 The charge of the 16th Queen's Own Lancers at Aliwal. Sir John Fortescue, the historian of the British army, wrote 'it was the battle without a mistake'.

23 The celebrated charger, Aliwal, who carried Sir Harry through his fiercely fought battles in India.

24 Sandile, by F. T. I'Ons. Handicapped by a withered leg and indecisive nature, the Xhosa chief took Sir Harry by surprise when he led a rebellion in Kaffraria (the Eighth Frontier War).

'Various Anecdotes and Events of My Life', he sent it on to Alice to decipher and edit. As an afterthought, he suggested that she might suppress the real names and submit it to Charles Lever, writer of romantic fiction, to rework. Harry expected half of the proceeds from 'a book that would take wonderfully'. The Sikh War, however, interrupted his plans. He added several more pages on his experiences immediately afterwards, but nothing came of it. Perhaps he grew more careful about putting into print that which might offend persons still living, for though the names may have been changed, the descriptions and events made them easily recognizable.

Some fifty years later the manuscript, which was preserved by his A.D.C., Sir Edward Holdich, was edited by a great-nephew, G. C. Moore Smith and submitted to a publisher. The timing was right because there was a renewed interest in the hero and heroine during the South African War, especially because of the celebrated siege and relief of the town of Lady-smith, which had been named after Juana.

While others savoured their rewards from the campaign, Ellenborough was punished with dismissal from office in June, 1844. His recall was unexpected by everyone but himself. For some time he had quarrelled with the Court of Directors in England over the annexation of Sind. They now had enough of his erratic behaviour and conquests. 'The only regret I feel on leaving India,' he declared in his farewell speech, 'is that of being separated from the army.' The most agreeable experiences he had in his life had been in cantonments and camps.

In the long run, Harry predicted to Alice, 'India will be the gainer by his removal by the man (if I mistake not) who succeeds him, my old friend Sir Henry Hardinge.' In the Peninsula Harry had known him well as a capable, honest soldier free from vanity. D'Urban knew him better as his deputy quartermaster-general with the Portuguese army; he commented, 'he was conspicuous where all were brave'. The consensus was that he was 'every inch a soldier'. Actually the delicate-featured Hardinge, now 59, could not boast too many inches, despite the efforts of his two maiden aunts who raised him. To increase his height they had often made him hang from a door by his arms. During the Waterloo campaign, Sir Henry lost his left hand at the battle of Ligny while serving on Blücher's staff. With the other hand he received Napoleon's

16

sword as a reward from his dear friend Wellington after Waterloo. Harry looked forward to renewing his old association, especially after Ellenborough told him that Hardinge was amazed that Nicolls had not put him, 'as the most fitting officer', in command of the army in Afghanistan.

It was encouraging to Harry to have so fine a soldier as supreme chief when a war with the Sikhs appeared inevitable. Privately, he informed D'Urban that

> Hardinge has in his pocket a Dormant Commission as Commander-in-Chief in the event of death, sickness, etc., regularly notified by the Duke himself to Sir Hugh Gough, which *he* regards as a hint, but does not mean, unless broadly stated, to take!!!

The Russians, he continued, were gaining ascendancy in Central Asia, but Gough drew as much inference from all this 'as a cow has of a side pocket'. Having served under Sir Hugh for a year, it was obvious he knew nothing of strategy, converging lines of concentration, base of operations and so forth. War to him was simply a matter of 'Lather away with your Old Oak Stick'. But Harry admitted that he 'never got on smoother with any of my generals, and he is as warm-hearted a fellow as ever breathed'. If war came with the Sikhs, Hardinge would surely give him a command and Gough would offer no opposition.

At the end of 1845, the Sikhs crossed the border in force and General Smith was placed at the head of a division.

[11]

The Sikh War: Mudki and Ferozeshah

War is a series of catastrophies that leads to victory.

Clemenceau

The Sikhs were a militant religious sect organized into the most powerful army ever to challenge British rule in India. Originally, in the late fifteenth century, the sect was an offshoot of Hinduism, though with a belief in one God and a desire to abolish the caste system. Savage Moslem persecution, however, turned the peace-loving community to increasingly militant activities: each male came to be designated a warrior at birth, with the young boys initiated early into a military brotherhood called the Khalsa ('the pure'). They adopted the appellation Singh ('lion'), abstained from alcohol and tobacco, and refrained from cutting their beards and hair, the latter covered by turbans. Before battle they were often stimulated by opium or bhang. The Sikhs ('disciples') regarded war as a natural way of life. Under no circumstances should they die in bed, even if it meant being thrown from their sick bed to the floor by their friends.

Early in the nineteenth century the Sikhs rose to the height of their power under Ranjit Singh, who hacked his way to supremacy and welded all the confederacies into one great kingdom. Through rigid discipline and the employment of foreign adventurers to train the Sikhs in the skills of modern warfare — most of all the use of artillery — he built an empire at the expense of his neighbours.

Goethe said genius is knowing when to stop. Ranjit recognized his limitations and refrained from testing British rule by crossing the Sutlej river border. Instead, he became a British ally and was content to rule the Punjab, a triangular-shaped tract watered by the great tributaries of the Indus in the north-west corner of the sub-continent.

Ranjit, the Lion of the Punjab, described by one English

visitor as looking like a one-eyed mouse with whiskers, was anything but disciplined in his private life. Debauched by tastes for liquor, opium, beautiful girls and painted boys, he died before his time in 1839. The absence of his firm hand led to chronic anarchy; as one observer put it, the old lion was succeeded by apes, wolves and tigers. The court became an inextricable tangle of intrigue, with rulers and rivals assassinated with bewildering rapidity. The Khalsa became a latter-day Praetorian guard that soon exercised undisputed control. Implacably anti-British, they looked upon the redcoats with unconcealed contempt after their retreat from disaster in Afghanistan. Since the Sikhs had defeated the Afghans in a previous war, they reasoned that they could easily vanquish the British. The Khalsa openly discussed plundering the wealth of India and boasted of building a bridge of boats from Calcutta to England.

The weak rulers lived in terror of the lawless, unpaid army and, therefore, were not averse to war. Jindan, the queen mother and regent; Lal Singh, her prime minister and paramour; Tej Singh, the commander-in-chief; and others at court believed the defeat of the Khalsa could only result in a recovery of their authority. To ensure defeat, they were prepared to betray their own soldiers to the British, who could be expected to offer appropriate rewards.

Hardinge, the governor-general, anxiously tried to avoid provocation. None the less, he recognized the imminent peril and gradually, and as quietly as possible, trebled the size of his forces on the northwest frontier, keeping the army scattered in isolated stations in order not to give offence or to betray their numbers. The army was in this situation when Lal Singh crossed the Sutlej on 11 December 1845, his Sikhs crying 'on to Calcutta!' Their numbers were estimated at 60,000, with 150 guns, though it should be noted that official reports tended to exaggerate enemy strength, thereby making a victory more glorious or a defeat more excusable.

The governor-general was inspecting posts on the frontier when he heard the news. He declared war immediately and ordered the army to concentrate at the point of danger, Ferozepore, where Sir John Littler commanded a small garrison. Since Hardinge was close to the frontier with the Ludhiana Division, Gough hastened to join him with his larger force from Umballa, for, as he said, 'It would be a fearful thing to have a Governor-General bagged.'

The First or Umballa Division was commanded by Harry Smith, who had recently resigned his post as adjutant-general and had come down from Simla where he left Juana recovering from one of her unspecified illnesses. Working with Gough in preparing the army for war, he complained to D'Urban: 'My gallant old Eagle-catcher is ready to fight anything to the best of his knowledge of the art, and courts the Moloch popularity with a full measure of ill-expended Blarney.' No one really expected 'the rabble of a rapacious army' to put up much of a fight; in fact, there was general fear among the British that the Sikhs would recross the border before they had a slap at them.

Making forced marches from Umballa, Gough's main force was hustled along over 114 miles in five days. On the fifth day, 16 December, they joined Hardinge's force. The army continued its march in a style 'more sporting than military', for the road was now altogether insufficient for such a vast host. The cavalry and most of the infantry spread out to the fields on either side, leaving the firmer ground to the slower moving artillery and baggage animals. The flat land was covered with light sand which caused great clouds of choking dust. The men having exhausted their water supply, each well on the way was surrounded by shouting, shoving men seeking to quench their thirst. Sometimes the water had a terrible stench caused, it was said, by evil Sikhs who had thrown dead carcasses into the well. There was, moreover, little time or means for the men to cook their rations.

On the morning of the 18th the van of the army trickled into the deserted mud village of Mudki, 20 miles from Ferozepore. Footsore stragglers were stretched out for miles. The 31st Foot of Harry's division reached the village with only 50 men, so covered with dust that their skin could not be distinguished from their clothes. The parched and hungry men lay about like the fallen after a battle as they waited for the outdistanced camels carrying their supplies. It was close to three o'clock before the weary men at Mudki began to cook their breakfast and pitch their tents.

Hardinge and his staff had just sat down to a meal in a large tent beyond the village, when a sowar rushed up to the governor-general and said, 'Lord Sahib, you are eating when

the Sikhs are at your door.' The presence of the enemy was
confirmed by other scouts; then clouds of dust appeared in the
distance. Sir Henry, swinging his one arm, called for his horse.
Trumpets, bugles and drums sounded everywhere. There was
a general commotion as soldiers darted from their tents, the
horse artillery bounced forward at breakneck speed and the
sepoys, shouting 'Bum! Bum!' frantically brandished their
muskets. Within half an hour the camp was deserted except for
the guard.

The opposing armies were separated by a mile or more of
level fields of ploughed ground interspersed with bushes and
small trees. They were roughly equal in numbers, for Lal
Singh, the pock-marked 'Potemkin of the Punjab', detached
only some 10,000 undisciplined irregular horsemen, 2,000
infantry and 22 guns from his encampment at Ferozeshah.
Whether the smallness of his force was designed to ensure their
defeat, or Lal Singh supposed that he had only Hardinge's
inferior Ludhiana Division to deal with will never be known.

The Anglo-Indian 'Army of the Sutlej' had a high-sounding
name and boasted over 11,000 men. But it was an unco-
ordinated field force that had until recently existed largely on
paper. Generals were unfamiliar with most of the battalions
brigaded under them, and officers and men were often total
strangers to the units serving next to them. Gough later
complained that it was beyond his power 'to arrest this evil'.

The battle opened with an exchange of cannon shots that
sent limbs and heads flying. The smoke grew so thick that the
gunners had little to guide them but the flashes from the other
side. The heavy clouds were stabbed with flames until it
'seemed to be tearing the air to pieces'. After thirty minutes
the Sikh fire slackened. By now Gough had had sufficient time
to form his infantry into line. Smith's division, with three
battalions under Wheeler and two under Bolton, occupied the
right. Gilbert's division, three native battalions, held the centre.
McCaskill's division stood on the left with four battalions.
There was no reserve. For a time Sikh horsemen tried to get
around the flanks, but they were driven off by the spirited
charges of three brigades of British cavalry (1,500 troopers)
and the horse artillery. The horsedrawn guns were then pulled
to the centre to join the rest of the artillery in support of a
general advance by the infantry.

Harry protested Gough's order for an infantry attack. It seemed foolhardy to attack an undetermined number of Sikhs ensconced in a jungle beyond the fields with recently brigaded and fatigued soldiers, mostly sepoys. (Hardinge said the sepoys were like the Portuguese: they had their 'fighting days'.) Moreover, they would be fighting blindly, for the short December day was almost over. Rather than hurry into action, Harry suggested that the troops stand on the defensive and await the enemy on open ground. But Gough was impatient for victory and never thought much beyond cavalry charges and infantry assaults with fixed bayonets. He held to the popular maxim that there was only one correct way of fighting Asians and that was by moving straight on.

The British advanced in echelon of brigades from the right, which placed Harry's men ahead of the others. The Sikhs held firm. Firing grapeshot, their batteries knocked down British gunners and horses going forward to support the infantry. Smith's division encountered the stiffest resistance. Wheeler's brigade on the far right was menaced by Sikh horsemen. The battalions formed into squares. As soon as the threat had passed, Harry ordered them to reform and advance once more in line. Only the 50th, called the 'dirty half-hundred' because of their dark facings, charged on. The two sepoy battalions, the 42nd and 49th, remained in squares and hung back. There was no more 'bum-buming'; their fear of the Sikhs dampened their ardour. They sent panicky fire in every direction and into the rear of the 50th. In the fading light it was difficult, except for the turbans, to distinguish Sikh units in red jackets from the redcoats. Elsewhere across the battlefield British shot British.

Realizing that the attack might falter, Harry spurred his black Arab, Jem Crow, forward, grabbed hold of one of the 50th's colours, raised it high, and rushed into the thick of the enemy. The entire battalion followed him. They were fired upon from every side—and from above. 'The bold rascals got into trees and shot our fellows in the rear,' Harry told his friend, Surgeon Ford. At first they did not know where the shots were coming from, but when the snipers were discovered high in the trees, Harry saw the most 'extraordinary thing' he had ever witnessed, 'half a dozen fellows out of each tree came rolling down like cock pheasants or caperaillie'. Some of the Sikhs who had been driven from their guns and other positions, threw down their muskets 'and came on sword and target (they all carry excellent swords) like ancient Greeks'. The British either ran them through or chased them to the rear.

All along the line the British had overrun the enemy and were heavily engaged. Gough in his white coat, Hardinge in a black one, and all their staff were in the middle of the fray. The enemy were dispersed by fire and steel.

The Indian night descending quickly, men became confused in the dark and continued to blaze away at nothing or at one another until the bugles sounded the 'cease fire'. The Sikhs had vanished. Some of the sepoys who had slipped over the edge of the battleground now quietly made their way back to camp.

The 31st, part of Bolton's brigade, had difficulty finding a bugler to sound the regimental call to form the battalion. After considerable searching they got hold of a sepoy who said he knew how to sound the instrument. He was producing some fearful squeaks when General Smith came by and nearly knocked it down his throat and asked what the devil the row was about.

Hardinge believed that half of the long list of casualties (215 slain and 657 wounded) were shot by mistake by their 'friends', particularly after dark. Smith's division had borne the brunt of the fighting and accounted for almost half of those lost. Some of the wounded were obviously murdered by the Sikhs, for the next day they were found 'frightfully disfigured; all had their throats cut and several were beheaded'. Sikh fire was generally high and, therefore, fatal to many senior officers on horseback. Of the generals, McCaskill was killed, his heart pierced by grapeshot; Bolton was mortally wounded and Wheeler severely. That night Harry saw General Sale, the quarter-master-general, who had 'attached himself' to his command, waiting patiently with a handkerchief over his face as the surgeons prepared to amputate his leg. He died the next day.

'Midnight Moodkhee', as the battle was nicknamed, was a costly and doubtful victory. There was no elation in camp that night. Not only were British casualties heavier (the Sikhs were estimated to have lost only 300 men), but enemy regulars had fought better than the sepoys. Moreover, Sikh guns had greater range and had been worked skilfully.

The Sikhs were anything but discouraged. They had lost

seventeen guns, but had nevertheless fought a fairly successful rearguard action. 'If a few thousand Sikhs required the united force of the British to conquer them,' a captured Sikh sowar told Surgeon William MacGregor, 'how much more difficult it must be to conquer the Khalsa army, and how infinitely greater must necessarily be the loss.'

Rumour kept most of the men standing in the sun all the next day, but the Sikhs had retired to Lal Singh's strongly fortified camp at Ferozeshah. Meanwhile, the wounded were carried in with great difficulty because of the shortage of doolies. Many of the dead, stripped by camp followers, were left to vultures and wild dogs. In temporary hospitals with improvised equipment the surgeons available worked as swiftly as possible. Still short of food, the men were fed what was called 'elephant's lug', large cakes of coarse flour and bran mixed with straw that was normally fed to the pachyderms. The Rev. Mr Coley, who tried to comfort them, wrote simply, 'religious conversation did not seem to be what they wanted'.

Four fresh battalions, two European and two native, came in that evening. Hardinge sent forth elephants and camels to bring in the exhausted stragglers and then ordered his fine band to play national airs as they marched through the camp. With a quixotic gesture which he would have cause to regret, the governor-general placed his talents as a general officer at Gough's disposal. Sir Hugh accepted the offer with pleasure and named him his second-in-command.

Preparations were now made for an assault on Ferozeshah nine miles northwest of Mudki. Gough ordered Littler to slip away from Tej Singh, who was watching him with a superior force at Ferozepore, and join him before Ferozeshah. Together they would number 18,000 men, with 65 guns and two powerful howitzers.

At dawn on the 21st, leaving the unfit behind with the baggage guarded by two native units, the army marched on a broad front towards Ferozeshah. Having reached their destination at 10.30 in the morning, the men consumed the meagre contents of their haversacks. Littler sent word that he would be late for the rendezvous so Gough, after a quick reconnaisance, decided to begin the attack without him. He rode over to Hardinge, who was sitting down to breakfast, and announced confidently, 'Sir Henry, if we attack at once, I promise you a

splendid victory.' Hardinge disapproved. The two generals
then retired behind a clump of trees to argue the matter out of
sight but not the hearing of their staffs.

Considering how well the Sikhs had fought at Mudki,
Hardinge favoured waiting for Littler's men. Gough held that
they must take advantage of the few daylight hours left in this,
the shortest day of the year. And there was the possibility that
Tej Singh might appear and increase the odds against them.
When Gough grew excitedly insistent, Hardinge said calmly,
'Then Sir Hugh, I must exercise my civil powers as Governor-
General, and forbid the attack until Littler's force has come up.'
This decision, Harry observed, was 'a most fortunate inter-
diction for British India'.

The Sikh position was a strong one. The village of
Ferozeshah was surrounded by a ditch and sloping ground in
the form of a parallelogram, surmounted by nearly 100 heavy
guns and defended by 30,000 men. As one officer said, 'This
bull was all horns'. Harry rode out that morning and carefully
surveyed the ground, concluding that the attack should be made
on the west side, facing Ferozepore, thereby facilitating a
junction with Littler and menacing the enemy's line of retreat.
Though the west side was strongly entrenched, he reasoned
that 'by a weighty attack on a given point, the half of the
enemy's cannon would have been lost to him and innocuous
to us'.

But Gough had no intention of discussing his plans, if they
can be called that, with his generals. Three divisions were to
be formed in line: Littler on the left, Wallace in the centre and
Gilbert on the right. Most of the guns were massed in the
centre and the cavalry was placed on the flanks. Smith was to
hold his strong and experienced division in reserve. The
attack was to be on as wide a front as possible, Harry wrote,
'thus presenting ourselves as targets to every gun the enemy
had'. He marshalled his two brigades on either side of the
artillery. Since there was almost a mile of ground dividing
them, he decided it would be impossible to control them both
effectively, so he placed himself on the left with the 2nd
brigade (Ryan's); Brigadier Hicks would direct the right-hand
brigade. Like the other division commanders, Harry was left
in the dark as to exactly how, what or where he was to fight.
He later remarked with bitterness: 'The army was one

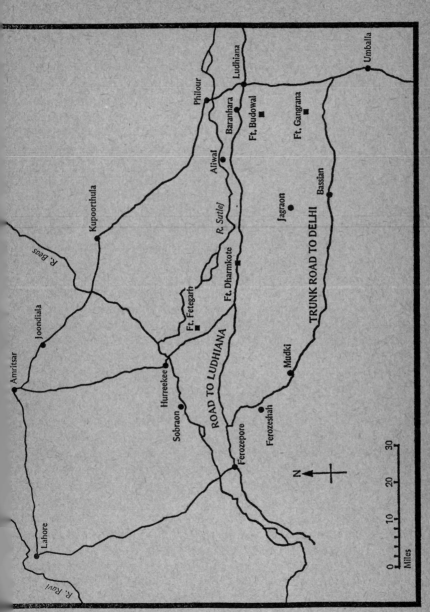

Map 5 The First Sikh War, 1845–6: Theatre of Operations

unwieldy battalion under one Commanding Officer who had
not been granted the power of ubiquity.'

When Littler arrived, the army began to deploy. It was an
awkward time-consuming business with Gough's and Littler's
battalions moving through the dust in opposite directions.
Harry's patience was tested as he watched the confused units
being sorted out in the waning sunlight. Gough refused to
start the battle until every soldier was in his proper place.
The men were so tired that they flopped into their assigned
positions. They were so thirsty, wrote Private Benjamin
Moore in Smith's division, 'they would have murdered their
father for a drink of water'.

Shortly before 4 p.m. the artillery opened what was to be
one of the most decisive and bloody battles in the history of
India. Sikh guns responded with a great roar. It was an unequal
duel. Except for the howitzers, the British artillery were
worsted by an enemy that worked their more numerous guns
rapidly and with precision. Brigadier 'Bully' Brooke, the
artillery commander, sought Gough and declared, 'I must
either advance or be blown to bits.' The guns moved ahead and
the infantry began to congeal into a long scarlet wall of human
bricks. The pageantry reminded Harry of the Peninsula; in
fact there had been very little change in thirty years. The bright
uniforms and accoutrements that made men feel bigger, braver,
more manly, were the same. They still carried the old flintlock
muskets, dubbed 'Brown Bess'. The leaders were all Peninsular
men. And before them they had the kind of flat field they had
wanted, one where they could advance in line, fire a volley and
sweep all before them with the bayonet.

Littler's division started prematurely against the west face
of the entrenchments. As they emerged from a belt of semi-
jungle, blasts of grapeshot splattered them; once they were in
range, the Sikhs hit them with musket fire. The division came
up unevenly. Reed's brigade moved ahead of Ashburnham's,
whose three native battalions had disintegrated at the sight of
a well. 'No power,' reported Ashburnham, 'could restrain the
thirsty sepoys from running out to drink.' Reed, meanwhile,
gave his men the order to charge too soon. The 62nd came
close to seizing their objective when the concentrated fire
brought them to a halt. Reed's two sepoy battalions seemed to
melt away. Without consulting Littler (who was near him),

Reed ordered the brigade to retire. One officer cried, 'India is lost!' The entire division pulled back out of range. Littler felt himself disgraced; Gough had waited half a day for this force which was put out of action in less than half an hour.

The reserve had also come under fire from long range cannon shot. Harry, with the bravado that was the prerogative of a general officer, exposed himself to it by riding up and down before the men lying on their stomachs and exhorted them, 'to be still as they could not get up and live'. None got up; they simply marvelled at the way the general stayed on his horse without being hit.

To see how the battle was progressing, Harry rode ahead, where he met Hardinge. The governor-general asked him what the commotion on the left was all about. 'I galloped forward to ascertain,' he wrote, 'and reported that they were Littler's force, that his attack appeared to me one of no weight from its formation, and that, if the enemy behaved as expected it would fail.' Hardinge told him to bring up his division and place it between Littler's and Wallace's, in the centre. Explaining that he had only one brigade (the other was operating independently), Harry was ordered by Sir Henry to use that.

Once advised of Littler's effort, Gough hurried the advance of the rest of the army. Howls of triumph were soon heard from the Sikh lines, announcing the repulse on the west face. Gilbert's division on the right, led by Sir Hugh, made for the south and east face. Wallace's centre division headed for the rest of the south face and a corner of the west. Commanding them was Sir Henry. With the governor-general was Prince Waldemar of Prussia, a nephew of King Frederick William IV. He had hoped to explore Tibet and had found a war instead.

The Sikhs redoubled their efforts to halt the approaching British with a hailstorm of grapeshot and musketry. 'To heighten our destruction,' recalled Captain John Cumming, 'mines had been dug before the trenches and sprung under our feet. The slaughter was terrible.' The trenches themselves were camouflaged with branches. Cursing soldiers tumbled on top of one another. Some fell back; others went over the slopes and penetrated the gun positions. Sikh regulars levelled their muskets for a volley. Close combat followed; the clash of tulwar and bayonet. As Sikh cavalry prepared to staunch the flow of redcoats, the 3rd Light Dragoons appeared on the scene. Having charged headlong over the works of the lightly manned eastern face, they tore their way clear through the enemy reserves and emerged on the other side with only half their men still in the saddle.

Darkness threw everything into confusion. Only an occasional flash from an exploding magazine revealed a *tableau vivant* of the inferno. The assaulting battalions became a snarled jumble of men uttering terrible oaths and firing at shadows. Generals could not gauge the extent of their success — or failure; colonels were separated from their regiments; soldiers found themselves alone or next to strangers.

By midnight, realizing there was little compensating advantage and much hazard in staying where they were, Gough and Hardinge withdrew the remains of their shattered battalions into a bivouac some 300 yards outside the entrenchments. Hardinge, who had lost all of his staff but his son, remarked 'another such action will shake the empire'. Disclosing his innermost fears, he gave orders that the State Papers he had left at Mudki be burned. He advised a reluctant Prince Waldemar, who had already lost one of his suite to return to safety.[1] Fearing that Napoleon's sword, his greatest treasure, would be lost, he had it sent back to his wife, with the assurance that his last thoughts were of her.

The two chiefs, Gough and Hardinge, agreed in thinking that their only hope was to resume the battle at dawn, which would lead either to victory or complete destruction. Their anxiety would have been lessened if they had known that Smith still had a fighting force somewhere to the west of them.

Smith, with only Ryan's brigade in hand (Hicks's had joined the main force) had moved into the gap caused by Littler's failure and Wallace's men crowding towards the centre of the line before them. The advance was somewhat impeded by Reed's reeling brigade on one side and broken troops from the centre on the other. Some stragglers took heart at the sight of Smith's formations and rallied behind them. Harry was about to order the charge when Major Broadfoot, the chief political officer, intercepted him with a shouted warning, 'Be prepared,

[1] The Prince later asked the British government to allow him to present the Iron Cross to the brave officers he had served with. The government politely turned down his request.

THE SIKH WAR: MUDKI AND FEROZESHAH   239

General. Four battalions of Avitabiles are close upon you in
advance; I have it on correct information — a man in my pay
has just left them.' Because of the smoke and dust that had
drifted across the lines, the Avitabiles could not be seen. But
Harry knew that these troops, rigorously trained by the
Italian soldier of fortune, General Avitabile, were counted
among the best of the Khalsa. The onslaught caused 'a storm
of musketry and cannon which I have rarely, if ever, seen
exceeded', declared Harry. The sepoys (42nd and 48th)
staggered and in some cases fell back; the 50th held and
returned the fire. Broadfoot was shot in the leg but fought
on until a second shot killed him. Major Arthur Somerset,
Lord Fitzroy's eldest son and great-nephew of the Duke,
was mortally wounded. Officers and men began to drop all
around.

'The enemy was at this moment in his bearing noble and
triumphant,' noted Harry. 'I saw there was nothing for it but
a charge of bayonets to restore the waning fight.' Placing
himself alongside Col. Ryan, he led the 50th into the trenches,
shouting, 'Into them my lads; the day is your own!' There was
a savage hand-to-hand contest, after which the guns were
taken and the enemy retired. The advance continued until Sikh
tents broke their order. 'But my orders and example,' recalled
Harry, were 'Forward! Forward! Forward!' Stragglers from
the main assault joined his men as they continued towards the
village of Ferozeshah, the heart of the Sikh defences. Some 400
yards short of its mud walls, Harry could see masses of the
enemy preparing to make a stand behind them. Because of
the dust raised to his left, he could not ascertain whether the
Avitabiles were gone or preparing to rush his flank. Nevertheless, he resolved to seize the village. Calling on his men in
sharp, imperative tones to follow, Harry rode forward and
planted the colours of the 50th on the mud walls. The general
himself was the first man into what proved to be the Khalsa
headquarters. The ensuing struggle was made more vicious by
the enemy's efforts to defend their richly ornamented horses
and camels, laden with valuables of all kinds. But the narrow
streets were soon cleared.

With no Avitabiles to his left and the British main assault
apparently successful on his right (officers and men were coming
up in small groups), Harry decided to take advantage of the

little daylight that remained to press on to the enemy's camp a half mile beyond the village. The camp was taken.

Once the darkness closed in, Harry tried to consolidate the miscellaneous accretions of his force. It was no easy task to reform some 3,000 excited and bewildered men. Only the 50th 'was well in hand'. To reduce casualties, he told the men to remove the covers from their hats and remain quiet. All the time Harry expected to hear British cheers of victory on his right, but he heard only the sounds of the enemy closing in around him. When he realized that the battle was not over and that he was cut off from the rest of the army, Harry made a desperate effort to form his men into a semicircle before the enemy. None too soon, for the Sikhs hit the 24th N.I. on his right and drove them in. Complete darkness, however, halted the enemy. Only the familiar sounds made by British troops told the general that his position was still intact.

A rising quarter-moon made Harry's position untenable. It disclosed to his adversaries how weak and isolated the British actually were. The Sikhs moved in to fire at closer range. Some of the men were so tired that they were killed while fast asleep. Harry had hoped to hold his ground as he drew his force into a tighter formation, but they were being speedily reduced and the survivors greatly agitated. Sensing victory, the Sikhs began to beat their drums and shout insults in French, English and Hindustani.

At three in the morning Harry made a feint to attack; he opened fire and under cover of the smoke his men, led by the 50th, pulled out as rapidly and silently as possible. They were gone before the enemy discovered their absence. Unopposed, the British went out as they had gone in, for the route was clearly marked by comrades who had been slaughtered in the advance.

Harry knew they were safe when he encountered a vedette who directed them towards a bivouac fire. The camp belonged to the 62nd and was being used by surgeons to attend the wounded. He placed some of his wounded in their care. All of his staff had been hit, and almost every officer's horse had been killed. Miraculously, neither Harry nor his horse, Jem Crow, had the slightest injury.

The officers in the camp knew nothing of the whereabouts of Gough. They presumed to tell Harry that his only course was

to retreat towards Ferozepore. In a voice made firm by
indignation, he told them that Gough must be near, contemplat-
ing an attack at daybreak — 'and find him I will if in hell, where
I will join him rather than make one retrograde step till I have
ascertained some fact'. At that moment he saw a great fire flare
up, obviously from another camp nearby. 'There is my point,'
he announced, 'friend or foe.'

The second camp was in a village appropriately named
Misreewalla. Huddled about the fires that bitter cold night was
a heterogeneous mass of several thousand tattered infantrymen
from every corps, along with some of the horse artillery and a
brigade of cavalry. Using his superior rank, Harry ordered rum
to be served to the men of the 50th and his oddments of other
Europeans.

To his surprise and delight, Harry met Captain Lumley, the
A.A.G. of the army, who, because of casualties, had taken over
the whole department of adjutant-general which had been under
his father, General Lumley (Harry's successor), before he
became ill. Assuming that he was in communication with
Gough, Harry was shocked to hear Lumley say, 'As senior
officer of the Adjutant-General's department, I order you to
collect every soldier and march to Ferozepore.' The old
campaigner asked sharply,

Do you come direct from the Commander-in-Chief with
such an order? If you do, I can find him and, by God, I'll
take no such order from any man on earth but from his own
mouth. Where is he?

The young captain admitted that he did not know, but in his
official capacity Smith was to obey *his* orders. 'Damn the
orders,' shouted Harry, 'if not the Commander-in-Chief's. I'll
give my own orders, and take none of that retrograde sort from
any staff officer on earth.' Harry's curiosity was now aroused.
'But why to Ferozepore?' he asked. Lumley explained that they
had been beaten; however, there was still hope that they could
buy the Sikhs. 'What!' exclaimed Harry incredulously, 'have
we taken no guns?' Lumley estimated they had captured fifty
or sixty. 'Thank you,' said the general coldly, 'I see my way,
and want no orders.' Turning to his adjutant-general, Harry
said, 'Now get hold of every officer and make him fall in his

17

men.' Lumley was dumbfounded. Harry thought the man was mad.[1]

Before Harry got under way, Captain Christie in charge of the irregular corps of horse appeared and told him he knew the way to headquarters.

The soldiers of the main force were nervously awaiting the dawn's first light, knowing they must conquer or die. To Gough's relief, Harry and his men arrived to participate in the fight. Smith's force was placed where Littler's had been the day before. At daybreak Harry saw, much to his astonishment, that directly before him was the village he had carried and held that infamous night.

The enemy had reoccupied most of the entrenchments during the night. There were fewer of them, however, because Lal Singh had taken out many of his men under cover of darkness. This time the British dislodged them completely, spiked their guns and went on unchecked as the Sikhs broke and fled. Thirsty soldiers, who had licked the dew from their gun barrels that morning, found that the enemy had committed one last act of vengeance, throwing corpses and gunpowder into the wells. As a result, many were soon afflicted with dysentery. (In extreme cases, surgeons applied leeches to the anus as a cure.)

All desultory firing ceased by midday, and the troops formed ranks to the north of the village. Gough and Hardinge were cheered as they rode along the ranks to congratulate each unit. The fagged and famished soldiers were promised comfort and rest—but another battle was about to begin.

A great dense, whirling cloud of dust appeared on the horizon and moved towards them. The gleam of steel and the bright silk flags soon announced the presence of 30,000 Sikhs. The army of Tej Singh, who had been uselessly watching Littler's abandoned tents, was about to attack. Gough called for the formation of hollow squares before the village. The exhausted men, uniforms ripped and faces blackened, put up a bold front as they stood steady and compact.

Tej Singh put his artillery forward and commenced a heavy

[1] Much later that day when Hardinge asked Lumley to explain his conduct, he found him wearing pyjamas. The staff officer told him that his trousers had been so riddled with bullets that they dropped off! His peculiar behaviour was attributed to sunstroke. He escaped a court-martial by pleading insanity, and then resigned. His father resigned his post and died the next day.

bombardment with 40 guns. All that was necessary was for him to stand and pound the squares to pieces, for the British gunners were down to firing their last few rounds of mostly captured ammunition. 'Who did not feel,' wrote Captain Cumming, 'that the field would be their burial ground?' Some of the sepoys ran away. At one point the chivalrous Gough galloped out with a single A.D.C. to draw the fire on to himself. Sikh cavalry thundered forward to turn the British flank. Gough ordered up the 3rd Light Dragoons, 74 exhausted men who mounted with difficulty horses barely able to gallop. Some native cavalry supported them. The Sikh horsemen halted and the Dragoons, whom the Sikhs called 'the Devil's Children', barrelled into them and they gave way.

To the astonishment of everyone on both sides, the rest of the British cavalry and horse artillery were seen moving away from the battle. This time the demented Lumley had succeeded in his mischief. Using the commander-in-chief as his authority, he gave the false order for them to retreat to Ferozepore, and they obeyed. Yet, Lumley possibly saved the day. For Tej Singh, already somewhat intimidated by the British victory over Lal Singh, later stated that he concluded the retreating column was manoeuvring to attack him from the rear. Or, perhaps, as some have suggested, he feared to allow the Khalsa the luxury of success. Whatever the reason, the Sikh commander threw away a cheap victory by pulling back across the Sutlej. Any attempt to dispute his withdrawal was out of the question.

Gough claimed a victory—to which Hardinge retorted, 'Another such victory as this and we're undone.' In two days they had 2,415 casualties, some 700 of whom were killed. As at Mudki, a good number had been shot by their comrades. Among them was a Catholic priest, the only one present, who had unfortunately worn a beard and a turban. Well over half of those lost were European, though the native troops were more numerous by far. 'The British infantry,' observed Hardinge, 'as usual carried the day. I can't say I admire sepoy fighting.' The governor-general tried to console the wounded 'with soldierly urbanity'. One man with grapeshot through both cheeks was told that he now had beauty marks to take home to his sweetheart. If a man lost an arm, Hardinge pointed to his own empty sleeve; if a man lost a leg, he told him that one of his sons had lost a foot in the battle. All the men were promised spirits and thousands of mince pies for Christmas.

To the average soldier, 'Paddy' Gough could do no wrong. Many an officer, however, questioned his competence. In a private letter, the governor-general told Peel, the Prime Minister, that Gough 'is not to be trusted with the conduct of the war in the Punjab'. He expected him to be replaced.

Harry agreed. In his opinion, Hardinge was right in forcing the commander-in-chief to wait for Littler, for there had been more than enough time to win a victory before nightfall, provided that Sir Hugh applied the correct strategy in the attack. Harry was incensed when his report of the battle was not included by Gough with the other public despatches. Moreover, the commander-in-chief in his own official despatch referred briefly and vaguely to Harry's success in taking the village by writing that Smith 'captured and long retained another point of the position'. It seemed clear that Sir Hugh was trying to conceal the fact that he had blundered in failing to support Harry in the advance position that he had seized, and that he accepted no responsibility for Harry's forced withdrawal.

Despite his differences with Gough, Harry informed Alice, 'Your old humbug of a brother's name is *up* in the army, I do assure you, especially with Sir Henry Hardinge and Sir Hugh Gough.' After the battle, the governor-general thanked him and declared, 'Smith, it was your boldness and audacity that saved to us the victory.'

[12]

The Sikh War: Aliwal and Sobraon

A health to ould Hardinge and Littler,
Hurrah for ould Smith and Gough,
Shures it's the Infantry settles their hashes
And lets the smoke out of their duff.
A soldier's song from The First Anglo-Sikh War

After 'muddled Moodki', and Ferozeshah, 'a bloody bull-dog fight' (as Harry termed them), both sides rested and were reinforced. The Army of the Sutlej remained idle while awaiting the powerful siege-train to batter down the walls of Lahore, capital of the Punjab.

The morale of the Khalsa, whose losses were probably equal to those of the British, was as high as ever. Captain D. H. Mackinnon wrote:

> It was confidently whispered amongst the natives of Hindustan that the British had met their match at last, and though the Sikhs had recrossed the river, they had left their opponents in such a condition as to be unable to reap any advantage from their victory.

It was obvious that the Sikhs, who had committed only a part of their army, would try again to wrest control of India from the British.

Gough had a problem: how could he prevent the enemy from crossing the Sutlej and interfering with his communications or attacking his scattered garrisons? It was impossible, Hardinge warned him: 'He who defends everything defends nothing.' Harry supported this view. However, he advised Sir Hugh that the army could be better posted along the river. Acting on his recommendation, Gough moved his centre up river, opposite Sobraon, with his left watching the fords to the west and maintaining direct communications with Ferozepore, and his right (under Smith) guarding the Hurreekee fords to the east.

The Sikh camp was at Sobraon. 'Hives of parti-coloured canvas speckled the country as far as the eye could reach,' recalled Mackinnon, 'and appeared to shelter a mighty host notwithstanding their recent losses.' The Khalsa made the first move, one 'unparalleled in the history of war', according to Harry, by constructing a bridge of boats over the broad Sutlej and moving their entire army across. They did so unmolested, for the entire operation was covered by their heavy guns on the high right bank. Hardinge told Gough that he should be satisfied to contain their strongly entrenched bridgehead with counter-fortifications until their own heavy guns arrived.

While the two main armies were stalemated at Sobraon, 10,000 Sikhs under Ranjur Singh went on the prowl. Moving east along the north bank, he could pounce on the four native battalions garrisoning Ludhiana, or strike farther south at the highly vulnerable convoy of heavy guns, ammunition and stores that extended over ten miles on the road from Delhi. The first threat to Gough's communications came when the Sikhs occupied two small forts south of the river, Dharmkote and Fetegarh, on the road between Gough and Ludhiana.

To counter the move Gough sent for Smith on 16 January 1846. He told him that the forts must be taken — but who should he send? Harry immediately volunteered. It was the answer Sir Hugh wanted to hear. When could he march? 'Soon after this time tomorrow,' Harry promised, 'I shall be writing my report that I have reduced them both.' Gough laughed and advised him that Dharmkote, the farther of the two, was 26 miles from his right. Harry replied that he knew the distance; all that he needed was the powder to blow the gates in if necessary. To himself he said, 'powder or no powder, I march'.

With all the provisions and transport he could lay his hands on in so short a time, Smith's small detachment was on the road two hours before daylight. Passing Fetegarh, which had been abandoned, he arrived before Dharmkote at two in the afternoon. It was occupied but Harry could see that it had no guns of consequence. The fort was quickly invested and Harry, under a flag of truce, met with the Sikh commander. Harry cut short his efforts to negotiate by offering all hands six weeks pay if they came out in 20 minutes and surrendered their arms. After waiting for 25 minutes, he gave his gunners the signal to fire. A few rounds were sufficient to have the Sikhs bring down their flag and to hoist a white one in its place.

The commander-in-chief received Harry's report of success shortly after intelligence told him that Ranjur Singh was in the neighbourhood of Ludhiana. To deal with this new development, Gough sent word to Smith that reinforcements were on the way, including the 16th Lancers, which would give him a total strength of three regiments of horse and 18 guns, besides the infantry brigade he already had with him. The 53rd was under orders to join him from Bassian at Jagraon, 18 miles southeast of Dharmkote. They, as well as the Ludhiana garrison under Col. Godby, would be under his command.

Once in Jagraon, Harry received urgent messages from Godby for help, and orders from both Hardinge and Gough to protect Ludhiana, where hundreds of wives and children were with the garrison. Ranjur Singh was said to be at Baranhara, only seven miles away. If he was not checked, the Sikhs would take Ludhiana and fall upon the great convoy coming through Bassian. Moreover, Harry learned that between Jagraon and Ludhiana the Sikhs held two forts: Budowal, 18 miles to the northeast, and Gangrana, ten miles south of Budowal. Enemy cavalry was at both places. To avoid harassment on both flanks of his relieving column, Harry decided to follow a road running just north of Budowal.

Once the moon was up, shortly past midnight on the 21st, Harry pressed on with every available man, about 4,000 plus 250 convalescents from Mudki and Ferozeshah. All wheeled transport were left with two sepoy companies in Jagraon. Their line of march that night was indicated by enemy spies, for Harry 'observed rockets firing, as if for signals'. To meet a possible attack on the morrow, he sent instructions to Godby every two hours to join him with every man he could spare at Suneth, half-way between Budowal and Ludhiana.

The sun's first rays revealed a lone despatch rider racing across a great sandy, featureless plain from the direction of Ludhiana. He had a terse message for the general: Ranjur Singh had moved from Baranhara and was camped with his entire force of 10,000 men and 40 guns at Budowal, only two miles away. This move, 'whether by accident or design', Harry told Alice, 'no French general could have exceeded in ability or conception.' As for Godby, whom he expected to join, 'the thick headed fellow never moved to help me,' he complained to D'Urban. (Actually Godby did move but only for a short distance in the wrong direction — and then back.) Without Godby's support, some senior officers advised Harry to fall back. 'I march, sir! to the relief of Ludhiana,' Harry shouted, 'then no earthly power shall deter me from going.'

But Harry was not so rash as to try to fight his way through and suffer the resultant heavy losses. He realized that should he fail, Ludhiana and its garrison would be lost, the convoy would be raided and 'all of India would have been ablaze'. He decided to give Budowal a wide berth by detouring two miles to the south. The order of march was changed so that at his command the entire column could wheel to the left in battle formation. Between the infantry and the enemy, Harry placed his cavalry, which would be shielded somewhat from Sikh guns by a low ridge of sand hills. The guns were kept to the rear to deal with any threat from that direction.

Once Ranjur Singh saw the British change direction, he put a force in motion parallel to their column. Travelling by road, the Sikhs were able to outdistance the British infantry. Sikh horsemen were soon a mile ahead of the redcoats. Sgt Pearman of the 3rd Light Dragoons recalled:

At about 10 a.m. I was looking at our Left Front, when I saw something glisten in the sun's rays. I said: 'Sergeant-Major Baker, there is the enemy.' He replied, 'You be damned!' He had been very drunk before he marched ... He had hardly replied when: 'Bang! Bang!' and two balls whizzed over our heads. A third went into a regiment of sepoys and knocked over three or four men ... another ball struck Henry Greenbank in the head. It sounded like a band-box full of feathers flying all over us.

Harry ordered his guns to reply, noting with satisfaction that they had 'a most auxiliary effect, creating slaughter and confusion'. Unfortunately, however, his baggage-train had fallen behind and several cannon balls, ricocheting through the camels, panicked the drivers. Suddenly there was chaos.

A large segment was cut off by Sikh cavalry, who rushed upon the unprotected baggage.

An even greater menace materialized to the rear. The Sikhs, 'with a dexterity and quickness not to be exceeded', drew up in a line of seven battalions, with guns at intervals, to attack the column from behind. Harry accepted the challenge and prepared to attack them by turning about part of the 31st to serve as a firm base. But he soon discovered that the sand was so deep and the men so knocked up that he had to abandon the idea. Instead, under heavy cannon fire, he 'changed front on the centre of the 31st Regiment and of the 53rd, by what is a difficult move on parade even — a countermarch of the centre by wings'. Disciplined and well-trained, the men executed the move with the precision of close-order drill at a review. Harry believed it was a sight never seen on a battlefield before. The sepoys were no less steady than the British. They all drew off in echelons of battalions towards Ludhiana. At the command 'Halt, Front', they would meet any attack. The cavalry, with horse-drawn guns behind, manoeuvred skilfully in their support and broke up all efforts of Sikh riders to dispute their passage. 'The whole were moving most correctly and the movement was so steady,' Harry reported to Gough, 'that the enemy, notwithstanding his overwhelming force, did not attack, but stood amazed, as it were, fearing to quit his stronghold of Budowal.'

Even without interference from the enemy, however, some never reached Ludhiana that day because of exhaustion aggravated by thirst, under a concussive sun. 'Men's tongues were protruding from their mouths,' recalled Pearman, 'Roberts made water in his cap and drank it.' Though the enemy cavalry was on their heels waiting to cut up stragglers, many men dropped, saying they could go no farther. When Sgt-Major Baker lay down, Pearman pleaded with him to think of his wife and children. He looked up and said, 'I can't.' Many of them were saved by the Lancers who picked them up. Stragglers came into Ludhiana that night and throughout the next day.

Harry halted three miles from Ludhiana to spare his men. Water from muddy cattle pools, almost as thick as molasses, 'tasted like nectar'. Outposts were established and strong patrols were sent out. On seeing Pearman and some of his comrades, Harry went to them. 'He looked at us with tears in his eyes. He said: "Poor boys, lie down now and rest for a time".' The general told them that two guides were supposed to have taken them wide of the enemy. The guides, however, treacherously led them within range of the Sikh guns. According to Pearman, 'Sir Harry shot the two guides himself.'[1]

Harry reported 214 casualties, convalescents with the baggage-train for the most part. Some were taken prisoner; but most were later found murdered in or near their doolies. Most of the baggage was lost. All of Harry's kit fell into enemy hands. 'I care not for the fine coats,' he told Kempt, 'but I lost my Waterloo medal and all other medals — Not my Peninsular one!' He also mourned the death of his new acting A.D.C., Captain Campbell, who had raced up from Calcutta to be with him. Whoever accompanied Sir Harry Smith in battle, commented Mackinnon, 'must be prepared to encounter the thickest fire'. During the confusion, Harry's dog, 'a large and handsome Newfoundland', was separated from his master. His appearance at Gough's camp, 70 miles away, was the first intimation that something was amiss with Smith's force. (The dog was later carried off by a leopard.)

General Smith ordered a day of rest, being compelled, as he told D'Urban 'to refit like a ship in a storm'. With reinforcements coming in, the Shekawati brigade from Bassian and Wheeler's from Dharmkote, Harry made preparations to attack Budowal the following day. However, Ranjur Singh was aware of the forces converging on him and prudently abandoned the place, going north to the Sutlej to meet his reinforcements.

'I was as you may conceive not a little delighted at seeing myself again between Ranjur Singh and the line of treasure,' Harry wrote D'Urban, 'and as quick as troops can traverse 9 miles, I was in possession of the Fort of Budhowal.' The fort was ransacked by the troops. The camp followers made a thorough wreck of the place and set fire to villages in the area. Some of the soldiers, on seeing the naked bodies of their murdered comrades, put the torch to some of the houses. Their one consolation was that the enemy might have mistaken

---

[1] The story is uncorroborated by Harry and others who left an account of the skirmish. Whether true or not, such tales enhanced his reputation with the soldiers.

the bottles in the medical stores they looted for wines and liquors.

The fires and looting were condemned by General Smith in the severest terms. Officers were ordered to suppress behaviour that might encourage hostility among the inhabitants who, after all, were not responsible for the initial hostilities.

Reinforcements were slow in arriving. The brigade under Wheeler, Harry related to D'Urban, 'was commanded by an ass, who listened to rumour, became alarmed, and actually made *one march* back to Head Quarters, in place of obeying my instructions and daily apprising me of his whereabouts'. When Wheeler finally came in on the 26th, Harry had 12,000 men, 32 guns — and a strong desire to 'teach the Sikhs how to swim' the Sutlej.

Adverse criticism of his conduct at Budowal sharpened Harry's desire for a victory. Irresponsible correspondents in India spoke of 'disaster' and 'defeat', and blamed him for the loss of the baggage. For a time it was feared that the great convoy would be lost. 'Nothing makes people in India so angry,' Hardinge observed, 'as losing their comforts.' The Sikhs were elated by what they claimed was a great triumph, and publicly displayed British prisoners in Lahore. Believing he had done 'that which *was right*' at Budowal, Harry was hurt by letters from friends who asked, 'Why did you not attack?' He said to himself and to them, too, 'I will soon be ready.'

Meanwhile, Ranjur Singh, one of the Khalsa's better generals and apparently no traitor, was also preparing for battle. On the 26th he was joined by battalions of Avitabiles, 4,000 stalwarts, mostly middle-aged veterans animated by a spirit of ferocity. Some wore armour, but most wore red jackets, blue breeches with a red stripe down the side and white turbans. Together with the 12 guns they brought, Ranjur Singh's strength stood at 18,000 men, with 67 guns. He was now emboldened to move on Jagraon and once more threaten the convoy.

Only after his men were well-fed and rested did Harry venture forth from Budowal on the morning of 28 January (1846) to seek and destroy the enemy. His force marched northwest in three contiguous columns with a regiment of native cavalry sweeping eastward to watch for a move against

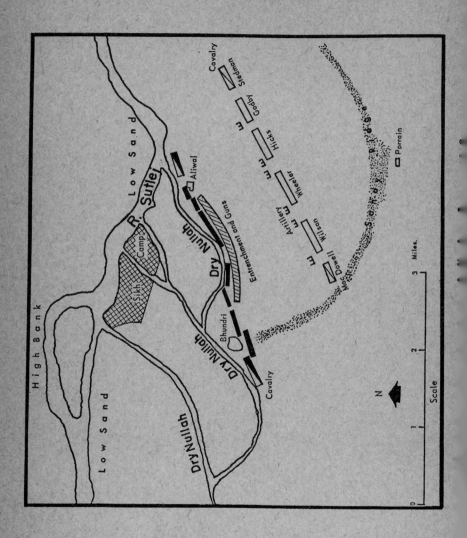

Ludhiana. Two hours out, a spy reported the enemy across the Sutlej heading for Jagraon. Harry was unperturbed, for he had anticipated such a move. As the Duke said, the business of war, as in life, is 'guessing what was at the other side of the hill'. Riding ahead with the cavalry, Harry was one of the first to reach Porrain, a village built on top of a sandy ridge. Climbing to the top of a house, he was delighted to behold Ranjur Singh's entire force spread out before him.

The enemy, forewarned, was hastily preparing a crescent line of shelter trenches on the crest of a sandy ridge extending for a mile between the fortified village of Aliwal on their left and the hamlet of Bhundri, masked by a sparse grove of trees, on their right. The alluvial ground behind the line descended for almost a mile towards the Sutlej where the Sikhs had their camp around a ferry-head. Harry noted with glee that what was otherwise a strong position, had one great weakness. Once the enemy was broken, his line of retreat would be hindered by the river. Moreover, the ground before their entrenchments was completely open with firm grass-land that would facilitate the movements of his three arms, most of all the cavalry and the horse artillery.

Once down from the house top, Harry ordered Brig. Charles Cureton, who commanded the two cavalry brigades of 3,000 sabres, to take the ground on the flanks so as to clear the front for his columns. The infantry was then told to deploy. 'We came to a halt,' recalled Pearman, 'and the infantry and foot artillery began to get into line, spreading out like a lady's fan ... It was a lovely sight.' Across the field the Sikhs could be seen drawn in battle-array, guns in front, drums beating to arms.

Having deployed his soldiers, Harry observed through his telescope that the Sikh left outflanked his line. He ordered that ground be taken to the right. The enemy was treated to the imposing sight of 12,000 soldiers acting as a unit: with drummers beating the step, the British wheeled into columns and then once more into line. It was all done with the nicety of field-day manoeuvres. The Sikhs, not to be outdone by this stately prelude, put on a show of their own, as one observer noted, 'Waving their swords, and cutting a great variety of dreadfully menacing capers.'

At ten o'clock the British went forward in a carefully dressed, compact battle formation to meet death in perfect order. Scarcely had they moved more than a hundred yards when wreaths of smoke appeared before the enemy guns. At first the shots fell short, but they soon reached the scarlet lines. To spoil the range and lessen the danger in the ranks, the order was 'Forward and lie down'. The men ran some fifty yards ahead and then fell like lightning down the line, allowing the balls to fly over them. When the fire slackened, they rushed for another fifty yards. All the while the British guns were blazing away as fast as they could.

Then an unexpected order to halt came from the general. It was not his intention to send his men headlong, like a herd of cattle, to trample down the enemy position whatever the cost. While the army waited under fire, Harry calmly reconnoitred the Sikh position that was now clearly visible in the bright sunshine. His eyes fixed on a decisive point—Aliwal. He rapidly decided to bring up his right to capture the village and, once this had been accomplished, hurl his men forward in a general assault on the enemy centre and left. Once the Sikhs were rolled back, their line of retreat would be threatened.

Two brigades were ordered to take Aliwal: the 1st under Hicks (31st Foot; 24th and 47th N.I.) and the 4th under Godby (36th N.I. and Nasiri Bn of Gurkhas). General Smith, recalled Corp. Cleveland of the 31st, galloped up and said, 'take that village, boys, and carry it along with you.' The 31st, mostly Irishmen, the sepoys from Bengal and the Gurkhas from the Himalayas, contended for the front. Then enemy gunners switched to salvoes of grape- and chain-shot, which thinned the ranks. The position, however, was held by untrained hillsmen who quickly lost heart before the onslaught. They discharged a straggling volley and then fled, leaving the gunners to fend for themselves. The village was won and two large guns were taken.

The general attack now followed. Wheeler's 2nd brigade (50th Foot; 28th N.I. and Sirmur Bn of Gurkhas) overran the centre, but Wilson's brigade (53rd Foot and 30th N.I.) found the hamlet of Bhundri strongly held by Avitabiles, 'proper varmint fellows', as Harry called them.

Ranjur Singh, recognizing the danger to his line of withdrawal, brought forward a large body of horsemen to retake Aliwal. Harry, who had stationed himself before the village, saw the move and ordered Cureton to attack with a portion of his right brigade (Stedman's). A second charge followed with the remainder of the brigade, including the Shekawati cavalry. The Sikh horsemen fell back in confusion on their own infantry.

Once on the summit of the ridge, Harry had a good view of the Sikh camp, crowded with milling infantry, along the river. Godby was told to change front with his brigade and charge the enemy's left flank and rear. They succeeded in driving the enemy before them. To save his army, Ranjur Singh drew back his shattered left and tried to form a new line farther back at right angles to the Sutlej, using the fortified village of Bhundri, which still held, as a pivot. To shield this move, the Sikh commander committed the rest of his cavalry.

Harry countered by having Cureton attack the Sikh cavalry with his left brigade (MacDowell's). Two squadrons, one of the 3rd Bengal Light Cavalry and one of the 16th Lancers, charged ahead. The former suddenly wavered, but the Queen's Own Lancers under Captain Bere went straight on. The Sikh cavalry were too light to withstand the crash of big British horses and men. Nor were their curved swords matches for the ten-foot lances. The Sikh horse, numbering thousands, were routed and virtually eliminated from the battle. They contented themselves with hovering around the fringes where they cut up stragglers and the helpless wounded.

Bere rallied his squadron of scarlet-coated troopers to go back. But the way was blocked by Avitabiles who had formed themselves into squares, or more correctly equilateral triangles. With the help of two horse-artillery guns, Bere fought his way through. 'Such stabbing and cutting,' declared Pearman, 'I never saw before or since.'

Witnessing this rare feat of breaking a 'square', even against Asians, Harry sent forth a messenger to bring up the remaining two squadrons under the command of Major Rowland Smyth.[1] The order, which proved to be well-timed, was to attack with the entire regiment.

The battle now reached a dramatic climax. The 16th wheeled into formation at the sound of a trumpet. It was a

---

[1] This was the Smyth that some had confused with Harry Smith after the death of Hintza. After killing O'Grady in a duel, he was sentenced to a year in prison. It did little damage to his career for he retired a general.

smart-looking (and expensive) regiment,[1] easily recognized by their *chapka*, or cap, and *ulinka*, or double-breasted tunic, modelled after the Polish lancers. Once the line was perfectly even, Major Smyth shouted, 'I am going to give the word to charge, three cheers for the Queen.' The troopers responded with wild, exulting cheers, which some Sikhs later complained was unfair, as it frightened them. The horses went from a trot to a gallop as they swept over the Sikh guns firing to the last second. Every one of the guns was taken. The Sikh regulars behind did not wait for the Lancers to assault them. They fired their muskets, then drew their tulwars and advanced boldly to engage them. Once the Lancers bowled into them, there was vehement destruction everywhere, the neighing of horses mingling with shouts and shrieks of death. Some of the enemy tried to maintain their orderly triangles; others lay on the ground to avoid the lances and fired or thrust their razor-sharp tulwars upwards at troopers and horses. When the 16th came out the other side, they turned, re-formed and charged again. After being ridden over and cleaved through three times, the howling, frothing Sikhs began to break formation.

As the Lancers rode past the loudly swearing General Smith, Sgt Gould heard him shout, 'Well done, 16th. You have covered yourself with glory.' On noticing C troop's officers had all fallen, Harry had the men join the left wing under Captain Bere.

The infantry, with the sepoys taking an active part, came up to attack the crumpled triangles. The 53rd cleared the streets of Bhundri with bayonets. The Sikh regulars, having been deserted by all the other units, as Mackinnon recalled, 'fell doggedly back, never condescending to run, though plied with musketry and shrapnel'. At intervals they faced about to fire an unco-ordinated volley into their pursuers. For the honour of the Khalsa, a gallant thousand took up a defensive position in a ditch. The British infantry, with considerable losses, nevertheless 'unkennelled' them for the artillery. The adaptable horse artillery dashed forward at top speed, and at 300 yards sent their projectiles into the closely packed Sikh ranks.

[1] To add to their fine appearance, one colonel of the regiment had sought to enlist only men with red hair, to ride only chestnut horses.

Hemmed in on all sides, the Sikhs fell back towards the river, a retreat which became a rout. Harry's despatch described them as 'precipitating themselves in disordered masses into the fords and boats, in utmost confusion and consternation'. He called his artillery forward to destroy the few guns on the river front that Ranjur Singh had left to cover the retreat. The infantry regiments, still maintaining their order, were sent across the alluvial plain to fire into the fleeing rabble.

'And oh, the fearful sight the river presented!' he told Alice, 'the bodies having swollen the float of men, horses, camels, bullocks, etc.' Some of the boats were sunk by the artillery pounding the river. All efforts by Ranjur Singh to re-form his men on the other side were soon blasted by the artillery. The Sikhs fled, leaving all their guns and 3,000 dead. 'Never was a victory more complete,' claimed Harry, 'and never was one fought under happier circumstances.'

The sounds of cannon fire had been clearly heard at Sobraon, 50 miles away. Gough insisted that he could determine by the sounds that Smith had carried the enemy position. When he heard the news that night, 'he was nearly frantic with joy'. Recovering control of himself, he fell to his knees and gave thanks to God. The anxiety of many officers and men was relieved when they heard that their families were safe in Ludhiana. A gala parade of the entire army was ordered the next day and, by Hardinge's order, a royal salute was fired. The Sikhs entrenched nearby, whether in defiance or to keep their troops in ignorance, fired a similar salute and their band played 'God Save the Queen'. But if there were any doubts concerning their defeat, they were soon dispelled by the sight of many dead comrades floating down the river.

The history of the battle of Aliwal rests on the descriptive records of a dozen participants, all different, yet apparently all correct. They were agreed on one thing, it was a battle in which not a mistake could be found. It was this rarity in the annals of warfare that made Harry Smith's reputation as a general. Unlike the clumsy battles of Gough, it was a scientific battle where reliance was placed on brains as well as bayonets. The three arms of the service were perfectly co-ordinated and committed with immaculate timing, so that every man on the field knew his place and contributed to the overall purpose.

Wellington, now 77, paid Harry a great tribute in the House of Lords:

> I have read the accounts of many a battle, but I never read the account of one in which more ability, energy and experience have been manifested than in this. I know of no one in which an officer ever showed himself more capable than this officer has in commanding troops in the field.

Peel moved a vote in the House of Commons to honour him. 'Thank God!' Queen Victoria wrote with relief in her journal. 'The news from India have been confirmed & are very good. Sir H. has obtained a decisive victory near Ludhiana ... '[1] Encomiums also came from the literary world. Thackeray wrote, 'Let those civilians who sneer at the army read Sir Harry Smith's account of Aliwal. A noble deed was never told in nobler language.' Throughout the land public houses were named after the 'Hero of Aliwal'. Harry liked to describe the encounter as 'a little sweeping edition of Salamanca, a stand-up gentlemanly battle'.

The success at Aliwal raised the spirits of the army, the sepoys in particular, whose dread of the Sikhs had been increased by previous encounters. The legend of British superiority that had been damaged at Mudki and Ferozeshah was restored.

And the British losses, for once, were light: 153 killed, 413 wounded and 25 missing. The number of dead was greatly reduced because hospital stores and conveniences were available to the wounded, who had been quickly and efficiently removed from the field.

The dead were properly buried. More than a quarter of them were Lancers. When the survivors of the 16th paraded the next day, their pennants stiffened with blood, General Smith told them that if Ranjit Singh had lived to see them at Aliwal, he would have spoken of them as devils, 'for you charged their ranks more like them than anything else'. Trooper Eaton noticed there were 'tears in the poor old man's eyes' as he said: 'God bless you, my brave boys; I love you.'

The proximate consequences of the victory were considerable: the convoy, upon which the prosecution of the war

[1] RA, Queen Victoria's *Journal*, 25 March 1846.

depended, was safe; the loyalty of cis-Sutlej states was restored; the tribes in the hills all the way to the borders of Tibet turned against their Sikh masters; and all the enemy posts south of the Sutlej were abandoned, except for their bridgehead at Sobraon.

Disposing of the wounded and most of the captured guns at Ludhiana, Harry blew up the fort at Budowal and marched his men back to the main army. Their arrival on 7 February was cause for a second celebration. With great emotion Gough expressed his thanks to Harry and each regiment that had served under him. That night there was a special reception and dinner for General Smith attended by 45 officers.

The enemy was waiting at Sobraon. They had no wish to attack, but were unwilling to retire. Negotiations with Lahore broke down because the governor-general made a demand which could not be met: the disbandment of the Khalsa. Tej Singh and Lal Singh remained apathetic while the various battalion commanders, with varying degrees of skill, kept their men busy on their own sections of the entrenchments. To accommodate so many men, 20,000 or more, a second line was built before the original one. Then a third was added to what was now a bulging semicircle extending for over two miles around the bridgehead, with the flanks resting on the banks. The breastworks varied from six to ten feet high and were strengthened with lumber, loopholed for muskets and provided with deep ditches. Sixty-five well-constructed emplacements for the guns covered the approaches to the bridgehead while thirty more were placed on the high north bank to play on the flanks of soldiers advancing on either the eastern or western front of the defences. About 10,000 troops, mostly cavalry, under Lal Singh, remained on the opposite side of the river.

Periodically the Sikhs came forward of their defences to taunt and tempt the British, who were instructed to hold their fire. Sometimes it was more than Gough could bear. Daily he saw the enemy position become stronger while he ran the risk of having his forces grow weaker, for the rainy season was upon them with all of its epidemic horrors. Once more he clashed with Hardinge who advised against any move until the heavy guns arrived.

The long-awaited convoy came in shortly after Smith's detachment. With 20,000 men and nearly 100 guns at his disposal, 18 of them heavy howitzers, Gough prepared to attack. The governor-general, still 'wearing two hats', once more interfered by suggesting that he move the bulk of his infantry and 50 guns across the Sutlej under cover of dark and thus fall on the surprised enemy's rear. But Sir Hugh contended that such a move would expose his communications. Reluctantly, Hardinge gave way and authorized a frontal assault, provided that heavy casualties were not anticipated.

Sir Hugh sent for his subordinate commanders and department heads to meet with him the next morning, 9 February, in order to explain his plan of attack. Relying on information provided by a native boy, the commander-in-chief told them that the enemy's works did not go all the way down to the river on the right or western side of the Sikh position. And what defences there were on that side were less formidable. Because of the sandy ground, they were only six feet high and manned mostly by poorly trained irregulars, supported by 200 1lb. swivel guns, a salient battery and some heavy guns on the farther bank. Following a heavy bombardment that would shake these defences, Dick's 3rd Division, the strongest, would move forward to attack with another brigade and cavalry in reserve. Sir Walter Raleigh Gilbert's 2nd in the centre and Smith's 1st to the east would divert the enemy with simulated attacks. Cureton's cavalry, stationed three miles up river, would threaten the ford at Hurreekee.

Sound tactics, Harry advised Sir Hugh, would dictate greater concentration rather than diffusion. The fundamental principle of battle, he observed, 'is being superior to your enemy on the point of attack'. Concealing his contempt for Gough's generalship, he did not press the argument. As he told Alice, 'Never catch a butting animal by the horns, though, as a good soldier, obey your superior's orders.'

The soldiers marched off in silence before dawn to take up their positions. At first light they were deployed, but the thick, white mist held up operations for an hour. Some of the gunners with their heavy pieces lost their way. When the sun burned through the mist, the Sikhs were surprised to see the British army formed up to attack them on all sides. British guns then shook the ground and shuddered the air.

The Sikh guns joined in the concert. As Harry stood waiting, the mist, the nearby river and Gough's tactics were depressing reminders of that fateful day when under similar circumstances he had stood before the American lines in front of New Orleans.

Just when the guns were beginning to have their desired effect after two hours of bombardment, Harry was astonished to hear their fire slacken and then cease altogether. All of the ammunition had been expended, for the officer in charge had brought up only half of the quota Gough had ordered. The gunners' excuse, in turn, was that they had not been given enough time. One would have expected Gough to be discouraged by the news; instead, he told the messenger, 'Thank God! Then I'll be at them with the bayonet.'

Sir Robert Dick was ordered to launch his attack at nine o'clock. Stacey's brigade ran into heavy fire of every description, for the British barrage was not nearly as effective as it might have been; some of the guns had been placed too far away and the mortar shells burst overhead because the fuses were too short. The Sikhs were more entertained by the fireworks than disabled. Regardless, the stormers fought their way through the first line and forced the enemy back to the second. At this point, many Sikhs who had concealed themselves in deep pits, or dug-outs, swarmed out to attack the advancing British from behind. To thwart a possible counter-attack, Wilkenson's brigade was sent forward, supported by Ashburnham's reserve brigade. But more Sikhs, undeceived by the feints on their left and centre, rushed over to defend the west side. Unable to hold their ground, the three brigades fell back slowly. Dick, who was in the act of encouraging his men, was mortally wounded. Gough's plan, as Harry foresaw, had failed dismally.

Sir Hugh had no choice but to convert the simulated attacks of the other two divisions into real ones. The works before them were very strong. Moreover, once the pressure on their right was relieved, many Sikhs ran back to man them. Watching Gilbert's men prepare to attack the centre, Gough exclaimed, 'Good God, they'll be annihilated.' This time he was right. The first attempt was stopped by the high, continuous barriers. The black-bearded Sikhs fired down into the redcoats as they tried to hoist one another up. Those who neared the top had their heads and shoulders bashed and slashed. A second effort was similarly unsuccessful, Gilbert himself being wounded. The division retired with heavy losses.

Smith's battalions, greatly reduced in numbers by previous battles to only 2,400 bayonets, faced what he described to Juana as 'the stiffest part of the trenches.—And, oh such trenches.' Manning these defences were the best warriors of the Khalsa.

As in two previous battles, he told D'Urban, 'I was placed in *Reserve*. I knew again what *that* would end in.' Harry, therefore, had prepared his men for a full-scale attack long before one of Gough's messengers came racing up with the expected orders. The soldiers were lying on the ground when the command was given. They sprang up, formed into solid lines and advanced with Hicks's brigade (31st; 47th N.I.) in front, supported by Penny's (50th; 42nd N.I. and Nasiri Gurkhas). Maintaining order was difficult because the ground was broken by water courses. Looking ahead, they saw that the batteries that covered their advance had little effect on the Sikhs crowding the parapets.

One Sikh gunner, Hookum Singh, left a record of what it was like to be standing on the wrong side of a British attack that morning:

Nearer and nearer they came, as steadily as if they were on their own parade ground, in perfect silence. A creeping feeling came over me; this silence seemed so unnatural. We Sikhs are, as you know, brave, but when we attack we begin firing muskets and shouting our famous war-cry; but these men, saying never a word ... appeared to me as demons, evil spirits, bent on our destruction, and I could hardly refrain from firing.

Cannon fire made great lanes in the ranks of Hicks's brigade, but it did not disrupt their formations or slow their step. The ramparts, however, stopped them and they were thrown back. Harry brought up Penny's brigade. The 50th, the leading battalion, formed in fours with great steadiness so as to allow the fragmented units of the 1st brigade to pass through them. Formed in line once more, it was their turn to storm the ramparts. Outwardly their movements were calm and correct but inwardly they were infuriated by the sight of Sikhs dropping down from their works to stab and cut the wounded of Hicks's brigade. The 50th made a furious attempt to surmount the obstacles to get at the enemy. Some men offered their backs for others to step on, but the loose sand underfoot was treacherous. 'Such a milling match I was never in,' Harry told D'Urban. 'Twice my gallant handful of 31st and 50th staggered back—but did not *turn*.'

Unable to break through, Harry shifted his men farther to the right, close to the river, 'where if left alone, I should have commenced'. The works here, being lower and less strong, were carried by 'dint of English pluck', the Gurkhas and sepoys not far behind. Sgt McCabe, 'a noble little fellow', took the perforated colours of the 31st and placed it upon one of the towers of the entrenchments. (He was rewarded with a commission.) The 50th overran the guns before them but failed to disable them, for they had no spikes. Enemy gunners who had survived the assault managed to turn their pieces to fire on their rear. The 50th turned to face the grape-shot that rattled through them, and charged. The enemy gunners, in the words of Lieut. Travers, 'died like trumps at their guns'.

For some 25 minutes, as Harry remembered, there was a hand-to-hand 'brutal bull-dog fight', with swords and shields pitted against bayonets, and firing on both sides. It was a case of two steps forward and one step back. Those of his men who could spare a glance saw their general in the middle of the fight swearing himself hoarse. Neither he nor Jem Crow, 'who sprang over the enemy's works like a deer', was hit as Harry on five occasions grabbed regimental colours and planted them forward. His face was bleeding from a slight cut on his cheek that had been caused earlier by a bursting shell. His blue uniform was sprinkled with the blood of others, including that of his A.D.C., Holdich, who received a bad wound in the arm and shoulder. The only thing Harry lost was a cane that had been shot out of his hand.

'By Jupiter!' Harry recalled, 'the enemy were within a hair's breadth of driving me back.' Yet, despite the fact that his men were fighting four times their number, 'I gained ground by inches and thank God, succeeded.' The enemy were staggered everywhere. Continuing his account to D'Urban in an admittedly egotistical vein, he wrote, 'Again, had I been beat back the day was lost—my authority the G.G. and C in C.' (i.e., Hardinge and Gough).

The tide of battle turned against the Sikhs all along the line. Taking advantage of the defenders' preoccupation in meeting the assaults of the other two divisions, Dick's Division came out of the ravines to attack once more. This time they tore through the western side. Engineers followed to make a way over ditches and through barricades for the cavalry. Led by the one-armed Thackwell, the blue-jacketed 3rd Light Dragoons, followed in single file, re-formed and flashed ahead. Harry saw it all and later told Thackwell, there you were 'shoving in your unwinged shoulder into the gap at Sobraon— the most gallant "go" of you and the 3rd Dragoons I ever witnessed'. Gilbert's Division made another effort and broke through the centre. Tej Singh, instead of bringing up fresh troops to hold the British, fled over the pontoon bridge and, according to some sources, deliberately cut adrift two centre-boats.

What had been a battle became simply carnage. Though defeated, the Sikhs refused to yield; and the British, who had passed over the bodies of mutilated comrades, were not inclined to be merciful. Pressed on every side, the enemy fell back towards the river. Grey-bearded old chiefs resolved to die rather than quit the field. Waving their tulwars, they rushed forward and hurled themselves on bayonets or risked themselves where the fire was the heaviest. A disordered mass gathered at the bridgehead. The bridge itself was crowded with guns, animals and Sikhs of all arms. The structure began to sway and finally crashed. Those who attempted the fords found that they had become impassable, for during the night nature had conspired against them by raising the level of the river seven feet. The swirling Sutlej seemed alive with thousands of struggling men clinging to one another. Those who did not drown were hurried into oblivion by the horse artillery that came down to the water's edge. Their guns 'swept the surface of the river with deadly precision', noted Mackinnon, and 'soon converted the greater portion of the Sikh army into a hideous struggling wreck of humanity'. Sikh batteries on the far bank contributed to the slaughter, since most of their shots fell upon their own men.

Harry, who was leading his men down to the river bank, told Alice that there was 'such a scene of shooting men fording a deep river, as no one ever saw before. The bodies made a bridge ... ' Someone heard Gough say that they were so thick that he believed he could walk across. Feeling little compassion, the victors looked on in stolid wonderment. The Rev. Coley, who saw nothing unChristian in his rejoicing, compared the destruction of the Sikhs to that of the wicked Egyptians by the Red Sea as they pursued the Israelites. The British press later condemned the massacre of a defence-less foe, but Gough had been by no means certain that this was to be his last battle.

By 10.30 a.m. not a Sikh remained standing on the south bank. What was left of the bridge was burnt and sunk by the British. Gough estimated that between eight and ten thousand had perished, more than half in the river. None had offered to surrender. 'The Sikhs met their fate,' remarked Hardinge's son Charles, 'with that resignation which distinguishes their race.'

The British, too, paid a heavy price. Their casualties totalled 2,283, of whom 320 were dead. Harry's division had 635 casualties out of 2,400. This was 100 more, he pointed out, than he had lost at Aliwal, when he had had 12,000 men. His staff were all wounded, some two or three times, and their horses killed.

Apart from the 67 guns that were taken, the loot in the Sikh camp was enormous. Many soldiers helped themselves. When Harry discovered some soldiers engaged in the act, he rode up without saying a word and laid into them, left and right, with a stick. The men returned to their camp laughing, recalled a young officer of the 31st, James Robertson, 'evidently thinking it was a good joke to be thrashed by a general'.

The spoils taken during the campaign and sold by the government brought to an end the financial difficulties that had haunted Harry for years. 'I have got a fine slice of Batta [prize-money],' he wrote to D'Urban joyfully, '47,520 Rupees, which pays everyone all I owe, the Lord be praised.' Just think, he told his old chief, had he been appointed lieutenant-governor by Sir George Napier, 'I should have been a beggar ... It shows we ought never to repine — for we do not know what is best for us.'

That night after the battle and again the next day, Enrique scribbled brief letters to 'My own dearest old woman'. Adjusting the spectacles he had borrowed from her, he wrote, 'The hand of Almighty God has again been upon me.' Once more he had gone through a battle virtually unscathed and taken 'three beautiful standards'. However, he revealed to Juana for the first time that he 'got a scratch on the chest at Budowal; it bled a great deal but no mark was left'. Hardinge and Gough were 'delighted with the achievement of my Division and so they ought'. His anxiety to see her put him in mind of those days he had yearned for her in King William's Town as she travelled out from Cape Town. The letters closed with those peculiar hieroglyphs that were part of their affectionate code.

The victory at Sobraon proved decisive. The Khalsa never rallied, leaving Lahore at the mercy of the British. Losing no time, Gough had a new bridge of boats thrown across the Sutlej. By 13 February the main body had passed over, along with 120,000 baggage animals. The next day, 'the soft and silky' Gulab Singh, Rajah of Jumma, who chose to remain neutral during the conflict, came forward to negotiate. The governor-general's terms were the reduction of the Khalsa, the surrender of their guns and £1½ million as an indemnity. To everyone's surprise, most of all the Sikhs, only a small stretch of territory was annexed for strategic purposes. The boy rajah and his mother made their submission to the British and conducted them to Lahore where the treaty was to be ratified. Thus, the scheming trio — Maharani Jindan, Lal Singh and Tej Singh — remained in power, this time protected by the British.

Meanwhile, Sir Charles Napier had organized a force of 10,000 men in Sind in case of need. When he arrived in Lahore looking as always the part of an eccentric, his long-flowing whiskers flaring out from under a pith-helmet that resembled an overgrown mushroom, the governor-general celebrated with a great dinner. Though always quick to find fault with others, Napier was full of praise for his brother generals. He told Harry that he 'did his work well'; but he could not resist twitting him about Budowal, saying he should have been court-martialled for losing the baggage. Those present that night at the banquet recalled what a fine sight it was to see the four old Peninsular warriors seated at the head of the table.

Sir Harry Smith was recognized by soldiers everywhere as he rode about on Jem Crow, now renamed Aliwal. He was the most popular man in the army, remembered a trooper from Ely who had served in India.

He always had something jocose to say. He would gammon us by complimenting us in comparison with some other regiment—then we should hear from the men of the other regiment that he had complimented them in the same manner. He would stroll round the tents and there would be a cry, 'Sir Harry Smith's coming'. Then he would call out 'Trumpeter, order a round of grog; not too much water; what I call "fixed bayonets!" '

With the signing of the treaty on 8 March 1846, the army broke up. Harry had a few warm words for the regiments under his command. Inspecting the guard of honour of the 50th, the 'dirty half-hundred', that was part of a grand durbar to receive Gulab Singh, he stood and scowled at them. They looked filthy, for it was raining and they were spattered with mud. In vigorous language that they knew so well, he told them, 'You well deserve your name; you are fit for nothing—' then he added, after a long pause, 'but fighting'.

Among the trophies of war that were sent to Calcutta by Hardinge in a triumphal procession were five of 'the most beautiful guns imaginable' that Harry had captured at Aliwal. He hoped that they would stand eventually in St James's Park. (Two ended up at Windsor Castle.)

Once more in Simla, he and Juana read with joy the many letters of congratulations. Some asked, as did Charlie Beckwith, 'But what did Juana do in all this row? Was she on horseback *abasco de los canonacos?*' By mid-June, Harry wrote to George Simmons that he had received nearly 150 letters of 'heartfelt gratification' from every old friend still left to them.

Then George, comes the *encomium* from *THE DUKE*. Dear old master! if I have done that which meets your approbation, then is the cup of glory full indeed, for it is to your example I have desired to apply any share of ability bestowed upon me.

The censure Harry had received 'from a set of old croakers' over the skirmish at Budowal was completely forgotten after Aliwal. Harry believed that in this case 'good comes out of evil'. If he had not lost his baggage, Ranjur Singh would probably have been less bold in seeking an encounter. Thus, Harry wrote to Alice, 'the battle of Aliwal became the offspring of Budhwal'.

Honours for Aliwal began to arrive that spring. The Prime Minister wrote to inform Harry that a baronetcy would be conferred upon him. To this title, as a special distinction, would be appended the words 'of Aliwal', which Peel indicated was 'unusual in the case of a Baronetcy'. Now that he had earned the privilege of adding supporters to his family arms, Harry wrote immediately for permission from Sir Andrew Barnard, colonel of the Rifle Brigade, and Sir Edward Gibbs, colonel of the 52nd, to use the figure of a Rifleman on one side and a soldier of the 52nd on the other.

Whereas Hardinge, now a viscount, and Gough now a baron ('of Chingkiangfoo in China and Maharajpore and the Sutlej in the East'), were awarded substantial annual pensions, Harry received nothing in the way of money. But the Queen insisted that he be advanced to the ultimate step in his Order, Knight Grand Cross of the Bath. He also was given a vote of thanks, along with Hardinge and Gough, from the cities of London and Liverpool. A more tangible reward came from the Horse Guards when he was appointed to the full rank of major-general to replace Sir Robert Dick, who had fallen at Sobraon.

Replacing Dick meant that Harry would be in charge of the troops at Cawnpore where the weather alternated between 'a fiery sun and torrents of rain'. Ignoring Harry's protests, Juana was determined that she would go with him, which meant a journey of 500 miles. Not only was it difficult for her to endure another separation, but Harry was in bad health after the exertions of campaigning and he needed her tender care.

The many letters he had received from England had a depressing effect upon Harry. He told Simmons:

I began to long to get once more to my native land, mine has been an awful banishment. I do so long to seize by the hand all those old friends who ... so kindly feel my success and honours *their own*.

But for financial reasons it would be difficult to leave his command. It was finally arranged through Lord Fitzroy Somerset that Sir Joseph Thackwell would temporarily take over while Harry went on sick leave to England.

He and Juana booked passage on a steamer for the first time. After what promised to be a swift voyage, they would not 'go mooning about the Continent', he informed Alice, but 'come straight home'. On 29 April 1847, after Harry's absence from home for 18 years, their ship docked at Southampton.

[13]

'I *will* be Governor'

We appear to want somebody here with much more of the devil in him, such as ... Sir Harry Smith.

Edward Napier, *Excursions in South Africa*

It was an age of heroes. For the moment none stood higher than Sir Harry Smith. Bells chimed and cannons boomed as the 'Hero of Aliwal' and his lady stepped ashore. They were greeted by the general commanding the South-Western District who stepped out from the throng of cheering thousands. On his heels came the Corporation with a flowery address. With becoming humility Harry told the crowd, 'If I have rendered good service to my country it is to the soldiers of the army I have commanded that I am indebted.'

Steam followed steam. The South-Western Railway placed at their disposal, free of charge, a saloon and special train for the journey to London. Travel by train was a novelty the Smiths had looked forward to for some time. 'These railroads will have an effect on the world,' Harry predicted to Alice, 'whether for good or for evil, and will change its population to one community, either saints or devils or a bastard mixture of both.'

Honours fell thick upon the national hero. There was an invitation for Sir Harry and Lady Smith to dine with Queen Victoria, still only 28, at Marlborough House. Her Majesty recorded the event in her journal:

> Sir Harry, a fine old man, was presented to me. He seemed so pleased at my praises, saying he would ever serve me in the same way, & hoped all my subjects would do so. He was so glad to see Albert, who asked him to come in the morning.[1]

Harry was deluged with dinner invitations from high society

---

[1] RA, Queen Victoria's *Journal*, 3 May 1846.

and various clubs. For once, at least, commented *The Times* 'the metropolitan season is supplied with a reasonable object of admiration and amusement'. Harry's speeches, whether giving thanks for the freedom of the city at the Guildhall or at private parties, conveyed the same message, Lord Brougham noted in his diary:

> He spoke of himself without scruple as the 'Hero of Aliwal' modestly, at the same time attributing his own great fame and position to the teaching of the Duke of Wellington and the bravery of the soldiers who fought under him.

In conversation, he entertained his listeners with anecdotes about the Sikh chiefs and the maharani. When asked if he faced great personal risk, his stock answer was, 'My horse did sometimes.'

The most memorable and moving dinner for Harry, one which called for no speech making, was the one attended by a hundred veterans of the Light Division. *The Times*, in a glowing article, described them as 'survivors of the most renowned division of the most famous army of England's most famous war'. There were congratulations for Aliwal and on his being gazetted colonel-commandant of the 2nd Bn of the Rifle Brigade from old comrades like the Duke of Richmond, Sir Andrew Barnard, Sir John Bell, Sir Hew Ross, Johnny Kincaid, Jonathan Leach and brother Tom. Many were embraced by Juana, beginning with Lord Seaton (John Colborne). She threw her arms round him, kissed him and cried, 'Oh, Colborne, Colborne, to see you again!' Colborne, 'by no means effusive or gushing,' later explained to his daughter, 'In the most trying circumstances for years no one could have behaved with more absolute discretion — I have the greatest regard and admiration for her.'

At the end of June another saloon car, specially fitted by the directors of the northern railway lines, puffed towards Whittlesea and home. Because the inhabitants of Ely clamoured to fête their local hero, the Smiths stopped there first. 'Thousands were assembled,' recalled Professor Adam Sedgwick, 'with flags, branches of laurel, and joyful faces.' The triumphal cavalcade, passing through decorated arches, was preceded by a standard-bearer and a mounted trumpeter. Then came the police, followed by gentlemen of the county on horseback four abreast. Behind them was the only sobering element, the 'Chairman of the Breakfast', escorted by two clergymen. The band of the Scots Fusilier Guards marched before their hero mounted on Aliwal. Those who expected to see him in uniform were disappointed, for he wore a blue surtout, with a star on his breast, and grey trousers. Lady Smith, riding in an open coach, brought up the rear. Dean Peacock presided at the magnificent meal, speaking of Harry's success and his ability 'to conciliate a foe and turn the foes of the British Empire into its friends'.

A similar procession took place later that day in Whittlesea before a crowd estimated at 10,000. The Whittlesea Yeomanry, with whom Harry had begun his military career, led the way, commanded by his brother Charles. 'He was much affected,' noted Sedgwick, 'and I saw tears roll down his weather-beaten, but fine face, as he passed the house where his father and mother once lived.' That evening there was a ball; Harry joined in the dancing but declined to take part in the polka.

There was a formal dinner the next night attended by 300 leading citizens of the area and a reporter of the *Cambridge Independent Press*. Harry was presented with an epergne valued at £300. Then he spoke. He recalled how he had left his native land with nothing but his sword and his mother's injunction — 'if ever you meet your enemy, remember you are born a true Englishman'. (Cheers.) Turning to Juana seated next to him, he related the awful conditions under which he had met a helpless but heroic 14-year-old girl and observed that he 'should have been less than a man if he had not sought her hand'. (Loud cheers.) Under the most extraordinary and often sanguinary circumstances she had followed him to every quarter of the globe with a devotion he found difficult to describe. 'Rightly,' he added, 'Lord Hardwicke said that he was urged on by the feeling that Spanish women would have none but the brave.' (Cheers.) She had watched him in the field of battle and tended to his needs in hours of pain. When they were parted, as in the Sikh and American wars, he regarded her as present 'as his guardian angel, for in difficulties and dangers he had often witnessed her shadow, as it were, in his path'. Then throwing back his head and raising his voice, Harry recited a poem:

Oh woman, in our hours of ease,
Uncertain, coy, and hard to please;
And variable as the shade
By the light quiv'ring aspen made;
When pain and anguish wring the brow,
A ministering angel thou! (Loud applause)
              Walter Scott, *Marmion*, VI, xxx.

Harry then thanked all for honouring his wife, 'an honour doubly grateful to his feelings because he knew in his heart that she deserved it all.' (Loud cheering.)

Academic honours were next on the agenda. On 5 July 1847 Harry received an honorary degree of LL.D. from the University of Cambridge, where Prince Albert was being installed as chancellor. Queen Victoria, the Duke of Wellington and other distinguished guests were present. In the Senate House, while waiting for the Queen and the Prince, the Duke and Harry were engaged in conversation when the students began to cheer the 'Iron Duke'. Wellington quieted them with a gesture and, putting his hand on Harry's shoulder, told them, 'No, no, this is the man you ought to cheer; here is the hero of the day.' The students lustily hailed the imperial conqueror, whereupon Harry burst into tears and was heard to say, 'I little thought I should live to hear such kind words as these from my old chief.'

After the ceremony, Sedgwick observed:

When the Duke of Wellington was leaving the Senate House, a loud peal of cheers was raised for him; and immediately afterwards Harry was caught sight of. 'Cheers for Sir Harry Smith' were called for; and the Duke turning back, laid hold of Sir Harry and turned him around, saying, 'There you have him.'

'Indeed,' thought the professor, 'he is more like the Duke's son, so much is he attached to him.'

There remained the question of Harry's future. Prominent politicians urged him to consider a seat in the House of Commons for Glasgow, where his handling of the 'Radical War' had won him so many friends. Meanwhile, admirers there made him a burgess of the city and presented him with a gift of plate valued at £400. But since members of Parliament were not paid in that day, Harry politely declined the opportunity.

Though he had discharged his debts, Harry required an income for support. Yet the thought of resuming his post in India was not an attractive one. Harry, therefore, sent discreet inquiries to Lord Henry Grey, the secretary of state for war and colonies in the government of Lord John Russell, concerning vacant governorships in the Empire where the climate would be more agreeable.

While still glorying in the intoxicating adulations of his countrymen, Harry heard that he was to be governor at the Cape and high commissioner. The good news leaked out in a conversation with the Duke while they were waiting to take part in a review. 'So you are going to the Cape,' his mentor remarked, 'and Sir Henry Pottinger is to go to Madras.' Harry immediately wrote to Grey, whose South African policies he had previously described ingratiatingly as 'notable, judicious and applicable', for confirmation. He learned that only the matter of emoluments remained to be settled, since he would have received more had he returned to India. It was arranged that he would be given extra allowances for the local rank of lieutenant-general and exemption from payment of fees on stamps on his commission as governor.

Harry Smith was the obvious choice for governor. His experience and vision inspired confidence in the colonial secretary. Public opinion in Britain and South Africa would support the appointment. As for the 'Saints' their influence had declined greatly. Their 'quixotic philanthropy' (in Grey's words), which had inspired the treaty system whereby the peace would be kept with independent and responsible chiefs, had been completely discredited by the outbreak of the Seventh Frontier War in 1846. The D'Urban–Smith policy was vindicated. The war had already led to the loss of many lives and cost the British treasury £1,000,000. The Sixth Frontier War had cost only £300,400. Smith's proven ability as a soldier promised a speedy end to the conflict.

No doubt Harry's earlier memorandum to the Duke, entitled 'Notes on the Kaffir War', strengthened his candidacy. He argued that a 'war against savages cannot be carried out according to acknowledged rules but to common sense and the peculiarity of circumstances which arise when applied to well-armed barbarians'. And clearly no one knew the circumstances better than he. He promised that 'the war would be terminated in two or three weeks'. As a soldier, Wellington was impressed. While the present governor, Pottinger, requested more troops in addition to the 5,000 soldiers and a large number of irregular levies he already had, Harry believed that 2,000 men, including burghers, would be ample to subdue the tribesmen. He noted encouragingly that 'as gratitude and docility progresses, so may the military force be considerably reduced'. But their management required 'energy and activity' —qualities which he obviously possessed. As an administrator, Grey was enthusiastic.

Elated by his appointment, Harry wrote to D'Urban, now in command of the army in Canada, that he was going to the Cape 'to *re do* what Lord Glenelg so ably did *undo*'. Of course, he added, 'you are far more qualified for the task of restoring *Confidence* — Peace, and a Prospect of Tranquility.' At least the former governor would have the satisfaction of seeing the policies he had initiated brought to fruition. Harry continued:

> Lord Grey appears very much disposed to place confidence in me, but all Governors and Ministers are great friends at the outset (!) ... Happen what may, I will steer *my own* course guided by his compass, but the helm is mine.

Much remained to be done before embarking. There were several conferences with the Duke during which they studied a large map and were in perfect agreement regarding military measures. The staff was chosen from many applicants, but Holdich was certain to be with him as an A.D.C. A large number of horses were selected, with Aliwal topping the list. Newly invented rubber pontoons for river crossings were approved and ordered on board.

Because the Church of England had begun to take a strong interest in the Cape, an area that had been left largely to the non-conformist sects, Harry sought an interview with the Right Reverend Robert Gray, recently consecrated as the first Bishop of Cape Town and soon to be Metropolitan of Africa. Mindful of the difficulties he had had with Dr Philip and other missionaries, Harry hoped to make of the Anglican prelate a powerful ally.

'Called on Sir H. Smith—much pleased with him,' Gray wrote to Miss Cole, daughter of the former governor. 'We have sent in a strong representation about additional chaplains for the forces in Kaffraria, where there are 5,000 without a single clergyman.' The Anglican parsons were soon on their way.

Before embarking on the *Vernon* on 24 September, Harry replied to an address at Portsmouth:

> If I can avert war, I will. If I can extend the blessings of civilization and Christianity in a distant land where, without any affectation of humility, I can say that some years ago I sowed its seeds, it will be a gratification to me beyond expression to do so.

On the anniversary of the abolition of slavery, 1 December 1847, a signal came down from the Lion's Rump heralding the arrival of the new governor and his lady. The same semaphore transmitted the latest news from shore to the *Vernon*: 'Five officers killed by Kaffirs.' Some of the passengers became alarmed, believing war parties had reached Cape Town. Harry reassured them by appearing wholly unperturbed and offering the amusing comment, 'Doing something they ought not, I'll be bound.'

All business was suspended to celebrate the governor's arrival. The rejoicings were even more ecstatic than they had been in Britain. The wharfs were filled with happy faces that raised a great cheer as the governor stepped ashore. The guns at the Castle were fired to announce his presence to those not close enough to see. A carriage with four splendid greys took the Smiths through lines of soldiers to Government House. From every window, door and roof top there were shouts of welcome. Harry responded by waving to old acquaintances that he recognized with every turn of his head. Once the oath of office was administered, the governor was bombarded with addresses, petitions and memorials. When someone alluded to the frontier, Harry struck a dramatic pose and announced emphatically: '*I* am now the governor and I WILL BE GOVERNOR!'

Liquor flowed freely as the festivities went on through the balmy summer night. Cheering, laughing crowds milled aimlessly along the thoroughfares. Guns were fired sporadically, causing dogs to bark and women to shriek. All houses were lit up and decorated; some displayed colourful transparencies depicting highlights of the governor's career. The most popular was his meeting with Juana. When a house was discovered without lights, a disapproving mob attempted to correct this oversight by applying torches. Another dark house had all its windows smashed.

Now 60, nearly white-haired and very spare with deep lines in his strong features, Harry looked to many like an old man. But the governor still behaved like a young one. Moving at a furious pace, he would say 'delay is ever reprehensible'. Daniel Lindley, an American missionary, described him as 'eagle-eyed and ubiquitous'. Even when he stood still, he held his body erect like a young recruit on parade. If anything, his voice seemed stronger, his temper more explosive and his oaths more terrible. His favourite threat was to jump down people's throats—boots, spurs and all. People took to calling him the swearing governor. Few dared to oppose him. 'He does what he likes with everyone,' observed Bishop Gray.

The very qualities that made Harry successful as a subordinate betrayed him when he was given sole command. Excessive praise and honours eroded his shrewd good sense. His bubbling self-confidence was often exaggerated into blind optimism. Rushing ahead with scant reflection, he had neither a D'Urban nor a Hardinge to restrain him. Harry believed that he could solve every problem by the sheer force of his own personality. 'But,' commented settler Jeremiah Goldswain, 'the odds were too great even for his dominant character.' In fact, in many instances his autocratic manners, emotional outbursts and outrageous eccentricities offended those whom he tried to charm. Critics saw him as an overbearing braggart; some thought him 'mad' and pointed to his subsequent conduct on the frontier as evidence.

Harry allowed himself only ten days in the capital. Entrusting civil affairs to the highly competent colonial secretary, John Montagu, he boarded a ship for Port Elizabeth and the eastern border where the war was sputtering to a conclusion.

The Seventh Frontier War, or War of the Axe, had begun in March, 1846, when a member of the Gaika tribe had stolen an old chopper from Fort Beaufort and was caught in the act. For some time the natives had been in an unsettled and defiant mood, and Tola, the arrested man's chief, insolently demanded his release. Col. John Hare, who had succeeded Stockenström in 1838, refused and sent the offender handcuffed to a Hottentot prisoner, to Grahamstown for trial. Seven miles outside of Fort Beaufort, the Hottentot escort was ambushed. The pilferer was freed by cutting off the arm of the man he was chained to. Governor Sir Peregrine Maitland, who had replaced Napier in 1844, insisted that Tola and Sandile, the most powerful chief in Kaffraria, deliver up the rescued prisoner and the murderers of the Hottentot. They spurned his demand. A punitive force under Col. Somerset was sent to occupy Sandile's kraal, but he was driven back by the chief's warriors with considerable loss. The entire frontier was soon ablaze as tribes that had sworn to be friendly turned against the Europeans. The war dragged on with great loss of life and property.

In the conduct of the war, it is difficult to decide who was more inept — Maitland, Hare or Somerset. Maitland, very old and fatigued, was recalled in January, 1847. Pottinger became the governor and was also given the new office of high commissioner, which would extend his authority beyond the colony. The army, now heavily reinforced, was placed under the command of Sir George Berkeley. He eventually gained some measure of success by employing Harry Smith's methods, such as using highly mobile patrols to strike at cattle and corn. One by one the Xhosa chiefs surrendered. In October, 1847, Sandile himself was taken and imprisoned in Grahamstown. Only Pato and Kreli beyond the Kei were still holding out when Harry Smith arrived.

Macomo, still regarded as a most formidable and crafty chief, half-heartedly participated in the war and had been one of the first to surrender. As he told Tshatsu on his return from England, trying to overcome the white man was 'like little boys attempting to shoot elephants with small bows and arrows'. But the settlers, having suffered much from his depredations in earlier years, viewed him, rather than his half-brother Sandile, as the chief culprit. Sandile was described as a boy in years and understanding, if not a simpleton, and it was said that he would not venture a move without Macomo's advice.

Macomo became increasingly addicted to drink, most of all a wicked brew distilled from peaches called Cape Smoke, which caused him to behave like a maniac. He treated his attendants and wives brutally, and knocked the brains out of one of his own children. Yet, he still had a great reputation among his people. They spoke of him as the most daring in war and cleverest in council. During the War of the Axe, he had been largely responsible for crippling British columns by advising them to cut off the supply wagons. Harry was very angry when he learned that Macomo, now detained in Port Elizabeth, had become a vicious, backsliding sot.

All of Port Elizabeth was lit up as the *Rosamond* sailed into the bay. The governor landed at four in the morning, 14 December, and there was another joyous reception followed by presentations. The most notable event was his encounter with Macomo. Looking out of a large window of the Phoenix Hotel at the cheering crowd, Harry spotted the chief and gazed at him steadily for some time. It was a practised look to put people down that Harry called 'a devil in my eye'. The onlookers grew silent. He then drew his sword halfway from its scabbard, held it there for a moment and then with a menacing gesture thrust it back. Macomo pulled back and the spectators laughed.

There was a more formal meeting later in the day. The governor upbraided the chief for his oath-breaking and murder, and then ordered him to prostrate himself before him. 'This,' said Harry as he placed his foot on his neck, 'is to teach you that I come thither to teach Kaffirland that I am chief and master here, and this is the way I shall treat the enemies of the Queen of England.' The look on Macomo's face, during this public humiliation, promised that the governor had not heard the last of him.

At Sidbury on the road to Grahamstown, Harry met with Pottinger. The ex-governor, who had the looks and reputation of a riverboat gambler, obviously had little interest in the colony and left, according to the historian Theal, 'without the esteem of a single colonist ... No other governor of the colony ever lived in such open licentiousness as he.'

The contrast between the disdainful Pottinger and the warm-hearted Smith heightened the enthusiasm of the welcome in Grahamstown. The prosperous and anxious citizens were delirious with joy. They saw Harry as the instrument which would resurrect the benevolent measures of D'Urban and believed as Pottinger did when he wrote to Grey, 'the very prestige of his name will awe the Kaffirs in an instant'.

On the morning of 17 December 'good old Sir Harry' was
met ten miles out of town by a large body of citizens on horseback. A special escort of the 7th Dragoon Guards took its
place at the head of the procession. Comradely sentiment
stirred Harry as he recognized friends from the past. 'Why,
there is old Japps,' he shouted, and his former Hottentot
soldier-servant was pushed forward so that he might shake
Harry's hand. More citizens joined the parade as it neared
the town. Hill-top beacons, so often in the past signalling evil
tidings, now announced the good news of his arrival. Rockets
flashed from one end of town to the other. Before St George's
Church there was a triple arch with banners reading: 'Truth
Triumphant' and 'Do Justice and Fear Not'.

Speaking from a high platform, the governor reminded the
citizens of his first visit when he had found them in a state of
siege and of how they had valiantly defeated a savage force.
He went on to tell of his thwarted efforts to civilize the natives.

> But gentlemen, though assailed, I ultimately triumphed
> and again appear on the scene to resume and carry out the
> very measures which were rendered abortive ... The
> Kaffirs shall be prostrated under our feet and the occur-
> rence of war shall be prevented. Let it be understood,
> I WILL BE GOVERNOR.

Proceeding to Government House, he ordered that Sandile,
who had been confined, be released and brought to him.
The slender young chief, one leg withered from birth, cringed
before the governor as he was severely rebuked. When
asked who was now Inkosi Inkulu, Sandile replied, 'Kreli',
the son of Hintza. Harry said angrily:

> No! I am your paramount chief—I am come to punish
> you for your misdoings—your treachery—and your
> obstinate folly. You may approach my foot and kiss it, in
> token of submission, but not until I see a sincere repent-
> ance for the past, will I permit you to touch my hand.

Once the chief performed the act 'crouched like a sneaking
spaniel', he was dismissed. Sandile said softly, 'I thank you
father', and wasted no time in hurrying out of town, for he
had been living in fear of being banished to Robben Island.

That day the governor issued a proclamation. All existing treaties with the chiefs were to be abrogated and annulled. The lands between the Fish and Keiskamma rivers, the so-called ceded territory, were to be annexed and named the District of Victoria East. The sparsely inhabited northern border of the colony was extended to the Orange river along nearly all of its length.

Before the governor left for the frontier, Pato surrendered. The war was virtually over.

On his way to King William's Town, Harry inspected various military posts. The soldiers were delighted to see him, all the more because he restored their liquor ration, at the same time lecturing them on the evils of drinking to excess. Hundreds of natives also greeted him and indicated their submission by kissing his foot.

The chiefs assembled in King William's Town to receive him on 23 December. Only Macomo was missing; he was said to be off somewhere drinking. With a ringmaster's glee, Harry arranged a theatrical spectacle to dazzle and impress 'his children'. Some 2,000 weaponless warriors were formed in a hollow circle with the chiefs in the centre. Harry rode up with his staff through lines of soldiers, his uniform ablaze with decorations. The band struck up the national anthem and 'See the Conquering Hero Comes'.

In a long speech, the governor praised the troops for their bravery and endurance. Turning to the chiefs he formally declared that Kaffraria was once more subject to British rule, not as an extension of Cape Colony but under the authority of Her Majesty's high commissioner with laws designated to enhance Christianity and civilization.

To impress the chiefs with his authority. Harry called for an ornamental pike and a broom-stick with a brass knob from a bedstead to be placed on either side of him. He then asked the chiefs by name to come forward and choose between war and peace by touching the instrument of battle or the brass knob. Already beaten in war and cowed by his presence, they all naturally touched the knob, symbol of peace. He then dwelt upon the punishment he had in store if they misbehaved and told each to kiss his foot and hail him as 'Inkosi Inkulu'. Throughout the kissing ceremony Harry sat proudly on his horse. Then he dismounted and shook their hands. The assembly was dismissed with an invitation to feed on a herd of oxen.

To preserve the peace and still satisfy Grey's demands for economy, Harry depended mainly on army officers. As commissioner in Kaffraria he appointed Lt.-Col. George Mackinnon. He warned Mackinnon against repeating the mistakes of Col. Hare whose one remarkable achievement had been in antagonizing the blacks, missionaries and settlers alike. Mackinnon was instructed to work through the instrumentality of the chiefs in enforcing obedience, and never, except when all else failed, to resort to military action—but then swiftly, with all the resources at his disposal.

There was an immediate and drastic reduction of troops. Those soldiers who wished to take their discharge could remain as independent settlers or take 12 acres of land and reside in military villages. They would help to stabilize the frontier while advancing the cause of civilization. The scheme had the additional virtue of saving the British taxpayer the cost of transporting discharged soldiers home. Initially four such settlements—Auckland, Ely, Juanasburg and Woburn— were founded on sites selected for their attractiveness and fertility.

To make up for the loss of regulars, Harry relied largely upon the C.M.R., with the addition of two divisions of Kaffir police, about 400 strong. Originally raised by Pottinger, they had remained steadfast during the last war. They would garrison posts and trust to their local knowledge and experience to forestall cattle raids. Too often regulars deteriorated in isolated 'wattle-and-daub' forts where duty 'was a bore and an abomination', wrote an old campaigner. Raw ensigns would ask themselves, 'What the deuce am I to do with myself today?' Some looked to the bottle for consolation; some took to shooting anything and everything; some sought 'discreditable "liaisons" with Hottentot women'. The settlers, however, were suspicious of native troops. To train them in the use of arms was looked upon as a dangerous experiment. 'Ah! but take care of these gentlemen,' Wellington warned Harry before he sailed, 'they may carry swords which cut two ways.'

In keeping with Harry's dream of creating another England, the sub-divisions of Kaffraria were given the names of home counties such as York and Middlesex. To facilitate the defence and attract more colonists, engineers were put to work building roads and bridges. King William's Town, already a market centre, was laid out for future expansion on both sides of the Buffalo. The Xhosas would again be given the chance to become like Englishmen. 'Gradual indeed is the progress from Barbarism to Civilization,' Harry advised Grey, 'but if not forced on, the latter will in the end prevail by the Will of the Almighty.' With this end in mind, missionaries were invited to resume their labours. Lands were allotted to them under the authority of the government, not under the chiefs, as had been previously done. The natives would be encouraged to send their children to missionary schools. Families would be given seeds, ploughs and goats with the hope that profitable farming would overcome their nomadic tendencies. In time the youth might be apprenticed to humane employers who would inculcate the useful habits of industry.

Traders were welcomed to stimulate commerce. (Licence fees of £50 would also be an important source of revenue.) However, the privilege to trade would be revoked if they trafficked in guns or liquor. In conversations with traders and settlers, Harry was informed of the need for a good port. Impressed with the facilities he found at the mouth of the Buffalo, he proclaimed it a port, named it East London and made plans to collect customs. All of these measures would serve the paramount wish of the colonial office that the colony become self-supporting.

Grey endorsed these arrangements. Dr Philip, who had seen his system collapse, remained silent. Except for the Byzantine practice of foot-kissing, even the *Commercial Advertiser*, formerly so caustic in its opposition, joined the other colonial newspapers in praise. 'Obscurity, uncertainty, confusion, which existed,' observed editor Fairbairn, 'vanished at his approach. Every man feels that within the last week the whole Kaffir question has changed colour. The black cloud has become transparent rain drops.' Old enemies and potential critics were, for the moment, content to wait and see. 'Time is needed,' one missionary told Dr Philip, 'and must be allowed for maturing an incipient scheme in the hands of such an extempore character as Sir Harry Smith.'

To inform the chiefs of his measures and to further intimidate them, Harry called for a second meeting to be held on the anniversary of the great gathering which had taken place on 7 January 1836. All the chiefs came as requested. Kreli and Buku sent representatives from across the Kei to express their desire for peace.

The arena was similar to that of 1836, with the same large ring of naked or nearly naked natives eight or more deep sitting on their haunches. Missionaries and other Europeans in the neighbourhood, attracted by curiosity, swelled the crowd. Standing on the same spot he had in 1836, Harry orated and then asked the chiefs to take an oath to acknowledge him as a representative of the Queen, to listen to the missionaries and repudiate murder, rape, witchcraft, the sins of wife-buying and other abhorrent practices. Furthermore, on this day each year the chiefs were to surrender a fat ox to show that they held their lands for the Queen. Producing a decorated rod, which he called 'the Stick of Office', Harry asked each chief to come forward, touch it and take the oath.

The chiefs being asked to speak their minds, Sandile was the first to limp forward. Contritely he thanked the governor for his life, but he could not refrain from pleading that the land allotted to him was too small for his needs. Kona was encouraged to make a similar request. Harry stared at them forbiddingly and advised them sarcastically that there was much vacant land towards the Kei. That ended all further supplication. The chiefs meekly professed their acceptance and expressed their thanks.

Addicted as he was to histrionics, Harry worked himself into a rage as he spoke of those who might dare to disobey. 'I will eat you up,' he growled, 'and drive you out of British Kaffraria.' Then, referring to the late war, his face became contorted with Jovian wrath. He choked:

And you even dared to make war, YOU DARE TO MAKE WAR, you dare attack our waggons! See what I will do if you ever dare to touch a waggon or the oxen belonging to it. Do you see that waggon I say?

All eyes were fixed, as he pointed, on a solitary wagon which had been secretly loaded with gunpowder. 'Now hear my word, FIRE!' At his command, a spark was laid by a hidden soldier. The blast was deafening and caused all to flinch, as thousands of particles showered the gathering. The smoke cleared and where the wagon had stood there was nothing. Quaking with terror, the natives groaned, 'Mawa!' and 'Que!'—'Ah! do you see the waggon!' Harry announced in triumph. He then pulled a large sheet of paper out of his pocket. 'Do you see this paper?' he asked. Vigorously Harry tore it to shreds and scattered the pieces to the wind. 'There go the treaties!' he shouted. 'Do you hear? No more treaties! No more Sarili, no more Sandile, no more Mhala. Hear! I am your Inkosi Inkulu!'

Harry's mood then suddenly changed, like the calm that followed the storm. Harry began to purr softly to his 'good children'. Gently he asked them to live in peace. Pato with the panther-like face, who had been chased through the hills for three months before he surrendered, came forth to speak for all of his people. 'I thank you as a great chief,' he blurted emotionally, 'today you have taken me from among the monkeys to sit in the sun.' In conclusion Harry called on them to give cheers for the Queen of England. Then in a stage whisper he bade them 'Farewell'. As he rode off, Harry directed the assembly to cry 'Peace! Peace!' which grew into a tremendous roar.

Once affairs in Kaffraria were adjusted to his satisfaction, the governor turned his attention to the northeast. Across the Orange was a vast land that encompassed what is now the Orange Free State, Lesotho and Natal, the latter being annexed in 1843. British interests had become entangled, with trekking Boers and warlike tribes disturbed by the encroachments of European settlers. In pursuit of order, Harry resolved to extend British rule in Trans-Orangia. Armed only with his authority as high commissioner, for he had no instructions from Grey, and accompanied by his staff and an escort of 60 C.M.R., he left King William's Town, moving, in the words of Sir John Wylde, Chief Justice at the Cape, 'as the whirlwind in energy and its effects'.

Confident of his powers of persuasion, he sought the chiefs Adam Kok and Moshesh to renegotiate existing treaties in order to clear the way for annexation. Much of the territory they held was either vacant or already occupied by settlers. On his way to Bloemfontein he stopped long enough at the confluence of the Ox Kraal and Klipplaats to select the site for

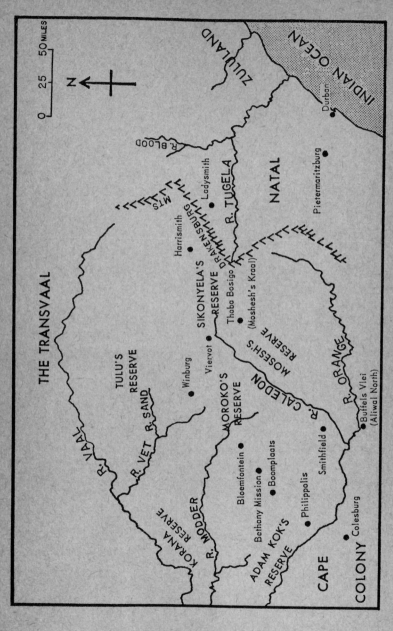

Map 7   The Orange River Sovereignty

a town that would be called Whittlesea. Not since Alexander
the Great would so many towns be founded or associated
with a great captain in so brief a period. There was to be a
Harrismith and Smithfield, a Ladysmith and Ladismith, an
Aliwal North and Aliwal South (Mossel Bay), and so on.

Arriving in Bloemfontein with its half-dozen houses on
24 January, the governor was received by the ruddy-faced
British magistrate, Major Henry Warden, whose one claim
to distinction was that he was the illegitimate grandchild of
'Bonnie Prince Charlie'. Warden arranged a meeting with
Adam Kok, the Griqua chief and protégé of Dr Philip. Harry
made him what he believed to be a generous offer, whereby
his people would be left with a large stretch of territory,
more than double their needs. For those lands relinquished,
he would receive an annual payment.

Kok, however, objected and assumed what Harry considered an overbearing manner. A quarrel ensued. 'What,'
shouted Harry, 'am I the conqueror of all Kaffirland to be
thwarted by a black fellow like you? There's the treaty and
there's the door!' Kok would accept neither. Thoroughly
riled, Harry pointed to a beam overhead and promised he
would hang him up unless he adopted a more reasonable
attitude. Warden tactfully intervened. He took the chief
outside and suggested that he would be wise to agree. Kok
signed the next day.

The Boers of the region came into Bloemfontein to see the
governor. They hailed him with a fervour unusual for a people
normally so imperturbable. Many, of course, had served with
him in 1836. Being reunited with old comrades was always a
moving experience for Harry. He told them warmly that he
came 'as a friend and not as a Governor'. Anxious to reconcile
these estranged emigrants who faced misery and uncertainty,
he offered them a chance to live once more under British rule
with the prospect of churches, schools and the construction
of roads and other public works. Naturally they would be
expected to pay taxes, but none of the money collected would
leave the territory. 'Had I been Governor,' he said, referring
to the time of their migration, 'I do not think you would have
done so, for I would have talked over your affairs with you.'
The Boers thanked him and, speaking for their community,
stated they were prepared to accept his proposal.

A gesture of kindness to these people conveyed more than words. At one point during the meeting, Harry observed an elderly man 'whose whitened locks told of some eighty years'. He instantly rose, beckoned him from the gathering and gave him his own chair, saying that he was sorry that a man of his age should have stood so long without being noticed.

The next stop for Harry was Winburg where he would meet Moshesh, or Moshoeshoe, so named in imitation of the sounds made by a knife in shaving. He was the founder of the Basuto nation, one composed largely of tribes displaced during the terror conducted by the Zulu chief, Shaka. Without exaggeration Moshesh could boast, 'I am Basutoland.' Skilled in war and diplomacy, he succeeded in maintaining himself against his enemies, black and white. Harry held him to be 'a superior man, possessing a strong mind adopted for government'. Rather than browbeat him as he had Kok, he would treat him with courtesy and respect.

Meeting outside Winburg, Moshesh was surprised that so great a man and his staff travelled with only two servants and two wagons. The chief himself was surrounded by many mounted followers; but he was easily recognized, for he wore a uniform similar to that of a French general. On closer inspection, Harry saw a well-modelled man about his own age with an almost aquiline profile, lively eyes and a soft smile. Through an interpreter, the Rev. Casalis of the Paris Evangelical Missionary Society, they chatted as they cantered towards town. Harry asked him if Winburg was part of his territory and the chief replied that it was.

Nearing the white washed mud-brick houses with thatched roofs, Harry held his hat aloft to Boers on either side, 'I salute you gentlemen of Winburg.' They responded by raising their big, round hats and firing their long 'roers' (elephant guns) into the air. Harry cried:

Moshesh! Musket fire is generally the sound of war, but today it is the sound of peace. I have fought much, but I declare there is no man in all the world who has as great a horror of war as I have.

Moshesh smiled. 'Peace,' he said calmly, 'is the mother of nations.' On dismounting, Harry presented him with two fine saddles, a gold watch and a marquee tent.

25 Moshesh, paramount chief and founder of the Basuto nation. Skilled in war and diplomacy, he maintained himself against the British, the Boers and powerful tribal forces.

26 Andries Pretorius, voortrekker leader and statesman, who championed Boer resistance to British rule in the Orange River Sovereignty. Sir Harry put a price on his head and defeated his forces at Boomplaats.

27 Convoy on the march, a common sight during the frontier wars at the Cape.

28 The action at Boomplaats, where Sir Harry moved his forces so swiftly that he crushed the Boer rebellion in the Orange River Sovereignty with one blow.

Their conference took place in the tent. Casalis, the chief's adviser for external affairs, spoke a broken English at best; and Harry's French was far from perfect. Consequently the conversants, long-winded by nature, became more animated than usual in trying to make themselves understood. The governor asked Moshesh to sign a treaty proclaiming as British all lands settled by the Boers. A commission would draw the boundaries and the Basuto would be compensated for lands they sacrificed. To demonstrate the tranquillity that would prevail as it did now in Kaffraria, Harry closed his eyes and pretended to fall asleep. All looked on in astonishment, recalled Casalis, as 'he began to snore with all his might'. With a sudden jerk he was wide awake. Turning to Moshesh with a broad, mischievous grin he declared, 'Everyone is to sleep this way now.'

Moshesh tried to press him on matters that involved disputes between himself and the Boers, but he brushed his questions aside by saying that he was in too great a hurry to go into details. The extension of the Queen's sovereignty, he asserted, would settle these problems. 'Moshesh,' he said earnestly, as he raised his hand a foot above the desk, 'is like this but,' and he raised his other hand two feet, 'Her Majesty is as this ... Trust me,' he asked with all the sincerity he could muster, 'and no one will dare to raise his hand against the great chief of the Basuto.' Moshesh indicated his acceptance by affixing his mark to the treaty.

That afternoon, the 27th, in the presence of the chief, the governor met with the burghers who had petitioned for British jurisdiction. 'Be thankful,' he told them, 'to Moshesh for your security.' Towering over them from the top of a table, he menaced them with condign punishment if they encroached on Basuto land. He swore that he 'would follow them up even to the gates of the infernal regions!'

In answer to their request for a church, Harry told them they could expect a grant from the government. To show his good faith, he dramatically emptied his purse on the table, £25. 'There is my share,' he declared. 'You are living without divine worship! What a state of degradation.' At a site on the principal street, he laid the foundation for the first Dutch Reformed Church in the Orange Free State. Kneeling before it, he asked Casalis to lead them in prayer. He then

20

took Casalis by the arm and croaked, 'Let us go.' To the
missionary's amazement, Harry's face was bathed in tears.
Nor was he able to speak above a whisper. Later Harry told
him, 'I never felt so much in my life.' Writing to a fellow
missionary, Casalis commented, 'I never met with one having
such a diversity of character—an iron will joined to a
surprising simplicity.'

Before dawn on 28 January, Harry and his saddle-sore party
were off in the direction of Natal. Commandant Gideon
Joubert in charge of the escort complained, 'He allows no one
to sleep.' There was even less sleep that night, the anniversary
of Aliwal, which he celebrated with Holdich, Major Garvock,
another nephew acting as his private secretary, and Richard
Southey, his official secretary.

The original plan was for the governor to return to Cape
Town, but in Winburg he heard that a large party of Boers in
Natal were trekking out of the colony to throw off British
rule. Their leader was Andries Pretorius, a veteran of the
Sixth Frontier War who had become a national hero. In his
efforts to establish a home for his people in Natal, the great
voortrekker had led a commando of 470 men in an astounding
victory over 10,000 Zulus in the battle of Blood River in
1838. When British authority was extended to Natal, he and
his followers had reluctantly submitted, but resentments soon
arose over native policy. Efforts by Pretorius to gain an
interview with Pottinger had been insultingly rejected. 'Had
Pretorius had an audience with the Governor of the Colony,'
Harry told the Boers in Winburg, 'I should not have been
here among you, I would sooner have lost five thousand pounds
than not have come.' That same day he sent an express
messenger to Pretorius to pause and meet with him. Harry
informed Grey:

> To deal with these honest but highly prejudiced Boers,
> both patience and temper are required, and if their case
> and supposed grievances are heard, reason will establish
> them in good faith towards the government—this shall
> be done however by a straight-forward honest course, as
> free from chicanery and duplicity.

It was a hard journey through heavy rains down the slippery
slopes of the Drakensberg or 'Dragon mountains'. Pretorius,

a sturdily-built man of 48 years, together with some of his men, welcomed the governor outside their large camp where they were stalled by the flooded Tugela. Harry presented him with a new saddle as a gift, but he asked him not to think of it as a bribe.

Harry was appalled by the sight that greeted him. 'These families,' he told Grey, 'were exposed to a state of misery which I never before saw equalled except in Masséna's invasion of Portugal.' Sickly women and children were crammed into tents and wagons only half-sheltered from the rain. When the governor rode among them, he was received 'as if among my own family'. He was deeply moved.

Three or four hundred men openly shedding tears assembled before him to express their grievances. Their main complaint was that the government permitted thousands of Zulus to squat among them where they pleased without any guarantee for their safety. Harry promised that if 'his children' returned, the Zulus would be relocated and the farmers would be given grants of land up to 5,000 acres.

Pretorius was not persuaded. He had visions of a great, independent Boer Republic extending from the Orange to far beyond the Vaal. In private conversation with this 'shrewd, sensible' man, Harry shattered his dream by displaying a draft proclaiming the annexation of the land between the Orange and the Vaal. 'Ah, admit there are faults on both sides,' Harry said soothingly, 'but we are taught to forgive.' Pretorius remonstrated against the publication of the annexation proclamation and declared that his people would either fight for their independence or retire far into the interior where the British could not reach them. Harry insisted that now that he was governor they would accept British rule. They finally agreed that Pretorius would meet with various Boer communities to ascertain their views. Only if four out of five favoured annexation, Harry assured him, would he issue the proclamation. Without further delay, Pretorius rode off on his mission.

Meanwhile, the governor remained in camp and induced some families to resettle in Natal. Without waiting to hear from Pretorius, on 3 February 1848 Harry went ahead with his plan to proclaim the Queen's sovereignty over the Orange river territory.

That day he wrote to Grey to explain the reasons for his action.

> My position has been analagous to that of every governor general who has proceeded in India ... The security of all Countries *within* depends not only upon their sound internal condition but upon their security from without, and the existence of a relationship on the borders calculated to inspire confidence.

He assured the colonial secretary that the cost of government would be borne by the inhabitants and that trade would thrive to such an extent that the treasury would benefit through the increase in revenue.

The jump beyond the Orange alarmed anti-expansionist sentiment in the colonial office. Grey, however, was more optimistic and prepared to give what Harry called his 'great experiment' a chance. The colonial secretary succeeded in overruling his critics and winning the approval of the Cabinet for such a radical departure from previous policy.

Major Warden, who was to be the chief authority as the British Resident in Bloemfontein, advised the governor that additional troops were now needed to maintain order in a territory of over 50,000 square miles. Harry took the opposite view. 'My dear fellow,' he replied, 'pray bear in mind that the Boers are my children; your detachments will march for the colony immediately.' He left Warden with a garrison of some 60 C.M.R. to keep the peace throughout the Sovereignty.

But Harry's influence with the Boers was never so great as he had imagined. He failed to appreciate their bitterness against British rule, and mistook their affection for him as an unqualified endorsement of the government he represented. Harry naively told Grey:

> To prove, if necessary, the faith I have in their loyalty, I may mention that on one occasion when the waggon in which I travel, and which they call 'Government House', was nearly upset when crossing one of the tributary streams of the Great Tugela, thirty or forty men on the bank stripped and sprang into the water, exclaiming 'Government House' shall not fall—and their efforts saved my only home from being carried down by the current.

To implement the generous promises he had made to the trekkers in the Tugela camp, Harry journeyed to Pietermaritzburg, capital of Natal, where a great reception had been prepared. Finishing his efforts to placate the Boers as quickly as possible — by handing out proclamations as others do handbills — he rushed down to Durban. Allowing only three hours for celebrations there, he boarded a steamer bound for East London. From there he galloped to King William's Town, arriving only 72 hours after he had left Pietermaritzburg. Travelling overland he reached Cape Town, according to Professor Cory, 'in a small waggon drawn by six tired horses and sitting upon bag and baggage, looking more like a post-contractor bringing in the mails than His Excellency the Governor of the Colony'. The return of the governor from his meteoric mission of peace touched off another round of festivities. Forewarned, Harry left his wagon, mounted a horse, summoned an escort and made an entry befitting his office. He was hailed on all sides as the 'Great Pacificator'. Once more Cape Town was lit up throughout the night with 'fireworks, flaming tar-barrels, volleys of musketry, drum-banging and trumpet-blowing'. New transparencies were displayed. One showed the governor offering his chair to an aged Boer. Fairbairn proposed an equestrian statue which would symbolize his virtues for future generations.

[14]

Rebellion: Boomplaats and the Convict Crisis

The Boers interfered with most people's arrangements.
Winston Churchill

In 1848 revolts broke out like an ugly rash across the face of Europe. South Africa was not immune from the contagion. Harry was still receiving kudos for his 'brilliant achievements' when reports of unrest came across the veldt. The abrupt annexation had sown anger and distrust among many Boers. Pretorius was outraged by what he regarded as a breach of faith. He had canvassed his compatriots and found to his satisfaction that the majority opposed the hoisting of the Union Jack beyond the Orange. The governor rejected the assertion that he had broken his word by maintaining that their agreement referred only to those Boers north of the Vaal. More than ever he believed that most of the Boers in the Orange River Sovereignty supported him.

It is conceivable that Harry, who talked better than he listened, misunderstood. It is more likely, however, that he was so confident of his popularity that he expected no opposition to his proclamation. This might also explain why he would encourage Pretorius, his staunchest opponent, to undertake such a mission. Pretorius himself was not altogether honest. In a meeting at Winburg on 7 February he misrepresented the governor by declaring that he had already violated his promises to these settlers; he urged them, if necessary, to fight for their independence.

After Harry's return to Cape Town, Warden relayed frequent charges that Pretorius, now a resident of the Transvaal, was encouraging the Boers in the Sovereignty to revolt. Instead of diverting the troops listed to return to England, as Warden expected, the governor sent words. On 29 March

he despatched a rambling, unconventional manifesto, reminis-
cent of Cromwell, in which he brandished the Old Testament
and 'the fatal sword'. Addressing the misbehaving Boers as
'half lost friends and wavering Christians', he bade them recall
the advantages he had recently conferred to rescue them from
hardship and raise them to the level of prosperity enjoyed by
their friends and relatives at the Cape. But if they listened to
'wicked agitators', who distorted the truth, they might find
'their generous friend turned into an Avenger of Evil'. He
swore that he would 'carry out or die in the attempt the
provisions of the Proclamations' that he had framed for their
exclusive advantage. ' "Vengeance is mine", saith the Lord,
and in his name, and for the benefit of his creatures, would I
smite those I love.' While his troops exulted as conquerors,
he would 'weep as you have seen me do over the fallen, the
defeated and deluded'.

The manifesto ended with an undoubtedly sincere appeal
that they join him in prayer.

> Lord of all Power and Might, Disposer of all things good
> and evil ... teach us *who* are our true friends ... defend us
> from the practices of wicked men ... When we must put
> off the mortal garment and lie down on the bed of Death,
> let us be at peace with Thee Oh Lord, at *Peace* with the
> world, and at *Peace* with our own hearts.

The governor might coo like a dove and growl like a tiger,
but a large number of Boers remained defiant. The bitter-
enders raised the standard of revolt and invited Pretorius
to lead them. Pretorius hesitated, for his attention was required
closer to home. His beloved wife lay dying. Declaring herself
beyond help, however, she pleaded with him to go. It was
to be the last time he saw her.

With a commando of Transvaalers he arrived at Winburg
on 12 July and frightened off Mr Biddulph, the British
magistrate. Riding as fast as he could, Biddulph warned
Warden in Bloemfontein. Possessing only a feeble force of
C.M.R. and a few armed civilians, he capitulated shortly
after Pretorius arrived on the 17th. The Boer leader put him
and his soldiers, along with the loyalists, in wagons, and
shepherded them ignominiously to the Orange river border.

Evidently Pretorius assumed that he had thereby ended the Sovereignty. But Harry Smith was hardly the man to tolerate open defiance. Apprised of events, he promptly ordered all available troops on the frontier to assemble at Colesburg, where he would join them. He proclaimed Pretorius a rebel and offered £1,000 for his head. When Pretorius heard of it, he laughed and said he would give 1,000 head of cattle for the apprehension of the governor.

Before departing, Harry scribbled a hasty letter to Grey in which he noted his expectation 'that this outburst will fall of itself to the ground as soon as Pretorius hears of his own value in my estimation, and my approach with the troops'. Aware of the government's concern over cost, he added, 'no apprehension need attach to the all engrossing subject, expense, for the Boers shall pay every fraction of it'.

The temper of Grey's colleagues was indicated by the chancellor of the exchequer. 'May the —— I won't say who, run away with some of your colonies,' he ejaculated. 'Here is a new insurrection at the Cape—pray write Sir H. Smith as to expense—for I really do not know what is to be done.'

With his staff and Dr Hall, the governor left on 29 July and arrived at Colesburg on 9 August. Holdich noted in his diary that they travelled '102½ hours at the rate of 6 miles an hour, making the distance about 615 miles'. The Boers were to be seen on the opposite bank where they had thrown up a trench. Meanwhile, some of the C.M.R. had arrived from Grahamstown, but most of the troops were delayed by heavy rains and snow that had caused the rivers to swell.

Both leaders still hoped that a battle could be avoided. A petition was received from Pretorius on the 16th, asking His Excellency to withdraw. Moreover, he added, the Boers would trek over the Vaal rather than accept British rule. The governor made no reply: time was on his side. Burghers pressed into service by Pretorius were deserting every day; some even volunteered to serve against the rebels. Native chiefs in the Sovereignty also offered their assistance. Harry, however, refused to enlist Boers to fight Boers or blacks to fight whites. 'A display of Her Majesty's Power', he believed, would be sufficient. A burgher crossed the Orange and confirmed this view by reporting that Pretorius and his men had broken up their camp of 62 wagons and fallen back. (Actually they had heard a rumour that another force was approaching from Natal.)

The crossing of the Orange began on the 22nd. Two india-rubber pontoons which had to be refilled every morning were brought up to ferry the troops. The current was so strong that there was a problem in getting the boats across. Baulked by difficulties, Harry stamped with rage and threatened to have the men in charge of the boats shot. Richard Southey solved the problem by advising the use of a thinner line. 'Why the hell didn't you say this sooner?' said Harry gratefully.

Ensign Fleming of the 45th, in a letter to his mother, wrote of the governor: 'He is the most extraordinary man I ever met, he is all energy and works from daylight to dark. Swears most awfully at everyone from his Aid de camps down to the drummer boy.' Most of all he cursed the rebels, announcing that 'he will make them all know who he is when he gets across'. But the soldiers believed that not a shot would be fired. 'If they mean to fight,' Fleming observed, 'they would oppose us crossing the River today which would be their greatest advantage.'

By sundown of the fifth day about 600 men and their impedimenta had been conveyed across without mishap. The procession moved out rapidly across the veldt the next morning, the 27th. Four squadrons of C.M.R., mostly Hottentots in dark green, with European officers, led the way. To avoid the onus of firing the first shot, the governor ordered them to remove the caps from the nipples of their carbines. Two companies of the Rifle Brigade followed. Like the rest of the regulars they were clothed in clay-coloured, leather overalls and wore forage-caps without peaks. A small detachment of engineers and artillerymen were in the centre with three guns. Two companies of the 45th and two of the 91st Highlanders marched towards the rear. One hundred and fifty wagons carried enough supplies for 30 days. Riding with the train were loyal Boers whose homes had been wrecked by insurgents, and who had offered to serve as scouts. Sixty men were left behind to guard the crossing. Riding up and down the column to encourage the marchers was the governor, conspicuously garbed in a blue jacket, white-cord trousers and a drab felt hat.

More colour was added to the force the next day, near

Philippolis where Adam Kok and a contingent of 250 Griquas joined them. They were attired in plumed hats and sheepskin karosses. Harry decided they would prove useful in augmenting his mounted troops.

The following morning (29 August), under a cloudless sky, the force pursued its march briskly for the air was refreshingly dry and cool. Ten miles out they breakfasted at the abandoned farm called Toufontein. The ground ahead was level for several miles before it rose into a series of hills around a farm called Boomplaats. Harry knew the region well. If Pretorius meant to oppose his advance, Harry was convinced that this would be the place.

He was right. Pretorius, an able tactician, expected to ambush the 'hero of Aliwal' in these hills. His commando, greatly reduced by desertions, numbered some 500 men, nearly 200 of whom stayed with the wagons an hour's ride away.

The Boers were strung out for a mile or more on two ranges strewn with stones and boulders. One range ran parallel to the road, on Harry's right. The other ran at right angles to the road and crossed it to the left. The road passed through this range and down into a valley with a small stream. Above it stood the Boomplaats homestead with huts enclosed by high stone walls. Beyond it lay a higher range with a gap through which the road to Bloemfontein continued. The ranges at right angles had pickets posted on forward spurs. The main party remained concealed behind breastworks of stone, the Transvaalers holding the centre before the road, the Free Staters were on the flanks. Once the column was well into the trap, Commandant Adriaan Stander on the Boer left (or east) flank was to fire the first shot as a signal for all to open up with rifles, muskets and elephant guns before the British had a chance to deploy.

As the Boers waited, the British finished their breakfast. Harry addressed the Riflemen, telling them—what they already knew—that he had fought with them from Montevideo to Waterloo. He recalled the glorious deeds that were their heritage. Pointing towards Boomplaats, he vowed that 'he would drive the arch-rebel Pretorius and his followers like rats from the hills'. The men responded with loud cheers.

At one in the afternoon a reconnoitring party moved into

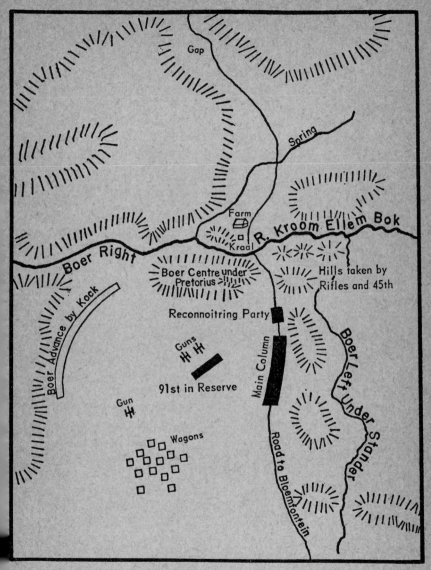

Map 8   The Battle of Boomplaats, 29 August 1848

the hills, where they encountered some 50 mounted Boers. Each side, mutually warned, galloped off in the direction they had come from.

Harry still hoped to win the insurgents over with words. He sent Lieut. Salis ahead with a company of C.M.R. in skirmishing order. Under no conditions, however, were they to fire unless fired upon. The governor and his staff rode behind them with the intention of opening negotiations with the first Boers they met. Southey warned him that they would fight. Harry answered, 'They dare not.' It was inconceivable that these farmers, his old friends, would try to shoot him.

The Boers, however, had no such inhibitions. Someone shouted, 'There they are!' The British looked up and saw the crests of the hills come alive with bearded men in duffle-jackets and great white hats. Not waiting for Stander's signal they blazed away. Salis had his left arm shattered and his horse killed.[1] Three of his men fell to the ground and lay motionless. One bullet grazed the nose of Harry's horse and another cut the stirrup leather and bruised his shin. More angry than hurt, he covered his retreat with ferocious curses. Spurring his charger back to prepare for battle, he passed some Hottentots. 'Maak klar, Papa se kinderen!' ('Get ready, dad's kids!'), he shouted in Cape Dutch. They immediately extended right and left.

It was the Boers' turn to be surprised. The guns, escorted by the 91st, rapidly opened up and blasted the Boer centre and left with grape and shrapnel. Harry later claimed that twelve Boers were killed by one cannon shot. The 45th and the Rifles, their bayonets glistening, rushed forward to envelop the enemy's left. The C.M.R., meanwhile, defended the wagons, which had been halted with the loyalists and Griquas, from the Boers galloping in from the west under Commandant Jan Kock. They were stopped by rifle fire and a 9-pounder that struck their flank. They retired back to the hills in the west and rode around to the high hills to the north.

The 45th and the Rifles, disdaining cover, pressed on despite their losses. Their movements were so swift that they completely dislodged the defenders. Many of Stander's men had

---

[1] As Salis lay helpless, some Boers came up to finish him off. The officer pleaded in Dutch that he had a 'vrouw and kinderen'. Mercifully he was allowed to crawl to safety.

no time to reach their horses. They ran to the ground behind the centre. Harry brought up the two 6-pounders to the captured high ground and directed their galling fire towards the centre which the 91st and C.M.R. were ordered to attack. 'Sir Harry was wherever the firing seemed to tell most,' observed Fleming, 'and when he saw a few falling and their comrades stopping to look at them he would ride up and shout "forward, boys, forward!" ' The rush broke the Boer centre.

Pretorius rallied his men for a stand along the stream to the north. The infantry continued to thrust ahead. The Rifles received sharp fire from the farmstead and their colonel, R. B. Buller, was severely wounded in the thigh. The artillery coming forward was too much for the Boers and they retired in disorder. Not until they were harassed by mounted Hottentots and Griquas did they stop at the gap and turn to fire, very angry that the governor should use non-whites against them. Many were short of ammunition, but they were reinforced by Kock's men. The Hottentots and Griquas were brought to a standstill. Harry charitably wrote, 'They did their best.'

On seeing the infantry reform and the guns come up and unlimber, the Boers decided that further resistance would be futile. They set fire to the veldt and 'ran like blazes across the flat ground', as the cannon fire reached out for them. Harry continued the chase with the C.M.R. in the lead. The few Boers they caught up with stubbornly refused to yield. By 4.30 p.m., having gone some eight miles, Harry halted his exhausted men. By now the fugitives had reached their wagons and dispersed to their homes.

Not until ten that night were the tents raised. Harry greeted the returning Hottentots: 'Here's all my kids. Dad has got lots of bisquits, tobacco, shirts and all sorts of things for you.' The Hottentots would never forget him. But one of them, Private Darling, remarked that the general 'was very fidgity; if we happened to touch the cords of his tent he would come out and swear at us'.

At one in the morning, Harry roused his men for the next day's pursuit towards Bloemfontein. There was evidence everywhere of the precipitate retreat: stray horses, arms and articles of clothing. The insurgents, however, had vanished. Two young lads said to be rebels were found at the mission station called Bethany. The only punishment they received, apart from the confiscation of their arms, was at the hands of a big grenadier whom Harry told to pull their noses and kick them out of camp.

'I have seldom seen a sharper skirmish,' Harry wrote in his report. Considering his career, this was more of a tribute to his men than the literal truth. Nevertheless, in two hours, under Harry's capable direction, his fast-moving, disciplined troops, supported by well-directed artillery, crushed a rebellion that threatened to be prolonged. It was a feat of British arms that grew in retrospect. Such successful actions against these highly mobile, straight-shooting frontiersmen would be notably absent from the First and Second Anglo-Boer Wars a generation or two later.

The cost of Harry's crowding tactics was high. Two officers were slain and 10 were wounded; 14 men were killed and 32 wounded. These figures did not include Biddulph, who fell down a hill, and six Griquas who were lost. Apparently for political reasons, Harry claimed that 49 dead Boers were counted in the field and estimated that upwards of 150 were wounded. In contrast, the Boers put their losses at 9 killed and 5 wounded. Reports of even more enemy dead were brought in by natives. Dr Hall, who attended to the British wounded, said the reports were not believed, but such stories would find their way into colonial papers and 'do good by showing the extent of the defeat'.

Queen Victoria was disturbed to learn that such 'a very large portion of those who were hit by the fire of the rebels were officers who appear to have been particularly aimed at'. Grey told her that Sir Harry had 'exposed himself very much',[1] but she was happy to learn that his 'wound was not of a serious nature'. Concerned by the possibility 'that Lady Smith might have been left a widow', the Queen insisted that Juana be awarded £500 a year.[2]

But the fighting had ended. Entering Bloemfontein on 2 September, Harry lost no time in restoring law and order. Forming up the troops, the Sovereignty was proclaimed with a 21-gun salute. Two prisoners taken by the Griquas the previous day were immediately court-martialled and sentenced

[1] RA, Grey to Queen Victoria, 25 Oct. 1848, B 10/224.
[2] RA, Queen Victoria to Grey, 26 Oct. 1848, B 10/225.

to be shot. One was a deserter named Michael Quigley. The other, Thomas Dryer, was a Boer who may have been compelled to join the rebel ranks; some described him as 'half simple'. Though there appear to have been mitigating circumstances in both cases, Harry justified the executions as necessary, telling Grey that 'if I can make a few public examples, a stern sense of duty and justice will banish all regret'.

At first some resistance was expected when Harry entered Winburg on the 7th. Not a shot was fired, however, as some rebels were seized. Harry told them they would be shot and ordered a rope to be placed around the neck of Frederick Schnehage as he was led away. His wife came to beg for his life. Blinded by tears, she stumbled over the tent ropes. Harry came out and was so affected by this heart-rending scene that he had her husband and all of the other prisoners released.

Following another 21-gun salute with proclamations, other rebels were encouraged to surrender their arms and to take an oath of allegiance. Some, like Commandant Paul Bester, had obviously been forced to support the insurgents' cause against their will. Harry not only pardoned Bester but appointed him civil commissioner of a newly created district. Those who had remained loyal during the Pretorian rule gave Harry much satisfaction; he loudly extolled their fidelity to the Crown.

Various tales were by now circulating through the Sovereignty, telling of the unflinching determination of the British soldier at Boomplaats. The one that pleased Harry most related how all the 91st were killed but one man, who continued alone to advance against the Boers. 'There is no use, they say,' wrote Dr Hall, 'in fighting against such desperate fellows.' The story grew out of the fact that Ensign Crampton and his soldier-servant were well ahead of their regiment in advancing over a hill. When the officer fell wounded at the top, the servant, faithful to his orders, advanced down the hill unremittingly alone.

For that 'cunning traitor' Pretorius, the governor raised the price on his head to £2,000. A reward of £500 was offered for various other ringleaders. They and others who had fled beyond reach across the Vaal had their property confiscated and all of those who had taken up arms were fined. 'Sir Harry,' Dr Hall noted in his diary, 'will make them pay every shilling

of it ... into the military chest.' Harry left behind his great
favourite, Richard Southey, to collect the fines since, in his
opinion, 'Warden is a weak man, Biddulph is an alarmist with
no more moral courage than a butterfly.' The Boers, notoriously
averse to taxes, paid in a surprisingly short time. Southey later
wrote that the execution of the two men at Bloemfontein 'had
a wonderful effect on the minds of those inclined to rebellion'.
The suppression of the revolt cost £10,378, but the war tax
and fines imposed wrung out · £10,812 — far more than Harry
had expected.

To deter future risings and afford greater security, Harry
put the recuperating Col. Buller in charge of a garrison of
three companies of infantry and half a company of artillery.
A small fort, Victoria, was to be built in Bloemfontein with
four 9-pounders on the walls.

Highly pleased with the 'staunch allegiance' of Moshesh
during the rebellion, the governor requested that he meet
with him in Winburg as soon as possible. On 8 September
Moshesh and various petty chiefs arrived to be entertained by
the governor. As always, Harry dominated the conversation.
He thanked them on 'sitting still' during the disturbances,
flattered them and recounted his exploits in many wars without
seeming to stop for breath. No further arrangements were
made affecting their positions towards the settlers or one
another; Harry merely asked them if they were willing to
support the Sovereignty when needed. They unanimously
declared their allegiance.

A review of the troops was held for their benefit the next
day, Holdich describing Moshesh as 'a clear-headed fellow and
very sharp ... who was much amused with the movements
and particularly astonished at the Artillery'. The Basuto chief
returned the compliment on the 11th by parading his 700
mounted men, many of them carrying muskets. This was
followed by a war dance and a great feast that lasted well into
the night.

A great mutual admiration appeared to have developed
between the two leaders. Harry was but a mile out of Winburg
when a message overtook him. Moshesh wrote:

Go, Great Warrior of your Nation, go under the shield
of your mighty God Jehovah, by whose help, you tell me,

29 Canteen at Fort Cox with Sandile drinking, by T. Baines.

30 Disguised as one of his escort of Cape Mounted Riflemen,
Sir Harry makes good his escape from Fort Cox.

31 Lord Grey, the reform-minded colonial secretary (1846–52). The renowned diarist, Charles Greville, was impressed by 'his contempt for the opinion of others, and the tenacity with which he clung to his own'. Sir Harry, as governor at the Cape, would learn the unhappy truth of this observation.

32 The best-known portrait of Sir Harry. It is an engraving by D. J. Pound, from a photograph taken in 1859, shortly before the general's retirement after 54 years of constant service in the army.

you have been able to do such great things in this country.
Go, Great Leader of the Soldiers of the Lady your Queen
... tell Her Gracious Majesty that I am sensible of the
great debt I owe to the brave General and her troops,
who has in a few days driven back and scattered the host
of the wicked Rebels.

Elated by his successful dealings with the chief, Harry told
Grey, 'The Chief Moshesh is really a wonderful man; but I
cannot induce him to embrace Christianity.' Moshesh was
never converted.

Leaving the soldiers to follow by regular marches, the
governor sped towards King William's Town. There was an
ovation at Smithfield and a loyal address of congratulation.
Through pouring rain the party crossed the Orange at Buffels
Vlei, where the governor approved the site of a town, Aliwal
North. In preparation for his customary durbar at King
William's Town, Mackinnon called in all the chiefs. Bishop
Gray, meanwhile, was riding on horseback from Grahamstown
to be present.

All was quiet on the frontier. Sandile, Pato, Macomo and
Umhala (who had named one of his sons Smith) responded to
the call. Though delayed, Kreli was on his way. Rumour had
reported that their Inkosi Inkulu had been killed at Boomplaats
—now they seemed genuinely glad to see him. As the chiefs,
in their military castoffs and shooting jackets, stood amidst a
thousand warriors, Harry strutted about and made magnilo-
quent speeches, alternately petting and scolding. The Staff of
Office was planted and all the British agents came forward to
report that the chiefs had behaved in a most exemplary manner.
The chiefs were invited to speak their minds, which they did
in the approved way. Harry then introduced the bishop as the
chief minister of the Queen's religion, 'whose business it was
to teach everybody in the land the way to heaven'. But when
the governor asked 'his children' for grain or cattle to found
mission schools there was an embarrassing silence.

Privately, the bishop had his doubts about the extent of
Harry's power over the natives. Though fully aware of Harry's
success among them, Gray had reservations about the future;
to his brother, Gray wrote of the character which Harry had
'earned for justice, kindness and determination, when in the

Colony ten years ago', but he wondered 'whether his [Smith's] personal influence will last long enough to induce them to keep sheep and cultivate their land.'

Harry, however, had no such doubts, and he considered the present durbar as a success. 'At first,' he told the colonial secretary, he had detected among the chiefs some questions as to 'the permanency of the present happy order of things', but the displays and ceremonies succeeded in their purpose, and 'a buzz of general contentment and satisfaction was elicited, showing the confidence which is reposed in the present order of things'. Harry was satisfied.

Back in Cape Town on 21 October there were congratulations and expressions of gratitude for the governor's prompt and decisive measures in restoring peace. The fund for an equestrian statue received more contributions. Expressions of relief and approval in both public and private letters were soon forthcoming from the colonial office. Grey, moreover, was gratified to hear that the cost of military operations would be recovered and that Harry could report after his travels among the Boers that he 'saw no appearance of slaves — much less traffic in them — which has been erroneously alleged to exist'.

The governor, for his part, was thankful to Montagu, who was described as 'the *mind* of the colony'. Not only had the colony in no way suffered during Harry's absence but in Montagu's experienced hands affairs were 'in a flourishing condition'. Montagu seemed driven to excellence by his earlier failures as colonial secretary in Tasmania. Diligent, single-minded and uncompromising, he often antagonized the colonists, especially in raising and collecting taxes. As one biographer noted, 'he tended to forget that the art of government is the art of the possible.' Nevertheless, since his arrival at the Cape in 1834 he had nearly doubled the revenue, using much of the money to improve harbours and internal communications. He was largely responsible for the great trunk road linking the capital with the east. Convicts from Robben Island were employed in these public works as part of his programme for rehabilitation. Harry detected one disturbing flaw in his secretary: he regarded the colonists with 'dislike — almost disdain'. Autocratic and unsympathetic to popular government, as one colonial editor observed, Montagu 'read the Bill of Rights with the Mutiny Act as a commentary'.

Harry felt secure enough about Montagu's abilities to rely on him for relief of some of his responsibilities as governor — especially during intervals of poor health. Before he set out on the campaign against Pretorius, Harry complained to Dr Hall of languor and indisposition; occasionally he felt nauseated and chilled, and these symptoms were often accompanied by an acute pain in his side, one which Harry attributed to a throw from a horse eight years before. The campaign itself had been difficult, and on his return, he frightened Juana by his jaundiced and fatigued appearance. Harry fretted, disturbed at the signs of age interfering with his past good health.

Juana's world continued to revolve around Enrique. She cared for little else and rarely left Westbrook to foster the well-ordered social life that was expected of a governor's wife. She found public functions distasteful, even more so now that ugly rumours, circulated by dissenters, that she was a 'worldly woman' had found their way into print. They frowned upon her costumes of Indian silks bedecked with dazzling jewels and her attendance at nautch dances in the Malay quarter. But what could one expect, they asked, from a woman who had adopted the vulgar life of a camp follower in her youth. Bishop Gray defended Lady Smith, 'a pleasant comfortable-looking dame with mild manners'. Writing to Miss Cole, he remarked, 'You will be pleased to hear that Sir Harry and Lady Smith are kindness itself. Nothing can be more considerate and warm-hearted than they are.'

Gray was also 'much struck with the religious turn which [Smith's] mind takes upon viewing any object'. But Gray soon learned that the governor did not understand church or education questions: 'I have to watch him very narrowly, lest he commit himself and hamper me.' Never a bigot, Harry was so broadly tolerant of other faiths that the bishop feared that he might be tempted 'to compromise the truth (not what he perhaps holds, but what the church does)'. Gray confided to his brother how one day the governor 'told me at luncheon that he was going to send for the Mahametan Imaums, and promise them schools. I could not say much, as there was a large party, but he frightens me.' (Such strains caused the bishop to suffer severe headaches, which had been diagnosed as 'rheumatism of the brain'.)

Harry's behaviour in church, moreover, could sometimes be disturbing. In a manner more regal than usual, he would peacock his way to the front pew with a solemn-faced A.D.C. carrying hymn books and prayer books. Nothing would please Harry more than to read part of the service, which, according to Shepstone, he did 'extremely well, and was very proud of it'. He was so eager that parishioners should hear him that during one period in Grahamstown he fined every absentee half-a-crown. Shepstone recalled:

> One Sunday, a dog came into the room where the service was going on, and began to create a disturbance. Sir Harry stood it for a little time, then in the middle of a prayer said suddenly, 'Take that damned dog away', after which he continued his prayer in the same tone as before.

The South African summer of 1848–9 was a time for relaxation. The pleasures of the holiday season were enhanced by the presence of six ladies as guests at Westbrook. One of them was a Mrs Sutherland, an attractive, wealthy young widow who resided there until she was married to Dr Hall, the 53-year-old bachelor twenty years her senior. 'Old Hall is no fool,' observed Harry, who gave the bride away. In a letter to a nephew, George Moore Smith, dated 17 March, Harry passed along some advice: 'Work hard through life as I have done.' Then using Hall rather than himself as an example, he added, 'do not be in a hurry in getting a wife — be well above the world ere you add to your cares'. Finally, he suggested: 'Take a common sense view of all matters and pitch the chicanery of the law overboard.' Little did he realize that within a few days his subjects were prepared to do just that.

Late in March it was revealed through English journals that a convict ship was on its way to dump 282 felons on South Africa's shores. The horrendous news shattered the tranquillity of the colony. After a large public meeting on 5 April the governor was asked to stop convicts from being turned loose among them. They gave notice that they would not employ them in any capacity or receive them on any terms. Their indignation was shared by all classes, British and Dutch, and spread throughout the colony. In every town and hamlet there were similar protest meetings, with angry speakers standing on platforms covered with funereal black. Even the Hottentots were stirred to protest. That South Africa should become a penal settlement, wrote Theal, 'was dreaded more than a dozen Kaffir wars'. The colonists were further outraged by the perfidy of Lord Grey, who had led them to believe that he would not force transportation upon them.

Grey, however, had a problem. In 1848 the prisons in Britain, as in the rest of Europe, were filled to overflowing. In the distant penal settlements of Australia, the non-convict communities were strongly objecting to the influx of more felons. In response, the character of transportation was altered. First, the convict was to be imprisoned up to 18 months. Then, as part of his rehabilitation, he was to labour on public works projects in such places as Bermuda. Finally, he would be exiled to a penal colony as a ticket of leave man, one who was reformed but restricted in his movements until his sentence had expired.

On 7 August 1848 the colonial secretary sent a public despatch to Cape Town requesting the governor to ascertain if the colonists were willing to accept ticket of leave men to alleviate the colony's acute shortage of labour. The money they earned in working off their passage would be turned over to the colony. These were not convicts in the ordinary sense, he added by way of assurance, but only 'Irishmen guilty of offences committed during the pressure of famine'.

But in a private letter Grey advised Harry, 'I believe we shall be compelled to make an Order in Council, declaring the Cape to be a place to which convicts may be transported.' Though he feared that the situation might be very unacceptable to the colonists, he asked the governor 'to reconcile them to it as well as you can'. Misled by the great popularity he enjoyed, Harry replied to Grey in November that he anticipated little dissatisfaction, 'as I shall endeavour to give it the colour of a duty to aid the Mother Country in all time of her difficulty'.

The patriotic appeal fell flat. Widespread opposition took the form of numerous petitions, especially against 'traitorous Irishmen who had incited their countrymen to wicked deeds of lawlessness'. The protesters at this time, December, 1848, were not unduly excited for they had successfully thwarted a similar proposal by the colonial office in 1842. In transmitting their petitions, Harry commented that resistance to this new proposal would 'most likely be very strong'.

Confident that the home government would not act against their wishes, the colonists were lulled into a false sense of security. Four months passed without any further word about transportation. By March, 1849, Harry too felt Grey would abide by the colonists' wishes.

Meanwhile, however, an Order in Council dated 4 September 1848 had made it legal to send convicts to the Cape. Disregarding the colonists' objections, Grey sent the *Neptune* to Bermuda where a shipload of convicts would be exchanged for ticket of leave men destined for the Cape. Among them was Ireland's renowned agitator, John Mitchel, sentenced to 14 years for opposing evictions and arming men with 'harvest snatchers'. Others had taken part in the only engagement of the rebellion, the battle of Widow McCormack's Cabbage Patch, Ireland's faint echo of the revolutionary struggles of 1848.

Harry was faced with a painful dilemma. He could not conceive of disobeying an order from his government or doing anything to offend the colonial secretary; on the other hand, he wanted to avoid sacrificing his popularity by enforcing such an objectionable scheme. The best he could do was assure the aroused colonists that April that he was opposed to convict labour except 'as a temporary measure', while at the same time pleading with Grey to reverse his decision. But Grey, in a despatch dated 20 January 1849, wrote with finality, 'I shall … persevere in the measure notwithstanding their remonstrances.' He did offer the suggestion that it might prove useful 'to scatter them around the country'. By the time this letter arrived, Harry was no longer certain that he could land the convicts, let alone distribute them throughout the land. His guarded response was, 'my desire will be to give effect to the general arrangement of Her Majesty's Government in any practical and discreet extent.'

This reply was dictated from his sickbed. On 18 April, Dr Hall recorded in his journal that Juana asked him to hurry to Westbrook to see her husband. The doctor found a carbuncle on Harry's neck which gave him much pain. Four days later, he lanced it and Harry fainted. The patient was revived and given enemas and 'blue pills'. Juana herself was so exhausted that for a time she too was a patient. For days no one was allowed to see the governor, not even the bishop whose first act was to appoint prayers to be offered for his recovery. It was a 'formidable affair for a person of Sir Harry's time of life,' wrote Hall, 'whose constitution has suffered so much from service, disease and climate. Had not Sir Harry been a man of abstemious habits,' he concluded, 'this disease, I am satisfied, would have proved fatal.' It would be weeks before he fully recovered.

While the *Neptune* was still at sea, excitement grew and leading citizens founded the Anti-Convict Association on 31 May 1849. The chairman was the highly respected merchant John Bardwell Ebden, who soon resigned his seat on the Legislative Council. Acting as the secretary was the journalist Fairbairn. A champion of constitutional liberty, he saw the movement as a means to advance representative government which was being considered in Whitehall. The Association pledged 'to hold in abhorrence any person who may aid the exiles in landing, and may have any communications with them whatever'.

Rarely in the history of the Empire had such an unauthorized body become so powerful in promoting disobedience. Every community in the colony had its branches. Those who did not support the Association faced public disgrace and financial ruin; in effect, they were to be treated as convicts themselves. Officials began to resign in droves.

Feeling rose to a frenzy when the Order in Council was published in Cape Town on 15 June. All business came to a standstill. Harry sympathized with the colonists; but when the Association asked him to ignore it, the old soldier told them bluntly on 18 June:

> This is the anniversary of the Battle of Waterloo — for four and forty years I served my sovereign — I say it with pride, — and I would rather that God Almighty strike me dead, than disobey the orders of Her Majesty's Government; and thereby commit an act of open rebellion.

The best he could do was to promise to halt disembarkation until he received further orders.

Harry's popularity vanished. 'Sir Harry Smith has disappointed the whole Colony,' announced the *Port Elizabeth*

Telegraph. 'How are the mighty fallen! Where is your vaunted high principle?' asked the editor. 'Your attachment to the Colony and its interests?' And what, he concluded mockingly, ever became of 'the oft repeated boast "I will be Governor!"'? The governor himself was interdicted and, at Fairbairn's suggestion, the fund collected for his statue was diverted to the Association.

The anniversary of the Queen's succession on 20 June was a time for the governor's backers to appear and be counted. Many returned their invitation with insulting refusals. Some who planned to go lost their nerve. 'The most violent of the Anti-Convict Association endeavoured to smash the Ball in honour of Her Majesty,' Harry reported angrily to Grey, 'and staid away, who shall never be invited to Government House in my time.'

The ball was a dismal affair. Guests noticed that Lady Smith, dressed in gold and black with 'a superb stomacher of diamonds', looked worried and constantly fluttered her fan. After 'See the Conquering Hero Comes', the governor in his full dress uniform appeared, supported by Garvock and Holdich. He looked as if he had stepped from his coffin. When he tried to speak, he was too weak to do so. Then he left. It had a depressing effect upon his followers, who were themselves divided as to how to deal with this challenge to authority. The bishop and Montagu advocated taking steps against the Association leaders. Harry, too, was inclined towards stern measures, but his Executive Council as a whole were fearful of an insurrection that might be joined by the Boers in the Sovereignty.

The Association offered a way out. Through public subscription they would indemnify the government for the expense involved in sending the *Neptune* to another land. Failing in this, a monster meeting was held on 4 July. For six hours in drenching rain their leaders harangued them. It was resolved that henceforth all relations with the government were severed.

A few days later the news that one of the members of the Legislative Council had died raced across the city and was hailed with delight. The number of members was now down to nine, one less than the minimum required by the constitution. If no one accepted the seat, a blow would be struck for popular government. The Association hastily met to threaten that if any person accepted or retained a seat, he would 'come under the pledge'.

A great crowd swarmed around the Court House where the Council convened on the 10th. Among them were local toughs who had boasted that they would assault the members when they came out. Another councilman resigned, but the governor then made his counter-move by appointing three new members. As the councilmen left the building there were groans and hisses. Rotten eggs and street filth began to fly. Those the mob could reach were assaulted. When the governor appeared, leaning on the arm of an A.D.C., there was a menacing silence; not a hat was raised. Calmly the veteran campaigner said, 'Gentlemen, I am glad to be amongst you. Believe me my heart is with you.' There was a faint cheer as he rode off.

Violence now became common. That night men danced like savages around the burning effigies of the three new members. They moved on to destroy the property of councilmen, until mounted police dispersed them. The three new members resigned. Only one non-official member, William Cock, a shipowner from the eastern part of the Cape, continued to resist by remaining aboard one of his vessels. To show that he could not be boycotted or starved into submission, he defiantly displayed a leg of mutton from the yardarm. The governor made no further attempt to fill the vacancies. The Association members crowed over their victory.

Over four months had rumbled by since the convict ship left Bermuda. 'Where is the *Neptune?*' people asked. All parties began to assume that she would never reach Cape Town. 'The non-arrival of the "Neptune" is most extraordinary,' Harry observed, 'unless your Lordship may happily have ordered her destination to be changed, some accident may have occurred.' But Grey had no intention of diverting the convicts. He expected from the colonists 'a regard for the general interest of the British nation', which had, after all, footed the enormous bill of the last frontier war. If nothing else, their common humanity towards these unfortunate men would allow them to land. So month after month, the colonial secretary sat Buddha-like, waiting for the governor to resolve this imbroglio to the satisfaction of all parties.

By September some clergymen complacently commented from the pulpit that the *Neptune* had been lost with all hands, which was obviously 'one of the most special Providences yet recorded'. But Providence did not interfere. On the night of 19 September the convict ship, detained by sickness at Pernambuco, hove into sight. The governor sent her an order to cast anchor in Simon's Bay. None was to go ashore or 'suffer communication between the ship and the shore till further notice'.

'The rumour of an invasion, or the fatal whisper that a pestilence had visited the shores,' wrote W. A. Newman, 'could not have spread greater agitation, or aroused a more general panic throughout the community.' At daybreak the fire alarm was sounded. The bells of all the churches tolled mournfully. Knots of excited men formed in the old square, where they waited for the governor's response to the Association's request that the ship be ordered 'to leave our shores'. They did not have to wait long. His Excellency informed them that the ship would ride at anchor until some word came from London with instructions; for him to act otherwise would be illegal.

For the next five months the *Neptune* remained in the harbour. The 'Plague Ship', the government and its supporters were placed in a state of siege. Soldiers were heckled and pelted with mud. But the governor kept his head and refrained from imposing martial law. In a general order to the army, he revealed his own standards of conduct: 'Your duty is to observe forebearance, obedience and moderation.' He went no further than prohibiting crowds or meetings in public streets in order to prevent hooliganism among the men who had been thrown out of work. As for the hard words that were hurled at him, Harry shrugged them off as he had missiles directed at him in battle.

With the assistance of loyalists, Harry adroitly campaigned to bring in food. Courageous farmers, risking life and property, ran the gauntlet to carry in supplies. Some were waylaid and their wagons overturned. One named Stanford was ostracized to the extent that medical attention was refused his children, resulting in the death of one of them. The soldiers were kept busy butchering and baking bread.

The ruthless, petty tyranny of the Association, whereby even children were punished and the convicts came down with scurvy, began to turn people against the boycott. Ebden the chairman, unwilling to sanction the extreme dictates of men like Fairbairn, resigned. Harry's position was further strengthened by Grey's despatch, received on 12 October, announcing that he had abandoned the idea of establishing a regular penal settlement. Furthermore, Harry declared that if he were ordered to land the convicts, he would resign rather than inflict so great an injury.

Each ship that arrived from England was hailed with the words, 'Did you bring the despatches?' Not until 13 February was an affirmative answer received. Grey finally recognized he had no alternative. Despite Harry's many messages to the contrary, the colonial secretary publicly stated, 'Had I been aware how strong was the feeling which existed at the Cape on this subject, I should not have advised the measure.' Forced to concede defeat, Grey directed his ire towards Harry. He peevishly described as 'inadvisable' his decision not to land the convicts, thereby inflicting further hardship on them, and reprimanded him for making his policy public before informing the colonial office. Grey never appreciated the harrowing ordeal that the governor had been put through in trying to reconcile the strictures of his government with popular opposition. Mitchel wrote in his *Jail Journal*:

> There is great rejoicing at Cape Town, a reconciliation of parties, moderates and immoderates burying their differences. There are to be high public rejoicings, a grand dinner, and illuminations such as South Africa has never beheld ... So the contest is over, and the colonists may now proceed about their peaceful business, with no worse enemies to disquiet them than the Kaffirs and panthers.

For a time there were rumours among the convicts that they would be sent to found a new penal colony in New Guinea, among the cannibals. '*Here* the people would give us nothing to eat,' Mitchel speculated, '*there* they will feed us indeed, but only to fatten us for their tables.' Grey, however, decided that their destination would be Tasmania where, because of the hardships of the voyage and detention, all would receive conditional pardons — except for Mitchel, who was a separate case. Never was a ship at the Cape more quickly supplied and refitted for the sea. The people of Cape Town raised £100 as a parting gift to be divided among the involuntary visitors.[1]

The crisis was over, but Harry never completely recovered his diminished popularity. Former supporters of the Association would never forgive his refusal to send the convicts away. On the other side, men like Montagu lost faith in a governor guilty of 'vacillation and infirmity of purpose'.

In an effort to restore favour with Grey, Harry explained in great detail why he had kept the convicts on board. In the matter of making his policy public before gaining approval from the colonial secretary:

> I cannot doubt that I committed a serious error. I do not feel that it is any humiliation for an old officer of Her Majesty who means to act uprightly, but who prefers no claim to exemption from mistakes to make this frank admission.

But Harry's handling of the crisis made Grey doubt the abilities he once held in such high esteem. And if the newspaper accounts about his poor health were accurate, Harry no longer possessed the energy he had once admired.

With the *Neptune*'s departure, Fairbairn said proudly, 'The people of the Cape of Good Hope have shown the world what it is that constitutes a state.' As was to be so often the case with the British Empire, the surest sign of a colony's readiness for self-government was rebellion. After over a decade of agitation, preparations were hurried to give the Cape a constitution.

Downing Street was not averse to self-government. By the 1840s the free-traders, with their abhorrence of unremunerative expenditures increased by costly native wars, had actively advocated such a policy. As early as 1846 Grey, who firmly believed that a self-governing colony was a less expensive one, sought the advice of Pottinger and then Smith on the matter of a constitution. On 29 July 1848, the very day Harry

[1] Mitchel later went to the United States where he chose the losing side in the American Civil War. After suffering imprisonment, he returned to Ireland and was elected to Parliament, but he was not allowed to take his seat since 'he was a felon who had not purged his felony'. His eldest son became mayor of New York. Others on the *Neptune* had distinguished careers: Sir Charles Duffy became prime minister of Victoria, Thomas Meagher became governor of Montana, Terence Manus and Patrick Donahue were generals in the U.S. army, Richard Gorman was made governor-general of Newfoundland and Morris Lyene attorney-general in Australia.

left for the Sovereignty to deal with the Boers, he transmitted a bundle of opinions collected from various sources. The main point of which all, including himself, were agreed was that the colony should have representative government.

At the end of January 1850 the Letters Patent arrived, providing for a constitution with the condition that there should be two houses, both elective, and the governor would have the power to dissolve the Assembly or both houses simultaneously. The Legislative Council would work out the details. This placed Harry in an awkward position, since he no longer had a Council. If he appointed moderates, he would antagonize the extremists of the Association; nor could he nominate radicals without offending the moderates. And because of his earlier unfortunate experience with unofficial members, it would be unwise to ignore popular opinion. To avoid responsibility for arbitrary appointments, he asked divisional road and municipal boards to elect a number of candidates from whom he would select five councilmen. To Harry's chagrin, the first five of the list of twenty-three were extremists—Fairbairn, Stockenström, Brand, Reitz and Wicht. He took the first four and then skipped over Wicht, a bitter foe, and went down to number eleven, Godlonton, a moderate and editor of the *Grahamstown Journal*, which he justified on the grounds that a better balance would thus be achieved between Englishmen and Dutchmen, between East and West. Porter, the attorney general who had organized the election, testified that this was legal.

With the spirit of dissatisfaction still running high after the anti-convict crisis, however, the governor was denounced for breaking faith in his selection of the fifth councilman. At the meeting of the new Council on 6 September 1850, the self-styled 'popular members', led by Stockenström (whom Harry called 'unscrupulous') and Fairbairn ('plausible but fickle') tried to protest. The governor cut them short by declaring he could appoint anyone he chose, and advised them to get down to business. Since they constituted a minority on the wrong side of every division, their resentment increased. After one stormy session the four extremists, led by Stockenström, bid the Council a dramatic farewell amidst 'tremendous cheering' from the galleries. The colonists treated them as heroes. A commission was formed which drafted a constitution taken by Stockenström and Fairbairn to London. There, the importuning pair were turned down with icy politeness by Lord John Russell. Later, in a debate in Parliament (15 July 1851) Grey spoke testily of how 'nothing but the factious, and vexatious conduct of the four retiring members of the Council had prevented those representative institutions from being at this moment in full and complete operation.'

The colonial secretary was also 'deeply disappointed' with the governor. Utterly failing to understand the difficulties Harry had to contend with, Grey censured him on 14 December 1850 for not complying with the instructions in the Letters Patent. Instead, the governor had made the mistake of combining the rump of the Council with the Executive Council in a commission to draft a constitution (which actually differed little from the one of the popular party). In an effort to make amends, Harry regretted that his despatches on the subject did not enable Grey 'to form a correct opinion of the peculiarity of my position', namely that the Legislative Council had legally ceased to exist. Privately, Harry told Montagu, 'I am very angry with Earl Grey.'

So, as Grey had expected him to do, Harry appointed four reliable men to the Legislative Council. Because that body would not have the confidence of the colonists, he suggested to Grey that the constitution be ratified in England. The colonial secretary agreed. The colonists, as was expected, vigorously protested. Reflecting their mood, *The Cape Town Mail* denounced this procedure as 'naked and undisguised despotism'.

Deluged once more with petitions, Grey was clearly unhappy with Harry's performance. In a despatch dated 14 February 1851 he hinted that perhaps he was not qualified for his office.

> It is very natural that having spent so large a part of your life in the Field ... you should not have accurate knowledge of matters of this kind which is necessary for your guidance in critical times, but I cannot but think that if you had consulted Mr. Porter and Mr. Montagu they would have prevented you from falling into some of the mistakes which I have been compelled very unwillingly to animadvert on.

Unable to contain his resentment any longer, Harry offered his resignation on 8 April.

Forty-six years of unmitigated exertion without previously a shadow of censure, naturally writhes under your Lordship's remark. If I have lost your Lordship's confidence whilst steering through the intricate shoals of political intrigue in this distracted Colony, and should I be any impediment to your Lordship's administration, I trust that you would not for one moment scruple or hesitate to relieve me by a man more competent for Civil Government than myself, in your comprehensive judgement.

Grey replied that Harry had misunderstood. His despatch was not one of censure: 'I only meant in case you should have overlooked the necessity in the hurry of affairs to caution you upon the subject.' He assured Harry that 'the loss of your services would be regarded by me as one of the greatest misfortunes that could happen to the Colony'.

But Grey's soothing words could not salve the wound. He told Alice four days later (18 June 1851):

I will be *censured* by no man, but I will endeavour to obey where I can. He affronted me by finding fault with an 'abortive attempt to reform the Legislative Council,' which made my blood boil, although my remonstrances were as mild as milk.

Later, in a confidential memorandum to the Cabinet, Grey admitted that he was 'greatly dissatisfied with his civil administration and his want of foresight as to the impending war'. However, he added, 'I have no doubt that when war was begun, as a soldier he was the best person that could be employed.'

The war Grey referred to was the eighth and most devastating of all frontier wars, sometimes called the War of Mlanjeni.

[15]

The War of Mlanjeni

How my achievements mock me!
Shakespeare, *Troilus and Cressida*

In 1850 Harry Smith committed the greatest blunder of his long career. For two years the frontier had enjoyed an unprecedented tranquillity. At the beginning of the year he boasted to Grey that his policies in Kaffraria had succeeded 'beyond the most sanguine expectations'. Grey responded by urging further troop reductions and Harry complied by sending home the Rifles in June. This left him with only 1,700 troops to keep the peace, nearly 1,000 of which were pinned down in a dozen or so isolated frontier posts. Vanity persuaded him to gamble on one great resource — himself.

The chiefs never regarded the peace as anything more than a truce. Under Smith's system they saw their dignity and power gradually diminished. No longer could they exact obedience or enrich themselves through the vicious practice of 'eating up' an individual by trumping up a charge of witchcraft. But the chiefs could still exploit the universal belief that disease and disaster were the work of wizards and witches. By suppressing the witch doctors, the people were told, the British put them at the mercy of the demons. And, as if in proof, there were sinister happenings. Throughout most of 1850 there was a severe drought, followed by a plague of locusts. A wild rumour told of a child born with two heads, who, immediately after birth, predicted that British rule would be overturned. The monster then died.

An emaciated young fanatic named Mlanjeni began to walk the land and to perform miracles, such as living underwater and wearing his face on one cheek. He claimed to receive messages from ancestors long dead who spoke of aiding warriors in driving the white men into the sea. He dispensed charms which would turn British bullets into water and soldiers

320

THE WAR OF MLANJENI

into cattle. Sandile and other chiefs patronized the prophet as a mouthpiece and exploited his influence. Efforts by authorities to arrest him failed. Thus, the ability to vanish at will was added to his other alleged supernatural powers.

The settlers were certain that war was imminent when their servants flocked homewards at Mlanjeni's behest. Loyalty prompted some to warn their white masters 'to flee as fast and as far as possible'. One missionary wrote that the prophet 'was drawing the whole after him'. Harry scoffingly called these apprehensions imaginary and breezily belittled 'this regenerated Mahomet'. Nor would he take seriously the supposed truculence of Sandile, 'a weak-minded man, possessing neither influence nor respect among the people'. On 10 October he wrote to Mackinnon, 'I cannot conceive that the majority of the Kaffirs are not most happy under our rule.' Nevertheless, he decided that his appearance in Kaffraria would 'at once put a stop to such evil intentions as may secretly exist'.

Going round by sea to East London, the governor galloped on to King William's Town. Passing through the lands of Pato and Umhala on the 21st, he saw no indications of unrest. The principal chiefs were ordered to assemble on the 26th. Many came wearing Glengarry bonnets and moleskin trousers that the governor had distributed as a reward for good behaviour. Sandile alone failed to appear, claiming that he had suffered an injury in a fall from his horse. The Inkosi Inkulu publicly denounced Sandile and that 'madman Mlanjeni'. In language that Harry described as 'highly dictatorial', he promised harsh reprisals against those who responded to incitements to make war. All denied any thought of breaking the peace — 'they were his dogs and thanked their father for giving them peace'.

The governor sent a message to Sandile. Unless he came forward now or gave proof of his injury, 'I will throw you away.' The chief replied with pretended innocence that none was more loyal or loving than he, but he was afraid that if he came he would be arrested. Harry immediately deposed the disobedient Sandile and appointed Charles Brownlee, the Gaika commissioner and son of the missionary John Brownlee, to take his place. The chiefs were summoned once more so that the governor might explain his action. They agreed that Sandile had misbehaved and deserved his punishment.

22

Satisfied that there would be no war, Harry made a quick tour among the settlers to allay their fears, assuring them that his investigation uncovered no 'direct evidence' of a war plot. By abandoning farms and taking unwarranted defence measures, the settlers had caused the Gaika tribe of the Xhosa nation to fear that they would attack them. When Goldswain protested this view, Harry rose and went to him. 'He caught hold of my hand and gave it a hearty handshake,' recalled the settler, 'and said that if there was a war within two years that he would forfeit his head.'

The settlers remained unconvinced as Harry rushed back to Cape Town to grapple with what he believed to be a more pressing matter, the proposed constitution. Shortly after his return, he reported his recent 'success' to Grey:

> I am happy to feel that my presence upon the frontier has borne its part in allaying an excitement which has extended to the Natal River, and it has been attended with no expenditure beyond the defraying of my ordinary travel expenses.

But Sandile's removal had the opposite effect. Harry's high-handed act made the Gaika chief, the hereditary ruler, more popular than ever and brought to his side other chiefs who wondered if they might not likewise be arbitrarily 'thrown away'. Macomo taunted the timid Sandile into resistance against the British. 'In the last war,' he declared, 'it was said Macomo was mad, but in this war it will be seen that Macomo is not mad.' He undertook a personal mission to the various chiefs to urge them to heed the predictions of Mlanjeni and called for their combined strength in a great assault to recover their waning independence. There would be little resistance offered, he promised, for most of the soldiers had been sent away and strife over the importation of convicts showed that many colonists would not support their own governor.

Early December saw portents of war in the rapid rise of cattle thefts and the feasting by warriors on meat. Somewhat depressed, Harry wrote to Grey on the 5th, 'The quiet I had reported in Kaffirland, which I had so much and just ground to anticipate, is not realised, and I start this evening.' Once more he boarded an eastbound ship, but this time with four companies of the 73rd. In East London on the 9th he received an offer from Pato of 1,400 warriors to guard the road from there to King William's Town. Harry was gratified. In a subsequent meeting, Pato, Umhala and chiefs of other non-Gaika tribes agreed with the governor that rebel Gaikas should be punished; they offered their support should it be needed.

Moving on to Fort Cox, Harry saw no signs of trouble. Over 3,000 Gaikas were gathered there to hear him speak on the 19th. The governor told them, 'I come not to punish the good, but the rebels.' He appealed to them to 'sit still', as he dealt with the wrongdoers in his own way. If necessary, more troops could be brought by many large ships. 'Can they sail up the Amatola mountains?' asked one chief scornfully. Harry fumed and threatened that those who resisted his authority would 'soon learn what troops are for!' To mollify the Gaikas, however, he named Sutu, widow of the great Gaika and mother of Sandile, to succeed Brownlee as their chief.

Harry's object was to avoid war at all costs. With less than 2,000 men, he planned a demonstration in force to overawe the recreants. Smith's line stretched from King William's Town through Forts White, Cox and Hare. The centre, under Mackinnon, was at Fort Cox, Harry's headquarters. The right wing was pushed forward to Kabousie Nek, 15 miles north-east of Fort Cox at the rear of the Amatola range, to check any combination of Gaika's with Kreli's men to the east. So soon as tidings were received that Sandile was to the east at Keiskamma Hoek, Harry sent out Mackinnon with a patrol of 600 men to dislodge him. They were ordered to be civil to the natives and not to load their weapons. There was to be no shooting unless they were fired upon.

All was calm that Christmas Eve. The column stopped for breakfast before entering a narrow and bushy gorge called Boomah pass. There the road furrowed a mountain side and dwindled to a winding footpath so that the C.M.R. in front could ride no more than two abreast. On the side of the precipice there was a jumble of loose rocks overgrown with small trees, bushes and monkey-ropes. To the valley below there was a sheer drop of 60 feet with a clear, cold stream gurgling at the bottom. 'What a jolly place it would be for a pic-nic,' remarked Ensign Lucas, 'with shade and good water at hand.' But the sudden brief appearance of an enemy scout turned his thoughts from picnic to ambush.

Sandile allowed the Kaffir police and C.M.R. to pass through, which in the light of later events suggested collusion. Once the last horseman left the pass, a line of a thousand warriors fired from above. The infantry, which had been chattering and laughing only a moment before, began to fumble for ammunition. It was impossible to dislodge the enemy from the impenetrable bush now clouded over with smoke. Nor could the police and C.M.R. turn the attackers' flank. The infantry eventually fought their way out but with a loss of 27 casualties and 3,500 rounds of ammunition at the rear of the column.

Mackinnon took his men back the next day by way of Fort White. The enemy swarmed in nearby hills and fired incessantly, but never close enough to do any damage. Close to the fort the column stumbled on the bodies of fifteen men who had been overpowered on patrol and flung in their path. All were naked, horribly mutilated and covered with flies. Some had their heads removed for the witch doctors, who were said to sprinkle the brains on warriors to make them invisible to the foe. The infantry remained at Fort White while Mackinnon took the mounted men on to Fort Cox. One officer wrote, 'Our Christmas had been anything but a merry one.'

It was far more miserable for those in the military villages. At Auckland the ex-soldiers invited visiting natives to join in the festivities. At a signal, the natives fell upon them, driving them into their huts until fire forced them out to be murdered. The other settlements, except for Ely, were also destroyed, with many inhabitants massacred. In former days marauders had as their object cattle; now the cattle were often ignored in the rush to destroy life and property. As before, however, women and children, except for being stripped, were spared.

Harry first heard of the ambush at Boomah pass from Brownlee, who repeated what an excited native had told him. 'Oh, it is some cock-and-bull story,' he said scornfully, 'I don't believe it.' But he learned quickly that it was true and that three military settlements had been wiped out; Fort White was under siege and nearly all of the Kaffir police had deserted to the enemy. Harry swore and raved from one end of the fort to the other. 'Dear man,' wrote Mrs Brownlee, 'he evidently wished for peace, and bitter must have been his awakening.' The governor declared martial law and advised the settlers to be ready to defend themselves.

To his mortification, the governor found himself shut up in Fort Cox. Thousands of 'his children' surrounded the large square of low buildings. They seemed intoxicated by the prospect of laying their hands on the Inkosi Inkulu. Twice Somerset tried to relieve the fort, only to be driven back with heavy loss to Fort Hare — which was itself invested.

Harry decided to make a dash for freedom to King William's Town 22 miles away. With 250 C.M.R., wearing the uniform of one of them as a disguise, he sallied forth on New Year's Eve. It was a running battle much of the way. At Debe Nek, about halfway, a strong effort was made to intercept them. In all previous engagements Harry had battled for victory, now he had to fight for his life. He vigorously spurred his horse and with his escort charged through to safety. Little did the enemy realize what a prize had slipped through their hands.[1]

Upon arrival at King William's Town the disenchanted governor fulminated a proclamation exhorting the colonists to rise *en masse* 'to destroy and exterminate these barbarous savages'. During his absence in Kaffraria, Somerset, whom he promoted to major-general, would have full powers to raise levies to 'form a nucleus for an invading army of Patriots' into Kaffraria. 'The Gaikas,' he added forcefully, *'must be driven out of the Amatolas and expelled for ever!'*

This unfortunate choice of words stunned the humanitarians and drew a sharp reprimand from the colonial secretary on 8 March. 'It is your duty as an officer representing a Civilized and Christian power,' he lectured Harry, 'to endeavour not to exterminate but to reclaim and civilize these fierce barbarians.' In a confidential comment, Grey added 'that a large part of the Dutch, and I am afraid not a few of the English settlers do ardently desire to enslave or exterminate the native races'. Aware of the gravity of the situation, he 'thought it better at once to send you reinforcements and this letter will go by the "Vulcan" which will carry the 74th Regiment'. A second despatch from Wellington, written the same day, told of how

---

[1] 'For gallantry in the field', Harry later awarded 30 silver medals to men of his escort, mostly C.M.R. The Fort Cox Siege Medal, one of the rarest in the world, was similar to the Waterloo medal and suspended from a Sutlej ribbon. The War Office was unhappy with the donor for having exceeded his authority. There was, he was told, no such procedure in the Queen's service. Harry's rejoinder was that precedence had been established by the governor-general in India, who granted medals to local forces.

he had advised the government to send another regiment. It was fortunate that a normally penny-wise Grey and a sympathetic Wellington acted on his behalf, for Harry was still optimistic enough to believe that he could crush the uprising with his own resources.

The Duke had a plan by which the insurgents could be effectively dealt with. It pleased Harry to learn, when the memorandum arrived two months later, that he had anticipated the suggestions of his great teacher by establishing a double line of operations. One ran from the marine base at East London with a chain of forts through King William's Town, his headquarters, on to Fort White and Fort Cox. The other was from Port Elizabeth with a string of posts through Grahamstown to Fort Beaufort and Fort Hare. Mackinnon was responsible for the first line, under Harry's watchful eye, while Somerset commanded the second, with his headquarters at Fort Hare. Though more than half of his 1,700 regulars and many of his native auxiliaries would be required for garrison duty, Harry never for a moment considered falling back or sacrificing one fort. By maintaining these lines of defence, he held back thousands of would-be invaders of the colony, ensured the loyalty of Pato and Umhala, and the neutrality of Kreli across the Kei. Once new levies of settlers, Hottentots and other loyal natives were raised, they could be sent forward along these lines to undertake the offensive. As commander-in-chief and governor Harry deemed it necessary to stay at headquarters to supervise the efforts of his subordinates, though Grey could never quite understand why an experienced bush fighter like Smith remained inactive while less competent officers were in command of large patrols.

With his plans of containment barely made, the rebellion spread to tribesmen north of the Amatolas and, worst of all, infected the Hottentots of the Kat river region. In previous wars Hottentots had given invaluable aid against their hereditary foes, the Xhosas. It was said now that they were disgruntled because they had not received a larger share of the spoils in the last war and that they were striking a blow for an independent Hottentot nation. Harry found it incomprehensible that civilized men, most of them Christians, should 'rush back, in nearly one torrent, to barbarism and savage life'. And since they were better disciplined and armed, they were more dangerous than the Gaikas, their new-found allies. 'This extraordinary proceeding,' he suggested to Somerset, 'must be ascribed either to the in-born evil propensities of man ... or agitation said to have been stirred up among these people.' He was referring to preachers of the London Missionary Society, 'white-faced devils' who persuaded the Hottentots that 'they were an oppressed and ill-used race'.

The rebel Hottentots were led by Hermanus, half Hottentot and half Xhosa, who swept through the Fort Beaufort district with fire and sword. During the 1835 war Harry had employed Hermanus as an interpreter and D'Urban had rewarded him with a large farm. To demonstrate his change in allegiance, the renegade sent the heads of two settlers to Mlanjeni. Emboldened by success, Hermanus directed an ambitious attack on Fort Beaufort itself. Col. Sutton, with 50 men of the 91st, supported by burghers and Fingoes, valiantly fought them off. Hermanus himself, wearing a lady's black bonnet, was shot from his saddle and was dead before he hit the ground. His body was placed in the market square on a table surmounted by a Union Jack to discourage other would-be rebels.

But the Hottentot revolt was far from crushed. William Uithaalder, a pensioner of the C.M.R. known as the 'general of the Hottentots', took over where Hermanus left off and threatened other districts with his followers. At first, the already inadequate forces at Harry's disposal could do little to restrain them. When Somerset was reinforced by Fingoes and burghers, he struck back on 22 February. Somerset shelled to bits the abandoned Fort Armstrong which the Hottentots had foolishly occupied. Those who were not killed fled in all directions. The Kat river uprising was smashed. Many rebel Hottentots, nevertheless, stayed in the field with the Gaikas. For once Harry was pleased with the conduct of that 'glossy hero' Somerset and wasted no time in congratulating this 'Hottentot hunter' on his 'most glorious and important victory ... It will surely quiet down the Rebellion, so unnatural, so unexpected, and so treacherous.'

The victory, won so 'neatly and cheaply', was followed by a trial by court-martial in Fort Hare. Forty-seven prisoners were condemned to death; but acting under his authority as governor, Harry commuted their sentence in July to transportation for life. The white settlers howled in protest against his clemency, feeling that 'hanging a few would have been a sovereign panacea'. Believing that he knew as much about their character as most men, Harry argued that if he had executed the condemned rebels, 'the torch of revolt would have blazed throughout the Colony'.

Another stroke of misfortune caught Harry completely unawares. That 'evil demon of ingratitude', he cursed, inspired the desertion of a large body of Hottentots in the C.M.R. early in March. Some of them had fought bravely to make possible his escape from Fort Cox. 'They were the best men here,' he told Montagu, 'many old and trusty soldiers, all Psalm singers.' He had pampered and indulged them; rode with them and chatted over the news; some he had intended to award medals. All the while they were 'brooding evil'. He told Grey:

> No event of my military career caused me so much pain as the defection of so large a portion of a corps to which I am as much attached as I am to that wearing the green jacket of my own regiment.

The 335 deserters made for the Kat river, Sandile having promised them a safe passage.

Taking no chances, the governor ordered a general parade on 14 March. The tainted remnants of the C.M.R. were flanked by the 6th and the 73rd. The guns behind them were loaded with grapeshot. The governor then rode before them and announced that 'in place of a gallant corps, as they used to be, they were a disgraced regiment, and that a disgraced corps should never serve under him'. They were ordered to put down their arms. They hesitated—and then obeyed. Those men who were white had theirs immediately returned to them. 'The war now seems Black against White,' remarked one officer present. 'Everyone asks, what is coming next?'

Another cruel disappointment was in store for the governor. Critically short of mounted men, he looked to the colonists to come forward as they had in 1835. But the commando system broke down. 'The English do not appear to volunteer in great numbers,' observed Bishop Gray, 'and the Dutch scarce at all.' The Boers lagged behind, even after the governor proclaimed that all cattle taken in the enemy's country would be lawful booty. They contended that they could not leave their homes while marauders were abroad. Moreover, they questioned the governor's judgment. Not so long ago he had laughed at their warnings and now he asked them to wage an aggressive war while lacking the necessary troops to defend the colony itself. In the western districts the hostile press claimed the war was a direct result of the governor's follies. Editors, still smarting from the convict crisis, tried to discourage burghers from signing up. The cry was raised that this was 'the Governor's war', or 'the settlers' war'. Sandile himself was quoted as saying: 'I have no quarrel with the Dutch. I have no quarrel with the Hottentots. They may all sit. I am at war with the settlers and with "Smith".' By mid-April, Harry lamented, 'Where are the men who so gallantly fought with me in 1835 — van Wyks, Greylings, Nels, Rademeyers, Rynevelds, etc.?'

English settlers were no less concerned for their safety. Many frightened families crammed the still open road to Port Elizabeth. With them was a Mr Smith, a commissariat officer as well as a local preacher who, not unlike Mlanjeni, had a vision from God telling him that the colony was doomed and that all should fly to the bay. Nor did Bishop Gray, with the conduct of the anti-convict agitators in mind, help matters by preaching in Cape Town that 'the hand of the Lord was upon us for our sins'.

Grahamstown once more took on the appearance of a besieged town, as refugees and their livestock rushed in for protection. Expecting instantaneous destruction, all citizens were armed, though some had never handled a gun. Women and children were crowded into the barracks and the Roman Catholic chapel where the windows were built up with bricks, leaving loopholes for the muskets. There were strong parties of Fingoes on the outskirts — but could they be relied upon?

Mounted companies of active young men were organized into units such as 'The Sporting Club' under the command of Thomas Stubbs. At their first exercise, one of them accidentally shot his horse in the head. Shortly after, one town sentry mistook another for an invader and shot him. Once the danger receded, 'The Sporting Club', along with other volunteers with such fanciful names as the 'Whittlesea Fire Eaters' and 'Cradock Bricks' rode off to join the regulars.

Stubbs was the first to go to the governor early in March to ask for supplies and more pay. Harry was sitting at a table when he came into the room. '[Smith] jumped up, put out his hand, and gave me a hearty handshake, then called Hooray! Hooray! — by God there are no more Caffers in the Colony, or you would not be here.' When he learned that Stubbs had managed to get through to King William's Town with only five men, he exclaimed, 'I can't move with five hundred. I am surrounded by a lot of damned rebels. If I had your men I would go through Cafferland.'

Stubbs then showed Harry a letter from the leading citizens of Grahamstown praying that more money be given to the 'Albany Rangers'. (Somerset told them the original name was too frivolous). 'He swore like a trooper,' the volunteer jotted in his journal, 'and said now Stubbs you know as well as I do it does not lie in my power to give them more than regulation pay.' Referring to the good citizens, he shouted, 'Why the Damned Hell don't they put their hands in their pockets and say here Stubbs, here is more pay for your men, who are protecting us while we are making fortunes.' The volunteer then asked for rations for his men's wives. 'No, no,' protested Harry, 'what the Damned Hell do soldiers want with wives?' The answer came easy, 'To use them in the same way and for the same purpose as officers.' Harry then complied. But when further pressed for rations for their children, Harry exploded. He could not agree to that, 'for if the men did their duty, I am sure they had not time to get children'. When Stubbs pointed out that they were born before the conflict, he promised additional rations.

Before Stubbs left, the governor told him the war would be over in a month. For the ride back, he insisted on giving him two guides, warning them that if anything happened to his friend, they would both be shot.

Stubbs took instantly to Harry Smith, but like so many settlers, he grew to distrust and dislike Somerset. It was said that Somerset had made a fortune by deliberately prolonging the last war; he, along with many officers, was paid a pound per diem for wagons they owned and entered under the names of civilians. Stubbs saw such wagons kept as store rooms in camp, stones placed under their wheels to prevent their rotting away. In the field, 'Hawk's-eye' travelled with every luxury for himself, including three or four Hottentot prostitutes. 'The Cape Corps is a species of family monopoly,' Captain W. Hall,

R.N., wrote in his diary, 'having his relatives in as officers, and they also as men, bastard children in the ranks.' (Unlike the C.M.R. serving with Harry, none of Somerset's deserted.) On patrol the volunteers did 'killing work', while his 'Tots', as Somerset called them, were spared. In a fight, such as at Fort Hare, the burghers grumbled that they had borne the brunt while C.M.R. and regulars took the credit. During a skirmish at Cowie Bush in 1835, Somerset had told Bisset, 'Oh, if you must go at them again, you may take volunteers; I won't order my men into the bush to be killed.'

Harry knew all this. Mrs Eyre, the wife of Lt.-Col. Eyre, believed that the governor was too lenient with his sub-ordinates. She wrote to a friend:

> Never *once* has General Somerset obeyed his orders and this is the secret of the losses we have had. One letter I *saw* from Sir Harry said that he had given the most stringent orders to General Somerset that only three wagons should accompany his patrol and he actually took 34, and then Sir Harry instead of bringing him to court martial for disobedience of orders contented himself with saying, 'Didn't I get in a passion?'

(This and other letters written by Mrs Eyre later came into the possession of Lord Grey.) That Somerset never lost his position as military commandant of the frontier force was a sure sign of powerful friends at the Horse Guards, which included his uncle Fitzroy Somerset, the military secretary.

Harry waited impatiently for reinforcements, which came in driblets. Sailors and Royal Marines were supplied by the frigate *Castor*. Steamers brought in detachments of regulars from Natal and Cape Town. Discharged soldiers, all veterans of the last war, came in, along with loyal Hottentots and Fingoes. Montagu worked overtime raising and despatching them. In bands of fifties and hundreds, the secretary sent bounty volunteers to the war. Within 17 days, 1,260 men of every caste 'from the Day-and-Martin coloured Mozambique nigger to the parchment faced Irishman' were armed and clothed in every variety of costume, and embarked. Altogether Montagu collected 3,900 mixed levies and 150 mounted men called 'Montagu's Horse'. Captain Hall, who transported them, called them something else. 'As bad a specimen of men as I ever met,' he wrote, 'lawless drunken fellows who had taken £23 bounty and purchased as miserable a horse as they could find.' Though Harry later complained that some had to be court-martialled for insubordination, he expressed 'grateful thanks' to Montagu for his efforts. Once 2,000 levies arrived, he declared, 'I shall be in high feather.'

On 17 March Harry requested from Grey 'four hundred young Englishmen between the ages of 18 and 21, not older, to be sent out as recruits, 400 double-barrelled carbines being sent with them'. Once they grew accustomed to bush warfare, he would get rid of the fickle Hottentots and make the C.M.R. exclusively British. Objections from the Treasury, however, scotched the proposal.

One wealthy, daredevil 22-year-old Englishman, Captain Stephen Lakeman, a hand-to-hand street fighter during the revolutions of '48, was allowed to go to the Cape to recruit a private army of 200 Europeans. Harry regarded him as a 'real soldier' and offered an extra bounty of £2 in addition to the two Lakeman paid out of his own pocket. Admitting that he shut his eyes in accepting those who proffered their services, the captain soon had a collection of the castoffs of Cape Town, plus a cripple or two. The Cape prison authorities were most co-operative in releasing desperate criminals to swell the ranks of his ruffians and rogues. The majority were seafaring men 'with big rounded shoulders, bronzed faces, and long hirsute appendages'. The captain bought them Minié rifles that he had seen the French use in Algeria; and he dressed them, like Roman centurions, in leather from head to foot—a costume which was well adapted for fighting in the thorny bush. Addicted as were these recruits to drinking and brawling, the good citizens of Cape Town were happy to see them hustled on to a man-of-war by their captain mounted on his horse, 'Don't-trust-me'. Under a born leader like Lakeman, who did not spare the lash, the ferocity of his 'Invisible Column of Death', as he dubbed it, was by the end of the year directed against the enemy.[1]

Cooped up in Fort Cox, Harry had thoughts of unleashing

[1] Lakeman was later knighted by the Queen. During the ceremony, Her Majesty momentarily forgot his Christian name. Suddenly the weight of the sword was too much for her. Sir Stephen ducked as it crashed to the floor. The Duke of Newcastle congratulated him after the ceremony for having his head still on, 'I thought at one time Her Majesty was going to cut it off.'

3,000 Zulus against their old enemies, the Xhosas. A message was sent to Natal where Panda, their chief, was eager to give his young men the opportunity of 'washing their spears' by raiding Kaffraria. The settlers were alarmed by the governor's proposal to call in 'wild and inhuman savages'. Shepstone, in charge of native affairs in Natal, eventually convinced Harry that the Zulus might become 'a worse scourge' by indiscriminately attacking friendly and neutral tribes.

By March the governor had 9,000 men, one-third of them regulars. 'Every eye now turned on Sir Harry Smith,' wrote one colonist, 'waiting with anxiety the steps he will take to bring down condign punishment on the murderous savages.' Harry's plan was to strike in swift raids, burning crops and kraals, seizing treasured cattle and killing as many of the enemy as possible. 'Among the natives,' he told missionary P. F. Gladwin, 'power must be exerted. I will assail as much and as often as I am able.'

Three strong patrols went out early in March but accomplished little against an elusive foe. These operations were handicapped by slow-moving wagons and a shortage of mounted men. As quickly as possible, Harry substituted pack animals and risked reinstating some of the disarmed C.M.R. He was also poorly served by Mackinnon, who was so cautious and slow that he threw away splendid opportunities. His men nicknamed him 'Regulate the Pace'. Captain Hall noted, 'I have never heard anyone mention him except to accuse him of very great incompetency only fit for an office.'

'A vigorous personal example was required,' observed Harry, as he prepared to take the field himself. Hall, who saw the 63-year-old governor at this time, anticipated meeting 'a careworn, slow-speaking General but I found an apparently active, energetic, and fine specimen of gallant soldier ... [with] a loud commanding voice.' Harry had not only recovered from his ailments but the thought of seeing action made him feel young again. When native spies reported large bands of Gaikas and rebel Hottentots assembling to rescue the Hottentot prisoners still at Fort Hare, Harry moved out on 18 March with 2,000 infantry, mostly from the 6th and 73rd, three guns and all the irregular horse he could muster.

Harry was only too aware that the enemy was far more formidable than in 1835. No longer were they a disorganized multitude, for they had learned much from previous wars. Like the British, they marshalled into columns with clouds of skirmishers; they sent out scouts and posted vedettes. By whatever means possible, they supplied themselves with fire-arms. Only in marksmanship and discipline were the Europeans still superior. Nor did the natives dread artillery any longer. 'Now they walk coolly up to the mouth of the cannon, and dare us to come out of our forts,' wrote one volunteer. 'Whenever a shell was seen to fall, the enemy all round were seen to fall flat on their faces.' Even when rockets or 'English assegais', as the natives called them, were employed, they showed little fear. But it was still guerilla warfare, all skirmishing, for they were rarely vain enough to fight out in the open like Zulus. Harry estimated that some 20,000 of them operated out of their favourite stronghold, the Amatolas, 'the Gibraltar of the Gaikas'. Directing enemy forays, Harry believed, was that 'clever scoundrel' Macomo. Topographical features, the dense undergrowth, precipice and crag were the chief's confederates, causing fatigue and privation among Europeans. While the heat of the day might be unbearable, the cold nights were equally intolerable. Ever present was the danger of a sudden attack by an enemy brave and shrewd, with 'feline and stealthy disposition'. But as Harry told Godlonton, 'War is always a game of hazard, and he who wages it must calculate the chances, then cast the die.'

On the morning of 19 March, the enemy was located at Mount Pegu, an isolated kopje west of Fort White. Harry sent levies around to cut off their retreat—then he attacked. Nearly fifty of the enemy were counted on the ground at the cost of one wounded. The force returned to Fort Hare for a day's rest before going out again on the 21st. On reaching a point halfway to Fort Cox, scouts came running in shouting, 'Kaffirs!' Harry spurred his charger and began to deploy his column for an attack on the long muskets protruding from the bush. Having inflicted heavy loss on the scurrying warriors, he sent the kraals and gardens up in smoke. 'For now's the time to devastate the flourishing corn fields,' Harry told Montagu, 'and teach savages there must ever be a day of retribution.'

After another day of rest, Harry swept the valley of the Keiskamma. The 73rd Highlanders, whom Harry was to rely on more and more for heavy bush fighting, were in the lead.

They were under the command of the unorthodox Lt.-Col. Eyre, one of the most daring, driving officers in the force — and, somewhat like Harry, a man with a fiery temper. To a great extent because of the efforts of Eyre and his men, the 73rd bagged over 1,000 head of cattle that day. Repeatedly the enemy attacked the rearguard to recover their herds, only to suffer heavy loss from volleys delivered by the 6th and the 73rd. Harry returned to headquarters on the 25th and wrote to Montagu that since so few Boers had come out, 'I can only carry on a very *little* war'. Their absence was felt even more keenly by Harry because of 'the outstanding conduct' of a few hard-riding, expert shots under Commandant Gideon Joubert, who had made possible the dispersal of marauders besieging Whittlesea.

Montagu sent back clippings from the press which had previously abused the governor and now praised the general. The *Cape Town Mail*, quoting the *Frontier Times*, wrote:

> Sir Harry Smith showed his usual energy, riding back-wards and forwards to where the different parties were engaged and cheering them on. A new spirit has been infused among the troops and levies, and all speak of the bravery and activity of His Excellency.

Colonists and soldiers, formerly depressed, were inspired with confidence. Mackinnon, combing the upper waters of the Buffalo, and Somerset, doing likewise in the Kat river region, appeared to be emulating the governor.

Morale was a vital factor in bush fighting. 'A Kaffir war is the snob of all wars,' complained Captain Lucas. A British soldier in this service 'neither lives nor dies like a gentleman'. Everything could be lost and not even glory gained in thrashing savages. Provided, of course, they could catch them, for the enemy 'retreats from bush to bush with marvellous dexterity, delivering his fire and sinking, as it were into the very earth, without offering any visible point of attack'. British casualties in any single skirmish could usually be counted on one hand, but no mention was made of the many who slumped from exhaustion. If they were taken prisoner, there were abominable tortures in store. One soldier of the 91st was said to have been roasted alive.

In England it was sneeringly said that 'Kaffir wars are nothing'. Conflicts were regarded by jaded spectators as of no account unless accompanied by reports of large numbers of killed and wounded. 'John Bull likes blood,' observed Captain Alexander, and the soldiers knew it. After one very bloody battle in the Peninsula, a redcoat was overheard telling a comrade, 'I think the people in England will be pleased with us today, at any rate, when they see our loss.'

The only comfort in this hard and discouraging service was that the governor kept the soldiers well fed and tolerated a relaxation of discipline in matters of dress. Forced marches, unavailing pursuits and bush skirmishes tore fancy tunics to ribbons. They were patched with canvas of every shade. Straw hats and wide-awakes replaced the regulation headgear. To further protect fair English skin from the sun, bushy jungles of beard and shoulder-length hair were permitted.

At headquarters, surrounded by heavy knapsacks that his soldiers had left behind in exchange for small canvas bags, Harry directed the movements of his men and waited restlessly for results in this hide-and-seek warfare. Often he dreamed of returning with Juana 'to our *old* Country and not to remain in these fractious Colonies of Radicals, Rebels and murderers'.

And Juana was unhappy. 'I never knew her to yield to so much dejection,' Harry confided to a friend in Cape Town. 'Pray tell her we are going right—and with God's blessing I hope to continue so doing.' He confessed that he had little time or inclination to write to his wife so long as the news was mostly bad. If he did send a letter, he tried to keep it light, but Juana read trouble between the lines. When some of the mail was intercepted by Uithaalder's Hottentots, she became alarmed. Writing on 24 May Enrique assured her that he was perfectly safe. He quipped:

I hope you may get this and not Genl. Uithaalder's Secretary, who wants an old shirt, a piece of soap, some coffee. He writes thus to one of those damned missionaries. I hope yet to see all the ringleaders hung while I would willingly forgive the poor wretches who have been led astray by the wickedness of others.[1]

---

[1] Harry was referring to missionaries like the Rev. James Read of the L.M.S., whom the settlers suspected of encouraging the Hottentot rebellion. When Read passed through Grahamstown in April there was a riot before his hotel. Not knowing the cause of the uproar, citizens in the other part of town thought they were under attack and panicked.

Ten days later Juana relayed the latest news to Alice:

Enrique's letter is almost all in Spanish, as he says, 'I don't think General Uithaalder will be able to *understand* that language.' It is a sad, sad thing, the mails being cut off. The Kaffirs now say they will fight no more, but act like wolves—attack and eat everything that comes in their way. God grant this is not true.

With her large map, Juana avidly noted every detail of the campaign. Nor did she hesitate to give advice and question tactics. 'Why form line?' she would ask, 'Porque no son Caçodores?' By the end of May Juana believed that Enrique had 'broken the *neck* of the rebellious black faces'. But her husband was not so sure. 'I hope so,' he replied, 'I wish with all my heart I had broken the *head*, too, or taken him whoever he may be. I doubt his wearing a black face unless he be a double faced scoundrel which is much more probable.'

'Poor Lady Smith,' remarked the bishop, 'is overjoyed at the arrival of troops.' There was the landing of the 74th Highlanders, part of the 12th and the news that the 2nd would arrive in August. But Juana was angered by importunate officers' wives who came to Cape Town and sought passage to the frontier to visit their husbands. When a tearful Mrs Campbell succeeded in so persuading Captain Hall—'a most chicken-hearted fellow' in such matters by his own admission—Juana was furious. She showed him a recent letter from the governor 'saying how much he deprecated it, and stating that his Nephew had as little idea of his Wife's coming as he himself had'. The naval officer nevertheless interceded on her behalf and managed to get a note from the governor: 'Pray let Mrs Campbell come up in Steamer and let her be the last.'

Just before boarding, Hall met Lady Smith, who casually asked him if Mrs Campbell was going. 'Upon my answering in the affirmative,' he recalled,

she opened a broadside of envy, hatred, malice and all uncharitableness which astounded me and showed the nature of her Country in its most unfavourable peculiarities. I quietly remarked, 'that I understood from her she always had followed Sir Harry to the field.' This caused a parting shot, and I was glad to ship and make sail.

23

All of Kaffraria soon knew of 'the arrival of many children of foam, whose great sea-waggons from the broad waters spit forth red men'. Harry hoped the enemy would become disheartened, for despite the addition of 600 of the 74th in June, he would soon have fewer men than he had before. The six-month enlistment of the Hottentot levies was up and out of 1,800 only a few could be induced to stay on. For a time it was feared that they might join their rebel countrymen. As Hottentots were 'terrible up and down' soldiers, 'equally devoid of restraint in success or calamity', Harry told Grey, they might as well be replaced with regulars who were more reliable and less expensive.

By June Harry was also uneasy about Kreli's professed neutrality—for it was apparent that his sympathies were clearly with his fellow Xhosas. To keep him in tow, the governor warned the chief, 'Look to yourself, or I will go and look at you!' Nor could Harry be sure of the continued loyalty of Pato, who during the last war had vowed to convert Somerset's skin into a tobacco pouch. The chief was given many presents of cattle and a guard of honour which, in reality, kept him under strict surveillance while he debauched himself with drink.

To maintain a bold front, the governor ordered four columns, 2,000 men, to converge on the centre of the Amatolas at the end of June. Following three days of sharp skirmishing, large stores of grain were destroyed and 2,200 cattle were taken. The 74th, which had marched off from Fort Hare to the inspiring strains of 'Hieland Laddie', came back 'unwashed and unshaven with tattered clothes and rusty arms'—but bush-worthy.

But Harry now frankly admitted to Grey on 3 July that these local successes had 'no perceptible effect on the termination of the war'. Victory was still a long way off in what had become a war of attrition, the purpose being to harass the enemy 'until they could bear no more'. All through July fresh patrols were sent out to keep the enemy busy, but as Harry observed to Fitzroy Somerset: 'These athletic brutes ... can move in an hour a distance it requires soldiers three; they have neither front nor rear nor commissariat; they can assemble like magic and disperse like a mist.'

In August, Sandile, possibly disenchanted by Mlanjeni's predictions, sent overtures of peace through Pato. But Harry

interpreted these as plays for time. He would accept nothing
less than unconditional surrender, to which Sandile swore he
would never agree. Grey supported Harry's views. 'It is thus
only,' Grey wrote, 'that a real peace and not a short and hollow
truce can be obtained.'

Coming to terms with Sandile was tempting, for the governor
had another war on his hands in the Sovereignty. The
Sovereignty's very existence rested on the acquiescence of
Moshesh, the co-operation of the burghers and the non-
intervention of the Transvaalers. And these conditions could
be met only if Harry, as high commissioner, could impose his
authority with force. Barely able to hold his own on the
frontier, Harry had neither troops nor time to spare when
disorder threatened.

Discord arose when Major Warden tried to draw boundaries
between burghers encroaching on native lands and between
the tribes themselves. Having once drawn a line, he was
burdened with the responsibility of punishing transgressors.
Cattle raids and bloodshed soon became common between
jostling tribes. A bewildered Warden was persuaded that
Moshesh, already suspected of being in league with the
Gaikas, was the chief offender, and he demanded restitution.
The Basuto chief's reluctance was interpreted as evasion.

Having only a handful of soldiers, Warden called on the
friendly chiefs and burghers for help. But the Boers curtly
refused to leave their farms unprotected to settle a quarrel
between tribes. Harry, meanwhile, felt that Moshesh, whom
he 'formerly had so much reason to respect and esteem ...
must be taught that British authority is Paramount'. He
prodded Warden to 'come to the point with Moshesh and if
you have sufficient force attack him at once if necessary'.

With even less skill as a soldier than as the Resident,
Warden attacked the Basutos at Viervot mountain on 30 June
with a scratch force of 160 regulars, 120 burghers, and 120
Griquas and nearly 900 of Chief Moroko's Baralong. As the
Baralong advanced, they found many beer pots which they
executed quickly on the spot. Meanwhile, the Basutos gained
the summit and surprised the ascending force. Over 150 were
killed, mostly Baralong stupefied by drink. British prestige
tumbled to a new low.

To recover control, Warden was given a contingent of 600 Zulus (with British officers), but they were so undisciplined that they plundered friend and foe alike. Further appeals to the Boers on the basis of race and greed (one-third of all cattle captured were theirs) failed. Instead it was rumoured that they were plotting with Moshesh and Pretorius against the Sovereignty. A bitter Warden denounced them, claiming that two-thirds were opposed to British rule. Harry advised him to sit tight while two assistant commissioners, Hogge and Owen, went north to investigate the causes of unrest.

Major W. S. Hogge, who had led a Hottentot force in the War of the Axe, and C. M. Owen, a former commander of the Kaffir police, had been sent out by Grey in May ostensibly to relieve the governor of administering the border territories. The colonel secretary assured Harry 'that they were made completely subordinate to you'. This was not the whole truth. Grey's confidence in Harry had begun to slip. The commissioners, reporting directly to Grey, gradually became more autonomous. Hogge, a man of 'energetic abilities' (according to Harry) and more capable than Owen, soon became Grey's confidant. Harry found the arrangement distasteful but accepted it with good grace. In effect, though he was at first unaware of it, he had lost control of the Sovereignty.

By mid-September, on hearing of Warden's fiasco at Viervot, the colonial secretary began to doubt the wisdom of Harry's annexation—which Harry had promised would prevent 'disorder and bloodshed'. It was now obvious that the majority of Boers would not support the Sovereignty and, thus, the British taxpayer would incur the expense of defending them. Pessimistic forecasts by Hogge and no less gloomy reports from other sources—including Harry Smith, who declared that Warden had all he could do to defend himself—convinced Grey that the situation was hopeless. Russell forcibly concurred: 'The ultimate abandonment of the Orange River Sovereignty should be a settled point in our policy.' Emotionally attached to that which he had created, Harry told Grey on 12 November that the abandonment would be regarded by the black man 'as an unprecedented and looked-for victory to his race'. Such a retreat, he prophesied, would become 'a signal for revolt or continued resistance to British authority from Cape Town to the territories and thence to Lake Ngami'. His

protest was ignored. Like a 'weary Titan' anxious to lessen
the load of imperial responsibilities, the British would formally
bring the precarious life of the Sovereignty to an end in
February, 1854.

Pretorius, meanwhile, exploited the unrest in the Sovereignty
to benefit himself and the Transvaal. If he intervened against
the British the situation could become dangerous. The commissioners decided to make a deal with him. Since they could
not negotiate with a 'proscribed rebel', the governor reluctantly
agreed to remove the price on his head. Though Harry considered it blackmail, Pretorius succeeded, by the Sand River
Convention (17 January 1852), in getting the commissioners
to recognize the independence of the Transvaalers, still
nominally British subjects, in exchange for non-intervention
in Transorangia. As for the Boers in the Sovereignty, Pretorius
left them in the lurch by telling them frankly, 'I cannot do
anything for you unless you cross the Vaal.'

Throughout the negotiations Harry, still technically the
high commissioner, was not consulted. Hogge persuaded
Grey that even if an angel had been the Resident, Smith's
system would have failed. Nevertheless, Warden was held to
be incompetent and Grey felt that Harry had made a grievous
error in not removing him sooner. Harry's defence was that
he had no one to replace him. Over Harry's objections, Warden
was dismissed from service without a pension. (He died in
poverty.)

Grey and his government never considered abandoning their
position in Kaffraria despite the mounting opposition of anti-
imperialist colonial reformers. A vigorous attack in Parliament
was led by the Radical, Sir William Molesworth, an 'intrepid
invalid' and professional protester who advocated colonial
self-government, most of all in the Cape, which he characterized
as the 'Algeria of England', to end the drain on the Treasury.
Deriding Grey and Smith for gilding Kaffraria as 'a sort of
terrestrial paradise', Molesworth accused the latter of gross
mismanagement, resulting in war. He observed bitingly:

Thus, by alternately coaxing and threatening the Kaffirs;
by playing up all manner of fantastic and mountebank
tricks, by aping the manners of the savage, Sir Harry
thought to civilize the Kaffirs to impose upon them; but

the Kaffirs laughed at him, turned him into ridicule and
imposed upon him.

During the following months other critics joined in the assault
on the Russell government. Gladstone, a rising star, condemned a policy which 'ensures the recurrence of war with a
regularity that is perfectly astonishing'.

The press added its protest. *The Times* had no doubts that
the 'hardy Sir Harry' would eventually quash the rebellion,
but asked, 'Who is to pay for the triumph we are to achieve?'
The *Daily News* and the *Spectator* echoed these sentiments.
The *United Service Gazette* was more constructive, recommending that dogs be used on every patrol in the bush: 'with
such allies, considering the strong scent of the Kaffirs, we
could not be surprised by them and this destructive war
would be brought to a close.'

Grey maintained a detached calm and the government
survived. To hasten the end of this seemingly interminable
war, one that menaced his own political future, Grey sent out
more unsolicited reinforcements. The 12th Lancers and the
60th Rifles arrived in October and the 43rd in December.
Grey was willing to take some of the blame for reducing the
force at the Cape before the uprising. But on the matter of their
substitution with native troops, a sepoy system in which he
had passionate faith, he faulted Harry for being too lenient
towards the Hottentot renegades. At the first sign of treasonable
activity among five or six of the C.M.R., he observed in a
despatch of 15 September, they should have been 'instantly
brought to Court Martial and shot on the spot'. Harry
demurred: it was 'not in my power from want of evidence —
Judge Jeffries could not have done so without sufficient
evidence'. Grey shocked Harry by persisting that 'even if it
had not been warranted by law ... it would have been no less
than just'.

Under pressure from colleagues and political opponents
alike, the colonial secretary became cantankerous, and continued to harp on the need for a constitution. Circumstances
had forced Harry to leave the matter to Montagu, who
procrastinated. When Montagu suggested, with the backing
of the majority of the Legislative Council, that they wait
until the end of the war, Harry remonstrated, 'I apprehend

far greater embarrassments to the Government by delay than by procedure.' Personally sympathetic to the expediency of Grey's order, he added, 'I do not view a war on the borders as affording cause for deferring the grant of representative government.' Because of the governor's firmness, the colonists' long cherished desire for self-government was introduced at the Cape in 1853.

'Oh! for one day's rest,' Harry confided to Montagu after reading one of Grey's contentious despatches, 'for I am weary of men and Public Life. I have done as well as his Civil Governors —Elgin, Torrington and Ward.'

In September, 1851, the war blazed unexpectedly with renewed fury. The enemy had suddenly become more aggressive and enterprising than ever. Macomo, it appeared, had completely forsaken the bottle and prepared his forces for a renewed effort. Warriors were concentrated in two main strongholds that were barely penetrable: to the north, the Kroome range, with its outworks of the Blinkwater and Waterkloof; and to the south their old haunts in the wild country between the Fish and the Keiskamma. Vast stores of powder and shot had been accumulated for an estimated 10,000 stand of muskets. Early in September marauders once more conducted raids into the colony to plunder and then retire. Macomo was spotted in the distance riding his great white horse.

Retaliation followed. On the 7th Harry ordered Lt.-Col. Fordyce and the 74th into the Kroome; and Mackinnon with the 2nd (Queen's) and the 6th to patrol the Fish. It was exhausting work chasing nimble-footed warriors through nook-riddled terrain. Soldiers fainted from heat and exertion as they tried to reach the naked foe bobbing out of rocky shelters and snaking through the scrub. And when the British retired, the enemy closed in on their flanks and rear to fight hand-to-hand. Fordyce lost 17 killed and wounded mainly because of the confusion caused by frightened Fingoes who ran into his cursing Highlanders. Mackinnon was even less fortunate. A detachment of the Queen's lost their way and were cut off, fighting their way out at a cost of 32 killed and 21 wounded. Once the patrols had gone, the enemy slipped back to reoccupy their lairs. Macomo celebrated, according to a native woman's sworn statement, by torturing for four days Fordyce's bandmaster who had been wounded and had fallen into his hands. Mlanjeni's influence had been restored and was stronger than ever.

Conversely, Harry's reputation as a soldier suffered. Angry colonists, once more exposed to enemy raids, magnified the loss of some 70 men into a disaster. The *Frontier Times*, which had previously lavished praise on the governor's martial talents, flatly asserted that the prolonged conflict, with its 'consequent ruin of thousands', was owing to his 'characteristic self-conceit' which robbed him of all military judgment. 'Sir Harry Smith stands revealed before the world as a mere talker,' announced the editor. 'The Kaffir shakes his assegai at him in scorn and the Colonists only respect the office which he has the undeserved honour to fill.' The *Cape Town Mail*, which had once commended 'the mingled fire and prudence of a veteran commander', began to wonder, more in sorrow than contempt, if 'the infirmity of age, or his recent illness ... or some other unknown cause—has deprived the troops of the advantages which were expected to result from the leadership of Sir Harry Smith'.

The press ignored Harry's difficulties. Even with the arrival of the 60th and the Lancers, he still had a mere 6,000 soldiers, 1,600 of whom performed garrison duty, to wage war against guerillas operating over thousands of square miles. Moreover, the number of volunteers and native auxiliaries he could muster were still far less than was possible three months before. Harry came to the inescapable conclusion that, for the first time, he would have to request more troops. Putting aside his pride, he sent a plea to Grey on 15 October for two more regiments and 400 British recruits, to bring his depleted C.M.R. back to full strength. Grey sent him the 1st Bn of the Rifle Brigade.

Like the prophet Mlanjeni, Harry had sold his credibility for future delivery. When Harry's political predictions did not materialize, the colonial secretary found him deficient as a civil administrator. And once the military situation worsened rather than improved, Grey began to lose belief in Harry's promises as a general. Grey, of course, received clippings from Cape journals, but he cared little for the opinions of colonial editors. Rather, he was influenced by the confidential, on-the-spot reports of Major Hogge, which documented what he had come to suspect—Smith's 'successes' were phantom triumphs. Between 24 December and 21 October, he claimed to have defeated the enemy on 45 separate occasions; Hogge, however, reported that Smith was waging a terrific war only on paper. Such notices might make good reading at the Horse Guards, but the commissioner found them absurdly bombastic. When the governor asserted after one engagement that 250 of the enemy were slain, Hogge scoffed that 247 were still very much alive and fighting; in another despatch, Harry spoke of having hurled back the enemy, but Hogge sneered that they had merely fallen back to a more favourable position. Exactly how Hogge obtained his intelligence is a mystery, for there is no evidence that he accompanied any of the patrols.

There were also reports that Smith's health was broken, sapping his energy and beclouding his comprehension. But if Harry was wanting in energy, it was belied by the offensive operations he prepared to launch in mid-October and carry on into the next year. He now commanded ten good battalions of infantry and one of cavalry, the Lancers having fully recovered from their ordeal at sea. Somerset was given 1,200 men for repeated assaults to 'clean out' the Waterkloof and Blinkwater, beginning on 12 October. Direct and flanking attacks supported by artillery proved a successful combination. On 9 November 'Hawk's-eye' reported that the bulk of the marauders had been rooted out and were fleeing eastward with their cattle to Kreli beyond the Kei. The moral effect of driving the enemy from a position they regarded as impregnable was incalculable.

The price of this success was slight, some 50 casualties. These losses added to those suffering from illness was more than compensated by the arrival of the 43rd in mid-December. The severest loss of the operation was the result of an ambuscade on 6 November in which the genial and conscientious Fordyce, along with two officers and six men of the 74th, was killed. The colonel had needlessly shown himself by stepping outside a bush with a telescope when a huge Hottentot picked him off and ran away laughing. The tragedy that befell Fordyce and his companions was used by the governor's critics to convert a success into a defeat.

The time was now at hand to deal with the slippery Kreli and his rebel sanctuary. Earlier the governor had asked the Xhosa chief to turn over some Hottentot deserters and pay compensation for a trader plundered in his territory. Kreli insolently rejected these demands, saying, 'I am only waiting until the troops cross the Kei, then I will fight and when I am beaten, as very likely I shall be, then will be the time to talk about payment.' Leaving the 74th and the 91st to patrol pockets of resistance in Kaffraria, Harry sent out 5,000 soldiers, plus native levies, in flying columns to invade the Transkei. The Pondos to the north were to fall on Kreli from behind. It was a nearly bloodless campaign, conducted almost wholly in the rain. Fleeing at the sight of troops, the enemy left behind their livestock, trophies acquired after a year's raiding. Six weeks of counter-raids in Kreli's country netted 30,000 head of cattle. Some 7,000 Fingoes were freed from bondage.

The sweep beyond the Kei also brought the rebel chiefs forward to sue for peace. Following a great meeting on 15 January, they sent emissaries to Charles Brownlee to intercede on their behalf with the governor. 'The war is over,' Harry told Grey, 'were I to accede to their terms.' The colonial secretary was advised to cancel any further reinforcements.

The chiefs wanted peace on the basis of letting bygones be bygones. 'Never!' declared the governor. He sent Brownlee back with a long message reciting their crimes and, as a preliminary, he expected them to prostrate themselves before him and beg his forgiveness. If they agreed to surrender unconditionally, he promised certain unspecified acts of clemency. The chiefs wavered. Macomo stiffened Sandile's resolve to stand firm by vowing that he would rather die fighting than put his neck under that foot again. Others feared that there might be something worse in store for them. And rightly so, for Harry informed Grey that in his opinion no settlement would 'be satisfactory which does not include the severe punishment of the guilty. Sandile, the prophet and some others, ought I think to be hanged, or at all events trans-ported.'

To hasten submission, Harry sent seven devastating columns to where they were thought to be hiding. Where once the troops had to struggle to hold the very ground on which they stood, they now were unopposed. The chiefs had no heart for further fighting. They requested an armistice to allow time to negotiate. Against Brownlee's advice, the governor agreed, reasoning that a tranquil atmosphere might be conducive to discussion. From the 12th through to the 14th of February the columns were halted. Harry informed the chiefs that a major condition was that the Gaikas leave Kaffraria and settle beyond the Kei. This was unacceptable and their harassment was resumed.

The governor, in turn, was now being harried by the colonial secretary. It would no doubt have been better if Harry had designated someone else to write his despatches, for his overly optimistic and inflated reports of events in October and November had the reverse effect upon Grey. Moreover, Grey's temper was tried by information from private sources that hundreds of barrels of gunpowder were being shipped coast-wise to the enemy. He demanded an explanation from the governor and Montagu. They tried to assure him that he had been misinformed and that every possible restrictive measure had been employed to prevent such illicit traffic. It appeared to them that the enemy had squirrelled large reserves before the war. Grey was unimpressed by their investigation.

Expecting some expression of approval from Grey over Somerset's initial success in the Kroomes in mid-October, Harry was dismayed to receive a peevish reproof instead. 'It is some relief,' Grey remarked sarcastically in his despatch of 15 December, 'that you regard the operations ... as having been attended with important success.' He saw it in a different light. The loss of two officers and 32 wounded, Grey felt, was 'very serious'. The colonial secretary then made the fatuous observation that

it was the rear, and not the van of the British force which was engaged with the enemy, and that the latter must therefore have been the assailants, would appear to me scarcely to justify the tone of satisfaction with which you relate these occurrences ... I am forced to believe that no real advantage whatever has been gained over the Kaffirs.

As a final thrust, he recalled 'that you more than once expressed to me in conversation an exceedingly low opinion of General Somerset's qualifications for Kaffir Warfare', which was at variance with 'the very exaggerated praise of this officer contained in your public despatch'.

By the time Harry received this carping despatch (5

February), he was sure that he could easily dispose of Grey's dissatisfaction by pointing to his recent success which had led to 'a general entreaty for peace by the enemy beyond the Kei, as well as by rebels in British Kaffraria'. In regard to Grey's last despatch, he condescendingly added, 'Those, my Lord, who have witnessed military operations, and are best acquainted with their varying character ... will not consider the affair of the rearguard as the criterion by which to judge of their general result.' He did admit that he had forgotten the opinion he had expressed about Somerset privately: '—he however possesses vast local experience and upon the whole was the only officer I have capable of doing so much as he has upon so extended a scale.'

By now Harry should have realized that Grey no longer put any stock in what he wrote. His sands had run out. Under ceaseless attack from the Opposition and leading journals over the soaring costs of the war, the colonial secretary had already suggested to Russell on 12 December that Smith be replaced. Though the Prime Minister was sympathetic, he cautioned him that Smith had powerful supporters. Only if Wellington agreed, which would help muzzle criticism, would Russell be willing. In a letter to the Queen on 18 December, Grey told of having 'had a long conversation with his Grace on the subject', but he learned that 'the Duke does not think it necessary that Sir H. Smith should be superseded'.[1] Wellington merely pushed aside the evidence Grey had compiled against him and stated that he approved of the way Smith was conducting the war. He went on to propose that the C.M.R. be completed by inviting volunteers from regiments now at the Cape, while drafts be sent from depôts at home to keep battalions up to strength. They would proceed in a few days on the *Birkenhead*.

To shorten the passage of the *Birkenhead* from Simon's Bay to East London, where the governor was anxiously awaiting reinforcements, the captain stood close to shore. In the early hours of 26 February the bottom of the iron paddle-wheel troopship was pierced by an uncharted rock off Danger Point. The world was appalled by the news that of 636 on board only 184 survived; and thrilled by the magnificent heroism of the officers and men who stood silently and steadily

[1] RA, Grey to Queen Victoria, 18 Dec. 1851, B 11/236.

to the very end as insufficient lifeboats took away the women and children. Only 68 soldiers and sailors reached the shore two miles away as the ship went to the bottom. Frederick William IV was so impressed by British valour that he had the full account of the epic story read to every regiment in the Prussian army.

With or without replacements, Harry was not about to give the enemy a chance to recover. The Kroome range, with its intricate defiles and battlemented crags, was once again becoming a running sore that demanded full and drastic attention. Anxious to be active in the field once more, Harry ordered the frontier forces to be concentrated under his personal command. Since it was the colony itself that was menaced by raids from these mountains, the governor made another appeal for volunteers in a final, all-out effort. The response was not too encouraging; 'One or two districts,' recalled Captain King, 'being alone the exception to what Sir Harry Smith termed melancholy shuffling'. Nevertheless, some 400 settlers, Britons and Boers, obeyed the summons. Harry galloped ahead to join his forces at Fort Beaufort, stopping only for a quick meal and rest for the weary mounts. While the governor chatted cheerfully, the staff scarcely opened their mouths except to eat and drink.

To squeeze the Kroome range, the governor had his columns close in like fingers into a fist. The Lancers and other mounted men were positioned so as to intercept those who attempted to slip through. The posts in the area were strengthened to provide large and frequent patrols. And should a possible distraction arise out of the dense scrub of the Fish river region, a detachment was sent to protect the rear. To be in a better position to direct operations, Harry moved his headquarters forward to the Blinkwater post. Once preparations were completed, he ordered the columns to advance on the morning of 10 March.

With the columns digging into the deep recesses and flushing the enemy towards the cannons and waiting horsemen, the durable governor threw himself into the extreme point of danger, yelling violent threats at those who encountered difficulty — or as Lakeman put it, 'basting the men with hot drippings of his martial wrath'. Nor were officers spared. It was reported that he sent a message 'seasoned with fearful expletives, to a colonel that if he kept his regiment so much to the front, he'd have him knee-haltered'.

Once, after moving on to unfamiliar ground, Harry was unable to find a guide. Brownlee kept insisting that he could direct them until Harry became so angry that he shouted, 'get out of my sight with your gigantic strides and consider yourself under arrest'. Eventually realizing that he was floundering about aimlessly, Harry sent a staff member to get the young man to assist him. 'Tell His Excellency,' was the reply, 'I am under arrest and cannot come.' That night Harry invited Brownlee to his tent for dinner and, before the entire staff, apologized for his behaviour that morning.

On 11 March, with a female prisoner to guide them, Eyre's column with four guns entered the area near Fuller's Hoek where Macomo had his hiding place. Macomo escaped after a hard fight, but three of his wives were captured. Within a few days the persevering columns had eliminated all resistance. The Lancers swept up the fugitives and their cattle.

His clothes torn by 'wait-a-bit' thorns and dripping with perspiration, Harry was none the less in high spirits when he began a despatch on the 12th to report the extraordinary progress of his troops. A messenger interrupted him with a letter from Grey dated 14 January. It contained the shattering news that he had been recalled. 'It is my painful duty to inform you,' went the words,

> there is evidence which it is impossible longer to resist, that you have failed in showing that foresight, energy and judgement which your very difficult position required, and that therefore ... the conduct of the war should be placed in other hands.

[16]

Epilogue

Old age is a bore!

Sir Harry Smith

Harry's luck, of which he had had more than his share in a long career, had finally run out. Earl Grey, determined to get rid of his governor, appeared to have been waiting for some untoward event to strengthen his case. Seizing upon Harry's despatch of 9 November, he found that Somerset's operations in the Waterkloof had been 'entirely barren of useful results'. Not only was a heavy loss sustained by the 74th on 6 November, including the death of Fordyce, but the enemy had reoccupied the ground the British had taken. Grey noted in his diary on 8 January:

> At first I was inclined to take a favourable view, but when I came to compare Sir H. Smith's account of affairs, with more detailed reports submitted by himself with the information contained in the newspapers I was so satisfied that he ought to be recalled that I brought the subject before the Cabinet and they all concurred as to the necessity of the step.

That same day Grey wrote to the Queen about the Cabinet's decision and sent Smith's recent despatches. He explained that on comparing them with 'information from other sources', the favourable impression created by the governor was not justified. It appeared to him, he told the Queen, 'that there is strong evidence confirmatory of the doubts [he] had previously entertained of Sir Harry Smith not being equal to the difficulties with which he has to deal ... '[1]

Two days later, after luncheon with the Queen, the captious colonial secretary armed himself with something more than

[1] RA, Grey to Queen Victoria, 8 Jan. 1852, 11/242.

351

hypercritical newspaper clippings. She was impressed by 'the absolute necessity of superseding Sir Harry Smith, who seems to have lost energy and not to be aware of what is going on around him. Our loss is very serious,' Queen Victoria noted:

> 3 very distinguished officers have fallen and I fear quite unnecessarily. A regular trade has been going on from Capetown of supplying the Caffres with gunpowder and Sir Harry Smith never found this out! This has been discovered and measures are taken to avert it, but it ought to have been done long ago. Genl. Cathcart is to go but the Duke does not much like Sir Harry Smith being recalled.[1]

The Duke, certainly better informed than the Queen on military affairs, recognized that the colonial secretary was twisting matters to his own ends. He was extremely angry with Grey and threatened to resign because of the odious despatch. In a letter dated 7 February, Lord Ellenborough wrote to Harry, 'What I am told is that Lord Grey recalled you, not without asking the Duke's opinion, but against it.' Wellington still regarded Harry as one of the two outstanding generals in the army (the other was Sir Charles Napier). The Cabinet went to great pains to persuade the Duke to stay on. He did. Privately, he told Lady Salisbury on 14 January, 'I did everything I could to save Sir Harry Smith, but in vain ... A monstrous inconvenience is the consequence of these eccentric courses of Lord Grey.'

Stung by being so flatly controverted by the colonial secretary, the Duke publicly disassociated himself from Grey's censure by paying tribute to Sir Harry in the House of Lords on 5 February. Wellington stated firmly that now that Smith had been recalled,

> it is but just to him to say that I, who am his commanding officer, though at a great distance, entirely approve of all his operations—of all the orders he has given to the troops, and all arrangements he made for their success ... I am proud to say I have not observed any serious error in the conduct of the whole of these operations of my gallant friend Sir Harry Smith.

[1] RA, Queen Victoria's *Journal*, 10 Jan. 1852.

In the House of Commons Mr Drummond called the despatch
'a shame and what was more unmanly', for the character of
Sir Harry was blackened before the House had a chance to
debate the merits of the case. 'It was a very dirty job.'

There were further outbursts of sympathy in Britain and
at the Cape on behalf of the soldier who had been 'viciously
wronged'. Sir George Napier wrote his brother Sir William,
'I am glad to see Lord Grey is abused by everyone for his
arrogant insolence.' That Harry's removal was a matter of
pique seemed to be supported by Grey's instructions to
Cathcart, which spoke of no change in policy but merely
ordered him to bring the war 'to a close at the earliest possible
period'. Letters of consolation from friends and admirers were
sent to Harry from all over the world. Dr Hall in Bombay
observed that Grey's 'uncivil despatch will damage his political
reputation more than it will injure your military fame'.

The adverse reaction to Harry's dismissal was of great
concern to Grey because his political enemies hoped to use it as
leverage to bring down the already tottering Russell government. On 27 February the Russell government fell as the result
of a spirited attack led by Palmerston on a Militia Bill. Wellington took a special delight in providing the Opposition with the
most telling arguments. Grey was out of office.

Harry refused to retort publicly to Grey's accusations. As a
soldier, it was his duty to obey orders cheerfully and maintain
an honourable silence. He acknowledged his recall without a
word of complaint, merely remarking, 'I thought it my duty to
continue operations.' Apparently to show that his health had
not deteriorated and to allay his frustrations through exercise,
Harry took three columns into the Amatolas to search for
fugitives concealed there. Mrs Eyre wrote to a friend on 30
March, 'his failures are not owing to want of energy, few have
so much'.

By 25 March he could declare that the Amatolas were
virtually cleared. To date, the enemy admitted the loss of
nearly 6,000 warriors and some 80,000 cattle. Few commanders have been more severely tried, but Harry's conduct
in the Eighth Frontier War matched his illustrious reputation.
Unfortunately, when the defeated chiefs heard that he had been
replaced, they held back from peace talks so as to test the
capabilities of Sir George Cathcart, who stepped ashore at

24

Cape Town on 31 March. Juana had the unhappy task of welcoming her husband's successor.

After bidding his troops farewell, Harry was relieved by Cathcart, a distinguished soldier and master of his profession, on 10 April in King William's Town, With the utmost courtesy and co-operation, reported Cathcart, the ex-governor devoted the whole day 'to the purpose of giving me every insight into affairs of the colony generally, and more particularly to the eastern frontier'. Cathcart did little that Harry would not have done if left in command, but he did it more slowly since he was unacquainted with bush warfare. It was the very thing Grey had wished to avoid.

The war lasted another year, though there was little actual fighting. Sandile was reinstated as chief of the Gaikas, but his people were expelled from the Amatolas. He was killed by a patrol at the end of the Ninth Frontier War. Macomo was later convicted for the murder of a petty chief and served on and off in a prison on Robben Island, where he died. Mlanjeni, whose last great 'miracle' was the sinking of the *Birkenhead*, fled over the Kei at the conclusion of the war and died an object of contempt. Cathcart died a hero's death, being shot while leading his men against the Russians in the Crimea.[1]

Ironically, in his last campaign, though branded a failure by Grey, Harry performed his greatest service. His calm courage averted a general race war between black and white; his tactics ultimately crushed the uprising, though another was given the credit.

The brusque manner in which their governor was relieved evoked compassion among the colonists. They gave him a send-off that almost paralleled his triumphal reception four years earlier. When the inhabitants of King William's Town expressed in a public address the wish that the final settlement of the war had been left in his hands, Harry gallantly defended the government by saying that they were naturally disappointed by the slow progress of the war 'and had not the various circumstances before them which were apparent to you'.

It was still dark on the morning of 11 April when citizens

[1] According to rumours about Mlanjeni's prophecies, resurrected warriors who had fallen in the Eighth Frontier War were now killing the British under the name of Russians.

and soldiers turned out to cheer the ex-governor on his way.
Pato was there with a body of warriors to shout 'Inkosi
Inkulu! Inkosi Inkulu!' Refusing all other escort to East
London, Harry placed himself in their hands. He was gratified
that his system had proved viable with nearly half the natives
of Kaffraria. Shaking hands with his officers, Harry choked
with emotion and finally said, 'Gentlemen, take care of the
soldiers. God bless you.' On reaching the man-of-war, oddly
enough named the *Styx*, Hall helped him over the gangway.
The naval officer was shocked by his appearance: 'He was
evidently suffering in mind and body.' After remarking on the
neatness of the ship, Harry told Hall that he was 'quite overcome taking leave of his soldiers' and went to his bunk.

The *Styx* steamed into Cape Town at noon on the 14th
with an ensign flying from every masthead. The whole population seemed to have flocked to the landing place. There were
magnificent arches bearing the inscription 'God Speed Sir
Harry' and simply 'Gratitude'. The loud cheers from shore
were answered by the sailors. Hall feared that his naval
superior, Captain Adams, might be annoyed with his men's
behaviour; 'However,' he reasoned, 'the natural respect one
has for a gallant old soldier who has fought his country's
battles for nearly half a century, added to the feeling that he
was a setting sun, conquered every other objection.' Carried
away by the general enthusiasm, Hall himself led his sailors
in a parting vocal salute, 'and well they obeyed the order I
gave to let the Dutchmen hear how an Englishman could
cheer'.

A somewhat surprised ex-governor was carried through the
arches and on to the waiting coach. The multitude quieted as
he thanked them and said, 'I have done my duty to the Cape of
Good Hope.' The carriage was drawn by admirers to the Castle
where Juana was waiting. The excitement being too much for
him, Harry declined a public dinner and went straight to bed.

For the next three days there were addresses of admiration
and affection and a gift of silver plate. 'They are beginning to
think Sir Harry was an excellent governor,' commented Hall.
Even those who had opposed 'the cocksure little veteran'
admitted that whatever his shortcomings he had always meant
well in all things he had done. People of all sections, rich and
poor, stood in line before his residence to wish Sir Harry and

Lady Smith well. Harry's aides were kept busy trying to 'choke off' the number of visitors. The ex-governor made a few brief speeches and asked the citizens of Cape Town and the colonists at large 'to keep alive old kindness and good feeling, and to bury all past differences and temporary estrangements in oblivion'.

One, at least, glad to see him go was Montagu, who was still smarting from Harry's rebuff over the question of representative government. 'A more thorough and lamentable failure is not to be found,' he wrote scathingly to the ex-governor, Sir George Napier, on 2 February 1852. 'In all he does he is guided by popularity — by favour or fear — the latter most frequently.'

Although far from well, Harry was determined to brook no delay in leaving. At mid-day on 17 April the man-drawn carriage made its way through the crowds and under the arches to the homeward bound frigate *Gladiator*. To an aide, Harry looked very sick and quite pale, but he none the less stood and responded to the applause 'with almost juvenile animation, while Lady Smith sat by his side in tears'. Once on board the indomitable old soldier broke down. Hall found him near fainting. He made him sit by the funnel until he had sufficiently recovered for his medical attendant to take him on to his cabin. No sooner was Harry there, Hall noted in his diary, 'than he roared out for me and said, "Where is the Skipper of the *Styx*, send him down here!"' Harry told the young officer that he would use whatever influence he had to gain a promotion for him. Hall, however, doubted whether he would survive the journey. Juana 'was very much overcome and cried bitterly'.

'At six o'clock in the morning of the 18th the ship steamed out of the bay,' recorded Theal, 'and the connection of the able and popular governor with the country was ended.'

Instead of returning home a beaten general, Sir Harry was hailed as a victor and fêted for his exertions. To his countrymen he was still a hero beyond reproach, one who had been made a scapegoat by the Russell government. There was a warm welcome, both official and private, when the *Gladiator* reached Portsmouth on 1 June. Having recovered his health on the long voyage, Harry went down to the Council Chamber the next day to receive an address which spoke of the 'capacity and fitness' for command that he had shown under the most difficult conditions. He replied succinctly: 'I became a Governor without a Legislative Council, a Commander-in-Chief without a British army.' But he refused to be drawn into any criticism of his superiors who had dismissed him.

Travelling on to London, Harry wrote, 'All of England upon my arrival again received me with open arms.' There were requests that he stand as a member for four different parliamentary constituencies, all of which he declined, along with invitations to public banquets that might be interpreted as partisan. He heeded the advice the Duke gave him: 'Mind what you do, everything is political and parties will try to make a tool of you. Your case as it stands cannot be improved but may be injured.'

Grey was relieved that Smith exhibited no animosity, which enabled him, he confided in his journal, 'to write a civil letter to [Smith's] lodgings'. He committed a *faux pas*, however, when he expressed the wish that Harry had recovered 'from the indisposition under which I am sorry to perceive that you were suffering when you sailed'. The injury that had given Harry so much pain began to fester. He shot back a reply on the same day (2 June):

> Your Lordship has from what source I cannot well conceive imbibed a very erroneous impression as to the state of my health while in British Kaffraria. I assure you there was never any military operation that was not in rapid progress and well provided for — no correspondence Civil or Military that was not put under immediate reply — and scarcely a day I did not ride fifteen or twenty miles.

But Harry's hot temper always cooled quickly. As Brownlee testified, he would swear at you one minute and cover you with kindness the next. So when Grey asked him to dine with him, he accepted. Friends and backers were astonished that he should bring himself to accept the hospitality of one who had so grossly affronted him. Some of the military journals were not a little disappointed that an officer of his spirit and renown should extricate Grey from the predicament he had placed himself in by writing that 'shameful despatch of recall'. *Colburn's Magazine* was to call it 'the most lowering act' of Sir Harry's career. However, Harry refused to see it that way: 'Why should I quarrel with a man for doing what he thought to be his duty?' Grey considered his conduct 'most handsome and honourable' and expressed himself as 'very deeply indebted to him for the kindness with which he has acted towards me since his return'.

That Wellington thought no less of him was indicated by his giving Harry the greatest honour it was his to bestow—an invitation to the Waterloo banquet at Apsley House on 18 June 1852. At the start the guests had been limited to royalty and those who held the rank of general, but over the years age and infirmity had taken its toll of high-ranking veterans. There were, of course, still many of the famed alive: 'The dashing Anglesey—the steady Maitland—the cool and strategic Hardinge—the accomplished Hew Ross,' reported the *United Service Gazette*, 'bask in the sunlight of their leader's eyes.' The host, it was observed, never looked better and 'was more than usually cheerful'. The great Duke himself proposed a toast to Sir Harry Smith's health, which was received with enthusiasm.

It was Wellington's final Waterloo banquet. In August the Smiths rented Belmont House, Havant, seven miles from Portsmouth and near the home of Sir Charles Napier. They were visiting him and his brother William on 14 September when they heard the news that Wellington, 'the greatest man in the world had died'. The funeral did not take place until 18 November. On that bleak, rainy day, the Duke rode again for the last time, and half of England seemed to ride with him while the other half looked on. Harry was mounted as a standard-bearer, with a large banderole containing ten heraldic inscriptions. The procession to St Paul's went on for hours with long pauses, some planned and some caused when the cumbersome, eighteen-ton catafalque sank through the surface of the road. The ostentatious funeral lacked for nothing except the simplicity that had been one of Wellington's most striking traits.

'We should all die in our boots, with spurs on, if possible,' Harry wrote to Beckwith; 'at any rate, the grand affair is to keep the game alive to the last.' Further employment, moreover, was a necessity, for his funds were hardly sufficient to maintain the appearance essential to his station. The Horse Guards was presented with the problem of finding suitable employment for a 65-year-old major-general, for both justice and political expediency demanded it. Harry was offered the

command of the army at Madras. After debating the matter,
however, he decided for reasons of health—Juana's as well as
his own—to turn it down. An agreeable solution was found in
January, 1853, when he was made Lieutenant-General in
Plymouth, with the command of the Western District.

Britain entered the Crimean War in March, 1854. With
Hardinge succeeding Wellington and Fitzroy Somerset (Lord
Raglan) commanding in the field, Harry expected to see
active service. But he was passed over. It was not a matter of
age alone; generals older than he were sent out. The truth
was that *by now* Harry was burned out. 'I suppose, old boy,'
he wrote to Beckwith, 'our share in coming events will be
reading the gazette at breakfast.'

For a brief moment, though Harry was never aware of it,
he was considered for the post of commander-in-chief. Late
in the war Raglan died and his temporary successor did not
feel himself equal to the task of commanding the army. The
crisis prompted a conference between Hardinge, Palmerston,
the Prime Minister, and Lord Panmure, the war secretary. In
passing down the list of lieutenant-generals (to which rank
Harry had been promoted in June, 1854), the respective merits
of each was weighed. 'We discussed those of Sir Harry Smith,'
Panmure reported to the Queen, 'but set them aside from the
circumstances of impaired health and liability to excitement.'[1]

Thus, Harry was reduced, somewhat pathetically, to fighting
mock battles in England while the war raged in the Crimea
and then in India during the Great Mutiny.

In September, 1854, he was stationed in Manchester to
command the Northern and Midland districts. If his health
was bad it was not apparent to those who served under him
there. Mr W. F. Collier recalled:

> He was an active General, to be seen everywhere. When
> inspecting or reviewing infantry, he usually rode his little
> Arab, Aliwal, and always, when the troops were in line,
> he would suddenly put his horse into a gallop and ride at
> the line as if he were going to charge through them (the
> men were, of course, well up to this trick and stood per-
> fectly steady); the little Arab always suddenly halted about
> a foot of the line.

[1] RA, Panmure to Queen Victoria, 11 July 1855, G 34/58.

A long drooping moustache he had grown in conformity with the Queen's regulations gave him a look of ferocity and added zest to the expletives he directed at 'bad riders, or men who used a spoon to their pudding, or left a glass of wine unfinished'. They soon learned that his manner was 'like sheet lightning ... terrifying yet harmless'.

At public balls and when celebrating such special events as the anniversary of the battle of Aliwal, he dressed in his tight Rifle uniform with the 'invisible-green' jacket, and equally constricting trousers to match. 'It was very trying to his figure,' noted Collier, 'and *his* then was rather spare and dilapidated, rather of the Don Quixote order.'

The highlight of the Aliwal dinner, reminisced the daughter of Major Payne, his A.D.C., came when someone proposed a toast to the health of Aliwal. Harry called out that the horse should be sent for.

> The groom would lead the beautiful creature all round the dinner-table, glittering with plate, lights, uniforms, and brilliant dresses, and he would be quite quiet, only giving a snort now and then, though, when his health had been drunk and the groom had led him out, you could hear him on the gravel outside, prancing and capering.

When the Manchester Art Treasures Exhibition was opened on 5 May 1857, Prince Albert wrote to the Queen that the six-mile procession was led by 'Sir Harry Smith upon his Arab "charging the multitude".' He performed a similar duty making military arrangements for the Queen's visit on 29 June. When Victoria knighted the mayor she used Harry's sword and informed the civilian that it had been 'in four general actions'. Afterwards, she asked Harry, 'Do you value it very much?' Without a word, he graciously presented it to her.

Giving his sword to the Queen symbolized to Harry the end of his fighting days. His only ambition now was to be raised to the peerage. In a long letter to the Prime Minister on 1 September 1857, he enumerated the various campaigns in which he had taken part. He concluded:

> Thus it is after 52 years unintermitted Service in every quarter of the Globe, worn out in Active Service, I venture to advance my claim in honorary distinction. I may

still serve my Country as a Senator and terminate it as I began it, in activity.

Palmerston expressed his appreciation of his long, distinguished military record. However, because the peerage 'depends upon a consideration of so many conflicting claims', he was not at liberty to submit his name to Her Majesty. 'Your title to the respect of your countrymen depends not upon what you are called,' he advised, 'but upon what you have done.'

Another petition was later sent to the Duke of Cambridge, the commander-in-chief, pleading for reappointment in order to avoid retirement. Though his feelings were 'strongly in favour' of allowing Harry to retain his command, Cambridge regretted that regulations would not permit an exception to be made in his case. On 30 September 1859 he was retired.

Before taking up residence in London, there was one unpleasant act to perform. Fearing that Aliwal's old age would be filled with unhappiness, he resolved to be merciful and shoot him. 'My father and the faithful groom,' wrote Miss Payne, 'were with Sir Harry when he did so, and I believe they all shed tears.' Harry disappeared that night and was not seen until the next morning. In his epitaph for Aliwal, Harry wrote: 'As a charger, he was incomparable, gallant and docile; as a friend he was affectionate and faithful.'

'I hear much talk of the happiness of old age,' Harry told George Simmons, 'and am grateful to be as I am, but the *fast* of youth is the fun.' Retiring to a rented home in London 'on a beggar's income', he missed the stirring exercise of '*a right good stud*'. Writing to Payne, the old spirit flared briefly: 'You would laugh to see me poring over two-pences. Hang me if I know how people in England live. I hate London but I love you, Tom.' He kept busy in his garden and at reading, most of all about South Africa.

There were many funerals as the circle of old friends and comrades grew smaller. Within the space of a few years brother Charles, Kempt, Hardinge, Simmons, William Napier and Barnard (whom Harry had succeeded as colonel of the 1st Bn of the Rifle Brigade in 1855) were gone. Beckwith and Harry remained to condole with one another. Harry bemoaned the fact that Westminster Abbey would not be the receptacle of his own remains, most of all because many with less claim upon England were interred there — such as architects who had spent untold millions on buildings 'which were now resting places for birds and bats, and owls'.

The Smiths took up spirit-rapping to reach beyond the grave. One who attended these sessions complained that Harry made them 'all sit round a table for ages, waiting for the spirits'. Particularly, he sought contact with his mother. Juana's dead relatives were another matter. Having been disowned by surviving relations as a heretic for becoming a member of the Church of England in 1835, there was some question as to how she would be received by those who had departed from this life.

In August, 1860, Harry had violent palpitations of the heart. He tried not to let Juana know how ill he was. Fearing that death was near, he made arrangements with Payne. 'I should not like to ship my wind without an attempt to secure for Juana the pension of my rank which must be an especial one.'

Many years before, Harry had written to Juana:

When I was first troubled with you, you were a little, wiry, violent, ill-tempered, always faithful, little devil, and kept your word to a degree which, at your age, and for your sex, was as remarkable as meritorious, but, please Almighty God, I shall have this old woman with me, until we both dwindle to our mother earth, and when the awful time comes, grant we go together at the same moment.

However, sentiment and reality often do not agree. On 12 October 1860 the grand old soldier died at 73 of an attack of angina pectoris at 1, Eaton Place West. Juana died twelve years later on 10 October 1872 and was laid to rest next to her husband in the new cemetery at Whittlesea.

A memorial chapel was dedicated at the end of the south aisle of St Mary's Church, which had been his schoolroom when he had been a boy: it is known as the Sir Harry Chapel. There is a monument of white marble surmounted by the veteran's bust. It bears an inscription listing the major battles in which he took part. 'His battle roll is one of singular splendour,' exclaimed an onlooker. 'It might of itself emblazon the colours of a regiment.'

Selected Bibliography

I MANUSCRIPTS AND PRIVATE PAPERS NOT INCLUDED IN THE PREFACE

ANDREWS, C., 'Personal Reminiscences', Library of the Royal United Service Institution, London.

BALFOUR, A. L., 'Journal', National Library of Ireland, Dublin.

BECHER, A., 'Diary', National Army Museum, London.

CARTER, G., 'Journal', India Office Library, London.

COLE, SIR LOWRY, Papers, Public Record Office, London.

COPE, SIR W. H., Papers and returns dealing with the troops at the Cape, National Army Museum.

CUST, R. H. H., 'Journals', India Office Library.

DICKSON, A., Papers, Royal Artillery Institution, Woolwich.

ELLENBOROUGH, EARL, Papers, Public Record Office.

Enclosures to secret letters from India, 1835 to 1850, India Office Library.

GODLONTON, R., Papers, Cory Library, Rhodes University, Grahamstown.

HAVILAND, R., Papers, National Army Museum.

HOLLAND, L., 'Diary', National Army Museum.

M.P. 'My Recollections of an Indian Battlefield', Hardinge Papers, Penshurst.

MICHEL, J., 'Diary', Royal Artillery Institution, Woolwich.

MOORE SMITH, G. C., Papers, Cambridge University Library, Cambridge.

NAPIER, SIR W., Papers, Bodleian Library, Oxford.

NAPIER, Papers, British Museum.

ORPEN, J., Papers, Cape Archives, Cape Town.

PALMERSTON, LORD, Papers, British Museum.

PHILIP, J., Papers, Rhodes House Library, Oxford.

PIERCE, T., 'Diary', British Museum.

PUGHE, J. R., 'Autobiography', National Army Museum.

Punjab Intelligence Reports, 1837 to 1849, India Office Records.

RUSSELL, LORD, Papers, Public Record Office.

SHEPSTONE, T., Papers, Natal Archives, Pietermaritzburg.

SITWELL, W. H., 'The First Sikh War', Hardinge Papers.

SOMERSET, H., Correspondence with Sir Harry Smith, Public Record Office.

SOUTHEY, R., Papers, Cape Archives.

VAN HOMRICH, H. D., 'Diary', National Army Museum.

WARDEN, H. D., 'Diary', Orange Free State Archives.

II   BRITISH PARLIAMENTARY PAPERS, IMPERIAL BLUEBOOKS

1836 vii (538) Report from the Select Committee on Aborigines, 1836.

1836 xxxix (279) Correspondence re death of Hintsa, 1836.

1837 vii (238) Further Report from the Select Committee on Aborigines, 1837.

1847 xxxviii (786) Correspondence re Kaffir Tribes, 1845–1846.

1848 liii (912) Correspondence re Kaffir Tribes, 1847–1848.

1849 xxxvi (1059) Papers re Natal, Boer rising, 1848–1849.

1849 xliii (217) Papers re transportation of convicts to Cape, 1841–1849.

1850 xxxviii (104) Cape, Papers re Convict discipline, 1849–1850.

1850 xxxviii (1137) (1234) Cape, Correspondence re establishment of Representative Assembly, 1848–1850.

1850 xxxviii (1138) Cape, Correspondence re reception of convicts, 1849–1850.

1850 xxxviii (1288) Papers re Kaffirs, 1848–1850.

1850 xxxviii (1292) Cape, Natal Correspondence, 1849–1850.

1851 xxxvii (458) Cape, Appointment of Sir H. Smith as Governor, 1847.

1851 xxxvii (1360) Correspondence re assumption of sovereignty over territory between Orange and Vaal Rivers, 1849–1851.

1851 xxxvii (1362) Cape, Papers re proposed Representative Assembly, 1850–1851.

1851 xxxviii (1334) (1352) (1380) Correspondence re Kaffirs, 1850–1851.

1852 xxx (516) Kaffir War expenses, Treasury Minute, 24th February 1852.

1852 xxxiii (57) Cape, Six Ordinances of Legislative Council, Nov.–Dec. 1851.

1852 xxxiii (1428) Correspondence re Kaffir tribes, 1851–1852.

1852–53 lxvi (1646) Correspondence re Orange River Territory, 1851–1853.

III   OFFICIAL PUBLICATIONS

Basutoland Records, compiled by G. M. Theal, 3 vols, 1883.

Further Correspondence relative to the State of the Tribes, and to the

recent outbreak of the Eastern Frontier of the Colony. Colonial
Office, 1851. Confidential.

Hansard's Reports of British Parliamentary Debates.

Report from the Select Committee on Aborigines (British Settlements); with the Minutes of Evidence. Ordered by House of
Commons, 1837.

Report from the Select Committee on Colonial Military Expenditure.
Ordered by House of Commons, 1835.

Report on the Select Committee on Kaffir Tribes. Ordered by the
House of Commons, 1851.

Summary of Correspondence relative to the Policy pursued towards
the Native Tribes in the Eastern Frontier of the Cape of Good
Hope, including the Wars of 1835, and 1846. Downing Street,
1856. Confidential.

The War in India. Despatches of Lt.-Gen. Viscount Hardinge,
General Lord Gough, Sir Harry Smith and other Documents.
London, 1846.

IV MEMOIRS, DIARIES AND LETTERS

BOOKS (published in London unless another location is given)

ALEXANDER, SIR JAMES, *Narrative of a Voyage of Observation and of a
Campaign in Kaffirland in 1835*, 2 vols, 1837.

ANGLESEY, MARQUESS OF, ed., *Sergeant Pearman's Memoirs*, 1968.

ANTON, JAMES, *Retrospect of a Military Life*, Edinburgh, 1841.

BALDWIN, J. W., *A Narrative of Four Months' Campaign in India* ...
1845—46, Norwich, 1850.

BANCROFT, N. W., *From Recruit to Staff Sergeant*, Calcutta, 1885.

BANKES, G. H., ed., *The Autobiography of Sergeant William Lawrence*,
1886.

BELL, SIR GEORGE, *Rough Notes by an Old Soldier*, 2 vols, 1867.

BISSET, SIR WILLIAM, *Sport and War*, 1875.

BLAKENEY, ROBERT, *A Boy in the Peninsular War*, 1899.

BROWN, GEORGE, *Personal Adventure in South Africa*, 1855.

BROWNLEE, CHARLES, *Reminiscences of Kaffir Life and History*, Lovedale,
1896.

BUCKLE, E., *Memoir of the Services of the Bengal Artillery*, 1852.

BUNBURY, THOMAS, *Reminiscences of a Veteran*, 1861.

BURFORD, ROBERT, *Description of a View of Sobraon*, 1846.

CASALIS, EUGENE, *Mes Souvenirs*, Paris, 1882.

CATHCART, SIR GEORGE, *Correspondence of Sir George Cathcart*, 1856.

CHESTERTON, GEORGE, *Peace, War, and Adventure*, 1853.

CLEVELAND, W., *Extracts from the Journal of* ... n.d.

CODRINGTON, SIR E., *Memoir of the Life of Admiral Sir E. Codrington*, 2 vols, 1873.

COLE, A. W., *The Cape and the Kafirs*, 1852.

COLE, M. LOWRY and S. GWYNN, *Memoirs of Sir G. Lowry Cole*, 1934.

COLEY, JAMES, *Journal of the Sutlej Campaign*, 1856.

COOKE, J. H., *Memoirs of the Late War*, 1831.

COOPER, JOHN, *Rough Notes of Seven Campaigns*, 1869.

COSTELLO, EDWARD, *Adventures of a Soldier*, 1841.

CURLING, H., ed., *Recollections of Rifleman Harris*, 1929.

D'URBAN, SIR BENJAMIN, *The Peninsular Journal of ...* , 1930.

DUGMORE, HENRY, *The Reminiscences of an Albany Settler*, Grahamstown, 1958.

FOREST, CHARLES, *The Battle of New Orleans; A British View*, New Orleans, 1961.

GILLING, J., *Life of a Lancer in the Wars of the Punjab*, 1855.

GLEIG, GEORGE, *The Subaltern*, Edinburgh, 1825.

—— *A Subaltern in America*, Philadelphia, 1833.

GORDON, C. A., *Recollections of Thirty-nine Years in the Army*, 1898.

GORDON-BROWN, A., ed., *The Narrative of Private Buck Adams*, 1941.

GRAY, C., ed., *Life of Robert Gray of Capetown*, 2 vols, 1877.

GREEN, JOHN, *A Soldier's Life: 1806–1815*, 1827.

GUTHRIE, G. J., *Commentaries on the Surgery of War*, 1853.

HAY, WILLIAM, *Reminiscences under Wellington*, 1901.

HENEGAN, SIR RICHARD, *Seven Years' Campaigning*, 1846.

HILL, BENSON, *Recollections of an Artillery Officer*, 2 vols, 1836.

HOOK, D. B., *With Sword and Statute*, 1907.

HOWELL, JOHN, *Journal of a Soldier*, Edinburgh, 1819.

HUMBLEY, WILLIAM, *Journal of a Cavalry Officer*, 1854.

HUTTON, C. W., *The Autobiography of the late Sir Andries Stockenström*, 2 vols, Cape Town, 1887.

KINCAID, SIR JOHN, *Adventures in the Rifle Brigade*, 1830.

—— *Random Shots from a Rifleman*, 1835.

KING, WILLIAM, *Campaigning in Kaffirland*, 1855.

KING-HALL, LOUISE, ed., *Sea Saga*, 1935.

LAKEMAN, SIR STEPHEN, *What I saw in Kaffirland*, 1880.

LIDDELL HART, B. H., ed., *The Letters of Private Wheeler*, 1951.

LONG, UNA, ed., *The Chronicle of Jeremiah Goldswain*, Cape Town, 1946–9.

LUCAS, T. S., *Camp Life and Sport in South Africa*, 1878.

LUNT, JAMES, ed., *From Sepoy to Subedar*, 1970.

MACKINNON, D. H., *Military Service and Adventures in the Far East*, 2 vols, 1859.

MENZIES, JOHN, *Reminiscences of an Old Soldier*, Edinburgh, 1883.

MITCHEL, JOHN, *Jail Journal*, 1854.

MOORE SMITH, G. C., *Autobiography of Sir Harry Smith*, 2 vols, 1902.

NAPIER, SIR CHARLES, *Lights and Shades of Military Life*, 1851.

NAPIER, SIR GEORGE, *Passages in the Early Life of ...* , 2 vols, 1884.

By an officer, *Narrative of the Proceedings of the Expedition under Craufurd*, 1808.

POWELL, A. G. B., ed., *The Barnard Letters*, 1928.

ROBERTSON, J. P., *Personal Adventures of an Old Soldier*, 1906.

RYDER, JOHN, *Four Years in the Service of India*, Leicester, 1854.

SCHAUMANN, A. L. F., *On the Road with Wellington*, 1924.

SCOTT, SIR JAMES, *Recollections of a Naval Life*, 3 vols, 1834.

SIMPSON, JAMES, *Paris After Waterloo*, 1853.

SURTEES, WILLIAM, *Twenty-five Years in the Rifle Brigade*, 1853.

THEAL, G. M., ed., *Documents Relating to the Kaffir War of 1835*, 1912.

VAUGHAN, SIR J., *My Service in the Indian Army and After*, 1904.

VERNER, WILLOUGHBY, ed., *A British Rifleman*; *The Journal of Major General Simmons*, 1899.

WALDEMAR, PRINZ VON PREUSSEN, *Zur Erinnerung an Reise des Prinzen Waldemar von Preussen nach Indien den Jahren 1844–46*, 2 vols, Berlin, 1853.

WARD, HARRIET, *Five Years in Kaffirland*, 2 vols, 1848.

WYLLY, H. C., ed., *Military Memoirs of Lt.-Gen. Sir Joseph Thackwell*, 1908.

ARTICLES AND PAMPHLETS

ACCOUNT OF AN EYE-WITNESS, 'The Night of Ferozeshah, 21st–22nd of December, 1845', *Orkney Herald*, 1910.

ANON., 'Operations in the Waterkloof', *United Service Magazine*, April, 1852.

ASHBURNHAM, LT.-COL., 'Letters on Ferozeshah and Sobraon', *Journal of the Society for Army Historical Research*, 1932.

BARTHROP, MICHAEL, 'A Soldier of the 73rd in the Kaffir War of 1852', *J.S.A.H.R.*, 1973.

BIDDULPH, G., 'Captain George Biddulph at Moodke and Ferozeshah', *J.S.A.H.R.*, 1934.

BROWN, WILLIAM, 'The Autobiography or Narrative of a Soldier', *Regimental Annual of the Sherwood Foresters*, 1921 and 1922.

BUTLER, CAPTAIN, 'My Volunteer Troop in Kaffirland', *Bentley's Miscellany*, 1851.

CAMPBELL, P. S., *Reminiscences of the Kafir Wars*, pamphlet, Cory Library.

EDGAR, A., 'Reminiscences of the Kaffir War, 1834–1835', *The Friend of the Free State and Bloemfontein Gazette*, April, 1874.

FLEMING, WILLIAM, 'An Irish Subaltern in South Africa', *Sherwood Foresters*, 1921.

GRANT, I. F., ed., 'Every-Day Letters Written During the First and Second Sikh Wars', *The Army Quarterly*, July, 1925.

HOFF, WILLIAM, 'Moodke and Ferozeshah, 1845: A Camp Follower's Account', Notes by G. Reeves-Brown, *J.S.A.H.R.*, 1934.

LESLIE, J. H., 'Two Letters Contributed by the Marquess of Sligo', *J.S.A.H.R.*, 1932.

NAPIER, COL., 'The Present Kaffir War', *United Service Magazine*, July, 1852.

NEWMAN, H. B., ed., 'Echoes of the Past. An Army Surgeon's Experiences in South Africa, 1843–46', *Journal of the Royal Army Medical Corps*, May, 1927.

OMAN, C., ed., 'Letters of Hodenberg', *Blackwood's Magazine*, March, 1913.

PARKHURST, HELEN, 'Don Pedro Favrot, A Creole Pepys', *The Louisiana Historical Quarterly*, July, 1945.

PEARSE, HUGH, ed., 'The Kaffir and Basuto Campaigns of 1852 and 1853', (as described by an Old Soldier who served in them), *Rifle Brigade Chronicle*, 1934.

WARD, MRS, 'Rebel Boers', *New Monthly Magazine*, Jan., 1849.

V SECONDARY SOURCES

BOOKS

BANCROFT, M. W., *The Bengal Horse Artillery of the Olden Time*, 1885.

BARRETT, C. R. B., *The 85th King's Light Infantry*, 1913.

BERESFORD, P. and S. MACA'GHOBHAINN, *The Scottish Insurrection of 1820*, 1970.

BOLITHO, HECTOR, *The Galloping Third, the Story of the 3rd the King's Own Hussars*, 1963.

BROADFOOT, WILLIAM, *Career of Major Broadfoot*, 1888.

BROWN, WILBURT, *The Amphibious Campaign for West Florida and Louisiana, 1814–1815*, Tuscaloosa, Alabama.

BRUCE, GEORGE, *Six Battles for India*, 1969.

BURGOYNE, R. H., *Historical Records of the 93rd Sutherland Highlanders*, 1883.

BURTON, R. G., *The First and Second Sikh Wars*, 1911.

BUTLER, LEWIS, *Annals of the King's Rifle Corps*, 5 vols, 1923.

CANNON, RICHARD, *The Thirty-First, The Huntingdonshire Regiment of Foot*, 1850.

CANTILE, SIR NEIL, *A History of the Army Medical Department*, 2 vols, 1974.

CHILD, DAPHNE, *Saga of the South African Horse*, Cape Town, 1967.

CLARKE, J. W. and T. HUGHES, *Life and Letters of Adam Sedgwick*, 2 vols, 1890.

CONNOLLY, T. W. J., *History of the Royal Sappers and Miners*, 2 vols, 1855.

COOK, H. C. B., *The Sikh Wars*, 1975.

COPE, SIR WILLIAM, *A History of the Rifle Brigade*, 1877.

CORY, SIR GEORGE, *The Rise of South Africa*, 5 vols, 1910–30.

CRAUFURD, A. H., *General Craufurd and His Light Division*, 1892.

CUNNINGHAM, JOSEPH, *A History of the Sikhs*, New Delhi, 1966.

DALBIAC, P. H., *History of the 45th 1st Nottinghamshire Regiment*, 1902.

DE KIEWIET, CORNELIUS, *The Imperial Factor in South Africa*, 1937.

DUNN-PATTISON, R. P., *History of the 91st Argyllshire Line Highlanders*, 1910.

FORTESCUE, SIR JOHN, *A History of the British Army*, 13 vols, 1906–20.

—— *A Gallant Company*, 1927.

FRASER, E. and H. E. N. JOURDAIN, *The Connaught Rangers*, 1924.

FYLER, ARTHUR, *A History of the 50th (the Queen's Own)*, 1895.

GALBRAITH, JOHN, *Reluctant Empire. British Policy of the South African Frontier, 1834–1854*, Los Angeles, 1963.

GOUGH, SIR C. and A. D. INNES, *The Sikhs and the Sikh Wars*, 1897.

GRAHAM, HENRY, *The Sixteenth, The Queen's Light Dragoons (Lancers) 1795–1912*, 1912.

GROVES, J. C., *History of the Princess Louise's Argyllshire Highlanders*, 1894.

HARDINGE, CHARLES, *Viscount Hardinge and the Advance of the British Dominions in the Punjab*, 1900.

HASTED, J. E., *The Gentle Amazon: The Life and Times of Lady Smith*, 1952.

HATTERSLEY, ALAN, *The Convict Crisis and the Growth of Unity*, Pietermaritzburg, 1965.

KINGSFORD, CHARLES, *The Story of the Royal Warwickshire Regiment*, 1921.

KILPIN, R., *The Romance of a Colonial Parliament*, 1932.

LEVINGE, SIR RICHARD, *Historical Records of the Forty-Third Regiment*, 1868.

LUNT, JAMES, *16th/5th the Queen's Royal Lancers*, 1973.

MACGREGOR, W. L., *History of the Sikhs*, 2 vols, 1846.

MARINE, W. A. M., *British Invasion of Maryland, 1812–1815*, Baltimore, 1913.

MEINTJES, JOHANNES, *Sandile. The Fall of the Xhosa Nation*, Cape Town, 1971.

METROWICH, F. C., *Frontier Flames*, Cape Town, 1968.

MOORE SMITH, G. C., *The Life of John Colborne*, 1903.

MOORSOM, W. S., *History of the 52nd Oxfordshire Light Infantry*, 1860.

NAPIER, EDWARD, *Excursions in South Africa*, 2 vols, 1849.

NAPIER, SIR WILLIAM, *A Life of Sir Charles Napier*, 4 vols, 1857.

NEWMAN, W. A., *Biographical Memoir of John Montagu*, 1855.

OMAN, SIR CHARLES, *A History of the Peninsular War*, 5 vols, 1902–30.

PEARSE, H. W. and H. W. SLOMAN, *History of the 31st Foot — The East Surrey Regiment*, 1898.

PETRE, F. L., *The History of the Norfolk Regiment, 1685–1918*, Norwich, 1919.

RAIT, R. S., *The Life and Campaigns of Hugh, First Viscount Gough*, 2 vols, 1903.

RIVETT-CARNAC, DOROTHY, *Hawk's Eye*, Cape Town, 1966.

SANDERS, PETER, *Moshoeshoe Chief of the Sotho*, 1975.

STEWART, P. F., *A History of the XII Royal Lancer (Prince of Wales's)*, 1950.

STUBBS, FRANCIS, *History of … the Regiment of Bengal Artillery*, 3 vols, 1895.

THEAL, G. M., *History of South Africa*, 11 vols, 1964.

TYLDEN, G., *The Rise of the Basuto*, Cape Town, 1950.

WILLIAMS, BASIL, *Record of the Cape Mounted Rifles*, 1909.

WILLIAMS, JOHN, *History of the Invasion and Capture of Washington*, 1857.

WILMOT, A. and J. C. CHASE, *History of the Colony of the Cape of Good Hope*, Cape Town, 1869.

WYLLY, H. C., *The Loyal North Lancashire Regiment*, 2 vols, 1932.

ARTICLES AND PAMPHLETS

DALTON, J. C., 'Buenos Aires and Monte Video 1806, 1807', *Journal of the Royal Artillery*, April, 1927.

EDWARD, S. E., 'Sir Harry Smith Medal 1851', *Bickel's News*, Oct., 1967.

EDWARDS, T. J., 'Soldiers' Wives with Wellington's Army', *Army Quarterly*, 1930–31.

FREMANTLE, A. F., 'Juana Maria de Los Dolores de Leon', *Army Quarterly*, 1933.

GAWLER, COL., 'British Troops and Savage Warfare', *R.U.S.I. Journal*, 1873.

HATTERSLEY, A. F., 'Unpublished Anecdotes of Sir Harry Smith and Sir Theophilus Shepstone', *Africana Notes and News*, 1963.

HUDSON, E. R. B., 'The English Invasion of the River Plate, 1806–07', *Army Quarterly*, 1956.

LANGHAM-CARTER, R. R., 'Arthur Murray and the Battle of Boomplaats', *Military History Journal*, 1969.

LECORDEUR, BASIL, 'The Relations Between the Cape and Natal, 1846–1879', *Archives Yearbook for South African History*, 1965.

LEY, A. E. H., 'The 3rd Light Dragoons at Moodkee and Ferezeshah', *Cavalry Journal*, 1911.

MACKENZIE, R. H., 'Brig.-Gen. C. R. Cureton, C.B.', *Cavalry Journal*, 1912.

MIDGLEY, JOHN F., 'The Orange River Sovereignty (1848–1854)', *Archives Yearbook for South African History*, 1949.

SINCLAIR, HUGH, 'The First Sikh War, 1845–46', *Proceedings of the United Service Institution of India*, 1899.

TYLDEN, G., 'Boomplaats, 29 August 1848', *J.S.A.H.R.*, 1937.

—— 'The Cape Mounted Rifleman, 1827–1870', *J.S.A.H.R.*, 1938.

—— 'The British Army in the Orange River Colony 1842–1854', *J.S.A.H.R.*, 1939.

—— 'Major-General Sir Henry Somerset, 1794–1862', *J.S.A.H.R.*, 1943–4.

WOOD, G. N., 'Burning Washington, the Lighter Side of Warfare', *Army Quarterly and Defence Journal*, 1974.

VI UNPUBLISHED THESES

BENYON, J. A., 'Basutoland and the High Commission 1868–1884', D.Phil., Oxford, 1968.

ENGELS, L. J., 'Sir Benjamin D'Urban's Handling of the Frontier Problems, 1834–1836', M.A., University of Cape Town, 1936.

KENT, J. P., 'Sir Harry Smith as High Commissioner', M.A., University of Cape Town, 1933.

RENWALD, SISTER MARY CASILDA, 'Humanitarianism and British Colonial Policy', Ph.D., St Louis University, 1934.

ROXBOROUGH, JAMES, 'Colonial Policy on the Northern and Eastern Frontiers of the Cape of Good Hope, 1834–45', Ph.D., Oxford, 1953.

SCOTT, JOHN B., 'The Role of the British Soldier on the Eastern Cape Frontier 1800–1850', Ph.D., University of Port Elizabeth, 1973.

VII NEWSPAPERS

Album of clippings from newspapers on the War of 1812, National Army Museum.

Calcutta Review

Cambridge Chronicle, Letters of Benjamin Moore from India in 1846.

Cambridge Independent Press

Cape Frontier Times

Cape of Good Hope Monitor

Cape of Good Hope Observer

Cape Town Mail

Eastern Province Herald

Graaff-Reinat Courant

Graham's Town Journal

Graphic
Illustrated London News
Natal Witness
Naval & Military Gazette and East India Colonial Chronicle
Observer
South African Commercial Advertiser
Spectator
Times
Zuid-Afrikaan

Index